Preparing for
Crises in the Schools

Preparing for Crises in the Schools

A Manual for Building School Crisis Response Teams

Second Edition

Stephen E. Brock

Jonathan Sandoval

Sharon Lewis

John Wiley & Sons, Inc.

New York • Chichester • Weinheim • Brisbane • Singapore • Toronto

---

Note about Photocopy Rights

The publisher grants purchasers permission to reproduce handouts from this book for professional use with their clients.

Library of Congress Cataloging-in-Publication Data:

Brock, Stephen E.
    Preparing for crises in the schools : a manual for building school crisis response teams / Stephen E. Brock, Jonathan Sandoval, Sharon Lewis.—2nd ed.
      p.   cm.
    Includes bibliographical references and index.
    ISBN 0-471-38423-2 (cloth : alk. paper)
    1. School crisis management—United States—Handbooks, manuals, etc. 2. Crisis intervention (Mental health services)—United States—Handbooks, manuals, etc. 3. School psychology—United States—Handbooks, manuals, etc. I. Sandoval, Jonathan.
II. Lewis, Sharon (Sharon E.)   III. Title.
LB2866.5 .B76 2001
371.7'13—dc21
                                                            00-033021

Printed in the United States of America.

10 9 8 7 6 5 4 3 2 1

To my family, Christine, Dyana, and David.

S.E.B.

To Susan and Marian Sandoval who know that the best way
to recover from a crisis is to go to the ocean.

J.S.

To Shirley and Tom Lewis for their love and support. To
Gary Campbell for his encouragement and understanding.

S.L.

Preface

The July 15, 1976, Chowchilla school bus kidnapping commanded international attention. On this date, all 26 children (ages 5 to 14 years) enrolled in the Alview Dairyland summer school disappeared for 27 hours. After their safe return, the children disclosed that their bus had been stopped by a van blocking the road, and that three masked men had taken it over at gunpoint. They had been transferred to two blackened, boarded-over, vans in which they were driven about for 11 hours and then transferred into a buried truck-trailer which the kidnappers covered with earth. The children remained buried for 16 hours until two of the oldest and strongest boys (ages 10 and 14 years) dug them out.

—Terr, 1981

ACCORDING TO Fullan (1991), schooling has at least two major purposes: to facilitate the cognitive/academic and personal/social development of our youth. Situational crises, such as the Chowchilla school bus kidnapping, have the potential to interfere with both of these purposes (Cowen & Hightower, 1986). Initially the distress generated by an apparently unsolvable problem will adversely affect the ability to learn. Perhaps more importantly, failure to adaptively cope with a crisis can impede multiple areas of social and emotional development (Slaikeu, 1990). On the other hand, successful crisis resolution can result in greater confidence and increased strength to deal with future stresses (Caplan, 1964). Kline, Schonfeld, and Lichtenstein (1995) have offered similar observations:

If a school-related trauma is not adequately addressed at school, temporary disruptions in children's ability to concentrate can create a downward spiral in academic performance. Likewise, how schools manage crisis in the short term can negatively affect long-term functioning. Staff morale and a school climate conducive to learning may be seriously impaired by unaddressed or unresolved crisis situations. (p. 245)

Given these observations, it is crucial that school systems develop plans and procedures to respond to crises (Young, 2000). Crisis response is not only consistent with the purposes of schooling, but can be essential to continued academic progress. Unfortunately, however, the authors' experiences have found school districts reactive, as opposed to proactive, when it comes to responding to crises. This reactive approach is dangerous. A lack of crisis preparedness magnifies the likelihood that a crisis will have adverse outcomes for students and staff (Newgrass & Schonfeld, 1996; Thompson, 1995). Because district personnel may not know what to do, the potential for mistakes is increased. At best, lack of preparedness results in a delayed response. Such a delay may make matters worse and necessitate more intensive remedial action (Gullatt & Long, 1996; Sandoval, 1988a).

Terr's (1979, 1981, 1983) work with the victims of the school bus kidnapping described earlier may illustrate the effects of failing to provide immediate crisis intervention assistance. Upon their safe return from the kidnapping ordeal, none of the children were provided crisis intervention (Terr, 1981). Although mental health personnel talked with the superintendent of schools, they did not interview any of the children. In fact, a local mental health center physician advised parents that only 1 out of the 26 children involved would likely be affected emotionally by this trauma. Despite limited treatment provided by Terr (1979, 1981) 5 to 13 months following the kidnapping, every child was found to exhibit posttraumatic symptomatology at follow-up 4 to 5 years later (Terr, 1983). The authors speculate that the extent and severity of the children's crisis reactions were influenced by the failure to provide immediate crisis intervention. The lack of an immediate helping response may have served to make a bad situation worse. Clearly, schools must do more than simply rely on the resiliency of children following crises (Poland, 1994).

In 1988, the authors' awareness of the importance of an immediate crisis response led to the development of crisis response procedures for their Northern California school district (Brock, 1994; Brock, Lewis, & Sandoval, 1991; Brock, Lewis, Slauson, & Yund, 1990, 1995). At that time, they found the task complicated by the fact that crisis preparedness plans in the schools were a relatively recent innovation. There were very few descriptions available of how to initiate school crisis response teams. Thus, after struggling with the process and achieving a good result, they decided to record their efforts along with what was learned of others' work. The result was the first edition of *Preparing for Crises in the Schools,* a book designed for educators interested in establishing school crisis response teams.

Unfortunately, recent events have only highlighted the need for school crisis preparedness. Since publication of the first edition of this book, our nation has been rocked by a series of tragic school shootings, including:

- *Pearl, Mississippi,* where a 16-year-old, after killing his mother, went to school and shot nine classmates (killing two).
- *West Paducah, Kentucky,* where a 14-year-old entered a school lobby and shot eight (killing three) as they completed a morning prayer circle.
- *Jonesboro, Arkansas,* where a 13- and an 11-year-old, ambushed their classmates, shooting 15 (killing five), as they assembled for a fire alarm.
- *Edinboro, Pennsylvania,* where a 14-year-old attacked people at his school dance, killing a science instructor.
- *Springfield, Oregon,* where a 15-year-old, after killing both his parents, entered the school cafeteria and shot 20 classmates (killing two).
- *Littleton, Colorado,* where a 17- and an 18-year-old terrorized an entire school with a shooting and bombing spree that left 15 dead and 24 wounded.

In addition to demonstrating the need for school crisis preparedness, these and other crisis events have also demonstrated the public's expectation for school crisis response. For example, the authors have noticed that news reports of school crisis events are typically followed by words to the effect "crisis counselors will be on hand to assist distressed students." Such reporting has created an expectation among the public that school crisis events will be followed by school crisis intervention. Consistent with this expectation, parents have become vocal and assertive when a crisis intervention is not what they think it should be (Brock, 1999a). Given these observations, it is more important than ever for schools to be prepared to respond to crisis events (Paine, 2000).

With these thoughts in mind, the second edition of this book expands on the first edition's discussion of crisis preparedness and response. From the authors' continuing crisis response experiences and evolving understanding of crisis research, this book examines some of the nuts and bolts issues of initiating and implementing school crisis response plans. In addition to reviewing how to intervene after a crisis has occurred, this book also examines how to get a school district in the best possible position to respond to crisis events.

As the subtitle indicates, this book is a *Manual for Building School Crisis Response Teams.* To actualize the concept of a *Manual* more completely, the second edition has been designed to make it easier for readers to actually use the work to initiate, implement, and continue a school crisis response team. Specific changes made to achieve this goal include an increased emphasis on crisis response forms, worksheets, and training materials. The second edition amends the copyright provisions to allow many of these materials to be reproduced for personal use.

Changes also have been made to the content of each chapter. First, using the ERIC and PsycINFO databases, the authors searched for all recent citations (1995 to present) that contained the words *school* and *crisis.* From this search, when necessary, content has been revised. Perhaps most significantly, readers will find that the authors have added a new chapter on identifying, assessing, and intervening with potentially dangerous students.

As was the case with the first edition, the authors believe that this book, if available, would have facilitated their own preparedness efforts. On the other hand, there is no substitute for personally going through the process of comprehensive planning. The authors do not expect readers to uncritically adopt this book. Prepackaged approaches to school change programs are typically too inflexible to permit necessary local adaptation (P. Berman & McLaughlin, 1980). Thus, this book is viewed as offering examples and strategies that would typically be modified to meet local needs and fit available resources. The authors expect that all school districts will find the need to customize their own crisis plans.

STEPHEN E. BROCK
JONATHAN SANDOVAL
SHARON LEWIS

Acknowledgments

WE ARE pleased to acknowledge the contributions of a number of individuals and organizations in the development of this book's first edition. First, we must cite the contributions of the Lodi Unified School District and school psychologists Steve Yund and Pat Slauson. In supporting the development of Lodi's crisis intervention team, they were critical to the success of the crisis intervention plan that served as the foundation for this book. Second, we wish to thank the Center for Cooperative Research and Extension Services for Schools (CRESS Center) at the University of California, Davis, for supporting a portion of this project. We are also pleased to acknowledge the assistance of John M. (Jack) Davis, who offered advice and counsel at every stage of the development of this project. Another key individual in helping with our thinking on this topic was school psychologist Mike Armstrong, whose professional experiences dealing with school crises provided us with a wealth of firsthand observations. Gerald Brock's editorial assistance on earlier versions of the manuscript is also greatly appreciated.

Last, but certainly not least, we would like to acknowledge Tracey Belmont and Nancy M. Land, whose contributions to the second edition were very important. As the editor for this project, Ms. Belmont provided important leadership. Her enthusiasm was also appreciated. Under the supervision of Ms. Land, the copy editing of the manuscript was superior.

S.E.B.
J.S.
S.L.

Contents

CHAPTER 1

Introduction

June 7, 1985, was an unusually hot, late spring day in California's Central Valley. A day that had begun with excitement for the students of a suburban Sacramento school district had ended in tragedy. On the way to an amusement park, a bus chartered for a sixth-grade graduation party had collided with a stalled truck and trailer rig on an interstate highway. The bus driver and several students were trapped in the wreckage for some time. Several students were hospitalized and, most tragically, one student was killed.

AWARENESS OF THE NEED FOR CRISIS PREPAREDNESS

ON THE day of this bus accident, each of the authors were looking forward to a summer vacation away from careers as school psychologists. Suddenly, however, attention was refocused on professional concerns as the first media reports of this tragedy were received. It was impossible to avoid thinking about this accident as the media bombarded the public with reports and updates. As this drama unfolded, school psychologists were portrayed as playing a critical role in assisting families, students, and staff cope with this crisis. It was at this point that each of the authors realized that *they* could someday be placed in a similar position. This realization heightened sensitivity to crisis events and the authors became aware that such events occurred with frightening frequency. This growing awareness generated anxiety as some unsettling questions were encountered. How does one conduct a crisis intervention? What does the school crisis response involve? What was the school's role during times of crisis? Each of the authors faced these questions in different ways.

Dr. Jonathan Sandoval, in his position as an academic school psychologist, has actively pursued answers to these questions through study and research while, as practicing school mental health professionals, Brock and Lewis addressed these school crisis response questions first hand. (Brock & Sandoval, 1997; Brock, Sandoval, & Lewis, 1996; J. Davis & Sandoval, 1991; J. Davis, Sandoval, & Wilson, 1988; Sandoval, 1985a, 1985b, 1987, 1988a, 1988b, 1989, in press-a, in press-b, in press-c; Sandoval & Brock, 1996; Sandoval, Davis, & Wilson, 1987; Sandoval, London, & Rey, 1994).

Dr. Stephen Brock's first crisis response occurred after an accidental shooting. One day after school, two intermediate grade students went to the home of one of the boys where a loaded rifle was accessible. They began to play with it. Apparently, one of the boys was holding the rifle on his lap when it accidentally discharged into the head of his friend. The wounded child's life was gravely threatened. Initially, there were fears that he would not live, but fortunately, he survived and eventually made a complete recovery. In the meantime, however, each of the intermediate grade classrooms at the boys' school was significantly traumatized. Both boys were popular students, and many classmates considered each their friend. Rumors ran rampant. Issues of blame, questions of the intentionality of the shooting, and punishment of the shooter were common. Students needed assistance dealing with the reality of a critically injured peer. They also needed answers to questions of how to respond to the student who had fired the rifle when he returned to school.

Ms. Sharon Lewis' first crisis response followed the accidental death of a student in a horseback-riding accident. Besides dealing with the various rumors about this death, Ms. Lewis was also faced with the task of identifying and assisting the students most significantly affected by this crisis. It was quickly recognized that the friends of the deceased student needed special attention.

For both Dr. Brock and Ms. Lewis, these first crisis interventions were unsettling. They knew that they needed to intervene; however, they were not exactly sure how to proceed, as responding to such events is not routine for most educators. Although each had given some casual consideration to crisis response, no formal crisis plans had been made. Because there were no school resources that could be turned to for guidance and support, both felt very much on their own. Looking back on these crisis responses, Brock and Lewis felt that they did an adequate job. However, as they realized they could have been much more prepared, the importance of crisis preparedness became more apparent.

Since the tragic bus accident 15 years ago and following a wide variety of professional crisis response experiences, each of the authors has invested significant time reading and writing about crisis theory, attending and giving numerous crisis response and intervention workshops and training sessions, and listening carefully to accounts of how other educators have helped their schools cope with crises. From these experiences, the authors have come to realize that it is not only possible to prepare for crises, but that it is necessary to do so. Having a crisis response plan in place significantly lessens anxiety about intervening during times of crisis. By providing a clear sense of direction, a crisis plan results in a more effective crisis response (Thompson, 1995). Systematic preparedness also helps to minimize the amount of trauma students may experience in times of crisis (Allen, Dlugokinski, Cohen, & Walker, 1999), and maximizes the likelihood they will adapt successfully to crises (Kline, Schonfeld, & Lichtenstein, 1995).

EVENTS THAT INFLUENCED THE AUTHORS' CRISIS RESPONSE VIEWS

In the pages that follow, you are provided with the authors' views on school crisis preparedness and response, which have been shaped by a variety of crisis response experiences. One experience played a primary role in the development of our views: On January 17, 1989, a gunman walked on to a crowded primary playground in a neighboring school district. Dressed in camouflage, he began shooting. Before taking his own life, the gunman killed 5 children and wounded 30 others, including a teacher (Cox & Grieve, 1989).

Along with other members of the local mental health community, we spent the next two weeks assisting the Stockton Unified School District as they helped the students, staff, and families of Cleveland Elementary School begin to cope with this disaster. Our experiences immediately following the Stockton schoolyard shooting are ones that we will never forget. Reassuring second-graders that it is safe to go out to recess, running a gauntlet of reporters, and helping families deal with having a child shot are all unforgettable memories. Our attempt to make some sense out of this tragedy, to make some good come of this great evil, was to redouble our crisis preparedness efforts. In large part, this book is a result of our experiences at Cleveland Elementary School.

Although primarily shaped by local experiences, our crisis response views have also been affected by events occurring outside California. Situational crises that have influenced thinking in this area are now briefly reviewed. This is done not only to further share origins of the authors' crisis response thinking, but also to reinforce that such traumas can occur at any place and at any time.

LANSING, MICHIGAN

On September 16, 1977, a truck crane struck a 231-foot pedestrian overpass next to an elementary school. Approximately 20 children were on the overpass at the time of the accident. Six students fell 15 feet to the street below and five were seriously injured (Blom, 1986). Blom's research report provided valuable information about the reactions of parents and children to such a tragedy. However, what was more important was Blom's account of his difficulty in obtaining the cooperation of the school in conducting this study. His report reinforced our experiences that research following crises is often made difficult by the fact that it can be perceived as a self-serving and exploitative activity. Given our belief that school crisis response research is critically needed, and to avoid such resistance, we recommend that research and evaluation of the crisis response be made a part of a school's crisis plan.

PETACH TIKVA, ISRAEL

On June 11, 1985, a train collided with a school bus that was taking a group of seventh graders on a year-end field trip. Nineteen students, one parent, one teacher, and the school bus driver were killed, and 15 other students critically injured. Three other school buses filled with the schoolmates of those who were killed and injured witnessed this accident (Klingman, 1987), thereby compounding this tragedy. The several published accounts of the mental health response to this disaster significantly influenced our school crisis response views. Klingman (1986, 1987) emphasized the importance of an awareness of cultural differences in reactions to crisis events, and of the need for a well-coordinated and organized response to such large scale disasters. Also influential was the article by Toubiana, Milgram, Strich, and Edelstein (1988), which reinforced our view that, to the extent possible, local or school site resources should provide direct crisis intervention services. Crisis intervenors brought in from outside an affected school should remain behind the scenes consulting with and supporting a school's primary helpers. Finally,

Milgram, Toubiana, Klingman, Raviv, and Goldstein (1988) provided data that verified the importance of prior friendships with victims in determining an individual's acute and chronic stress reactions.

COKEVILLE, WYOMING

On May 16, 1986, at 1:00 P.M., a husband and wife team invaded and held hostage approximately 160 students and adults at the Cokeville Elementary School. Reportedly, a ransom was demanded to help finance a "revolution." Two hours after it had begun, the siege ended when an explosive device was accidentally triggered. The bomb injured 80 persons including one of the hostage takers. Realizing that their plans had failed, the husband shot and killed his already wounded wife and then took his own life. Sandall's (1986) report of the school's response to this disaster further reinforced our view that school site resources should provide direct crisis intervention services and that outside crisis intervenors should remain behind the scenes. Additionally, this article verified our belief that the structure and routine of school can be reassuring. Returning students to school as soon as possible can be very helpful, and helping children talk about what has happened to them facilitates an optimal recovery.

WINNETKA, ILLINOIS

In May, 1988, a 30-year-old woman walked into the Hubbards Woods Elementary School, shot six students (killing the son of a school board member), and then committed suicide (Pitcher & Poland, 1992). Dillard (1989, 1990, cited in Pitcher & Poland, 1992), the head of psychological services for the school district affected by this tragedy, made several suggestions that influenced our views on crisis response. Among them, that it is important for the school to be familiar with available mental health resources; that clear and honest information be provided about the trauma; that the school faculty be made aware of the symptoms of posttraumatic stress; and that a plan be developed for reactions on the anniversary of crisis events.

JONESBORO, ARKANSAS

On March 24, 1998, two boys, 13 and 11 years old, opened fire on their middle school classmates as they assembled for a fire alarm. In less than four minutes, the pair had fired 22 rounds of ammunition, killing five and wounding 15 (Labi, 1998). The magnitude of this tragedy, and the national-level crisis response it required (Poland, 1998), emphasized the importance of multiple-level crisis response teams. While school site crisis teams can manage most school crises, some events are so overwhelming that outside crisis intervenors are necessary. This led us to consider the concept of crisis intervention mutual aid (Brock, 1998b).

SPRINGFIELD, OREGON

In May 1998, the 15-year-old son of two schoolteachers discharged 51 rounds of ammunition from a semiautomatic rifle and two pistols. When the shooting stopped, two students had been killed and 18 others wounded. Later, both of the boy's parents were found at home shot to death (Hornblower, 1998). Paine's (1998a, 1999) articles on this shooting reinforced our awareness of the profound effects that responding to such a tragedy can have on caregivers. They also emphasized that recovery is an ongoing process, that media management is an essential part of crisis response, and that a cadre of trained crisis responders is essential. Paine (1998b) emphasized the importance of actively involving all affected individuals in memorial development.

LITTLETON, COLORADO

The most violent and deadly act ever to occur on U.S. schoolgrounds took place on April 20, 1999 when two teens, aged 17 and 18, terrorized their entire school with a shooting and bombing spree that left 15 dead and 24 wounded. Before committing suicide, the killers fired approximately 900 rounds of ammunition from two sawed-off shotguns, a 9-mm semiautomatic carbine, and a semiautomatic handgun. More than 30 bombs placed throughout the school were later found by police (Gibbs, 1999). In addition to reinforcing virtually all of the other lessons learned about school crisis response, this event and the media attention that followed also suggested to us that media attention may have a contagion effect. It led to thoughts on the most appropriate and productive role for school personnel when working with the media in times of crisis (Lazarus, Brock, & Feinberg, 1999).

EVOLUTION OF THE SCHOOL CRISIS RESPONSE

There has been an increasing interest in school crisis preparedness and response. In 1987, results of a national survey suggested that most school psychologists felt that crisis intervention was important and were interested in learning more about it (Wise, Smead, & Huebner, 1987).* However, despite this interest, in the early 1990s, school crisis intervention was judged to still be in its infancy (Pitcher & Poland, 1992) and many school professionals reported that they had inadequate training for crisis intervention (Wise et al., 1987).

As with any infant, it is safe to say that early school responses to crisis events were reflexive in nature. From first-hand experiences, we observed that most school crisis responses were reactive. Very little prior planning had taken place. It was in response to the need for crisis planning that books, such as this volume's first edition, were written. Because of this increased attention, school crisis teams have begun to mature. Evidence of this maturation includes a growing school crisis response literature (e.g., Canter & Carroll, 1999; Fairchild, 1997; Johnson 1993; Petersen & Straub, 1992; Pitcher & Poland, 1992; Poland & McCormick, 1999). Perhaps even more convincing evidence of the growth and development of school crisis response can be found by observing media reports of school crises. The authors have observed that most of these reports end with words to the effect: "crisis counselors will be on hand to help distraught students."

As expectations for school crisis teams continue to increase, educators must further their ability to consciously reflect on the provision of these services. Soon it will no longer be acceptable to respond in a reflexive fashion to crisis events. As we enter a new century, the authors anticipate that school crisis preparedness will be *expected.*

RECENT LEGISLATION

STATE GOVERNMENT EFFORTS

Evidence supporting our suggestion that crisis preparedness will become "expected" can be found in recent state and federal legislative efforts. For example, at the state level in 1999, both Alaska and Virginia adopted legislation requiring their public schools to develop written school crisis emergency or response plans. In Alaska, SB 125, the School Crisis Response Planning Act, requires all school districts to develop a model crisis response plan for each of its schools. It further specifies the composition of

---

*Interest in crisis preparedness was particularly high among those who had dealt with crises (Collison et al., 1987). Poland and Pitcher (1990a), for example, reported that those school administrators who had experienced a school crisis advocated for crisis planning and the formation of crisis intervention teams.

each school's crisis response team, and details the specific components of plans. Finally, the Act requires annual review of the plan and annual crisis response team training. In Virginia, SB 827 amended its code relating to school safety (Code of Virginia, § 22.1–278.1) to include school crisis and emergency management plans. As with Alaska, this amendment requires each school district to develop a written crisis plan. It also specifies the range of critical events or emergencies that may require a crisis response.

Taking a more conservative approach, California's School Violence and Response Act of 1999 (AB 1366) authorizes funding to create a School Violence Prevention and Response Task Force. This task force will analyze and evaluate current statutes and programs in the area of school crisis prevention and response and then make appropriate policy recommendations. In Illinois, the "Safe to Learn Initiatives" sponsored by the Attorney General's office includes recommendations for the development of a School Emergency Response Team. This state-level team will assist schools during and following crisis events. And finally, a resolution by the Kansas legislature (House Concurrent Resolution No. 5018) "strongly urges every public and private elementary and secondary school to create a school crisis plan tailored to that school."

FEDERAL GOVERNMENT EFFORTS

Two federal legislative efforts may also be seen as developing an expectation for school crisis preparedness and response. First the School Safety Enhancement Act of 1999 (H.R. 1898; S. 973) proposes the establishment of the National Center for School and Youth Safety. Among the duties of this Center would be emergency response (designed to assist local communities respond to school safety crises), and information and outreach (designed to compile and share information about the best practices in school violence prevention, intervention, and crisis management). Also, the School Anti-Violence Empowerment Act (H.R. 1895) would authorize the Secretary of Education to provide grants to school districts to help them establish or enhance crisis intervention programs.

PURPOSE AND PLAN OF THIS BOOK

With the growing expectations and mandates for crisis response in mind, this book shares the knowledge we have gained developing and implementing our own school crisis response plans. This book is not intended to be a theoretical treatise. Rather, its primary goal is to provide school personnel with the practical information needed to meet the growing expectations for school crisis preparedness and response. It is anticipated that the information provided will be applied in the development of local and regional school crisis response teams.

Chapter 2 of this book presents a brief review of crisis theory. Following this discussion is a review of techniques or strategies found helpful in getting crisis response planning started (Chapter 3). Specifically, the processes schools may go through in educating themselves about crisis response are reviewed. Also reviewed are strategies designed to increase a district's receptivity to crisis preparedness. This discussion investigates the process of team building and includes suggestions for forming a Crisis Response Planning Committee, identifying priorities, conducting needs assessments, creating a tentative plan, and obtaining a consultant.

After presenting suggestions for getting started and for creating an environment receptive to crisis preparedness, we review recommendations for securing a commitment to crisis response planning (Chapter 4). Here we examine strategies aimed at developing and implementing a school district crisis response policy.

Chapters 5 through 13 examine the specific components of a model crisis response plan. These components include planning for crisis responses; delineation of specific crisis intervention procedures; risk screening or triage procedures; crisis intervention; working with the media, security, and safety issues; identifying and preventing student violence; emergency medical and health procedures; and evaluation of the crisis response.

Although an important focus of this book is on preparing for and responding to the immediate mental health needs of students and staff, this volume also addresses multidimensionality of crisis response. Given this reality, we distinguish between the terms *crisis intervention* and *crisis response.* You may be more familiar with the term *crisis intervention* as a descriptor for the team that intervenes following traumatic events. However, we describe such teams as crisis "response" teams because of our observations that the direct crisis intervention services provided to traumatized individuals are only a part of the crisis response. As will be described later, crisis response involves much more than crisis intervention. Thus, *crisis response* is used as a more inclusive term designed to refer to the variety of activities required to manage the aftermath of a crisis event. The term *crisis intervention* is reserved for those psychological first aid and mental health activities that involve provision of direct intervention services to traumatized individuals. Additionally, although not a primary focus of this book, we also address the important role schools can play in the prevention of crises in the first place (primary prevention), and in providing the long-term follow-up often required by crises (tertiary prevention).

It is our hope that this book will assist school districts in completing crisis preparedness plans, which can benefit both students and staff. Crisis response plans not only allow educators to provide students with more effective support, but they also make the process of crisis response less anxiety provoking for educators.

CHAPTER 2

Crisis Theory

The Coconut Grove fire was a tragedy never to be forgotten in New England history. It took place in the evening following the Harvard-Yale football game, in a Boston nightclub where couples and families had gathered to celebrate the occasion. Four hundred and ninety-one persons lost their lives; thirty-nine living casualties were brought to the Massachusetts General Hospital and segregated on a ward where they received the most recently approved burn treatment.

—Lindemann (1979, p. 47)

A LTHOUGH THIS book is not considered a theoretical volume, we believe a brief review of crisis theory is necessary before continuing the discussion of crisis preparedness and response. Without the conceptual framework provided by crisis theory, it is difficult for crisis response planners to develop meaningful crisis management plans. This discussion of crisis theory provides a basic understanding of the terms *crisis* and *crisis intervention* and what it means to be *in crisis*. For more complete discussions of crisis theory, the reader is encouraged to refer to Aguilera (1998), Caplan (1964), and Slaikeu (1990).

THE ORIGINS OF CRISIS INTERVENTION

The origins of modern crisis intervention can be found in the pioneering work of Eric Lindemann following the Coconut Grove fire (e.g., Aguilera, 1998; Pitcher & Poland, 1992; Slaikeu, 1990). Lindemann's (1944, 1979) work describes his efforts with the survivors of this fire and explores

11

their grief reactions. It provides the foundation on which our current understanding of crisis reactions is built.

In 1946, Gerald Caplan joined with Lindemann in establishing one of the first community mental health programs. Together they continued the pioneering crisis intervention work started by Lindemann. Although Lindemann presented a brief description of crisis types, it was Caplan who discussed them in depth (Smith, 1990). This major contribution to crisis theory came from Caplan's observation that crises are generated not only by situational factors (such as the Coconut Grove fire), but also by developmental transitions. Caplan (1964) suggested that a failure to negotiate transitions from one developmental stage of life to another (such as from adolescence to adulthood) plays a role in the development of psychopathology. He also suggested that personal and social resources are important in determining how an individual resolves both developmental and situational crises.

Caplan was also one of the first theorists to address the concept of *homeostasis* (Smith, 1990). This concept suggests that people constantly employ problem-solving strategies to maintain a state of emotional equilibrium. Following a crisis, however, the individual may not have access to the problem-solving strategies needed to cope with the crisis reality. The resulting disequilibrium is associated with the crisis victim's lack of emotional control. In other words, Caplan (1964) views a crisis as an upset of and an inability to maintain a steady emotional state.

Caplan's (1964) work with children also represents a major contribution to crisis theory (E. Nelson & Slaikeu, 1990). He suggested that children who cope with crises are those who have the resources necessary to endure emotional disequilibrium. These children also have the resources required for making the changes crises necessitate.

CRISIS TAXONOMIES

The term *crisis* has a variety of meanings and connotations in our society (Pitcher & Poland, 1992). It can be used to describe financial, environmental, governmental, and educational problems, as well as personal emotional trauma. Simply stating that you plan to develop a crisis response plan can mean different things to different people. Crisis response planners need to specify (both for themselves and others) what it is that they are preparing for.

Building on the work of Lindemann and Caplan, today's crisis theorists typically differentiate between *developmental* crises and *situational* crises (Aguilera, 1998; Mitchell & Resnik, 1981; Parad, 1965; Slaikeu, 1990; Smith,

1990). These concepts are based primarily upon Erikson's (1963) model of developmental and accidental crises (Smith, 1990). Developmental crises are defined as those events associated with movement from one developmental stage of life to another. Examples include entering school for the first time, becoming an adolescent, and beginning adulthood. Whether these events become crises depends on a number of variables, including timing; and personal, financial, and social resources. Crises of this type and the issues they generate are somewhat predictable. On the other hand, situational or accidental crises are defined as incidents that are unexpected in nature. For example, Lindemann's (1944, 1979) work provides us with possible reactions to a situational crisis (the Coconut Grove nightclub fire). Besides being unexpected, situational crises have a sudden onset and seem to strike from nowhere. They have an emergency quality to them and have the potential to affect an entire community. Like developmental crises, many situational crises (such as the death of a loved one) are an inevitable part of life. They are also times of both danger and opportunity. Although the crisis event itself is perceived as dangerous, the new coping strategies these events require create an opportunity for personal growth (Slaikeu, 1990). Unlike developmental crises, however, the timing of situational crises is unpredictable. In making this point Slaikeu states:

> Not all life crises are directly tied to the natural process of maturation; many are completely unpredictable. The loss of one's entire family in an automobile accident, leukemia in an eight-year-old boy, rape, being held hostage under the threat of death—events such as these are called *situational* crises. The most salient characteristic of these crises is that the precipitating event (flood, physical attack, death of a loved one) has little or no association with the individual's age or developmental stage in life. Situational crises can strike virtually anyone at any time. (p. 64)

From several sources (Carlson, 1997; Green, 1993; Matsakis, 1994; Slaikeu, 1990; Young, 1998), six classifications are offered for potentially traumatic crisis events. These classifications are severe illness or injury, violent and/or unexpected death, threatened death and/or injury, acts of war, natural disasters, and manmade/industrial disasters. Examples of events fitting into each of these categories are provided in Table 2.1.

"Crisis" as Defined by the School Crisis Response

School systems need to be prepared to deal with all kinds of crises, both those that they can anticipate and those they cannot. However, the unpredictable or situational crisis is the one most commonly associated with

Table 2.1

Crisis Event Classifications and Examples

Classification	Examples
Severe illness and injury	Life-threatening illnesses; disfigurement and dismemberment; road, train, and maritime accidents; assaults; suicide attempts; fires/arson; explosions
Violent and/or unexpected death	Fatal illnesses; fatal accidents; homicides; suicides; fires/arson; explosions
Threatened death and/or injury	Human aggression (e.g., robbery, mugging, or rape); Domestic violence (e.g., child and spouse battery/abuse); kidnappings
Acts of war	Invasions; terrorist attacks; hostage-taking; prisoners of war; torture; hijackings
Natural disasters	Hurricanes; floods; fires; earthquakes; tornadoes; avalanches/landslides; volcanic eruptions; lightening strikes; tsunamis
Man-made/industrial disasters	Nuclear accidents; airline crashes; exposure to noxious agents/toxic waste; dam failures; electrical fires; construction/plant accidents

the need for a crisis response plan, and it is the one that constitutes the most appropriate definition of *crisis* for the school crisis response planner.

In most cases, existing school mental health programs are prepared to address developmental crises. When available, these resources typically do an excellent job of preventing, identifying, treating, and/or referring individual students as they enter developmental crises. However, one or two counselors, psychologists, nurses, or social workers serving the typical elementary, middle, or high school are not sufficient following situational crises. These events have the potential to affect the entire school community. At these times, the need for more planning becomes evident. It is simply not practical to employ full-time all the support staff needed to react in such emergencies (Pitcher & Poland, 1992). Therefore, school systems must make contingency plans capable of dealing with situational crises. Chapters 3 (Getting Started), 4 (Developing and Implementing a Crisis Response Policy), and 5 (Components of a Crisis Preparedness Plan) of this book will assist schools in preparing for the unexpected and frightening reality of situational crises.

THE CRISIS STATE

The student or staff member who, as the result of a situational crisis, has entered a crisis state is an important focus of a crisis response. Thus, it is essential for crisis response planners to have an understanding of what it means to be *in crisis*.

The most important cause of this state is a stressful or hazardous event (Roberts, 1990). However, of equal importance is the individual's perception or subjective interpretation of this event (Silverman, 1977; Slaikeu, 1990; Taplin, 1971). In other words, whether or not an individual enters a crisis state has as much to do with how threatening the event is perceived to be as it does with the crisis itself.

The crisis state results in significant upset, discomfort, anxiety, disorganization, and/or disequilibrium. This distress is associated with an inability to cope with or adapt to the crisis circumstances (Cohen & Ahearn, 1980; Rapoport, 1965; Roberts, 1990; Slaikeu, 1990). Further, individuals who enter a crisis state will have perceived the crisis event as one that has significantly changed their life situation (Cohen & Ahearn, 1980). M. Lewis, Gottesman, and Gutstein (1979)* suggest that the crisis state follows an unexpected event that causes extreme psychological discomfort and that cannot be dealt with by customary coping strategies. Consequently, new methods of problem solving must be employed. However, if these methods also fail, the individual in crisis will feel anxiety, depression, helplessness, and lowered self-esteem. The intensity of the crisis state's psychological discomfort is so severe that it cannot be allowed to continue indefinitely. Thus, the individual will continue to try different coping strategies until one is found that alleviates the discomfort. This crisis resolution is typically accomplished within eight weeks or less. However, it is important to note that there is no guarantee that this resolution will be adaptive. For example, following a crisis at school a student may cope with the crisis by becoming truant. The student's refusal to attend

---

*Lewis, Gottesman, and Gutstein (1979) summarizes the work of Caplan (1961, 1964), Hansell, Wodarczyk, and Handlon-Lathrop (1970), and Taplin (1971).

school, although maladaptive, will solve the problem at hand (i.e., the emotional pain now associated with school).

The definition that appeals most to the authors has been offered by Slaikeu (1990), who defines the crisis state as: "... a temporary state of *upset and disorganization,* characterized chiefly by an individual's *inability to cope* with a particular situation using customary methods of problem solving, and by the *potential for a radically positive or negative outcome*" [italics added] (p. 15).

Upset and Disorganization

The individual in crisis will feel exhaustion, helplessness, inadequacy, confusion, and anxiety (Slaikeu, 1990). Physical symptoms may also be seen. Disorganization or disequilibrium may be experienced in all spheres of the individual's life. Disorganized functioning may occur in work relationships, family relationships, social relationships, and in social activities. Part of this state of upset and disorganization is a lessening of the individual's natural defenses (which in a crisis may no longer appear to be functional) and increased suggestibility.

Inability to Cope

As we mature and face new and varied problem situations, we develop a variety of coping strategies that help us adapt to the changing reality of life. For example, with minor or everyday problems, it may be helpful to talk to a friend, take a vacation, or even ignore the problem. In a crisis, however, the presenting problem is so overwhelming that previously developed coping strategies are viewed as ineffective (Slaikeu, 1990). The result is a sense of being out of control and unable to adapt or adjust. Children who lack the perspective of adults and have yet to develop a broad array of coping strategies are particularly vulnerable to a crisis event.

Potential for Radically Positive or Negative Outcomes

Slaikeu (1990) points out that crises are events that redefine how we perceive the world and our place in it. As such, they are situations where the potential for change is great. Defenses are down and suggestibility is high. In other words, crises motivate change. Individuals who successfully work through a crisis not only no longer feel upset and disorganized, but also have developed new coping strategies and have grown psychologically. On the other hand, those who are unable to resolve the crisis adaptively may find that they need to withdraw from many areas of their life (Caplan, 1964).

This state is more than simple stress. Crises differ from stress in several ways (Slaikeu, 1990). First, the defenses of an individual in crisis are down and he or she is very open to suggestion (Halpern, 1973). The individual who is stressed, on the other hand, is typically very defensive. Second, a crisis has the potential for a radically positive or negative outcome. The typical outcome for the individual experiencing stress is either adaptation and survival, or a return to the status quo. Finally, a crisis state has a sudden onset and is of fairly short duration. The stress state, on the other hand, usually builds gradually and is many times a chronic problem.

In concluding his discussion of the crisis state, Slaikeu (1990) indicates that although the symptoms of the crisis state are in many ways similar to those of pathological states, they are not signs of mental illness. Anyone, regardless of how psychologically ill or healthy, can enter a crisis state. Simply put, it is a normal reaction to abnormal circumstances.

THE SCHOOL CRISIS RESPONSE TO THE CRISIS STATE

It is essential that the school system be prepared to respond immediately whenever a student enters a crisis state. The potential for a radically negative outcome makes it dangerous not to do so. As a result, one of the hallmarks of an effective crisis response plan is the use of available school and community resources to identify individuals who have entered into a crisis state and to then provide immediate crisis intervention and, if needed, ongoing therapy. Chapters 6 (Components of a Crisis Response), 7 (Psychological Triage and Referral), and 8 (Crisis Intervention) of this book assist schools with the tasks of identifying and working with those students affected by a situational crisis.

CRISIS INTERVENTION

Crisis intervention models and techniques are directive, time-limited, and goal-directed procedures designed to assist individuals who have entered a crisis state (Roberts, 1990). Mitchell and Resnik (1981) state that the goals of crisis intervention are to "(a) Shield the crisis victim from any additional stress. (b) Assist the victim in organizing and mobilizing his resources (family and community). (c) Return the victim, as much as possible, to a pre-crisis level of functioning" (p. 11).

Several authors offer descriptions of what steps or activities might be involved in a crisis intervention (e.g., Aguilera, 1998; Burgess & Baldwin, 1981; Sandoval, 1988a; Slaikeu, 1990). Roberts (1990), for example, offers a model that he feels synthesizes the work of a number of authorities. He identifies the following procedural steps for working with an individual in crisis:

> (1) Make psychological contact and rapidly establish the relationship. (2) Examine the dimensions of the problem in order to define it. (3) Encourage an exploration of feelings and emotions. (4) Explore and assess past coping attempts. (5) Generate and explore alternatives and specific solutions. (6) Restore cognitive functioning through implementation of action plan. (7) Follow-up. (p. 12)

Beginning with the work of Lindemann (1944), crisis intervention has always had a preventative focus (Slaikeu, 1990). Its primary goal is to prevent psychopathology resulting from a failure to cope with crises in a healthy manner. However, crisis intervention, is not the only type of preventative mental health intervention. Caplan's (1964) three-part conceptual model, widely regarded as the most appropriate for use in the public health setting, differentiates between primary, secondary, and tertiary prevention. To place crisis intervention in context with these other mental health interventions, Slaikeu (1990) points out that whereas primary prevention is aimed at preventing entry into the crisis state, and tertiary prevention is the long-term care often necessitated by crises, a crisis intervention, or secondary prevention, is provided immediately upon entry into the crisis state, when the risk for negative outcomes is greatest.

CRISIS INTERVENTION AS DEFINED BY THE SCHOOL CRISIS RESPONSE

From the perspective of the school crisis response planner, Slaikeu's (1990) description of crisis intervention has the greatest practical value. In his discussion, he points out that crisis intervention is a twofold process that involves both ". . . immediate psychological first aid (offered by those closest to the event) and short-term crisis therapy (offered by trained counselors and therapists)" (p. 12). The reestablishment of immediate coping is the chief goal of psychological first aid. Crisis therapy continues the crisis intervention process begun by psychological first aid and attempts to assist the individual work through and resolve the crisis event. It is his distinction between first aid and therapy that gives Slaikeu's definition of crisis intervention its practical utility. It allows school crisis response planners to develop procedures that place school personnel in appropriate roles. For example, although it would be appropriate to involve just about all school staff members in the provision of psychological first aid, only mental health professionals should be involved in the provision of crisis therapy. Chapter 8 (Crisis Intervention) of this book clarifies for crisis response planners the process of crisis intervention. It includes discussions of psychological first aid and psychotherapeutic treatments. In addition, Appendix A provides a description of an in-service program designed to facilitate the development of psychological first aid skills.

SCHOOL CRISIS RESPONSE: THE UNTOLD STORY

The nature of most situational crises does not allow schools to focus on providing crisis intervention to those who are in crisis. The untold story of school crisis response is that it requires activities other than crisis intervention. For example, following crises, schools might anticipate that the media will create a series of challenges and opportunities that need to be addressed (Paine, 1998a; Poland & McCormick, 1999). Issues of physical safety and problems associated with physical injuries may require significant attention (Poland, 1994). In addition, it is important to have strategies available to debrief the crisis team (Mitchell & Everly, 1996a) and evaluate the crisis response. Ultimately, a crisis response plan must be prepared to deal with a number of issues and concerns. Chapters 9 through 13 of this book provide the reader with concrete suggestions for addressing these issues and concerns.

SUMMARY

This discussion of crisis theory reviewed the origins of crisis intervention and presented different crisis taxonomies. School crisis response plans typically address the situational crisis. The crisis state and the crisis intervention techniques employed to help people in this state were also briefly reviewed. A crisis intervention model that distinguishes between immediate psychological first aid and professional psychotherapeutic treatments will be most useful to the school crisis intervention planner.

CHAPTER 3

Getting Started

The Crisis Response Planning Committee meeting was scheduled to begin at 2:00 P.M. on January 17, 1989. Agenda items included the development of a tentative crisis plan and discussion of a proposed school board crisis response policy statement. However, this agenda was immediately cast aside as the magnitude of what had happened earlier in the day became apparent. At about 11:40 A.M., a heavily armed lone gunman, wearing a flak vest, had walked on to the crowded primary playground of Cleveland Elementary School in Stockton, California. After setting his own car on fire, as an apparent distraction, the gunman began shooting. The 105 AK-47 assault rifle rounds, fired from two different locations in less than 2 minutes, tore holes through concrete walls and penetrated metal playground equipment. The damage done to almost three dozen young bodies was unspeakable. Before taking his own life, the gunman had killed five children and wounded 29 others and one teacher (Cox & Grieve, 1989). Besides these physical injuries, the psychological damage done to the entire school was profound. After our offer of assistance was accepted, the Planning Committee found itself participating in the Cleveland School crisis intervention response. With this intervention came the realization that crises were not going to wait for the development of a response plan. They could, in fact, happen at any time.

—Author recollection of the day of the Stockton schoolyard shooting (January 17, 1989)

THERE ARE several prerequisites to beginning crisis response planning. These include finding at least one committed individual who is available to take a leadership position, having access to knowledge about crisis management and working with a reasonably receptive school district (Sandoval et al., 1994). Ideally the previous chapters have (1) helped provide a sense of the importance of crisis intervention, (2) interested the reader in assuming a leadership role, and (3) begun to provide a theoretical crisis intervention framework. This chapter focuses on acquiring the additional knowledge necessary to complete crisis response planning and on increasing school district receptivity to this planning. Once these ingredients are in place, crisis response planners will be able to secure a school district commitment to crisis preparedness, which is discussed in Chapter 4 (Crisis Response Policy Development and Implementation).

Before going further, it is important to point out that the process of crisis preparedness planning is time-consuming. According to Cultice (1992), officials in districts where crisis response plans are already in place caution that it takes one to two years for a program to become operational. The authors' experiences support this conclusion.

The first step is to learn as much as possible about crisis preparedness and response. This book provides a compendium of useful information about getting ready for the inevitable crisis. However, reading and self-study constitute only one method for self-education.

STRATEGIES FOR SELF-EDUCATION

REVIEW THE LITERATURE

There are several strategies useful in educating yourself about crisis preparedness and response. One of the more important, yet also the most time-consuming, is to study the crisis literature. Sample resources are presented in Table 3.1.

USE THE INTERNET

A second strategy for self-education that has become a valuable resource is the Internet. Recently, there has been a significant growth in crisis-related sites, many of which are helpful with crisis response planning. Table 3.2 provides a review of useful crisis intervention Web sites.

PROFESSIONAL DEVELOPMENT

A third strategy for self-education is to attend conferences and workshops dealing with crisis intervention. Such workshops are available at

Table 3.1
Annotated Bibliography

A library computer search revealed 347 entries of books that are in some way related to the topic of crisis intervention. Since it is impossible to review each of these works, 16 books that one or more of the authors found helpful are listed.

Aguilera, D.C. (1998). *Crisis intervention: Theory and methodology* (8th ed.). St. Louis, MO: Mosby.

What started back in 1970 as a joint effort with Janice Messick is now in its eighth edition and perhaps one of the two classics in the field. It is well-written, pragmatic, and a must for any practitioner. Although somewhat medically and adult-oriented, its longevity speaks to its usefulness. One of the most often cited works on crisis intervention.

Brooks, B., & Siegel, P.M. (1996). *The scared child: Helping kids overcome traumatic events.* New York: Wiley.

Written especially for parents and other caregivers, this three-part book facilitates a general understanding of children's responses to trauma and provides guidance on how adults can promote coping. Part one includes a general discussion of trauma, its effects at different ages, and how to recognize signs of distress in children. It concludes with a discussion Brooks' debriefing model. Its greatest use will be as a resource to offer caregivers following crisis intervention consultations. It may also serve as a helpful addition to community and teacher crisis intervention in-service programs.

Canter, A.S., & Carroll, S.A. (Eds.). (1999). *Crisis prevention and response: A collection of NASP resources.* Bethesda, MD: National Association of School Psychologists.

This volume is a collection of previously published papers on crisis prevention and response. It provides parents, teachers, and crisis response planners with information on a variety of crisis topics. Specific issues addressed include violence prevention, warning signs of youth violence, cultural issues, suicide, posttraumatic stress, as well as sample checklists and forms.

Carlson, E.B. (1997). *Trauma assessments: A clinician's guide.* New York: Guilford.

Designed to help mental health professionals understand and assess psychological trauma, school crisis response planners will appreciate its discussion of what makes a crisis event truly traumatic. Also informative are the detailed profiles of measures designed to assess children's trauma reactions.

Table 3.1 *(Continued)*

Fairchild, T.N. (Ed.). (1997). *Crisis intervention strategies for school-based helpers.* (2nd ed.). Springfield, IL: Charles C. Thomas.

This collection of chapters, addressing a variety of child and adolescent crises, was written for school-based helpers. From the information provided it is hoped that this text will (1) help to reduce the number of students who require crisis intervention, (2) assist students who have experienced various crises, and (3) provide guidance for working with students who display maladaptive coping. Specific crisis issues addressed include separation and divorce, stepfamilies, disabled students, abused and neglected students, substance abuse, death and grief, violent and disruptive students, suicide, eating disorders, teen pregnancy, and stress. Each of the 12 chapters includes assessment devices, curricular materials, and suggestions for further study and support.

Johnson, K. (1993). *School crisis management: A hands-on guide to training crisis response teams.* Alameda, CA: Hunter House.

Designed as a crisis response team training resource, crisis response planners will find the full page masters that can be reproduced to provide handouts or transparencies especially useful. Chapter titles include the following: Crisis, The Traumatic Stress Reaction, School Intervention, Group Intervention, and Taking Care of Yourself.

Lindemann, E. (1979). *Beyond grief: Studies in crisis intervention.* New York: Aronson.

Perhaps the other classic of the field. Lindemann began his studies of crisis intervention after the Coconut Grove fire in Boston, which essentially began the field of crisis intervention. Although initially tied to the study of acute grief following disaster, his work expanded to other areas and is probably one of the best works on the psychodynamics of crisis intervention.

Matsakis, A. (1994). *Post-traumatic stress disorder: A complete treatment guide.* Oakland, CA: New Harbinger.

Designed as an introduction to PTSD for psychotherapists, school crisis response planners will find the first part of this volume especially helpful. In it the author defines trauma, reviews theories regarding the causes of traumatization and provides a brief description of trauma symptoms. The discussion of the biochemistry of traumatization is also very interesting. Found throughout the volume are a series of client handouts that can be used to gain needed information about, and provide helpful information to, the person in crisis.

(continued)

Table 3.1 *(Continued)*

Mitchell, J.T., & Everly, G.S. (1996). *Critical incident stress debriefing: An operations manual for the prevention of traumatic stress among emergency services and disaster workers* (2nd ed., rev.). Ellicot City, MD: Chevron.

Although designed for those working with emergency service personnel, applications to school crisis response planning can readily be made. Perhaps the most important feature of this book is its description of the Critical Incident Stress Debriefing model, a technique that can be used to help groups cope with a common crisis event.

Monahan, C. (1997). *Children and trauma: A guide for parents and professionals.* San Francisco: Jossey-Bass.

This volume provides a review of the effects of traumatic events (such as accidents, abuse, and violence) on children and offers guidelines for helping youngsters cope. Especially helpful for the school crisis response planner is the discussion of warning signs that indicate a child is in need of professional mental health counseling.

National School Safety Center. (1990). *School safety check book.* Westlake Village, CA: Author.

Designed for school-based professionals, this book reviews crime and violence prevention in schools. It includes sections on school climate and discipline, school attendance, personal safety, and school security. Each section includes a review of safety problems and provides prevention strategies. Charts, surveys, and tables plus descriptions of model programs are also provided.

Petersen, S., & Straub, R.L. (1992). *School crisis survival guide: Management techniques and materials for counselors and administrators.* West Nyack, NY: Center for Applied Research in Education.

A very readable, user-friendly work designed specifically for educators. It is one of the few books found that offers crisis preparedness suggestions. Additional chapters examine crisis counseling and provide specific activities for the resolution of trauma and grief. The copyright provisions of this book make it especially useful. They allow individual administrators and counselors to reproduce worksheets and activity pages for use at individual schools.

Poland, S., & McCormick, J.S. (1999). *Coping with crisis: Lessons learned.* Longmont, CO: Sopris West.

Intended by its authors to be a "quick read," this volume focuses on the immediate school response to violence-related crises. This is an applied work that includes numerous real life examples of school crisis response,

Table 3.1 *(Continued)*

as well as two expanded case studies. It also includes one chapter on suicide and one chapter on long-term crisis interventions.

Sandoval, J. (Ed.). (1988). *Crisis counseling, intervention, and prevention in the schools.* Hillsdale, NJ: Erlbaum.

As with Fairchild's book, this is a collection of chapters covering a diversity of crisis areas (e.g., divorce, abuse, death, and suicide), all child and adolescent focused. This book is very readable, and it is written for a school-based practitioner audience. An added value of this particular work is that it not only looks at crisis intervention, it also addresses the issue of how to try to prevent and/or prepare for predictable crises again, with a school-based orientation. A second edition of this work is in press.

Slaikeu, K.A. (1990). *Crisis intervention: A handbook for practice and research* (2nd ed.). Boston, MA: Allyn & Bacon.

One of the most popular handbooks available on crisis intervention. Slaikeu has long been involved in this area and does an excellent job of coalescing the available knowledge and presenting it to the reader in a clear fashion. Although not specifically a child-focused book, he does one of the best jobs of explaining the basics of crisis intervention practice. Helpful additions to this second edition are chapters on providing crisis intervention training.

Table 3.2

Internet Web Sites of Interest to the Crisis Response Planner

http://www.aacap.org
American Academy of Child and Adolescent Psychiatry
Available in both English and Spanish, this Web site's "Facts for Families" page includes pamphlets that cover a variety of mental health issues. Specific topics that crisis planners will find helpful include: "Children and Grief," "Children's Sleep Problems," "Children's Threats: When Are They Serious?" "Helping Children After Disaster," "Teen Suicide," and "Understanding Violent Behavior in Children and Adolescents."

http://www.aaets.org
The American Academy of Experts in Traumatic Stress
This Web site provides information about Academy membership, publications and certifications. Its most practical feature is access to the

(continued)

Table 3.2 *(Continued)*

document "Crisis Response in Our Schools: An Overview (which is based upon the Academy's publication *A Practical Guide for Crisis Response in Our Schools*).

http://www.apa.org
The American Psychological Association
Located on this Web site's "Consumer Help Center" page, viewers will find a copy of "Warning Signs," a violence prevention guide for youth from the Association and MTV. Hard free copies of this document can be ordered online. Another helpful article found on this site is titled: "Coping with the Aftermath of a Disaster."

http://www.childlaw.law.sc.edu/manuals/user/crisisi
South Carolina Children's Law Office
This Web site provides access to a "Crisis Intervention" user manual that may be viewed online. Manual contents include: "Understanding Crisis," "Crisis Intervention Goals and Steps," "Crisis Intervention Assessment," "Crisis Intervention Treatment Approaches and Techniques," "Termination and Follow-up Services," and "The Crisis Intervention Worker."

http://www.ncptsd.org
National Center for PTSD
This Center, and its Web site, are programs of the U.S. Department of Veteran Affairs. It provides information on a broad range of research and training programs. A helpful document found within this site is "Information About PTSD." Also, found on its "Fact Sheets" page are the following: "PTSD in Children," "Survivors of Natural Disasters," and "PTSD and the Family." In addition, viewers can download a PDF file titled "Disaster Mental Health Services: A Guidebook for Clinicians and Administrators." This document, which is in the public domain, addresses the reactions of survivors; how to help survivors, helpers, and organizations; and mental health team and program development. Finally, PDF files for the *PTSD Research Quarterly* can be viewed. An index for this journal is available.

http://www.ed.gov/offices/OESE/SDFS/
U.S. Department of Education (Safe and Drug Free Schools Program)
Here the document "Early Warning, Timely Response: A Guide to Safe Schools" can be accessed.

http://www.fema.gov
Federal Emergency Management Agency
This is one of the best Web sites for crisis response planners. Available in both English and Spanish, it contains a variety of resources which parents and students will also find helpful. By accessing this site's Virtual Library

Table 3.2 *(Continued)*

and Electronic Reading Room, viewers can browse the *FEMA for Kids* room, which contains disaster preparedness activities, curriculums and games for children. It also includes resources for adults such as a mental health checklist and a discussion of how to help child victims. In addition, viewers can download a PDF file titled "How to Help Children After a Disaster: A Guidebook for Teachers." The *Preparedness, Training and Exercise* room includes an emergency preparedness checklist and a disaster supply kit list. It also includes suggestions for how to prepare for and respond to a variety of specific crisis events. Finally, another PDF file titled "Disaster Preparedness Coloring Book" can be downloaded. This document includes coloring activities for children and "Action Steps for Adults" on helping children respond to and prepare for a variety of disasters.

http://www.hhpub.com/journals/crisis
Hogrefe & Huber Publisher's Journal "Crisis: The Journal of Crisis Intervention and Suicide Prevention"
This Web site allows for online viewing of previous editions of this journal. It includes a table of contents.

http://www.icisf.org
International Critical Incident Stress Foundation
This Web site provides several documents that crisis response planners will find helpful. Titles found on the site include "School Crisis Response: A CISM Perspective," "Signs and Symptoms," and "Some Things to Try to Mitigate CIS Effects." In addition this site contains descriptions and outlines of courses offered by the Foundation, and has a description of the Foundation's 24-hour emergency hotline of obtaining crisis intervention assistance.

http://www.istss.org
The International Society for Traumatic Stress Studies
The most interesting document on this Web site is a preliminary draft of the Society's "Treatment of Posttraumatic Stress Disorder: Critical Reviews and Treatment Guidelines" (istss.org/quick/toc.htm/). Online discussion groups with many topics of interest to crisis response planners can also be found on this site. Finally, it also provides an excellent list of resources and related links.

http://www.naspweb.org
National Association of School Psychologists (NASP)
By visiting this Web site's search engine and entering the word "crisis," viewers can gain access to NASP's "Resources on Crisis Prevention

(continued)

Table 3.2 *(Continued)*

and Violence Prevention." Specific documents found here include "Children's Reaction to Trauma," "Helping Children Cope with Disaster," and a variety of crisis response materials provided by the Association's National Emergency Assistance Team. This site also provides a PDF file of a special edition of the *Communiqué* (NASP's newsletter) which addresses the topic of crisis and loss.

http://www.nssc1.org
National School Safety Center
A helpful resource found on this Web site include a "Check List for Characteristics for Youth Who Have Caused School Associated Violent Deaths." This site also provides a PDF file of the Center's report on "School Associated Violent Deaths." For a small fee, viewers can order a variety of resource papers, the video "School Crisis: Under Control" and the book *School Safety Check Book.*

http://www.psych.org
American Psychiatric Association
This site contains a link to the Association's "Disaster Psychiatry" page. This page is specifically designed to provide information useful for preparing for and responding to disasters. Found on the "Public Information" page are a variety of handouts addressing mental health issues. "Fact Sheets" of particular interest to crisis response planners include "When Disaster Strikes" and "Teen Suicide." Also, found among the "Let's Talk About . . ." series is a handout on PTSD.

http://www.pta.org/programs/crisis
National PTA: Violence, Kids, Crisis. What You Can Do.
This Web site provides a list of topics providing parents and educators with guidance on how to prevent youth violence. Issues addressed include the warning signs of emotional problems, school violence prevention and response plan development, and media management. A helpful crisis intervention bibliography includes links to other related Web sites. This site also provides a PDF file of the PTA's "Community Violence Prevention Kit."

http://www.redcross.org
American Red Cross
This Web site includes the handout "Helping Children and Adolescents Cope with Grief and Loss." This site also provides a PDF file of the Red Cross' pamphlet "Talking About Disaster."

Table 3.2 *(Continued)*

http://www.schoolsecurity.org
National School Safety and Security Services
Operated by a national consulting firm specializing in school security and crisis preparedness training, this Web site includes a variety of free school security and crisis preparedness training materials. Links with other related sites are provided.

http://www.suicidology.org
American Association of Suicidology
This Web site's online resources include the following titles: "Understanding and Helping the Suicidal Person," "Suicide in Youth" and "Suicide Statistics." For a small fee, viewers can also order school guidelines for responding to suicide.

http://www.try-nova.org
National Organization for Victim Assistance (NOVA)
This Web site's online resources include documents titled "The Crisis Reaction," "Why Did This Happen to Me?" and "The Psychological Aftermath." For a small fee, a variety of training materials and informational packets and bulletins can be ordered. Found on its "Crisis Resources and Links" page is a comprehensive list of crisis-related toll-free phone numbers.

http://www.uncg.edu/edu/ericcass/violence/index.htm
School Violence Virtual Library
Produced by the ERIC Counseling and Student Services Clearing house, this Web site includes pages for students, parents, and practitioners. Topics include "Punishment and Intervention," "School Environment," "Security Measures," "Avoiding Violence," "Dealing with Violent Children," "Crisis Intervention," and "Media Impact."

http://www.wm.edu/TTAC
The Training and Technical Assistance Center at the College of William and Mary
This Web site is part of a program designed to assist educators serving disabled school-aged students. Crisis response planners will find several of the articles contained within this site useful. Available titles include "Managing a Crisis," "Origins of Violence and Aggression," "Developing a Plan for Crisis Intervention," and "Verbal Interventions with Aggressive Children and Youth."

Note: The PDF files offered by some Web sites can be viewed with free viewing software, Acrobat™ Reader.

state and national conventions of organizations such as the National Association of School Psychologists and the American Psychological Association. Additionally, a variety of specific training programs, available on a national level, can provide crisis response planners with essential crisis intervention skill development. Information about helpful training programs is provided in Table 3.3.

Review the Work of Others

A fourth strategy is to review crisis intervention policies, plans, and procedures used by other school districts (Purvis, Porter, Authement, & Boren, 1991). There are a number of excellent crisis management plans in place in today's schools. Planners will find it helpful to examine those plans already in place and to modify them to fit their local needs. For example, materials prepared by the Los Angeles Unified School District (1994; Wong et al., 1998), Oklahoma State Department of Education (1995), Nettleton Public School District (1998), Lodi Unified School District in Lodi, California, (Brock et al., 1995) and the Parkway School District in Chesterfield, Missouri, (Colombo & Oegema, 1986) are excellent examples of a school crisis response plan.

Discussion with other educators about their experiences dealing with crises and developing crisis intervention plans is also an excellent strategy for self-education. In addition to face-to-face conversations, journal articles are another excellent source of information regarding how schools have responded during times of crisis (see Table 3.4). The National Association of School Psychologists' (NASP) monthly newsletter, *Communiqué* provides insightful descriptions of how school psychologists have responded to crises. Recently, these articles and other NASP publications have been collected together in a single publication (Canter & Carroll, 1999).

Form a Crisis Response Planning Committee

A final strategy is to form a Crisis Response Planning Committee (CRPC). Through the establishment of a CRPC, a district is not only able to spread the responsibilities of self-education across a number of individuals, but is also able to begin the process of disseminating the information as it is gathered. Additionally, with more individuals involved, more people have ownership in self-education and team development.

Table 3.3

Crisis Intervention Skill Development Training Programs

Basic and Advanced Critical Incident Stress Management

Mitchell, J.T., & Everly, G.S. (1996). *Critical incident stress management: The basic course workbook.* Ellicott City, MD: International Critical Incident Stress Foundation.

Description: The two-day Basic *Critical Incident Stress Management* (CISM) course prepares participants to provide a crisis intervention services. Topics covered include preincident education, defusings, demobilizations, and crisis intervention team development. Special emphasis is placed on the development of *CISM.* The two-day Advanced *CISM* course continues this preparation. Topics covered include post-trauma syndromes and special (or difficult) crisis intervention issues. A recent addition to the *CISM* course offerings is a two-day workshop titled *School Crisis Response: A CISM Perspective.* Other course titles typically available during CISM trainings are *CISM Application with Children, Disaster Management,* and *Suicide Prevention, Intervention and Postvention.*

Prerequisites: The Basic *CISM* course is open to anyone. However, the Advanced *CISM* is only for those who have already had training in Critical Incident Stress Debriefing.

Registration Information: For information on a training near you contact: International Critical Incident Stress Foundation, Inc., 10176 Baltimore National Pike, Unit 201, Ellicott City, MD 21042, phone: 410-750-9600, or Fax: 410-750-9601, http://www.icisf.org.

Suicide Intervention Workshop

Ramsay, R.F., Tanney, B.L., Tierney, R.J., & Lang, W.A. (1996). *Suicide intervention workshop.* Calgary, AB: LivingWorks Education.

Description: The two-day *Suicide Intervention Workshop* is a superior learning experience that helps to develop the basic confidence and competencies needed to assist a person at-risk of suicidal behavior until the danger of injury has passed or until additional resources are mobilized. It is one of the best workshops of its type that the authors have attended. Learning modules explore participant attitudes toward suicide, provide knowledge about suicide risk assessment, and train participants in a suicide intervention model. A five-day training of trainers is also available to those who are interested in becoming Workshop facilitators.

(continued)

Table 3.3 *(Continued)*

Prerequisites: There are no prerequisites for this training program. It is purported to be appropriate for any individual who is (or might be) in a caregiver role. The authors have provided this training to groups ranging from mental health professionals to high school student peer helpers.

Registration Information: For information on facilitating and/or attending a *Workshop* contact: LivingWorks Education, Inc., #208, 1615 10th Ave. SW, Calgary, AB, Canada, T3C 0K7, phone: 403-209-0242, living@nucleus.com

Nonviolent Crisis Intervention

Steiger, L.K. (1987). *Participant workbook. Nonviolent crisis intervention: A program focusing on management of disruptive, assaultive, or out-of-control behavior.* Brookfield, WI: National Crisis Prevention Institute.

Description: The two-day *Nonviolent Crisis Intervention*® workshop provides the skills needed to resolve potentially violent student crises. The techniques taught include nonverbal and verbal deescalation skills, techniques to better ensure personal safety, physical control and restraint techniques, and therapeutic postvention procedures. A one-day seminar, emphasizing early intervention and nonphysical methods for preventing or controlling disruptive behavior is also available. A four-day Instructor Certification is available to those who are interested in being certified to train others in nonviolent crisis intervention.

Prerequisites: There are no prerequisites for this training program.

Registration Information: For information on these workshops/seminars contact: National Crisis Prevention Institute, 3315-K North 124th Street, Brookfield, WI 53005, phone: 800-558-8976, http://www.crisisprevention.com.

National Community Crisis Response
Team Regional Training Institute

Young, M.A. (1998). *The community crisis response team training manual,* 2nd ed., Washington, DC: National Organization for Victim Assistance.

Description: The five-day *National Community Crisis Response Training* provides comprehensive training in crisis intervention. Topics covered

Table 3.3 *(Continued)*

during day one include acute and chronic stress reactions. Day two reviews the topic of death and dying. Day three introduces participants to a model of individual and group crisis intervention. Days four and five provide further review and practice of crisis intervention skills. This is an ideal training for an entire local team to attend together and can help to ensure a common level of crisis intervention skill.

Prerequisites: There is an application and screening process for those interested in this training program. It is expected that all participants will be involved in local crisis preparedness and response activities.

Registration Information: For information about this training program contact: National Organization for Victim Assistance®, 1757 Park Road, N.W., Washington, DC: 20010, phone: 202-232-6682, http://www.try-nova.org.

Table 3.4
Journal Articles Describing School Responses to Crises

Article	Description
Adami & Norton (1996)	Describes one school's response to student-on-student violence.
Adams (1996)	Documents the response of a residential high school for gifted students to a three-student suicide cluster. Responses included development of screening/prevention programs and workshops/conferences.
Arena, Hermann, & Hoffman (1984)	Describes a crisis intervention model for helping children deal with the death of a classmate.
Blom (1982, 1986)	A university child psychiatrist describes a school's response after a truck crane struck a pedestrian overpass next to the school. Five students were seriously injured after falling 15 feet.

(continued)

Table 3.4 *(Continued)*

Article	Description
Blom, Etkind, & Carr (1991)	Describes how a community mental health center helped schools deal with an accidental auto death disaster and a family murder-suicide.
Boylan (1987)	The author interviews five administrators who have handled crises at their schools. It presents what administrators can expect and how they can prepare for crises in the schools.
Brooks, Silverman, & Hass (1985)	Describes the behavioral and emotional adjustments of students following the sudden death of their third-grade teacher. Intervention strategies are also reviewed.
Catone & Schatz (1991)	Describes the school's response to the event of suicide.
Collison et al. (1987)	Five pupil service personnel describe their efforts in responding to student, teacher, and parent needs after a 14-year-old boy wounded two teachers and a student and killed the principal in a shooting spree.
Cornell & Sheras (1998)	Uses five crisis case examples (alcohol-related fatality, self-injurious behavior, school homicide, racial/ethnic conflict, and community violence) to demonstrate the importance of leadership, team work and responsibility in successful crisis management.
Dallas (1978)	A director of a hospital's social services department describes how he and a school's counseling services assist pupils and parents after at least 50 elementary students witnessed a 23-year-old man stab and partially decapitate his father.

Table 3.4 *(Continued)*

Article	Description
Foley (1986)	A school principal describes his experiences dealing with two major crises. First, a student was shot after taking two peers hostage. Then teacher-astronaut Christa McAuliffe was killed in the Challenger disaster.
Goldman (1996)	Uses the sudden death of a six-year-old to illustrate a special child-oriented memorial service.
Klingman (1986)	Describes the role of mental health professionals in providing emotional first aid to parents following the collision of a train with a school bus.
Klingman (1987)	A report detailing a coordinated crisis intervention undertaken in response to a collision of a railway train with a school bus.
Klingman (1989)	Describes a brief (three-day) school-based intervention following a tenth-grade student's suicide.
Klingman & Ben Eli (1981)	Describes how local school psychological services provided crisis intervention in schools following a terrorist attack on an Israeli town's neighborhood.
Kneisel & Richards (1988)	Describes a school crisis intervention following the suicide of an elementary school teacher. Argues that a broad multifaceted response contributes to the healing process and minimizes subsequent mental health difficulties.
Mathers (1996)	A high school principal discusses how his school responded to the bomb attack on the federal building in Oklahoma City.

(continued)

Table 3.4 *(Continued)*

Article	Description
Meyers & Pitt (1976)	Describes a consultation and in-service program implemented by the authors to help the staff of a K-8 parochial school intervene to help children cope with the accidental deaths of two classmates.
Nye (1997)	From experiences dealing with an armed disturbed student, who terrified a rural high school, the author offers suggestions for how administrators can prepare for such crises.
Ponton & Bryant (1991)	Two child psychiatrists describe their role in developing a total school program designed to address the ongoing emotional needs induced by an earthquake.
Rohrer (1996)	Discusses children's reactions to televised war. Suggests that schools should be prepared to address such reactions.
Sorensen (1989)	Describes a school's response following the suicide of a third grade teacher to illustrate the importance of a preplanned intervention approach.
Toubiana, Milgram, Strich, & Edelstein (1988)	Provides a different perspective of the same intervention described by Klingman (1987, 1986).

CRISIS PREPAREDNESS AS AN EVALUATION OBJECTIVE

After beginning self-education efforts, it is suggested that the commitment to crisis preparedness be formalized by establishing it as a professional growth objective. In California, a school professional's personal goals or objectives are a part of the evaluation process. Thus, for those working in this state's public schools, the establishment of such an objective serves

several purposes. In addition to meeting professional growth requirements, it provides motivation to complete crisis planning, and it also
serves to involve the immediate supervisor. By accepting crisis preparedness as one of the objectives used during this process, a supervisor gives
his or her tacit approval.

BUILDING A TEAM

After committing to crisis planning and obtaining a degree of administrative support, the next step is to begin team building. In addition, once
the crisis planners feel comfortable with their own crisis preparedness
and response education, they must begin to think about how to share
their knowledge with the school district. At the same time, they may start
working toward a district policy regarding crisis preparedness. The best
vehicle for moving forward in this planning may well be a Crisis Response Planning Committee (CRPC). Through this Committee, or task
force, interested individuals will continue their own self-education efforts and begin to sketch out crisis preparedness plans. The CRPC is also
a way to begin the development of common goals, well-defined roles, and
the ability to work together. These elements have been suggested to be essential to the effective functioning of a crisis response team (Cornell &
Sheras, 1998). The CRPC must be large enough to broaden the base of support for crisis planning within the district, but small enough to meet and
get tasks accomplished—between eight and 10 individuals is an optimum
committee size.

The formation of this team need not be time-consuming or complicated.
When ready, the crisis planners set a date, write a memo stating their perceptions regarding the need for crisis preparedness, and send it to selected
staff members. The crisis planners may choose to select from different con-
stituencies, such as school principals, nurses, elementary and secondary
counselors, social workers, district level supervisors, school psychologists,
child welfare and attendance workers, and so on. It is recommended that
the CRPC represent a variety of staff positions.

One option to consider at this point is whether to include parent, teacher,
and classified employee representatives on the Committee. Teachers are the
central individuals in a school district and can be important contributors to
any planning. Thus, it is important that they be involved as early as possible
in the process of crisis planning. Similarly, parental support is often a prerequisite to obtaining the school board and district-level administrative
sanction needed to continue crisis planning. However, an argument against

including parents, teachers, and classified personnel on the CRPC is that to get things going quickly, it is important to involve those who would be most significantly affected by this policy (i.e., support staff), and at the same time keep the number of committee members low enough to function efficiently. Having parents, teachers, and classified employee representatives may be important later on in the implementation stage, but at this point, especially in a large district, they may increase the size of the CRPC past the recommended efficiency level. In addition, teachers and other school staff may be least able to attend planning meetings held during school hours. A possible compromise would be to designate specific CRPC members as parent, teacher, and classified employee liaisons. These individuals would be charged with the task of disseminating crisis response planning information to their respective groups. In doing so, these liaisons would also attempt to solicit support for crisis planning and bring back to the CRPC any ideas or suggestions parents, teachers, and classified employees may have. Parent-teacher associations or organizations also would be important contacts for the liaisons.

Once formed, the CRPC may meet as often as weekly or as seldom as monthly. The first few sessions will be exploratory in nature, without much structure. The committee needs to get to know and trust each other before firm decisions can be made. As the group progresses, it begins to get more specific in conceptualizing how a crisis response team might function in the district and what components need to be included in developing district policy and a plan. A primary activity for the CRPC may be to review other model plans and to debate options and local modifications. In addition to the parent, teacher, and classified employee liaisons, the CRPC may also want to designate certain committee members to focus on specific response issues such as crisis intervention, media management, emergency medical, and safety and security procedures.

Next, a choice needs to be made about crisis team structure. Does a district wish to have multiple and hierarchical crisis teams, or a single crisis response team? A major factor in deciding this issue is the size of the district. A small district may easily manage with a single team. The advantage of having school site-level teams, as will be discussed later, is that they will be familiar with the individuals involved in a crisis, and will be able to act immediately when disaster strikes. Therefore, the recommended crisis response model consists of several levels of crisis response teams. At a minimum, a school district should have a single district-level team and multiple school site-level teams. Also, whenever possible, a third level of crisis response should also be available. This level would be a regional team, usually composed of representatives from several neighboring school districts. This level would be available to assist the school district that finds its own resources overwhelmed by a crisis.

Given the reality that a crisis can happen at any time, it is suggested that the committee begin by developing the district-level crisis response team as soon as possible. Crises that could occur before school-based planning is implemented may be addressed by having a district-level team in place. The district-level team may be used in two additional ways: (1) It can serve as a resource for materials, consultation, support, and validation, and training for individuals and school staff; and (2) once school-site crisis teams are developed, a district-level crisis team can provide direct intervention in conjunction with a site team when a school's resources alone are unable to manage a crisis.

IDENTIFYING PRIORITIES

Another CRPC activity will be to identify crisis intervention priorities for the district. Although it is suggested that first priorities include increasing support staff's (counselors, psychologists, and nurses) knowledge of crisis intervention, other things may occur first. In some districts, the first priority will be to develop a set of district-level policies regarding crisis intervention. In other districts, it will be to develop a detailed list of procedures to follow and to assign individuals to different roles they may assume during a crisis. In examining priorities, choose a starting point only—all of these activities need to be undertaken eventually in the process of developing a comprehensive plan.

Many committees will come to the realization that a crisis is not going to wait for the district to develop a finished, comprehensive plan. In fact, disaster could strike at any time. Thus, it seems reasonable to initiate crisis preparedness efforts with those who will be on the front lines of any crisis response. The CRPC meetings themselves will be very helpful in this regard because many of the members of the committee will ultimately be functioning on either a district-level or school-level crisis response team. Discussions of setting priorities will also continue the process of preparing individuals to act. The authors' experience suggests that the priorities identified will likely include the following: (1) conducting a needs assessment to determine support staff needs for education, training and supervision; (2) developing a tentative or working plan; (3) creating a conception of which crises the district/school should respond to and development of a crisis response policy statement; (4) educating school principals about crisis preparedness and crisis intervention; (5) adoption of a school board policy regarding the need for crisis intervention; (6) implementation of the crisis response policy by constructing a plan of procedures and deciding who will be responsible for following them; and (7) the education of individual school site personnel about crisis intervention and the district plan. The first two of these activities are discussed in this chapter and the second two in Chapter 4 (Developing and Implementing a Crisis Intervention Policy).

NEEDS ASSESSMENT

At some point early on, it is appropriate for the CRPC to conduct a needs assessment (Purvis et al., 1991). This assessment would be a critical component of CRPC efforts to involve parent, teacher, and classified employee groups in planning. To complete the needs assessment systematically, crisis response planners may refer to H. Davis and Salasin (1975) and/or Maher and Illback (1985) for helpful advice.

Needs assessments are usually conducted with questionnaires, focus groups, and interviews. Different questions will lend themselves to different methods of data collection. For example, a superintendent might be interviewed, but teachers or parents might be asked to respond to a questionnaire.

It is useful to collect hard data. Later, when others such as the school board need to be persuaded to invest in a plan, it is helpful to have facts and figures available derived from a local assessment.

Needs assessments will also reap benefits if a tentative plan has been under consideration. Planners often make assumptions that need to be verified, for they are sometimes inaccurate. Thus, a needs assessment often yields needed modifications to a tentative plan.

CREATING A TENTATIVE CRISIS RESPONSE PLAN

It may not take long before a CRPC wishes to move toward a tentative plan. It is useful to have a set of ideas on the table as long as everyone is aware that they are subject to modification as the planning process continues. The process of developing the first draft for a crisis response program should be a team effort. The team should begin by holding discussions in which the goals and objectives of the crisis response program are explored. Next, the team should delineate the nature and scope of the program. Doing so results in an outline of methods and activities that will make up the program. Once the nature and scope of the program are clarified, the committee must determine who will make up the crisis intervention team, assuming that more than one trained person is available. Finally, a relevant timeline for program development and implementation should be created. It will take time for training, changing expectations of how a professional's time is spent, and producing the necessary forms, check lists, stockpiles of equipment, and so on.

The outcome of this initial preparation should be a rough draft of a plan for delivering crisis response services to the school. Once the plan has been prepared, the team should circulate it among school staff for comment and discussion. Although the goal of eventual proposal implementation may not be negotiable, there may be areas where parent and teacher reactions will be important (e.g., the possible use of substitute teachers to free classroom teachers to participate in school-level crisis response planning sessions, how parents may assist the process of a school crisis response). The school community should be encouraged to examine the plan and to indicate which program elements are not clear and raise other issues or difficulties with the plan. Now is the time to obtain these reactions and not in the middle of a crisis response.

ELEMENTS OF A PLAN

A draft plan should include the following elements:

- A set of program goals and objectives including intended outcomes
- A set of procedures to follow when a crisis occurs
- Clarification of the roles of the team members and who they will be
- How the crisis response team will be coordinated, supervised, and evaluated
- A set of expectations for counselors and coordinators
- Discussion of incentives for participating in the program
- Discussion of what, when, where, and how records and reports will be kept
- Recommendations for modifications to the facility (e.g., rooms where crisis intervention will take place)
- A timeline for the implementation of the crisis response program
- An explanation of how the crisis response program will interface with other programs in the school (e.g., special education or teacher in-service education)
- A set of procedures for evaluating the program

OPERATIONAL POLICIES AND PROCEDURES

A program for crisis response necessitates a number of systemic changes, and these changes must be considered when developing the tentative crisis response plan. First, individuals need to be freed from other duties to participate in the program. For example, the demands on school psychologists to test children need to be modified so that they will have time to talk with teachers and parents and to counsel students. Ideally, crisis intervention would be made a part of the job description of all school mental health professionals. Similarly, a teacher needs to have time released from classroom instruction to participate in crisis response planning, training, and intervention. It is important to be aware of the probability that this will require some financial backing by a school district.

The crisis intervention program will have to respect the due process and equal protection rights of parents. When possible, parents need to be informed and give their permission for their children to be seen as part of counseling activities. Procedures must be established so that the program operates in an ethically responsible manner in other respects as well. General "rules of thumb" should be specified in any plan. For example, the following questions should be addressed:

- How will children become the subjects of crisis intervention activities?
- How much time will be spent on crisis intervention for an individual child?
- What limits might there be on working outside of the regular counseling services provided to school children in the district?
- How will the issue of confidentiality be handled and what limits might be placed on confidentiality during a crisis?
- When and how will parental consent for crisis intervention services be obtained?

AN ALTERNATIVE TO COMMITTEE PLANNING

The foregoing is not to suggest that a CRPC is the only way a district may proceed. It may be possible for a single individual to be placed in charge of creating a district-level system of crisis response. If the crisis response system is planned from the top down, rather than by a committee made up of interested personnel, a mid-level administrator should be assigned at the district level to coordinate efforts across school sites. Some goals and timelines for implementing the crisis plan would probably be developed first, but otherwise an individual might follow the same steps as the committee.

The district might also designate pilot sites for developing a crisis response team. Success might be assured by selecting a site where (1) the principal displays strong leadership and is receptive to having staff engage in crisis response activities; (2) there is high staff morale and a good sense of professionalism; (3) the support services staff is already well trained and enthusiastic about assuming crisis intervention roles; and (4) the school is representative of the district. This latter consideration is important if district personnel are to learn how to export any model of crisis response to other schools in the district. Having a model program also allows interested personnel in the district to closely review a good program.

Leaders who are able to create a shared vision throughout a district, school, and community mount effective programs. Programs at a particular school must have the backing of the district particularly when change of the magnitude discussed here is projected.

OBTAINING A CONSULTANT

After conducting a needs assessment, it is often a good idea to obtain a consultant to assist in meeting the identified priorities. Consultants can provide useful expertise and critical validation of crisis response plans. The most important thing to look for in a consultant is an established level of expertise in the area of crisis response. Additionally, the consultant must be willing and available to help. Knowledge of school systems and how support personnel fit into them is also a desirable characteristic. One place to look for such an individual is in a regional school psychology or counseling training program. Besides training program professors, instructors, or both, other potential experts might be found in local mental health systems.

One possible way of making a district more attractive to a consultant, especially one from a university, is to offer research opportunities. For example, one of the consultants used in the Lodi project was interested in studying suicidal ideation among high school students. He was pleased to work with the staff in return for assistance in research planning. Another practical way of attracting a consultant is to offer a stipend for their services. Besides attracting the consultant, obtaining funding for such a purpose can serve as a measure of a district's willingness to continue development of a comprehensive crisis response plan. The district that is willing to make a financial commitment to crisis response is one that is more likely to follow through on crisis response proposals. In addition, the financial commitment could also serve as a motivating force as the more one invests in something the more important it typically becomes.

Consultants can be helpful in several specific ways. First, they serve as a valuable resource when it comes to providing staff with crisis response training. They may be able either to provide staff development or to locate qualified speakers for the staff. An important point to be made here is that a school's personnel may be more receptive to an outside expert than they will be to in-house staff. Second, consultants can be helpful in developing components of a crisis plan that are beyond team member's expertise. For example, a consultant may be knowledgeable about working with the media or creating good security services. Finally, consultants may be helpful in giving the planning committee a sense of direction by validating their plans and proposals. Consultants are perhaps most effective when they are presented with previously developed plans they can review, comment on, and help to refine. Do not expect a consultant to do all the work. Rather, expect the consultant to offer comments on what the committee or crisis response planner has already done.

SUMMARY

This chapter has examined the critical strategies and/or elements required when beginning to prepare a school district for crisis response. Critical steps in getting started are self-education and team building. Strategies have been provided that should help educators become more knowledgeable about crisis response. Additionally, the chapter offered suggestions for forming a Crisis Response Planning Committee that should further these self-education efforts, as well as begin to build a team of individuals committed to the idea of crisis preparedness. A situational crisis is not going to wait for a district to develop a comprehensive crisis response plan, thus the first steps in crisis planning should include the training of support staff and the development of a tentative response plan. The elements of a tentative plan and the operational policies and procedures that this plan will require have also been examined. The chapter concluded with a discussion of alternatives to committee planning and an examination of the use of a consultant in getting a crisis response plan started.

CHAPTER 4

Developing and Implementing a Crisis Response Policy

On March 15, 1982, 14-year-old Brian Kelson confronted a teacher with a .38 caliber revolver. Brandishing the gun, he forced the teacher to place a small amount of coins on a desktop. After complying with this request, the teacher persuaded Brian to accompany him to a room where the vice-principal was waiting. During discussions with the vice-principal, Brian placed the gun in the waistband of his pants, revealed a suicide note he had prepared, and asked to speak to his favorite teacher. He did not receive permission to do so. During this conference, school officials contacted the local police, who in turn called Brian's parents and informed them of the situation. When Brian and the vice-principal left the room in which they had been talking, they were confronted by a police officer who told Brian that he was "in trouble with the law." After a further 5-minute conference, Brian left the vice-principal, entered the restroom, and shot himself with the gun that had never been taken from his possession. Later that morning, he died.

—*Kelson v. City of Springfield* (1985)

AFTER HAVING committed to crisis preparedness, invested signifi- cant time and energy in crisis response activities, and developed a common vision of crisis response (through the Crisis Response Planning Committee), the crisis planners will have set the stage to secure a district commitment to crisis preparedness. This chapter discusses the development and implementation of a school district crisis response policy. Simply put, the purpose of a crisis response policy is to help ensure the provision of effective and efficient crisis intervention services following traumatic events.

PURPOSE, NATURE, AND LIMITATIONS OF A DISTRICT CRISIS RESPONSE POLICY

Most school district leaders and boards of education are aware of, and concerned about, school crisis events and their effects. However, relatively few districts have gone so far as to create a district-level policy addressing such circumstances (Palmo, Langlois, & Bender, 1988). Yet, according to Cultice (1992), "A written crisis intervention policy . . . is essential" (p. 70). Having a policy in place is useful, because it focuses attention on the problem. Additionally, the process of policy development leads to careful planning and thought about local problems and needs.

An important reason for developing a crisis response policy statement is to protect the staff and school from charges of negligence (Palmo et al., 1988). School districts have been the targets of litigation whenever they do not follow best practice and there are negative outcomes for children. For example, in the court case that followed the student suicide described at the beginning of this chapter, the courts held that parents have the right to sue a school district if it can be shown that a student suicide is the result of inadequate district suicide intervention procedures. J. Davis and Sandoval (1991) point out that this case is especially important in that it was "the first in which the court permitted a lawsuit when there was no intentional act to harm the child on the part of school district employees but the child's death could be linked to the *inadequate training* [italics added] of district employees" (p. 174).

An effective policy statement documents school staff members' responsibilities, affirms the district's intention to be aware of crises and to prepare individuals to cope with traumatic events, and announces the district's general stance on crisis preparedness. It is an institutional record of guidelines that can be communicated to the public and used to hold the district accountable.

However, it is not enough to simply adopt a policy. It must be successfully implemented. The district, from the board of education and superintendent on down, must not only commit itself to crisis preparedness, it must also be provided with the knowledge it needs to carry out a crisis response. Additionally, the district must recognize that time and resources must be given to support the policy. Most preparedness activities do not cost much more than staff time, but budgeting for planning-time is essential. Often the expertise is available among staff, but those individuals must be given release time from other duties.

CRISIS DEFINITION AS A STEP IN THE DEVELOPMENT OF A CRISIS RESPONSE POLICY STATEMENT

In the process of developing a district-level policy statement, a first step is to define what is meant by crisis. On the basis of this definition it will be much easier to develop a policy statement. Without agreement about which situations will require a response, and which will not, the task of developing a crisis response policy will be impossible. Different individuals will understand the term *crisis* differently. An example of a definition of crisis developed by the authors' CRPC is as follows:

- A sudden and unexpected event
- An event that has the potential to affect a large number of students and/or staff
- An event that might affect the health, safety, and/or social and emotional well being of students

The features of this definition eliminate a number of events that might typically be seen as crises for children. For example, the divorce of parents or an isolated instance of child abuse, although crises for the child, would not require a crisis response (per item 2). Children experiencing these problems would probably be dealt with individually by the appropriate school and community mental health personnel. On the other hand, events such as a teacher's death, or a natural disaster with many injuries, would fit all the features of this definition. This definition is just an example, however. Each district would have to decide the range and scope of its crisis response policies.

THE SCHOOL BOARD CRISIS RESPONSE POLICY STATEMENT

An effective crisis response policy statement should include the following components:

- A definition of what types of "crisis" situations will require a "crisis response
- A statement of staff responsibilities during a crisis response
- A statement of the district's general stance on crisis preparedness

Table 4.1

Policy Regarding Administrative Response to Crisis Situations

The governing board recognizes the need to provide support to students and staff in the event of a crisis. A crisis is defined as a sudden, unexpected, and accidental event. These events will have an emergency quality to them and will have the potential to impact the entire school community. Examples of such situational crises include physical illness and injury, unexpected/untimely deaths, being the victim of a crime, natural and man-made disasters, and war and related acts.

These events may cause entry into a *crisis state.* This is a temporary state of distress, characterized chiefly by the inability to cope with the situation using customary methods of problem solving, and by the potential for a radically positive or negative outcome. This crisis state is more than simple stress and not necessarily a sign of mental illness. The crisis state is a normal reaction to abnormal circumstances.

It is the intent of the governing board that the administration shall develop procedures to identify and assist students and staff who enter into a crisis state as the result of a situational crisis.

It is the policy of the governing board that the district have a plan in place for the provision of immediate crisis response and crisis intervention, as well as for follow-up support.

A sample policy statement is provided in Table 4.1. The authors strongly recommend that a policy statement, such as this one, be adopted in all school districts undertaking crisis preparedness efforts.*

With this policy, individual schools within a district will not have a choice regarding whether to undertake crisis response planning. It will be board policy and they will be required to initiate such planning. Before policy adoption, the authors found it difficult to obtain the support needed to develop school crisis response teams. Frequently the question: "Where are we to find the time to do this planning?" was asked. While things progressed slowly at first, attitudes quickly changed when a memo from the assistant-superintendent was sent to all schools. This memo indicated that a newly adopted school board policy required the development of school crisis response plans. Subsequently the authors no longer had to ask permission to initiate crisis planning; they were asked to do so.

---

*School board associations may provide other examples of policy statements. For example the Oregon School Board Association has a sample policy "Crisis Prevention and Response" [On-line]. Available: http://www.osba.org/hotopics/crismgmt/crispol.htm.

One component of the policy statement (in Table 4.1) that deserves special attention is its provision for follow-up support. Although there is often little argument about the need for crisis intervention assistance immediately following a crisis event, some school systems are reluctant to provide the resources needed for long-term follow-up support. School psychologist Mike Armstrong's (1990) experiences following the Stockton schoolyard shooting validate this point. He reported that three weeks after this shooting, which left five students dead and 29 wounded, he was given a list of over 300 students in need of counseling assistance. Armstrong reported he was provided with assistance only after he and his fellow staff members demanded that it be provided.

The need for long-term follow-up support is documented by the research of Nader, Pynoos, Fairbanks, and Frederick (1990). This study found that a majority of students directly exposed to a school yard sniper attack continued to display a number of Posttraumatic Stress Disorder symptoms 14 months after the event. These researchers conclude: "The findings of this study suggest that psychological first aid at schools exposed to violence must be accompanied by a more comprehensive program of follow-up for highly exposed children" (p. 1530).

Along with a general crisis response policy, there may be a need for additional policies addressing specific crisis events such as a student suicide intervention. Table 4.2 provides an example of a district policy on suicide prevention. This policy statement is based upon one suggested by J. Davis et al. (1988). Palmo et al. (1988) provides additional suggestions for the development of a suicide prevention policy and the California School Boards Association (1987) provides a comprehensive sample board policy statement.

Table 4.2
Suicide Prevention Policy Proposal

It is the policy of the governing board that all staff members learn how to recognize students at risk for suicidal behavior, to identify warning signs, to take preventive precautions, and to report suicide threats to the appropriate parental and professional authorities.

Administration shall ensure that all staff members have been issued a copy of the district's suicide prevention/intervention policy and procedures. All staff members are responsible for knowing and acting upon them.

Source: Adapted from "Strategies for the primary prevention of adolescent suicide," by J.M. Davis, J. Sandoval, and M.P. Wilson, 1988, *School Psychology Review, 17*, pp. 559–569.

HOW TO GET THE CRISIS RESPONSE
POLICY ADOPTED

Adoption of any school district policy statement requires a broad base of support encompassing most if not all of a district's hierarchy. We offer the following suggestions on how to obtain a district commitment to a crisis response policy.

Obtain District-Level Administrative Support

It is essential that district-level administration support the idea of a crisis response policy (Gullatt & Long, 1996; Kline et al., 1995). Without such support, it will be very difficult to approach a school board with the proposed policy statement (Cultice, 1992).This step is facilitated by prior work and planning. Administration will not be receptive if approached with a vague idea. Thus, crisis response planners will need to educate themselves, broaden their base of support (e.g., by establishing the CRPC), and develop tentative crisis response policy and procedures. These steps combined may take up to a year.

From this point on, it would not be surprising if crisis response planners were to meet with some resistance. Crises are an unpleasant reality that people naturally try to avoid. This natural tendency may transfer to resistance toward preparing for crises (Klingman, 1987, 1988). Thus, it would not be unusual if a school system is resistant to the idea of a crisis response policy (Pitcher & Poland, 1992; Poland, 1994). In such a circumstance, it is recommended that planners continue self-education efforts, work out the specifics of a crisis response plan, and share crisis intervention expertise with peers. Unfortunately, in the life of every school district there will come a time when it experiences a significant crisis. Following such events, school districts will be more willing to develop and implement formal crisis response plans and procedures (Poland, 1994). In fact, following crises, school mental health professionals are often asked to undertake such development and implementation. By being prepared, crisis planners will be able to take advantage of the heightened sensitivity to crisis preparedness generated by crisis events.

Depending on the financial status of the school district, its receptivity to crisis planning, or both, at this stage it may be appropriate to look not only for administrative support, but also for financial backing. Budget items might include crisis response books and resource materials, in-service funds, consultant fees, duplication costs, release time expenses, and so forth. Although it is possible to get by without a financial commitment, it is helpful if one can be obtained.

OBTAIN THE SUPPORT OF SCHOOL PRINCIPALS

The next step is to approach site-level administrators and solicit their support. It is critical that principals have an opportunity to review and comment on the policy and procedures proposals before they are adopted. Just as crisis response planners will need the support of their colleagues before approaching district-level administration, district-level administration will find the support of site administrators helpful when these procedures are brought before a school board. Additionally, such a review has the potential to strengthen crisis response plans. From their knowledge of a district's schools, principals are in an excellent position to provide critical suggestions regarding crisis planning needs and feasibility.

OBTAIN THE SUPPORT OF THE SCHOOL BOARD

Before actually presenting the policy to the school board, it is useful to do preparatory work with them (Cultice, 1992). For example, it may be helpful to have a school board member participate in policy development. Another strategy is to get on the school board agenda for a presentation. A cooperative administrator should help a CRPC with this task. It is important not to make a school board presentation independently. What crisis response planners will be doing will reflect upon their district administration. Thus, it is important that the district administration, directly supervising crisis planners, be not only aware, but also actively involved in the process and presentation.

At the first brief school board presentation, the committee members might introduce themselves to the school board and review their activities. It would also be helpful to share plans for the future, including hopes for the development of a district crisis response policy.

The authors' experience with such a board presentation was extremely productive. However, although the board's reception to this presentation was positive, it should be noted that a school shooting had occurred just weeks before the presentation. Because the need for crisis response had just been demonstrated, the board was very receptive to the idea of crisis preparedness. There are clearly moments where school systems are more responsive to crisis preparedness than others.

A district administrator such as a director of pupil personnel services may handle subsequent board presentations. Although the committee may do all the work in preparation for these presentations, it is often expedient for board presentations to be done by an administrator. In this way, district-level administrative support for crisis preparedness is clearly communicated to a school board.

The final step before implementing crisis preparedness procedures is to request that the school board adopt a policy statement (e.g., Table 4.1) regarding their support for administrative response to crisis situations. During a final meeting, if all the concepts and language of the statement can be worked out, the policy should be placed on the board consent agenda for adoption.

EDUCATION AS A FIRST STEP IN THE IMPLEMENTATION OF THE CRISIS RESPONSE POLICY

For the sake of this discussion the development and the implementation phases of the crisis response policy have been separated. However, they are not necessarily separate activities. In fact, some of the in-service activities designed to facilitate policy implementation are critical in obtaining crisis response policy support. The following discussion reviews the in-service or educational activities that are typically the first step in the implementation of a crisis response policy. The importance of this first step cannot be overstated. As Weatherley and Lipsky (1977) have noted, school change will fail if this training is not given careful thought.

TRAINING SUPPORT STAFF

Besides broadening the support base needed for policy adoption, in-servicing of support staff can also provide support staff with the knowledge and skills needed to conduct crisis response and intervention. A crisis response plan is useless without personnel capable of conducting crisis interventions.

Typically, the needs assessment described in Chapter 3 will identify areas where support staff may need training. On occasion, in-service needs will be in areas in which existing district staff are not qualified. As was mentioned in Chapter 3, this circumstance is one where an outside consultant can be extremely valuable. The consultant can either provide this in-service education or will be able to locate the personnel who can. Topics for support staff in-services include suicide risk assessment, the child's concept of death, psychotherapeutic treatments, and psychological first aid. A comprehensive two-day training model for providing educators with psychological first aid skills is provided in Appendix A (School Crisis Intervention: An In-Service for Educators).

TRAINING ADMINISTRATORS

Although in-service models for support staff and those for administrators will be quite different, both have at least one common goal. Both should be intended to solicit support for attempts to implement a district crisis response plan. In other words, not only do we hope to increase the crisis intervention knowledge of in-service participants (and thus increase their ability to implement a crisis response policy), but we also hope that an educational program will heighten their awareness of the need for a comprehensive district crisis response policy.

An in-service model for school principals must consider that the demands placed on principals are many, and their time is very much in demand. Thus, the time for planning and preparation by principals is extremely limited. They may be so busy with the day-to-day operations of running a school, it may be difficult for them to take time to plan a new program. Consequently, it is recommended that any orientation program for administrators be relatively short. Crisis response planners should be direct, to the point, and very applied in describing how a plan might work. With this group, for example, it may not be profitable to spend time discussing crisis theory or techniques of crisis intervention. Rather, deal with the basic issues of crisis preparedness and response. This training should not last any longer than one hour.

It is suggested that a training for school principals begin by reviewing the crisis response policy statement (Table 4.1). After discussing the need for such a policy, review with principals a set of rules that would govern how the policy would be implemented. Rules such as those in Table 4.3 should appeal to most building-level administrative personnel.

The rules for policy implementation presented in Table 4.3 refer to *Administrative Guidelines*. These *Guidelines* can be developed to give principals further direction on how to implement the proposed crisis response policy. They should also be reviewed during this in-service training. The Planning Checklist referred to here is one that can be constructed to summarize such *Guidelines*. A second checklist might be developed with procedures to follow in times of crisis. Chapters 5 (Components of the Crisis Preparedness Plan) and 6 (Components of a Crisis Intervention Response) provide

Table 4.3

Rules for a Board Policy Dealing with Administrative
Response to Crisis Situations

Crisis Preparedness

1. At least annually, school administration will review Administrative
   Guidelines for Crisis Intervention with site staff.
2. A current copy of the Planning Check List (from Administrative Guidelines for Crisis Intervention) must be on file in the superintendent's
   office by October 1 of each school year.
3. Annually, district administration will select a sample of school sites
   that will have their crisis preparedness evaluated through a readiness
   check or drill. Supervision and evaluation of this drill will be facilitated
   by district-level administration.

Crisis Response

4. Once a crisis situation has stabilized, school administration must
   make efforts to determine facts surrounding the crisis. Assess degree
   of impact on the school and begin to determine the level of response
   required.
5. The superintendent's office must be notified immediately following a
   crisis that occurs at school. District Crisis Response Team assistance
   (if needed) is requested through the district office.
6. Implement procedures for crisis intervention as specified in Administrative Guidelines for Crisis Intervention.

Source: Adapted from Lodi Unified School District (1989) Governing Board Policy
5141.5. (Available from Lodi Unified School District, 1305 East Vine Street, Lodi,
CA 95240).

examples of these checklists. Validation for the use of checklists has come
from the authors' work with school principals who indicated that they
would appreciate a document giving them a clearly defined procedure to
follow. They also indicated that they were unlikely to read, let alone follow,
a long narrative description of how to prepare for and intervene during
times of crisis.

To summarize, a principal training may be composed of a review of the
proposed policy and accompanying rules, plus an examination of check lists
outlining steps in policy implementation and crisis response. At its conclusion, crisis response planners would not only have a clear idea whether this
is a policy that principals can support, but will also have begun to provide
them with the knowledge needed for implementation.

TRAINING INDIVIDUAL SCHOOLS

Due to the magnitude of this step, especially in larger school districts, it is best that training individual schools not be attempted until after crisis response policy adoption. It involves developing individual crisis response plans at each school within a district. To prepare schools for developing these plans, it is advisable to hold orientation and training meetings for all certificated, classified, and administrative personnel at each school site. In a large district, it may be difficult for crisis planners to do all of this training independently. Thus, it is suggested the crisis planners write a training manual that illustrates how to implement the policy. Included in this manual should be a detailed outline of what to cover in each training session. This training-of-trainers program will be discussed further in Chapter 5.

The model chosen for school-site in-services involves a combination of awareness activities and short lectures regarding crisis theory and crisis intervention. Appendix B provides a handout titled *Tips for Teachers in Times of Disaster* (Marin County Community Mental Health Services and Santa Cruz County Mental Health, 1985) which may be helpful in conducting this in-service. Similarly, Appendix C provides a handout titled *Helping Your Child in a Disaster* (National Institute of Mental Health, 1985). These same handouts may also prove useful immediately following a crisis event.

Lectures chosen for this in-service can be based on the information in this book. The presentations may be planned to last from 1 to 2 hours. The purposes are to solicit interest in school crisis response and to provide a knowledge base that would allow individuals to be more active participants in the development of the Site Crisis Response Plan. An outline of a site-level school crisis response in-service program is provided in Table 4.4.

To begin the site crisis intervention in-service, a brief introduction should be provided stating the purpose of the training (i.e., to review crisis preparedness and response). Next, a brief history of the events that lead to adoption of the crisis response policy should be provided. The introduction should conclude with a brief review of the board policy on crisis response. It is important to emphasize how the policy affects school sites (e.g., requirements for site crisis preparedness).

After these introductory remarks, the in-service begins with an activity. During this activity, participants are divided into small groups and assigned a crisis scenario to review and discuss. Table 4.5 contains some

Table 4.4
School Crisis Intervention In-Service Outline

Introduction
  -Review of board policy statement

Activity
  -Reacting to Crisis Scenarios

Videotape
  -*School Crisis: Under Control*
  -*Children and Trauma: The School's Response*

Crisis Theory
  -Inability to Cope
  -Extreme Distress
  -Potential for Radically Positive or Negative Outcomes
  -More than Stress
  -Not Mental Illness

Crisis Reactions
  -Preschool and Kindergarten
  -Elementary School
  -Junior and Senior High School
  -Teacher's Reaction to Crisis

Crisis Intervention
  -Classroom Management Following a Crisis
  -Psychological First Aid
  -Crisis Therapy

Summary and Needs Assessment

---

examples of scenarios. Returning to the large group, participants share their perceptions of what they felt their role would be during their assigned crisis. This activity gains the attention of the audience quickly and makes the in-service personally relevant. Because of this personal connection with the topic, it is not uncommon for school staff to generate specific questions or areas of concern. For example, during the authors' school site in-services, one school was particularly concerned about visitors ignoring the school policy to check into the office before proceeding to classrooms. At another, staff discussed the legal ramifications of an armed person entering a classroom and to what extent the teacher is held responsible to intervene. It will be important to begin to address these

Table 4.5

Crisis Scenarios: Examples of Crises in the Schools

Scenario 1: A local gang, in response to the physical beating of a fellow gang member by a student at your high school, has come on campus. A fight breaks out in the student parking lot between the gang and the student's friends. A 15-year-old gang member is hospitalized with a stab wound, and one of your students is killed by a gunshot wound to the head. The principal was in the immediate area and tried to intervene; she was hospitalized with serious stab wounds and is not expected to live.

Scenario 2: A very popular fifth-grade teacher at an elementary school was supervising his students on a field trip to a local lake. He tragically drowns after hitting his head on a rock while trying to rescue one of the students who had fallen into the lake.

Scenario 3: A seventh-grade student enters your classroom and begins shooting a handgun at random as he runs through the room, exiting through an outside door. He takes up a position in an adjacent building within full view of your classroom. He continues to fire at any movement he observes within the classroom. Other classrooms not within his sight are safely evacuated. Initial attempts by school staff to enter the classroom are turned away by gunfire. The Police Department is notified. Police authorities cordon off the school grounds. Parents arrive on the scene due to immediate news coverage.

Scenario 4: An irate father has come on to your elementary school site at 8:30 A.M., a half hour after school has started. He heads to his daughter's kindergarten classroom without checking in with the office. The father enters the classroom and begins to hit his daughter. As the astounded class and the teacher watch, he severely beats her. Leaving the girl unconscious, he storms out the door and drives off in his pickup truck. The event took place in less than five minutes.

Scenario 5: The principal assembles the School Crisis Response Team at 1:30 P.M. on a Friday afternoon. He reports that a neighbor found a popular tenth-grade girl unconscious at home, after not showing up at school today. It looks like a suicide attempt (probable overdose of unknown substance). She is on her way to the hospital by ambulance. Rumors are rampant. Some stories relate a type of "suicide pact" involving an eighth-grade girl from a middle school. Apparently, the girl told some friends of her suicidal thoughts the day before, but nobody took them seriously. Teachers are beginning to report increasing tension among students and the school office is filling up with kids who are complaining of stomachaches, headaches, and so on. Others want to call home. Parents are calling

(continued)

Table 4.5 *(Continued)*

the office asking about the incident. The media has already tried to reach the principal for comment. Just before school is dismissed, a teacher panics when another tenth-grader runs sobbing from the classroom. The girl can't be located.

Scenario 6: A third-grade teacher is presenting a lesson to her students. She has just soundly reprimanded students for continuing to talk out; in fact, she is still very upset. Suddenly, she turns pale, clutches her chest and keels over in front of 20 horrified children. Two frightened children run to the office, sobbing the news. The teacher is taken by ambulance to the nearest hospital, where it is discovered that she has suffered a massive heart attack. She never regains consciousness and succumbs the next morning.

Scenario 7: The primary grade children at an elementary school have just returned to their classes from recess. Suddenly, the walls begin to shake, the lights flicker and go out, windows break and glass shards fly across the rooms, books and equipment fall from shelves. Several children have been hit by books and broken glass; they are bleeding. Some children are screaming; others are pale and silent, obviously in shock. Communication with the outside world is limited, phone lines are jammed, rumors suggest that there has been a major earthquake just south of San Francisco with thousands injured and dying.

Source: Adapted from Sacramento City Unified School District, Psychological Services (n.d.).

unique school site issues as a part of this in-service training. However, keep in mind that some issues will be so complex that immediate solutions will not be found. Thus, after some initial discussion, it may be necessary to place them aside for further discussion and study.

Following the introductory activities, a video presentation designed to illustrate the school's role in crisis intervention will be helpful. Two excellent productions, are titled *School Crisis: Under Control* (National School Safety Center, http://www.nssc1.org) and *Children and Trauma: The School's Response* (Emergency Media Services 800-480-2520), produced by the National School Safety Center (1991) and the Federal Emergency Management Agency (1992), respectively. These videos do an excellent job of giving faculty an idea of what a crisis response in a school setting might involve.

The next section of the in-service is devoted to crisis theory and gaining an understanding of the definition and characteristics of a crisis and the crisis state. The material provided in Chapter 2 might be used to develop this section of the in-service.

Following the crisis theory discussion is a section on reactions typically seen during a crisis. The importance of providing staff with such information has been previously mentioned by Dillard (1989, 1990, cited in Pitcher & Poland, 1992). This information is best organized from a developmental perspective. It provides for understanding of how children react to crisis events at varying age levels. This section is easily modified to reflect site needs. For example, an elementary school in-service would provide a detailed review of the preschool/kindergarten and elementary school reactions and point out the availability of similar information for older students as a handout. (See Appendices B and C for examples.) A portion of this session is devoted to preparing teachers for their own possible crisis reactions. In conducting a school site in-service, it is useful to provide examples of actual student and teacher reactions from personal crisis intervention experiences. In doing so it is important to normalize and give permission for the expression of a range of emotional reactions following a crisis.

The next in-service section should focus on classroom management following a crisis and offer suggestions for curriculum modifications. It is very important to give teachers permission to modify the classroom routine. For example, in one classroom following a school shooting, a teacher returned from an illness several days after the crisis had occurred. She had missed the meetings that had discussed the need to modify instruction. The teacher began her usual classroom routine of a math and then a reading activity. She was then surprised during the regular sharing time that followed when the children did not talk about their experiences and feelings about the shooting. The teacher had given the crisis event a low priority in her daily schedule. She had not taken time to address the incident and therefore the children followed her model. A handout that may be useful in guiding this discussion is provided in Table 4.6.

This in-service component should also review the components of the psychological first aid response school personnel will employ when working with students during a crisis. Information provided in Appendix A and Chapter 8 (Crisis Intervention), should assist in the preparation of this in-service component.

In closing the school-site in-service, a brief summary of the workshop should be provided. Staff should also be asked to complete a needs assessment to assist in the planning of future in-service programs. This needs assessment provides an excellent opportunity to validate any

Table 4.6
Classroom Management Following a Crisis

The teacher's reaction to crisis: Following crises, adults can expect to react in many of the same ways as children. Somatic, emotional, and behavioral reactions are expected. As is the case for children, not all adults will respond to a crisis event in the same way. Some will be more affected than others will and each individual's reactions are unique. Perceived threat, proximity to the crisis, familiarity with victims and prior trauma will play a significant role in determining degree of traumatization.

Complete control of all crisis reactions by the teacher is not necessarily effective and it is certainly not natural. Following a crisis the teacher should feel comfortable letting his or her emotions show in a controlled fashion. While it would be counterproductive to become hysterical in front of students, it would be okay to shed a tear or two. Unpleasant feelings and resulting emotional reactions are a normal response to crisis. By displaying crisis reactions, the teacher models appropriate responses to crisis. Doing so may also let students know that they are not alone in what they are feeling and normalize these feelings.

In some instances, however, crisis reactions may significantly adversely affect the teacher's ability to manage a classroom. Teachers and administrators should understand that not all teachers will be able to continue to run a classroom without assistance. If a teacher's emotional reactions interfere with the ability to manage a classroom, he or she should not be afraid to ask for help.

Do not expect a quick return to normal routine: Following a crisis, the teacher should not expect an immediate return to the normal classroom routine. A significant change has taken place and there will be aspects of teacher and student life that will never again be the same. Time to adjust and adapt to this reality will be needed. In fact, a worst case scenario for a crisis intervention is an environment that attempts to ignore the crisis and immediately returns to a precrisis mode of operation.

Provide factual information and facilitate discussion: Students and teachers will need time to digest what has happened to them. Lacking adult perspective, children will need repeated opportunities to review what has happened. It is helpful to provide students with as much factual information as they request. The one exception to this rule is student suicide. Here you will want to avoid giving out excess detail to avoid glorifying the event.

Structure can be reassuring: Although one should not expect a normal routine, daily classroom structure is important. For example, by following the normal bell schedule children are reassured that not everything has changed.

Table 4.6 *(Continued)*

The curriculum will need to be modified: Because crises present their own opportunities for learning, it is more than appropriate for curriculum to be adjusted and adapted. Curriculum following a crisis should avoid presentation of new academic materials. Much of what is typically called "busy work" might be appropriate for the classroom dealing with crisis. It might also be appropriate to integrate activities designed to help children process what has happened into the curriculum. For example, students could write letters to the injured and/or families of the deceased. They could discuss and/or write about how to avoid/prepare for future crises. Art projects could include creation of memorials for those who have died.

Recognize the importance of taking action: Teachers will need to help students become "actors" rather than "victims." Taking some concrete action can be an important element of crisis resolution. To the extent possible, teachers should help students see the situation as a challenge rather than a threat. They also need to teach and assist with problem-solving skills and efforts. This can be done by involving students in the decision-making process regarding such things as crisis prevention and preparedness, memorials, condolences, gifts, belongings of deceased individuals, and so on.

Recognize signs of distress and make referrals when necessary: When symptoms of distress become severe and/or persist beyond a reasonable length of time, the teacher should refer the student(s) to school mental health professionals for individual crisis intervention.

Source: From "Administrative response to crisis situations: Recommendations for the implementation of Board Policy 5141.5" by S.E. Brock, S. Lewis, and S. Yund, 1990. (Available from Lodi Unified School District, Special Services/SELPA, 1305 E. Vine St., Lodi, CA 95240.)

specific crisis response issues that participants may have brought up during earlier discussions.

SUMMARY

The last two chapters have reviewed of how crisis response planners facilitate the establishment of a crisis response team. These chapters have provided suggestions and recommendations for increasing school district receptivity to crisis planning as well as for obtaining a district commitment to crisis preparedness. Before moving on to a more detailed description of the components of a crisis plan, this chapter concludes with recommendations that summarize the most important ideas just presented.

RECOMMENDATION 1

The first step is to commit oneself to the idea of crisis preparedness and response. At this stage, simply do everything possible to learn about crisis preparedness and response.

RECOMMENDATION 2

Formalize this commitment by establishing crisis preparedness as a professional objective and announce it to others. This step serves two purposes. First, it provides motivation to complete the task. Second, it will involve the immediate supervisor. By accepting crisis preparedness and response as an objective, the supervisor lends support to the project.

RECOMMENDATION 3

Initiate team development. Begin by establishing a Crisis Response Planning Committee which should include district administration and support staff. Through this Committee begin to develop crisis response plans.

RECOMMENDATION 4

With the support of supervisors and peers firmly established (by establishing a crisis response evaluation objective and the Crisis Response Planning Committee), approach the superintendent and/or other district-level administrators regarding the desire to establish a district crisis response policy.

RECOMMENDATION 5

To gauge district willingness to engage in crisis preparedness and to increase their investment in the idea, obtain some sort of financial commitment from administration. If possible, obtain release time from traditional duties to develop and implement the crisis policy.

RECOMMENDATION 6

Do not be frustrated if crisis preparedness proposals are met with resistance. Rather, continue self-education, policy development, and in-service efforts. Remember that the occurrence of a crisis will motivate a change in attitudes regarding crisis preparedness. Be prepared to strike while the iron is hot.

RECOMMENDATION 7

Next, approach site-level administrators and attempt to solicit their support. Just as crisis response planners needed the support of their colleagues before approaching district-level administration, the district-level administration will need the support of their own site administrators before this procedure can be brought before a school board. The strategy is a very direct one; ask for time to make a presentation and review the proposed district policy, a tentative plan, and suggestions for its implementation.

RECOMMENDATION 8

The final step in the initiation of a crisis response policy is to bring crisis preparedness proposals to the school board for discussion and approval. We strongly recommend that the crisis response planners formalize a district's commitment to crisis preparedness and response through adoption of a school board policy. This will ensure that preparedness proposals are implemented district-wide.

RECOMMENDATION 9

Begin crisis intervention in-service efforts with support staff. Crises will not wait for the development of a comprehensive plan. Thus, it makes sense to begin by in-servicing those who will be on the frontline of a crisis response.

RECOMMENDATION 10

Extensive school site-level in-service efforts are typically needed to implement a district-wide crisis response policy. These efforts should serve the dual purposes of increasing receptivity to crisis preparedness as well as providing participants with the knowledge they will need to implement a crisis response policy.

CHAPTER 5

Components of a Crisis Preparedness Plan

It was a Saturday evening when Ms. Smith, a sixth-grade teacher, got into her car to return home from a social event. She was traveling along a two-lane highway when suddenly a van, driven by an allegedly drunk driver, crossed the median and crashed into her car, killing her instantly. Ms. Smith was remembered as a well-liked, energetic, and resourceful teacher and as a caring human being. The next morning, the school's principal called the school counselor to relay this tragic news and to begin to make plans for Monday morning. After consulting with the district's Crisis Response Team, the counselor was able to assure the principal that crisis intervention services would be available at 8:30 A.M. on Monday.

—Adapted from Brock, Lewis, Slauson, and Yund (1995)

BUILDING ON the foundation described in Chapter 4, this chapter and the ones that follow continue to describe the implementation of a crisis response policy. The remainder of this book focuses on the specific components of a model crisis response plan.

The crisis preparedness plan discussed in this book has four important components. First, and perhaps most importantly, it mandates crisis preparedness and crisis response through the adoption of the school board policy statement already discussed in Chapter 4. Second, it features crisis response teams at the regional, district, and individual school-site levels. Third, it emphasizes crisis preparedness by delineating various intervention tasks and specific individual responsibilities that should be in place before a crisis occurs. These latter two elements are the focus of this chapter. Finally, this plan offers specific crisis response procedures to be followed in times of crisis. This last component is discussed in Chapter 6 (Components of the Crisis Intervention Response).

Surprisingly, attempts at creating crisis response plans are a fairly recent development (Klingman, 1988). The rationale behind their development is the need to respond quickly to a crisis (Kneisel & Richards, 1988; Newgrass & Schonfeld, 1996). Delay fuels rumors that can make a bad situation worse. However, a quick response is often made difficult by the fact that group cooperation is undermined by crisis-induced stress (Murray, 2000). Further, a crisis can immobilize an entire school. Crisis team training and response plans minimize these difficulties (Murray, 2000; Pitcher & Poland, 1992). They place staff members in a better position to provide students with timely, effective support (Klingman, 1988). Another important reason for crisis preparedness is that the ability of nurturing adults to cope with crises is a strong predictor of how children cope (Kline et al., 1995).

CRISIS RESPONSE TEAMS

Crisis preparation can emphasize regional-level, district-level, and/or school-site teams. All three are needed to some extent. In forming regional- and district-level teams individuals with special skills, interests, and training are identified and brought together from various community agencies, school sites, school districts or a combination of these. Following crisis events, one or more of these teams can be drawn from their regular jobs and sent to the school where crisis response is needed. However, even though the regional- and district-level teams will typically have significant crisis response expertise, they will still need the assistance of school site teams, school personnel (Poland & McCormick, 1999), or both. These are the individuals who best know the children and parents affected by the crisis event. This fact highlights the principle advantage of school-site teams. Its members will be more familiar with the individuals affected by a crisis and will be able to act immediately when disaster strikes. Nevertheless, some crisis events are so traumatic that individual school or district resources may not be sufficient to manage the response. Consequently, the preferred model for a crisis response program consists of multiple hierarchical crisis response teams.*

---

*Some smaller school systems may not have enough school mental health professionals on staff to create multiple crisis response teams. Regardless, some school-level planning and coordination will be necessary.

THE HIERARCHICAL CRISIS RESPONSE TEAM MODEL

The hierarchical crisis response team model typically includes at least three levels of crisis response: school site-level, school district-level, and regional-level crisis response teams (Kline et al., 1995). Figure 5.1 illustrates how these crisis response teams are related to each other.

The basic structure of regional-level, district-level, and school-site crisis response teams is almost identical. Although the regional- and/or district-level teams will have greater responsibility for community- and district-level crisis preparedness, the basic team structures should not be different. This parallel structure helps to ensure that the school team is comprehensive and that it has support for all crisis response tasks by the district or regional teams. It also facilitates communication among crisis teams. Thus, the crisis plan components discussed in this and subsequent chapters apply to regional-level, district-level, and school-site crisis response teams.

SCHOOL SITE-LEVEL CRISIS RESPONSE

As a rule, individual school teams are the first lines of defense. To the degree possible, local school resources should handle most if not all of a given crisis response. School site resources should have superior knowledge of their school(s). Therefore, they are typically in the best position to offer an efficient response. Numerous sources have been identified that support this view (Caplan, 1964, 1974; Kline et al., 1995; Klingman, 1989; Sandall, 1986; Stacy, 1988; Toubiana et al., 1988; Weinberg, 1989). For example, Klingman (1988) states: ". . . preference in carrying out a prevention in disaster should be given to intervention within the natural setting (i.e., the school, the classroom), by those *most closely identified with and most familiar with this setting (i.e., school staff), through pedagogical and social means rather than through direct clinical intervention* [italics added]" (p. 206). Similarly, Doll (1999), reflecting on the response to the Columbine High School tragedy, in Littleton, Colorado, stated:

> While our thanks go out to the national leaders and experts who came to Littleton to help, it was the local "insiders" who led the community's response who were most valued by the Columbine students, staff, and their families. Many of these leaders had participated in national training on crisis intervention in the recent past. They were insider experts, familiar and trusted faces, who knew the history of the school and the community, were part of a shared culture and shared the loss. We especially appreciated the fact that these local leaders were here, in the community, and prepared to intervene. (pp. 66, 97)

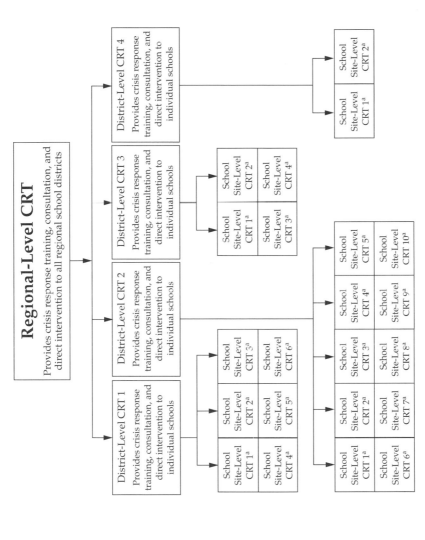

Figure 5.1 The Regional-Level CRT Flowchart depicts the relationship and roles of a model hierarchical crisis response team (CRT) in a hypothetical region (e.g., county or state). *Note:* Each school site provides crisis response training and direct intervention on its own campus. In this hypothetical region there are four separate school districts. District 1 has six schools, District 2 has ten schools, District 3 has four schools and District 4 has two schools.

In this model, school-level crisis response teams are responsible for initiating and eventually concluding all crisis responses. Following a crisis event, a school's first actions will be to convene their own school team and begin to assess the circumstances of the crisis event (e.g., what happened, how many will likely be effected, to what degree will they be effected). From this initial assessment of the crisis facts, and many times after consultation with the district-level team, an initial determination regarding the level of the crisis response will be made. Crisis response options include a school-level response; a combined school- and district-level response; and a combined school-, district- and regional-level response.

DISTRICT-LEVEL CRISIS RESPONSE

Despite this model's clear preference for site-level intervention, it is suggested that the district team always be available to provide individual school teams with consultation services and direct crisis intervention support. District-level teams will typically have superior crisis response training and knowledge, as well as more crisis response experience. Thus, these teams will usually have helpful advice and suggestions to offer schools as they respond to a crisis.

Even if school resources are initially judged sufficient, site-level teams should always have the option of calling on the district-level team for direct intervention support at any time. Crisis events affect staff members as well as students. In some cases, staff may be so devastated by an event that they may not be able to respond to the crisis situation emotionally or physically (Pitcher & Poland, 1992). In practice, as the authors have implemented this crisis team model, they have often placed the district-level team on stand-by. Doing so allows a school to begin the crisis response independently, with the knowledge that additional personnel could be brought in at a moments notice.

If needed, a district team would remain involved until the situation has stabilized to the point that site resources can independently manage the crisis response. Although the district team members will have more crisis intervention expertise, they will still need the assistance of that school's personnel. It is also important to note that although there is no time limit for how long district team assistance would be provided, this model suggests that site resources are responsible for concluding the crisis response.

In addition to providing consultation and direct services to individual schools following crisis events, district-level crisis response teams would also have crisis response training responsibilities. This team is the school district entity that would ensure that each school has the knowledge and skills needed to conduct a crisis response. Additionally, to assess crisis response readiness, district-level crisis response teams may, for example, conduct crisis drills at individual school sites (Kline et al., 1995) (see Chapter 13). A final district-level crisis response team responsibility is to, when needed, make a request for regional-level crisis response assistance.

REGIONAL-LEVEL CRISIS RESPONSE

Requests for regional-level crisis response team assistance are typically made very infrequently and only following crises that have significantly traumatized large numbers of students and staff members. For example, the tragic school shootings at Jonesboro, Arkansas; Springfield, Oregon; and Littleton, Colorado, are all examples of crisis events that would require a regional-level crisis response. Following such instances, the crisis response resources of even relatively large school districts would not be sufficient. It is important to note that while an individual school should have a significant voice in determining the need for district-level assistance, the regional-level crisis response would be a district-level decision.

Before requesting regional-level crisis response assistance, the requesting school district should ensure that all available district resources have either been exhausted or are unavailable. This requirement is based on the observation that the staff of the affected school or school district usually most effectively manages crises. However, it should be acknowledged, that regional-level support might be needed sooner in some school districts than in others. For example, smaller school districts with fewer support staff may need such support sooner than larger districts.

DEVELOPMENT OF SCHOOL SITE-LEVEL CRISIS RESPONSE TEAMS

The district crisis response team can facilitate the process of developing school site crisis response teams. If the district team is large enough, or has sufficient release time from other responsibilities, or both, members can personally visit each site and assist in the process of school crisis team development. In most cases, however, this will not be practical, especially in larger school districts. Thus, as an alternative it is suggested that a "training of trainers" workshop be provided. A sample outline for such a workshop is presented in Table 5.1. Many of the materials provided in this book would serve to facilitate such a workshop.

The training of trainers model involves asking schools to send to the workshop one to two representatives who can, after being trained,

Table 5.1

Trainers' Workshop Outline

---

1. Review of the school board policy
2. Crisis theory
   - What is a crisis?
   - What is the crisis state?
   - Principles of crisis intervention
3. Developing school crisis response teams
   - Implementation recommendations
   - Completing the crisis preparedness checklist
4. Members of a crisis response team: roles and responsibilities
   - Crisis response coordinator
   - Crisis intervention coordinator
   - Security liaison
   - Media liaison
   - Medical liaison
   - Crisis intervenors
5. The crisis response in-service model
   - How to prepare your school to develop a crisis plan
6. The crisis team in action
   - Use of the procedural checklist
7. Role plays
   - Review and respond to crisis scenarios

Source: From "Administrative response to crisis situations: Recommendations for the implementation of Board Policy 5141.5" by S.E. Brock, S. Lewis, and S. Yund, 1990. (Available from Lodi Unified School District, Special Services/SELPA, 1305 E. Vine St., Lodi, CA 95240.)

become trainers for their school site colleagues. Ideally, these representatives should include a school administrator and a school psychologist or counselor. Involvement of the school's support staff is critical given that they are most likely to have had some crisis intervention experiences and are also likely to be key members of the school's crisis response team. At this workshop, the district team can review components of an effective crisis response plan and make specific recommendations for the development of site crisis response teams. An example of such recommendations is found in Table 5.2. Note that the school level in-services mentioned in these recommendations may follow the outline specified in Table 4.4.

Table 5.2

Recommendations for the Development of
School Site-Level Crisis Response Teams

The following steps are offered as suggestions for how to develop school site-level crisis response teams:

1. The school principal, counselor(s), and psychologist(s) meet and discuss the crisis response policy and develop a calendar for its implementation.
2. The psychologist and counselor present a one- to two-hour in-service to all school staff members (classified as well as credentialed) introducing the concept of school crisis response.
3. Following this in-service, invite staff participation in the development of a site crisis response plan and conduct a needs assessment to determine crisis response issues that may require further staff development.
4. Form a committee of all interested staff members to develop a site crisis response plan. In addition to teacher representatives, this committee should include the principal, vice principal(s), school psychologist(s), school counselor(s), custodian(s), and school secretary.
5. The committee meets to review and discuss the crisis response policy, rules, and administrative guidelines. It then develops the site crisis response plan.
6. The committee discusses how to make staff aware of the site crisis response plan.
7. The committee reviews with all staff the site crisis response plan.
8. From the needs assessment, the committee provides additional school crisis response in-service(s).

Source: From "Administrative response to crisis situations: Recommendations for the implementation of Board Policy 5141.5" by S.E. Brock, S. Lewis, and S. Yund, 1990. (Available from Lodi Unified School District, Special Services/SELPA, 1305 E. Vine St., Lodi, CA 95240.)

DEVELOPMENT OF A
DISTRICT-LEVEL CRISIS RESPONSE TEAM

As mentioned in Chapter 3, the Crisis Response Planning Committee often naturally evolves into a district-level crisis response team. Many of the activities involved in self-education and in team building are necessary to the development of a district-level team. Additionally, training such as that provided in Appendix A, School Crisis Intervention: An

In-service for Educators, is important. Such training needs to be available on an ongoing basis, as it cannot be assumed that once in place all members of the team will remain with the district. Ideally, training for district-level crisis response teams will be made available by the regional-level crisis response team.

DEVELOPMENT AND USE OF A REGIONAL-LEVEL CRISIS RESPONSE TEAM

A regional-level crisis response team's collaboration with local County Mental Health and Office of Emergency Services personnel is essential (Brock, 1998a). In the authors' case, this level of team development relied upon the California Emergency Services Act (Government Code Section 8550). This Act is designed to help mitigate the effects of natural and manmade disasters. Among its provisions, the Act calls for disaster response partnership agreements within and between the various regions of the state. These response partnerships institutionalize the practice of *mutual aid* already employed by many emergency response personnel (e.g., firefighters). Mutual aid allows regions to share emergency response resources whenever a given disaster is beyond local control. Recently, the practice of mutual aid has also been applied to the mental health response to disasters. The regional-level crisis response team is modeled after this application.

Regional-level crisis response teams might be considered an insurance policy that a school district purchases by agreeing to send its own trained staff to other school districts in times of crisis. With such an agreement, districts are able to access a much larger cadre of crisis intervenors than any one district could ever hope to employ. A template for an agreement, or memo of understanding, to be signed by school districts agreeing to participate in a regional-level crisis response team mutual aid system is provided in Table 5.3. Although written primarily with California public schools in mind, it may be easily adapted for use within other regions.

A primary strength of having a regional-level crisis response team includes greater control over exactly who is responding to a crisis event. Following mass disasters, there is a need for a large number of crisis intervenors. While there is usually an abundance of volunteers willing to provide such assistance, it is difficult to quickly assess the qualifications of these volunteers. This creates the possibility that individuals without crisis intervention skill may become a part of the crisis response. A

Table 5.3
Sample Memorandum of Understanding for
School Crisis Response Mutual Aid

Date: _____

    This Memorandum of Understanding addresses agreements between the _____ County Office of Education, _____ County Office of Emergency Services, _____ County Mental Health Services, and those school districts within _____ County who agreed to participate.

Purpose

    Disasters of a large scale that occur within school districts may overwhelm the resources of that district. While this is an infrequent occurrence, it is best to be prepared for the possibility of such an occurrence by entering into mutual aid agreements with other school districts, county emergency services and county mental health services. Such mutual aid agreements help institutions offer services to each other following major disasters. Past experience has shown that when a large scale disaster occurs, it is difficult to coordinate services without some planning.

Background

    The origins of this Memorandum can be found in two pieces of legislation. The first is the state Emergency Services Act. This Act is designed to help mitigate the effects of natural and man-made disasters. Among its provisions, the Act calls for disaster response partnership agreements within and between the various regions of the state. These response partnerships institutionalize the practice of mutual aid already employed by emergency response personnel (e.g., firefighters). Mutual aid allows regions to share emergency response resources whenever a given disaster is beyond local control.

    The second origin of this agreement can be found in school safety legislation. According to this legislation, all school districts are required to have a school safety plan in place. Part of the safety plan includes Disaster Response procedures.

    Typically, it is expected that individual schools and/or school districts will manage their own crises using their school safety plan. This Memorandum addresses those occurrences, infrequent they may be, which tax the resources of the school district to the point where outside help is required.

(continued)

Table 5.3 *(Continued)*

Agreement

1. Each individual school district has the responsibility of responding to its own crises. Additionally, it is district administration's responsibility to determine when the resources of the district are no longer adequate to deal with a situation. It is district administration's responsibility to ask for assistance when it is deemed necessary. Mutual aid support is not provided without a request from a district-level administrator.

2. If school disaster mutual aid response assistance is needed, a district-level administrator or designee will contact the Regional-Level Crisis Response Team Mutual Aid Coordinator to request assistance. The Mutual Aid Coordinator may be reached Monday through Friday 8:00 A.M. to 5:00 P.M. through (phone number) or through the 24-hour crisis line at (phone number).

3. The Regional-Level Crisis Response Team Mutual Aid Coordinator will record requests for help on a call out form developed specifically for that purpose. This documentation will indicate who is requesting help, what type of help is requested, when it is needed, where it is needed and whether the help being requested is volunteer help or is paid help.

4. The issue of payment is raised because it is possible that an emergency situation can turn into a disaster, which will require federal assistance, at which point there may be reimbursement for costs for disaster response.

5. Following a request for mutual aid assistance, the Regional-Level Crisis Response Team Mutual Aid Coordinator will contact appropriate resources for the first response. The choice of which resources or school districts to contact may be based on geographic considerations (i.e. proximity to requesting district), but can also be based on other considerations (i.e., choosing a district that has not already been asked to provide mutual aid support).

6. School districts offering to provide mutual aid to a requesting district will provide only credentialed personnel. Mental Health Services staff responding will be either licensed clinicians or registered interns (psychiatrist, psychologist, licensed clinical social worker, or marriage, family counselor). Generally speaking, only staff trained in crisis response will be deployed.

7. Responding districts will provide assistance for up to three days. At the end of the three days, further agreements between individual

Table 5.3 *(Continued)*

districts, Mental Health Services, Office of Education and Office of Emergency Services will be necessary in order to provide further assistance.

8. Unless otherwise specified, shifts of work shall be eight hours long for the three-day period.
9. The district requesting the help shall supply supplies for classroom activities, such as art supplies, writing materials, unless otherwise specified in the request for assistance.
10. Participating districts agree to meet annually to ensure appropriate response procedures are still viable.

The signatures below indicate an agreement to abide by this Memorandum of Understanding for crisis response to school districts, pledges cooperation and problem solving, and by responding appropriately for the good of the district and the County.

Term

This Memorandum will be in force on the date first signed below, and will be self-renewing. This Memorandum will be reviewed annually. Districts that no longer wish to participate in this Memorandum of Understanding shall notify, in writing, within 30 days, the following departments:

_____   _____

Superintendent, County Schools   Director, County Mental Health Dept.

_____   _____

_____   _____

_____

Director, Office of Emergency Services

_____

_____

Source: Adapted from "Memorandum of Understanding: School Crisis Response Mutual Aid," by Roger Speed, Director, San Joaquin County Mental Health Services, October, 1998. This document is in the public domain.

regional-level crisis response team eliminates this concern. As will be discussed, a mutual aid program can specify uniform crisis intervention qualifications.

Another strength of the school crisis intervention mutual aid program is the simple fact that it makes use of individuals who know schools and how they operate. Many times "expert" crisis intervenors, who are not school employees, make simple mistakes (e.g., not accounting for a bell schedule) because they do not understand how the school functions. By having a cadre of school-based professionals, with crisis intervention skill, this concern is also eliminated.

MUTUAL AID REQUEST AND CALL-OUT PROCEDURES

The following illustrates the sequence of events that may result in a regional-level crisis team response.

1. A crisis affects a school or schools.
2. If the individual school(s) does not have resources sufficient to manage the crisis event, then it requests school district-level assistance.
3. If the school district does not have sufficient resources to manage the crisis event, then consultation with the regional crisis response team is obtained.
4. If consultation confirms that local resources are overwhelmed, then neighboring school districts would be contacted and asked to provide crisis intervention mutual aid support.

Figure 5.2 illustrates this process of determining what level (or levels) of crisis response would be used following a traumatic event.

Proximity to the crisis will determine which school districts are called and asked to help provide mutual aid support. However, it is possible that other factors will be considered as well. For example, the district that has recently had to manage a significant crisis of its own may not be asked to participate, even though it is closest to a given crisis. Similarly, the district that has recently already provided mutual aid support to a neighbor may not be among the first asked to respond to a new incident.

To facilitate the call-out of mutual aid support, a Regional Coordinator must have a list of district crisis response coordinators for each participating school district. Figure 5.3 provides a sample of a form Coordinators use when a request for mutual aid is received. Twenty-four hour phone numbers, pager numbers, or both should be specified and

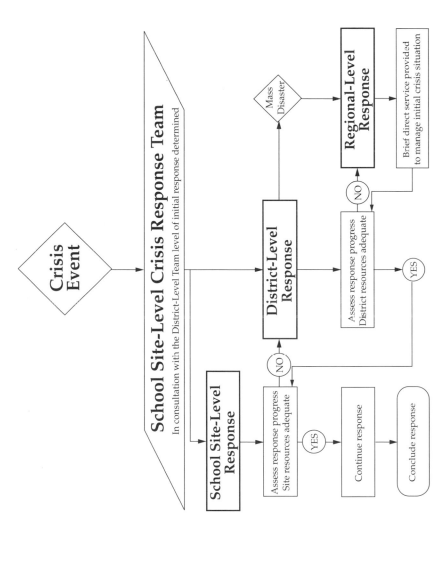

Figure 5.2 The Crisis Event Flowchart depicts how decisions to use the various levels of crisis response are made.

Regional-Level Crisis Response Team Mutual Aid Request
SCHOOL INCIDENT REPORT

Incident and Request Information

Request date: _____ Request time: _____

Person requesting mutual aid: _____ Phone number: _____

Known incident facts: _____

_____

Specific mutual aid request: _____

Law enforcement contacted? _____ Yes _____ No

Office of Emergency Service contacted? _____ Yes _____ No

Incident Location

School Crisis Response Coordinator: _____

Name of school: _____ Phone number: _____

Address of school: _____

Cross Streets: _____

Mutual Aid Call-Out Information

District	Crisis Response Coord. Name/24-Hr. Ph. #	# of Crisis Intervenors		# Sent to Incident		
		Available	Needed	Day 1	Day 2	Day 3

Figure 5.3 Sample request for mutual aid form.

alternates identified in case a district coordinator is not available. Once contacted, each district-level crisis response coordinator will inform the Regional Coordinator of the resources available. The Coordinator will in turn give directions on how to get to the affected school and to whom crisis intervenors are to report.

Each supporting district is responsible for determining which staff members they feel are most qualified to provide the regional team with mutual aid support. However, it is recommended that participating districts establish some general guidelines. For example, a high school counselor should not typically be sent to work with the students of an elementary school. In addition, certain minimum standards should be explored for what level of crisis intervention training is expected from regional-level crisis response mutual aid crisis intervenors. All mutual aid crisis intervenors should be credentialed (or certificated) personnel. Typically, these individuals are district psychologists, counselors, social workers, or nurses. However, because crisis intervention is a form of psychological first aid (not a professional mental health intervention), regional-level mutual aid crisis intervenors may include teachers and administrators with the proper training. Crisis intervenors might also appropriately include licensed staff from local mental health agencies. These individuals would typically already have a high level of crisis intervention training.

LIMITS OF MUTUAL AID SUPPORT

An important topic to be discussed by districts participating in any mutual aid system is how long selected support staff will be committed to another school district following a given crisis. Young (1998) recommends that this type of mutual aid last about three days. If crisis intervention support is needed for more than three days, it may need to be obtained from another district. Regarding long-term psychological treatment, other resources will need to be identified (e.g., state and federal resources). The mutual aid program described in this chapter is designed to facilitate the immediate crisis intervention response. It is not designed to provide long-term mental health treatment.

RECOMMENDED CRISIS RESPONSE TEAM ROLES AND RESPONSIBILITIES

An important first step in the development of crisis response teams is identifying crisis response resources and assessing areas of need within the school district. As stated previously, in large districts individuals with special skills, interests, and training can be formed into a team that can be taken from their regular assignments and sent to a school where a traumatic event has occurred. Smaller districts, on the other hand, may not have enough school mental health professionals on staff to create a viable team. Nevertheless, some district-level planning and coordination will need to be done.

Inclusion of individuals on the crisis response team should consider a number of variables. Purvis et al. (1991) suggest team members should be reliable, level-headed, available, and have the physical and emotional strength needed to face crises. Thompson (1995) recommends that members of a crisis response team have "strong individual and group facilitation skills, knowledge of how the school and community functions, and experience with crisis intervention and management procedures" (p. 269). Pitcher and Poland (1992) indicate that the following "personal needs" can interfere with the ability to be an effective crisis team member: "(1) The need to be a hero. (2) The need to be in control. (3) Difficulty tolerating unhappiness or strong emotions in others. (4) Taking on too much responsibility for the organization. (5) Discomfort with consultation, indirect roles. (6) The need to have things go perfectly" (pp. 157–158).

Crisis response team structure is based on a number of crisis-preparedness and response roles. The process of creating a team involves identifying individuals to fill each role. At a minimum, a team should be made up of individuals prepared to fill the roles of *crisis response coordinator, crisis intervention coordinator, security liaison, medical liaison,* and *media spokesperson.* As a rule, it is appropriate for an administrator to fill most of these roles. However, any individual with special training in any one of these areas may take on any one (or under extreme circumstances, more) of these roles. This team must also have a group of crisis intervenors.

CRISIS RESPONSE TEAM ROLE RESPONSIBILITIES

In delineating crisis response team role responsibilities, we use Caplan's (1964) three-part conceptual model that differentiates between primary, secondary, and tertiary prevention. Primary prevention activities include those tasks undertaken before a crisis event occurs. These activities are aimed at either preventing crises from occurring in the first place (e.g., development of a school safety plan) or are designed to minimize the adverse consequences of crises (e.g., preparing for crisis intervention) when they do occur. Secondary prevention activities take place immediately after a crisis and are also designed to minimize adverse consequences (e.g., providing crisis intervention). Tertiary prevention activities refer to the long-term followup that may be required by a crisis (e.g., professional psychotherapeutic treatments).

CRISIS RESPONSE COORDINATOR

This individual should be an administrator or his or her designee (Pitcher & Poland, 1992; Purvis et al., 1991). The crisis response coordinator should be someone who is responsible, able to get things done, and who is knowledgeable about the district or school and staff (Pitcher & Poland, 1992). It would be beneficial for the coordinator to have an awareness of the objectives, methods, and limitations of crisis intervention in the schools.

The crisis response coordinator's primary prevention responsibilities include coordinating the development of crisis response plans, and reviewing these plans with school staff members at least annually. Secondary prevention responsibilities include declaring that a crisis exists (Cornell & Sheras, 1998), making a determination regarding the level of crisis response required, and overseeing all initial crisis response activities. Tertiary prevention duties include ensuring that the long-term needs generated by the crisis event are met. This individual may also be responsible for evaluating each crisis response (discussed in detail in Chapter 12). Such evaluation includes examining how to prevent crisis reoccurrence and how to improve the crisis response plan.

As with all crisis team positions, it is critical to appoint at least one alternate to serve in the coordinator's absence (Kline et al., 1995; Purvis et al., 1991). This backup person must be as familiar with his or her role as the primary coordinator or liaison.

CRISIS INTERVENTION COORDINATOR

The individual filling this role should have a clear understanding of the objectives, methods, and limitations of school crisis intervention (Pitcher & Poland, 1992) discussed in Chapter 8. Implementation of the triage and referral suggestions offered in Chapter 7 are the responsibility of this individual. Ideally, the crisis intervention coordinator should meet Frederick's (1985) specific requirements for key workers in major emergencies. These requirements include a facility for administration when groups of victims are involved, a facility for providing emotional support, a facility for recognizing emotional problems, the ability to handle emotional reactions, and a facility for providing information. Typically, an individual with a background in school social work, psychology, or counseling is assigned to this position. The crisis intervention coordinator has several primary prevention responsibilities, including:

- Maintaining an up-to-date list of mental health or counseling referral sources (e.g., county mental health, crisis centers, hospice) (Purvis et al., 1991)
- Developing and maintaining a supply of crisis intervention referral forms
- Keeping support staff up to date on crisis intervention literature
- Developing a psychological triage or risk-screening procedure
- Facilitating the development and training of the team of crisis intervenors

Immediately following a crisis event, the crisis intervention coordinator's secondary prevention responsibilities include:

- Making referral forms available to staff
- Establishing a procedure for self-referral
- Conducting a psychological triage to estimate individual traumatization risk
- Working with the crisis intervenors in planning and implementing crisis interventions (e.g., classroom crisis intervention and individual psychological first aid)
- Maintaining a referral list
- Distributing referral summaries to support staff

Tertiary prevention responsibilities include:

- Identifying the need for long-term counseling interventions (e.g., crisis therapy)
- Ensuring the provision, when necessary, of professional mental health psychotherapeutic interventions
- Facilitating the return to school of psychological trauma victims
- Keeping track of crisis anniversaries
- Writing a detailed summary of crisis interventions in order to determine how to improve future crisis responses

MEDIA LIAISON

The media liaison is responsible for establishing procedures for working with broadcast and print journalists. At the district-level, this individual is many times an associate superintendent; on the school-site team this individual is typically the school principal. In districts that have a media spokesperson, this individual will naturally fill this role. Pitcher and Poland (1992) suggest that this individual should have good interpersonal skills and be comfortable with radio and television appearances. Chapter 9 (Media Relations) is especially helpful to individuals filling this role. Additional training in media management and previous experience working with journalists is desirable.

Primary prevention tasks include establishing an ongoing dialogue with local media as shown in Table 5.4. This dialogue helps to ensure effective and efficient communication following a crisis, and that the media is an aid, rather than a hindrance, to the crisis response. Immediately following a crisis, the media liaison is responsible for disseminating crisis facts (Nye, 1997) and for ensuring that the media is able to assist and not hinder the response.

Table 5.4
Sample Policy Statement Regarding Responses to the
Media during Times of Crisis

Following a crisis event, it is possible that members of the press may contact staff members. Because of the need to control rumors (which can run rampant following a crisis) it is our policy not to speak to members of the press immediately following a crisis. Rather the journalist should be referred to the crisis spokesperson. The principal will identify the crisis spokesperson to all staff members.

As the given crisis situation stabilizes and the facts become clear, it may become appropriate for staff members to be interviewed. Such interviews should either be cleared through or arranged by the crisis spokesperson.

In some instances, it may be appropriate for office staff to be given prepared statements (developed by the media liaison), that they could read to journalists over the phone.

Whenever possible all staff members will be briefed on press releases before they are given to the press. However, it needs to be recognized that there may be some situations where this is not possible.

Source: Adapted from "Administrative response to crisis situations: Recommendations for the implementation of Board Policy 5141.5" by S.E. Brock, S. Lewis, and S. Yund, 1990. (Available from Lodi Unified School District, Special Services/SELPA, 1305 E. Vine St., Lodi, CA 95240.)

Tertiary prevention responsibilities include assisting with or managing the follow-up coverage that often accompanies crisis events. Along with helping to ensure that the media has the access needed to make an accurate report, the media liaison would also try to minimize coverage that might serve to rekindle crisis reactions. For example, it would be preferable to have the media use pictures or scenes that reflect the current school situation and not use those obtained during the crisis.

SECURITY LIAISON

The security liaison is typically a school administrator. In some cases, a school, district, or both may have its own security personnel who will naturally fill this role. Ideally, this person will have ongoing contacts with local police or sheriff's departments. Chapter 10 (Security and Safety Procedures) will be helpful to an individual in this role. Primary prevention activities include both general safety planning and the development of plans designed to ensure security following a crisis.

The security liaison's secondary prevention responsibilities include implementing the previously mentioned procedures, plans, and strategies. Similarly, tertiary prevention responsibilities include modifying the general safety plans and procedures suggested by a given crisis event to prevent crisis reoccurrence, escalation, or both.

MEDICAL LIAISON

The medical liaison is typically a school nurse or district health administrator. This individual is responsible for several medical and health-related procedures to be followed during and following a crisis event. Chapter 11 (Emergency Medical and Health Procedures) provides additional information on fulfilling this role. Specific primary prevention responsibilities include providing first aid training (e.g., CPR); ensuring that medical first aid materials and equipment are available; and establishing communication links with local doctors, hospitals, and emergency medical personnel. Providing curricula designed to promote student health may also be an appropriate task.

In some cases, the medical liaison's secondary prevention responsibilities may include participation in, or management of, the medical triage of crisis victims (Young, 2000). However, in most cases emergency medical personnel (e.g., paramedics) will do this. In these instances, the medical liaison facilitates communication between paramedics and the crisis response team. Once immediate medical needs are taken care of, the medical liaison facilitates communication between hospitals, doctors, and other medical personnel and the crisis response team. An especially important intervention issue to be addressed is to find a way to shield those students who were uninjured from unnecessary exposure to carnage (Nader et al., 1990). Additionally, the medical liaison assists in communicating to parents and staff the medical conditions of those who were injured.

Tertiary prevention responsibilities of the medical liaison include assisting the crisis intervention coordinator in facilitating the return to school of students who were physically injured during a crisis event.

CRISIS INTERVENORS

Typically, psychologist(s), social worker(s), nurse(s), and counselor(s) comprise the majority of those filling this role. Although the other crisis response plan roles are assigned to one individual and an alternate, several individuals are needed to deliver direct crisis intervention assistance (such as classroom crisis intervention and individual psychological first aid) to children and staff. It may be appropriate to have teachers and classified employees functioning in this role. However, they would first need to receive special training.

The more individuals who are capable of providing direct crisis intervention services to students, the better. For example, it would be ideal if every classroom teacher were able to meet the crisis intervention needs of his or her students. As discussed in Chapter 8, teachers and other school personnel may learn to administer psychological first aid, however, not all will have the inclination or aptitude for this role. As a compromise, it is suggested that the crisis intervenors at the very least be representative of the school. For example, in an elementary school a primary and an intermediate grade teacher should be included in crisis intervention team training.

Another essential factor to remember when creating a team of crisis intervenors is the cultural background of the student body. It is essential for crisis intervenors to be sensitive to cultural differences. Perhaps most important, it is critical that crisis team members be aware of the different cultural norms for responding to crises (M. Armstrong, 1990). Klingman (1986) highlights the importance of this type of cultural awareness. In describing the interventions conducted by crisis workers as they notified parents of their children's death in a school bus accident, he states that cultural "awareness on the part of the workers proved valuable in that they were prepared for various culturally based manifestations of traumatic grief reactions, and thus refrained from requesting the use of sedatives in cases in which the parents' reactions to a death notification on the surface seemed extreme but were in line with their cultural norms" (p. 55).

Along with providing an understanding of culturally appropriate crisis reactions, cultural awareness also allows for an understanding of the resources available to the crisis victim. For example, Stack (1974) reports that urban African-American families may have several different households available to act as a resource in times of crisis. Resources available to the families studied by Stack went well beyond the extended family and into the community. Conversely, O. Lewis' (1970) study, *A Death in the Sanchez Family*, illustrates how the lack of resources (the financial strain of burying the dead) can exacerbate a trauma for the Mexican poor. On the basis of these observations, it appears critical for crisis intervention team members to include individuals who are aware of a student body's cultural identity and differences.

All crisis intervenors are under the direct supervision of the crisis intervention coordinator. However, once identified and trained, the crisis intervenors assist the entire crisis response team (crisis response coordinator, crisis intervention coordinator, media liaison, security liaison, medical liaison) in carrying out its primary, secondary, and tertiary prevention responsibilities.

PLANNING FOR A CRISIS RESPONSE

Crisis intervention may be necessary following a variety of traumatic events. Examples of such situations include death of a student or staff member, an accident with major injuries, attempted suicide, community disaster, terrorist threat or attack, or gang violence. No matter how hard we try to prevent them, crises such as these are an unpleasant reality of life for which we need to prepare.

In developing a regional and/or district-level crisis response team, members need to prepare materials and procedures for use during times of crisis. For example, a regional or district crisis response coordinator may facilitate development of a crisis response handbook and establish a mechanism through which school crisis teams can obtain district team assistance; the referral coordinator will establish referral and triage procedures; the security liaison may prepare crisis team member identification cards and develop crowd control plans and other procedures to ensure student safety; and the media spokesperson could prepare prototype press releases and plan for a media center to be used during times of heavy press interest. The summation of these efforts is the creation of a regional or district crisis response handbook. The remaining chapters of this book provide an expanded version of what this handbook might look like. In fact, some of what appears in this book is an adaptation of the authors' school district crisis response handbook (*Administrative Response to Crisis Situations*; Brock, Lewis, & Yund, 1990). This handbook can serve as a model for the school crisis team manuals developed for each site. The utility of a crisis response handbook is especially apparent when conducting a training of trainers workshop. The handbook will provide participants with concrete crisis response procedures.

Before a crisis, team members should establish communication links, outside and within the district, and keep them up to date (Toubiana et al., 1988). For example, the district crisis response coordinator might set up telephone trees so the district personnel on the crisis team can be reached 24 hours a day. This coordinator may also establish links with local mental health organizations, hospitals, and other community agencies. Similarly, the security coordinator could meet with police personnel, and the media spokesperson could hold meetings with local newspaper editors and reporters and keep lists of names and phone numbers on file.

Following a crisis event, it is essential to respond quickly. A quick response is, however, often made difficult by the fact that a crisis can immobilize the entire school. Crisis response plans can minimize these immobilizing effects. They place staff in a better position to quickly provide students with effective and efficient support. To facilitate the development of such plans the *Crisis Response Planning Checklist* (Figure 5.4) was developed. The primary purpose of this *Checklist* is to identify specific individuals to fill specific crisis preparedness and intervention tasks. Such delineation helps to ensure that everything that needs to be done is addressed during the chaotic, overwhelming times following a crisis event.

This checklist is specifically designed to give school personnel general crisis response planning procedures and to assist in the development of a crisis response plan. It specifies the identification of the crisis response team roles previously discussed. Additionally, it directs the crisis response team to assist the crisis response coordinator complete the tasks discussed next.

IDENTIFY CRISIS INTERVENTION LOCATIONS

As many locations as possible need to be identified for use as crisis intervention offices following a crisis. In doing so, remember that some crisis

Crisis Response Planning Checklist

1. **Designate a crisis response coordinator.**
   The coordinator would be in charge of implementing and overseeing the crisis response.

   NAME: _____ DATE ASSIGNED: _____
   a. **Designate an alternate** to serve in the coordinator's absence.

2. **Designate a crisis intervention coordinator.**
   Responsible for planning and implementing the crisis intervention referral/triage procedures.

   NAME: _____ DATE ASSIGNED: _____
   a. **Designate an alternate** to serve in the coordinator's absence.

3. **Designate a media liaison.**
   Responsible for establishing media management procedures.

   NAME: _____ DATE ASSIGNED: _____
   a. **Designate an alternate** to serve in the liaison's absence.

4. **Designate a security liaison.**
   Responsible for establishing safety and security procedures.

   NAME: _____ DATE ASSIGNED: _____
   a. **Designate an alternate** to serve in the liaison's absence.

5. **Designate a medical liaison.**
   Responsible for establishing medical and health procedures.

   NAME: _____ DATE ASSIGNED: _____
   a. **Designate an alternate** to serve in the liaison's absence.

6. **Designate a crisis intervention team.**
   Provides crisis intervention services and advises the crisis response coordinator.

   NAME: _____ DATE ASSIGNED: _____
   NAME: _____ DATE ASSIGNED: _____
   NAME: _____ DATE ASSIGNED: _____
   NAME: _____ DATE ASSIGNED: _____

7. **Members of the crisis response team should work cooperatively to complete the following crisis preparedness tasks:**

   a. **Identify crisis counseling locations.**

      Individual crisis intervention locations: _____

      Groups crisis intervention locations: _____

      Student/Parent waiting area: _____

      _____

Figure 5.4 Sample Crisis Preparedness Checklist. *Source:* Adapted from "Administrative response to crisis situations: Recommendations for the implementation of Board Policy 5141.5," by S.E. Brock, S. Lewis, and S. Yund, 1990, pp. 6–8. (Available from Lodi Unified School District, Special Services/SELPA, 1305 E. Vine St., Lodi, CA 95240.)

b. **Designate specific phone lines to be used for specific reasons.**

Press or media line: _____

Parent information line: _____

Emergency line: _____

c. **Designate a base of operations for the crisis response team.**

Location: _____

Alternate location: _____

d. **Establish a phone tree among all staff.**

Date completed: _____

e. **Establish a crisis response tool box.**

Date completed: _____

f. **Account for substitutes.**

Substitute names posted: _____

8. **Review administrative guidelines for crisis intervention at least annually.**

Date last reviewed: _____

Figure 5.4 *(Continued)*

intervention sessions will be individual whereas, others will be group. Additionally, a waiting area needs to be designated. Keep in mind that if teacher or staff rooms are used for crisis intervention, alternative areas for the staff to relate, eat, and consult will need to be designated.

DESIGNATE SPECIFIC PHONE LINES TO BE
USED FOR SPECIFIC REASONS

Incoming calls following a crisis may quickly tie up all available lines. Thus, it is important to designate that specific lines be used for specific purposes (Young, 2000). Especially important is the establishment and maintenance of "hidden phone lines." These are numbers not available to the public that could be used by staff for emergency communication following a crisis. Using cellular phones is another alternative. Another option is to identify a phone company representative who would be able to obtain additional dedicated phone lines for a school in times of crisis (e.g., Nettleton Public School District, 1998).

DESIGNATE A BASE OF OPERATIONS

Office staff needs to be involved in designating a base of operations because they may take on important responsibilities during its operation. Procedures need to be established for identifying and monitoring the additional support personnel that may be brought in following a large-scale crisis. Sign-in procedures need to be established so that school administration is always aware of who is on site at a given time. Additional procedures for getting messages to crisis response team members and support staff need to be developed. According to Purvis et al. (1991), the chosen location should be equipped with telephones, paper, pens, telephone directories, emergency power, and portable two-way radios. The base of operations should also be equipped with a computer.

ESTABLISHING A PHONE TREE

A system of quick, effective communication of crisis situation facts during nonschool hours needs to be established (Newgrass & Schonfeld, 1996; Petersen & Straub, 1992; Sorensen, 1989). A phone tree is one such method. A phone tree model is provided in Figure 5.5. Such a system is especially important given the Purvis et al. (1991) observation that crises may be better resolved if staff members are informed of an incident before students.

ESTABLISH A CRISIS RESPONSE TOOLBOX

Thompson (1995) acknowledges that during the initial phases of a crisis response it is "difficult for people involved to clearly think through all the details necessary to manage and contain the crisis" (p. 267). Thus, she recommends that a toolbox be created. This toolbox should centrally house all of the documents and materials developed by team members as part of their primary prevention responsibilities (e.g., psychological triage or risk screening materials; a list of mental health referral resources; prepared statements; evacuation, bomb threat, and traffic management procedures; medical first aid materials). Other materials recommended by Thompson for inclusion in the toolbox include a detailed school map, a complete set of school keys, a master schedule of all classes and a current list of all students enrolled in the school. The State of California's Office of the Attorney General has developed a guide that is extremely helpful to crisis

Emergency Telephone Tree

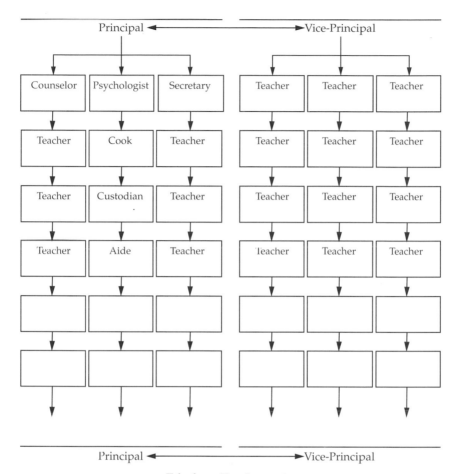

Telephone Tree Instructions

1. When you receive a message write it down, exactly as you received it. Read it back to the caller to ensure correctness.
2. Phone the person on the tree directly below your name. Tell the person you have a message from the principal and to get a paper and pencil. Ask the person to write down the message.
3. Ask the person you have called to read the message back to you to ensure that it has been received correctly.
4. If the person directly below your name is not immediately available, skip her/his name and call the next name below that on your branch. Continue down the list until you successfully relay the message.
5. Keep trying to contact persons you were unable to reach. When you do so, inform the person of the message and of the fact that you have already called the person she/he should have called.
6. If you are the last person on your branch of the tree, be sure to call either the principal or the vice-principal.

Figure 5.5 Model Emergency Telephone Tree. *Source:* This phone tree was adapted from a model developed by Resa Matteoli, a teacher at Beckman Elementary School in Lodi, CA. Used with permission.

planners as they start to assemble their own crisis response toolboxes (Crime and Violence Prevention Center, 2000).

ACCOUNTING FOR SUBSTITUTES

A centrally located message board on which the names of absent staff members and their substitutes are posted needs to be created. Substitutes need to be assisted during crises because it is probable that they will lack familiarity with the crisis response plan. Ideally, all substitutes within a district should be aware of the existence of school crisis plans. Also, school site plans should be placed in an accessible location (e.g., in the front of lesson plan books), and substitutes made aware of this location.

It is important to note that the final item of the Checklist (Figure 5.4, Item 8) specifies that the crisis planners review the crisis response plan at least annually. In doing so, the crisis response coordinator should make sure that individuals designated to fill crisis response roles are still willing and available to serve. It may be helpful to have crisis response teams discuss the crisis scenarios found in Chapter 4, Table 4.5. Such discussion will help each team member to better understand his or her responsibilities during a crisis intervention.

SUMMARY

Implementation of recommended crisis response plan components places a school district in a position to respond to crisis events. Development of regional- and district-level crisis response teams provides school districts with individuals well versed in responding to crises. The regional or district teams can also serve as models for individual school-site teams.

Complementing the crisis response plan are crisis response procedures. The *Crisis Response Planning Checklist* provides a framework for developing a crisis response team, while the *Crisis Response Procedural Checklist*, to be discussed in Chapter 6, offers guidelines for how teams should respond to crisis situations.

CHAPTER 6

Components of a Crisis Response

The response to Ms. Smith's tragic death on Saturday, in a head-on car crash, began the next day. The phone tree was used to inform all staff of the accident. Teachers, in turn, contacted parents. They were notified that counselors would be available on Monday and were encouraged to discuss this tragedy with their children. Besides the students in Ms. Smith's classroom, her former students would also be affected. Thus, middle school counselors were also notified of this death. With this exception, it was determined that the School Site-Level Crisis Response Team could manage this crisis. However, the district office was notified and District Crisis Response Team personnel placed on standby. A staff meeting was held on Monday morning. During this meeting, crisis facts were provided. Also, teachers were informed of possible emotional and behavioral reactions to anticipate among their students, given an opportunity to express their own grief and told that it would be appropriate to do so (in a controlled fashion) with their students. Primarily, the crisis response was directed toward Ms. Smith's students. Individual and whole-class discussions were provided. Especially vulnerable students were identified. Absent students were contacted at their homes. Requests from the media to interview students were received. Plans to attend the memorial service were made. At the conclusion of the school day, a letter from the principal was sent home to all parents. In this letter parents were notified of the memorial service, provided information about the grieving process, and provided a list of grief counseling services available both within and outside the school.
          —Adapted from Brock, Lewis, Slauson, and Yund (1995)

THIS CRISIS scenario illustrates many crisis response tasks. While at first glance these interventions might seem basic, imagine how you might respond if Ms. Smith had been your friend and/or colleague. Doing so should illustrate that crises have the potential to affect staff as well as students. Just as a crisis may immobilize students, they may immobilize staff as well. Crisis response procedures can minimize this immobilization.

It has been documented that during crises the ability of an organization to work as a team crumbles; individuals tend to become less socially cognizant and more focused on themselves than on the team. Further, it has been suggested that team training is the best way to overcome the effects of stress on the team (Murray, 2000). Thus, the crisis response procedures discussed in this chapter presuppose that a crisis response team has invested significant time in crisis preparedness. At a minimum, at the school site-level, it is assumed that the school principal has designated specific individuals to fill various crisis response roles or functions. By completing the Planning Checklist (Chapter 5, Figure 5.4), a school site places itself in position to implement these procedures.

The initial crisis response task is for site administrators to assess the impact of a given situation and determine if school resources will be able to deal with the crisis. If school resources are not able to handle the situation then district crisis response team assistance should be obtained. In case of a mass disaster, regional-level crisis response team mutual aid support may be utilized. As discussed in Chapter 4, site resources should be exhausted before outside crisis responders are requested. However, regardless of the level of response required, consultation with a district team should always be encouraged.

Once the initial crisis is brought under control, follow-up support will be needed. All individuals respond to crises differently. Some students will be more significantly affected than others will. These individuals need to be identified, and follow-up intervention plans made accordingly.

REGIONAL-, DISTRICT-, AND SCHOOL-LEVEL CRISIS RESPONSE

As mentioned in Chapter 5, a hierarchical or multiple crisis-team model is recommended. This means that parallel crisis response teams should exist at the school, district, and regional levels. The primary difference between these three teams is that one (the school site-level crisis team) is responsible only for crises affecting its school, whereas the other two (the district- and regional-level crisis teams) could be called into any one of a number of different schools. Additionally, it is likely that the regional- and district-level crisis teams will have a greater level of crisis response expertise than will school-site team members. With these exceptions, these three levels of crisis response teams are identical in form and function. Thus, the crisis response procedures about to be described can be used at any level of crisis response.

Because of their superior knowledge of school assets and liabilities, school crisis response teams should handle most, if not all, of a given crisis intervention. Involvement of an outside crisis response team should not mean that a school team is any less active or involved in a response. It simply means that school resources are not sufficient and support from outside the school is required. In implementing the crisis response procedures, school site-level crisis response resources should take the lead. Except under extreme circumstances, regional- and district-level teams

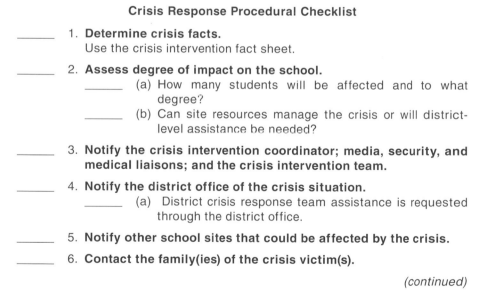

Crisis Response Procedural Checklist

_____ 1. **Determine crisis facts.**
Use the crisis intervention fact sheet.

_____ 2. **Assess degree of impact on the school.**
_____ (a) How many students will be affected and to what degree?
_____ (b) Can site resources manage the crisis or will district-level assistance be needed?

_____ 3. **Notify the crisis intervention coordinator; media, security, and medical liaisons; and the crisis intervention team.**

_____ 4. **Notify the district office of the crisis situation.**
_____ (a) District crisis response team assistance is requested through the district office.

_____ 5. **Notify other school sites that could be affected by the crisis.**

_____ 6. **Contact the family(ies) of the crisis victim(s).**

(continued)

Figure 6.1 The Crisis Response Procedural Checklist can be used by a crisis response coordinator to help guide the crisis response. *Source:* Adapted from "A Handbook for Crisis Intervention," by Los Angeles Unified School District, 1994. (Available from Los Angeles Unified School District, Mental Health Services, 6520 Newcastle Ave., Reseda, CA 91335-6230.) Also from "Administrative Guidelines for Crisis Intervention," by S.E. Brock, S. Lewis, P. Slauson, and S. Yund, 1995, pp. 23–23. (Available from Lodi Unified School District, Special Services/SELPA, 1305 E. Vine St., Lodi, CA 95240.)

_____ 7. **Determine <u>what</u> information is to be shared with**
  _____ (a) Students
  _____ (b) Parents/Community
  _____ (c) Staff
  _____ (d) Media
  Remember to keep in mind parental rights to confidentiality.

_____ 8. **Determine how the information is to be shared.**
  _____ (a) Written bulletins and/or letters
  _____ (b) Assemblies
  _____ (c) Phone calls
  _____ (d) Parent/Community meetings
  _____ (e) Classroom presentations/discussions

_____ 9. **Initiate the psychological triage and referral process.**
  _____ (a) Make referral forms available to staff.
  _____ (b) Designate who will maintain the referral list and where it will be kept.
  _____ (c) Designate interview/counseling locations.
  _____ (d) Distribute a summary of referrals to support staff.
  _____ (e) Establish a procedure for self-referral.

_____ 10. **Identify high-risk students and plan interventions.**
  _____ (a) Designate who will maintain the high-risk list and where it will be kept.
  _____ (b) Decide upon interventions (i.e., individual, small group, classroom).

_____ 11. **Hold a staff meeting.**

_____ 12. **Activate the base of operations.**
  _____ (a) Set up a sign-in/sign-out system.
  _____ (b) Set up a message board.
  _____ (c) Give each crisis team member an ID badge so that the individual is easily identified.

_____ 13. **Computers, attendance registers, and student belongings.**
  _____ (a) Following a student's death, delete the name from computers and attendance registers.
  _____ (b) Be sure that no one calls reporting the student absent.
  _____ (c) Determine how the deceased's belongings will be dealt with.

_____ 14. **Debriefing held at the end of each day.**
  _____ (a) Review the intervention process.
  _____ (b) Plan follow-up actions.
  _____ (c) Review the status of the referrals.
  _____ (d) Provide mutual support.
  _____ (e) Prioritize needs.

_____ 15. **Schedule a morning planning session.**

_____ 16. **Plan memorials.**

_____ 17. **Debrief and evaluate the crisis response.**

Figure 6.1 *(Continued)*

should avoid implementing any intervention plan that does not meet with the approval of the school they are assisting.

THE PROCEDURAL CHECKLIST

The Procedural Checklist (Figure 6.1) is specifically designed to give response teams general guidelines to complete essential crisis response tasks. The following discussion details each Checklist item.

DETERMINE THE FACTS

The first and perhaps most important crisis response procedure is to determine the facts surrounding the crisis (Blom, Etkind, & Carr, 1991). The crisis response coordinator needs to determine specific information such as who was involved, when it happened, and so on. The *Crisis Fact Sheet*, provided in Figure 6.2, will assist the coordinator with this essential task. Possible sources of information might include police or sheriff's departments, FBI, coroner's offices, fire departments, hospitals, parents, and students.

Especially if there is a death, these facts will need to be checked and rechecked (Poland & McCormick, 1999). This verification is particularly important following a suspected suicide. It is critical that school staff not accept statements from students or even teachers that a death by suicide has occurred without checking out the facts first (Garfinkel et al., 1988a). The legal classification of a suicide is complex, typically made by medical examiners working within a coroner's office. Therefore, it is usually advisable to avoid labeling even what appears to be an obvious suicide as such until an official determination is made. The ramifications of immediately notifying a student body that a peer committed suicide, only to later have the cause of death be ruled an accident could easily serve to alienate students from the school staff.

As facts are gathered, it is important to identify specific individuals involved in the crisis event. Degree of exposure and crisis intensity are critical variables in determining entry into the crisis state. Resnick, Kilpatrick, Dansky, Saunders, and Best (1993) report that among crime victims, traumatic stress reactions are a function of life threat, physical injury, or both. Crime victims who are not injured or threatened are much less likely to be traumatized. Thus, when determining crisis facts special attention should be directed toward identifying those who had the most direct and intense exposure to the crisis. (For a further discussion of risk assessment, see Chapter 7.)

Crisis Fact Sheet

Date: _____ Response Coordinator: _____

Summary of known facts:

_____

_____

_____

	Information Sources:
1. What happened? _____ _____ _____	
2. Who was involved? _____ _____ _____	
3. How were they involved? _____ _____ _____	
4. How did it happen? _____ _____ _____	
5. Where did it happen? _____ _____ _____	
6. What caused the crisis? _____ _____ _____	
7. When did it happen? _____ _____ _____	
8. What is the prognosis for those involved? _____ _____ _____	
9. Other information and potential information sources _____ _____ _____	

Figure 6.2 The Crisis Fact Sheet can be used by a crisis response coordinator to record crisis facts. These facts are used to help guide the crisis response. *Source:* Adapted from "Administrative Guidelines for Crisis Intervention," by S.E. Brock, S. Lewis, P. Slauson, and S. Yund, 1995, pp. 22–23. (Available from Lodi Unified School District, Special Services/SELPA, 1305 E. Vine St., Lodi, CA 95240.)

ASSESS DEGREE OF IMPACT

As soon as the crisis facts are verified, the crisis response coordinator should begin to estimate the impact that the event has had on the school. Determining the appropriate level of crisis response is important because there are dangers associated with both under- and overreacting to a crisis.

Lack of sufficient response resources may result in delay of critical services (e.g., media relations). As mentioned in Chapter 5, delay fuels rumor, which can make a bad situation worse. The effectiveness of crisis intervention is directly related to its temporal proximity to the crisis event (Slaikeu, 1990). In other words, the greater the delay in providing crisis intervention, the less effective this response becomes. While some authorities suggest "It's almost impossible to have too much assistance during a crisis" (Poland & McCormick, 1999, p. 133), there are dangers associated with over-reacting. Perhaps most importantly, children (especially primary grade students) are very sensitive to the anxiety of adults in their environment (Nader & Pynoos, 1993). Thus, if personnel respond as if the event was very severe (by over-responding), when in fact it was not highly traumatic, there is a chance some students will be unnecessarily stressed. A second reason for not wanting to over-respond to a crisis is that school crisis resources are limited and the crisis response is expensive and time consuming.

Variables to consider when estimating the level of crisis response include the type, the severity, and the number of individuals involved in the crisis event. In Table 6.1, factors that increase the likelihood that school site-level resources will be able to manage a crisis response are labeled "Traumatization Minimized." Those that make it more likely that regional- or district-level crisis response personnel or both may need to be included in the crisis response are labeled "Traumatization Maximized."

Some crisis events are more traumatic than others (Breslau, 1998; Carlson, 1997; Kilpatrick & Resnick, 1993; McFarlane & De Girolamo, 1996). Posttraumatic Stress Disorder (PTSD) literature suggests that the risk of traumatization is influenced by several variables. First, the predictability of a crisis event affects how traumatic it may become. Relatively predictable or gradually unfolding events (e.g., floods, death following a long illness) may be less traumatic than those that are sudden and unexpected (e.g., flash floods, sudden death, earthquakes). Second, the source of injury or threatened injury will affect how traumatic the event may become. Threatened injury or death due to war or assaultive violence is the most traumatic type of crisis event (Breslau, 1998; McFarlane & De Girolamo, 1996; Pynoos

Table 6.1

Crisis Event Variables

Traumatization Minimized	Traumatization Maximized
Less traumatic crisis type	**More traumatic crisis type**
1. Predictable/gradual onset	1. Unpredictable/sudden onset
2. Nonassaultive injury and/or threat	2. Assaultive injury and/or threat
3. Natural disasters	3. Man-made disasters
4. Nonfatal trauma to significant other	4. Fatal trauma to significant other
Low crisis severity	**High crisis severity**
1. Brief crisis duration	1. Long crisis duration
2. Low crisis intensity	2. High crisis intensity
Few individuals involved	**Many individuals involved**

Source: From "Estimating the Crisis Response," by S.E. Brock (in press), in *Best Practices in School Crisis Prevention and Intervention*, Bethesda, MD: National Association of School Psychologists. Copyright by the National Association of School Psychologists. Reprinted with permission.

et al., 1987). Third, the type of disaster affects how traumatic it may become. Natural disasters (e.g., floods, earthquakes) are less traumatizing than are manmade crises (e.g., war, assaultive violence) (Breslau, 1998; McFarlane & De Girolamo, 1996; Salyor, 1993; Shore, Tatum, & Vollmer, 1990). Finally, the presence or absence of fatalities greatly influences how severely individuals are affected by a given traumatic event. Simply learning about a nonfatal trauma (i.e., sexual/physical assault, serious injury/accident) experienced by a friend or relative conveys the lowest risk of traumatization (Breslau, 1998).

An important caution needs to be offered here. While the type of crisis event can give crisis response coordinators a general idea of the level of response required, it is important to remember that each event and each individual is unique. Events that are typically not highly traumatic may become overwhelming given the right set of circumstances. While survivors of manmade crises are reported to suffer more than survivors of natural disasters (Matsakis, 1994), natural catastrophes that are extremely destructive and have a high death rate can be highly traumatizing (Pynoos et al., 1993). Also, while learning of the sudden death of a significant other is typically associated with only a moderate risk of PTSD (Breslau, 1998), Milgram et al. (1988) found that over 40 percent of Israeli seventh graders who learned that 19 classmates had been killed in a school bus disaster displayed PTSD reactions. These clear exceptions to the typical traumatizing potential of specific crisis types emphasizes the importance of also considering the severity of the trauma when determining the level of crisis intervention response.

Numerous studies have suggested that the more severe the crisis event, the greater the likelihood of traumatization (Carlson, 1997; Kulka et al., 1990; Matsakis, 1994; Shalev, 1996). Thus, more severe crisis events require a greater crisis response. As defined by Brock (in press-a), crisis severity includes duration and intensity of the crisis. The *duration* of the crisis refers to the amount of time that the event presents on-going problems that are perceived by victims as unsolvable. Crisis events that last longer are generally associated with more severe distress (Matsakis, 1994; Saylor, 1993). The *intensity* of the crisis refers to the more extreme instances of crisis events. More intense crises are associated with greater amounts of property destruction, fatalities, and personal physical and emotional damage. The importance of this event variable is emphasized by Pynoos et al. (1987) who state: ". . . the extreme intensity of some situations will lead to initial symptoms [of traumatization] in virtually anyone" (p. 1061).

The number involved in, or affected by, the crisis is the final variable that needs to be considered. Arguably, when it comes to estimating the required level of crisis response, this variable is perhaps most important. Simply put, the more individuals directly or indirectly exposed to a crisis the more involved the crisis response. When estimating the number of people involved in a crisis event, it is important to include not only those persons who would be considered trauma victims/survivors (i.e., those that the event directly affected), but also those who had a relationship with the victims (i.e., friends and relatives).

To help crisis response coordinators use this information in estimating crisis response level, the Crisis Response Estimation Scale (Figure 6.3) has been developed. This Scale can be used as a *rough* guide to estimate the level of response. However, because crisis events are unique, it should only be used to provide an estimate; it is not an exact tool. Additional variables to consider when assessing the impact of a crisis event on a school are summarized in Table 6.2.

NOTIFY THE CRISIS RESPONSE TEAM

If they are not already aware of the crisis situation, the crisis response coordinator should notify the crisis intervention coordinator, media liaison, security liaison, and medical liaison and brief them on the crisis facts. It is important to keep in mind that crisis team members may need to contact

Crisis Response Estimation Scale

Crisis Type

What happened?

30	15	3	0
Man-made disaster/Violence (with threatened/ actual death)	Unexpected/ Sudden death	Natural disaster (without fatalities)	Accident victim/ Learn of nonfatal trauma to others Event was predictable/ gradual

Crisis Severity (Duration)

How long was the perception of threat present? How long did the event present problems that may have been perceived as being unsolvable?

10	5	1	0
Days	Hours	Minutes	Seconds

Crisis Severity (Intensity)

Relative to other examples of the current crisis type, how intense was this trauma?

10	5	1	0
High	Moderate	Mild	Low

Number Involved/Effected

How many individuals were physically and/or emotionally involved in (affected by) the crisis?

Witnessed the Crisis/Aftermath	Victims (threatened/ injured)	Close Associates of Victim(s)

Crisis Type   _____

Crisis Severity   + _____

Number Involved   + _____

Total   = _____

Total	Possible Level of Crisis Intervention Response
60+	Regional-level crisis team response
20–60	District-level crisis team response
6–19	School-level crisis team response
0–5	No crisis team response (use traditional resources)

Figure 6.3 The Crisis Response Estimation Scale is a tool that can be used by crisis response coordinators to provide a rough estimate of the level of crisis response required.

Table 6.2

Variables to Consider When Assessing the
Impact of a Crisis on a School

Variable	Crisis Impact Questions
Popularity of the victim(s)	How popular were/are the crisis victim(s)? If they were/are well known in the school and/or community a more significant impact can be expected than if the victim(s) were not well known. For example, if the victim(s) had just moved into the area the impact is likely to be less severe.
Exposure to or involvement in the crisis	To what extent were students and staff exposed to or involved in the crisis? The greater the exposure or involvement the greater will be the impact of the crisis. For example, a schoolyard shooting would be likely to affect an entire student body. On the other hand, a crisis event occurring well off campus and involving only a few students will have a less severe effect.
History of similar crises	Have similar crises happened to the school in the past? If they have, it is possible that the current event will rekindle old crisis reactions in addition to generating a new trauma. This may result in a more significant crisis reaction.
Recency of other crises	Have other crises happened to the school recently? If so it is possible that this will reduce resiliency. This may result in a more significant crisis reaction. On the other hand, a less dramatic impact can be expected if the crisis is an isolated incident.
Resources available	What personal, family, school, and community resources are available to help individuals cope with the crisis? Fewer resources are likely to result in more significant crisis reactions.
Crisis event timing	When did the crisis event occur? If the crisis occurred during a vacation its impact on the school may be less than if it occurred while school was in session. In this case it is possible that students will have dealt with the crisis away from school, on their own or with their family. Additionally, rumors are spread more quickly when children are congregating in groups at school. Finally, when a crisis occurs during a vacation the school has more time to prepare and is thus able to respond more effectively.

their own families to verify that all are safe before beginning a crisis response. Allowing them to do so will help to ensure that they are emotionally available for the work ahead. Members of this team play a critical role in completing the remaining response tasks. We briefly describe these team member roles and their activities next.

Crisis Response Coordinator

During a crisis response, the crisis response coordinator (who is typically an administrator) gathers information about the crisis event, declares that a crisis exists, estimates the level of crisis response required, and oversees initial and follow-up interventions. This coordinator is also responsible for ensuring that the crisis response is properly evaluated.

Crisis Intervention Coordinator

The crisis intervention coordinator (who is typically a school psychologist or counselor) implements psychological triage procedures, makes referral forms available to staff, maintains a referral list, distributes a referral summary to support staff, establishes a procedure for self-referral, and helps to plan and implement interventions. Also, following a student death, it is important for the crisis intervention coordinator to be sure that a school staff member is available to walk through the decedent's class schedule to help students in those rooms who are affected by the "empty chair" (A. Berman & Jobes, 1991). At the conclusion of the intervention, this individual is responsible for writing a detailed summary of the crisis interventions. This summary will be a key document used by the crisis response coordinator when evaluating the effectiveness of the crisis response. Following certain types of crises, such as death by suicide, it may be appropriate for a mental health consultant to help the school plan its response. The crisis intervention coordinator is responsible for obtaining such assistance.

Media Liaison

According to Davidson (1989): "Providing reasonable access to information, controlling rumors, and protecting students from intrusive news reporters are important concerns" (p. 96). From such observations, it is recommended that all school systems identify a spokesperson (A. Berman & Jobes, 1991; Davidson, 1989; J. Davis & Sandoval, 1991). The media liaison fills this role. This liaison is typically a school- or district-level administrator. This individual is responsible for ensuring that staff knows how to productively respond to the media (i.e., what to say or to whom to refer), for creating an environment that would facilitate media cooperation with school requests, and arranging for interviews. Additionally, this individual plays a major role in determining what and how information will be shared with the press and community. It is important for this individual to be familiar with guidelines for the media, such as those developed by the American Association of Suicidology (1987) and proposed by Lazarus et al. (1999). Also, Table 6.3 provides J. Davis and Sandoval's (1991) guidelines that may be useful as the media liaison prepares a press release following a suicide.

SECURITY LIAISON

The security liaison's (who is typically a school principal or other administrator) responsibilities include implementing plans designed to ensure student safety following a crisis, and acting as a liaison with local law enforcement officials. For example, crowd control can become a problem following some crises. If a student suicide took place at a school, and students are aware of this fact, students may congregate at this location. In such a situation, the security liaison is responsible for appropriate crowd control procedures. This liaison is also the person from the school who would have contact with the local police department. Garfinkel et al. (1988a) recommend that the school let the police know that this liaison is the person whom they can contact day or night with any reported crisis. Having all the facts is essential to quelling any rumors that may arise about the crisis. In addition, it might be appropriate to have someone, such as the security liaison, walk the halls to monitor common areas such as bathrooms, parking lots, and cafeterias. In this way the liaison observes and connects with students in need who are not in their classrooms (A. Berman & Jobes, 1991).

MEDICAL LIAISON

The medical liaison (who is typically a school nurse) is primarily responsible for facilitating communication between emergency response personnel, hospitals, doctors, other health care providers, and the crisis response team. The liaison also assists in communicating to parents and staff members the conditions of those injured. Once injured students have recovered, the medical liaison may help to facilitate school reentry.

NOTIFY THE SCHOOL DISTRICT OFFICE

Especially when a crisis occurs at school, it is essential that district-level administration be notified of the crisis event. This contact needs to be made as soon as possible. Once word of a crisis reaches the community, it

Table 6.3
Press Release Guidelines

1. Report what happened. Avoid sensational or romantic accounts of what occurred, and omit precise information on methods used in the attempt or the suicide so that impressionable individuals will not be able to copy the tragedy. For example, one might announce that a suicide was committed by carbon monoxide poisoning but not provide details (e.g., about how a hose acquired from a local store was connected between the tail pipe of a car and the driver's window, and the individual then sat in a running car in a closed garage).

2. Report who was involved in general terms. Use general terms and not names of individuals, unless this information is public knowledge and next of kin have been notified. A victim may be described in terms of sex and grade in school and other relevant demographic facts but usually not by name. If others were involved, that fact can be generally indicated without identifying data.

3. Report when the suicide or attempt occurred or was discovered. Give this information as precisely as known.

4. To the extent relevant, report where it happened. The location of the suicide or attempt can be reported. Although addresses of private residences or businesses should not be released. If the location could lend itself to sensationalism, it would be best if it could be omitted, played down, or only vaguely mentioned.

5. If someone is injured, report what the prognosis is for those involved. Prognosis and status can be given as long as they have been verified. This information can often be left to the hospital.

6. Indicate what the district will do or has done. The emphasis should be on positive actions taken by school personnel or students. Communicate the fact that the district is concerned about the health and safety of all students and will provide resources as well as work with other community agencies to help the student body recover from the event and return to the basic tasks of learning.

7. Indicate where troubled individuals in the community can get help. Indicate what counseling services will be available to those upset by the event or who are having suicidal thoughts. The phone number of the suicide hot line, for example, might be listed.

8. If asked, provide other sources of information. The reporter may wish to consult with other individual experts or organizations who can supplement the story.

9. In interviews, avoid "no comment" answers. These sorts of statements suggest that the spokesperson has something to hide. If you cannot make a comment, you might respond, "I have not had enough time to talk to others" or "We have just received the information and must study it before giving an answer."

Source: From "Suicidal Youth," by J. Davis and J. Sandoval, 1991, pp. 162–163, San Francisco, Jossey-Bass. Copyright (1991) by Jossey-Bass. Reprinted with permission.

is not uncommon for district-level administrators to receive calls from concerned citizens as well as from the media. Thus, it is critical that they have knowledge of what happened and what is being done to assist students cope with the tragedy. Also included in this step would be a mechanism for obtaining district-level crisis response team assistance. If necessary, requests for regional-level crisis response team assistance would be made by district office personnel. A method of arranging for such help during nonschool hours should also be provided.

Notify Other Schools

Whenever a crisis occurs at school, attention needs to be given to how other sites might be affected. Issues to examine include whether the students involved in the crisis have siblings or friends who attend other schools. When teachers are involved in a traumatic event, examine whether there are former students, now attending different schools, who may be affected. For example, as a sixth-grade teacher, the students Ms. Smith had during the previous school year were now all attending middle school. As a result, the middle school counselors were contacted and asked to monitor these students to determine if they needed assistance and support and, if necessary, to help them express their feelings.

Contact the Family(ies) of the Crisis Victim(s)

Many times parental contact will be one of the first crisis intervention tasks as the school attempts to verify the facts surrounding the crisis. If the family(ies) of the victim(s) have not already been approached, now is the time to do so. Following a student suicide, for example, this call should be made within the first 48 hours (Thompson, 1990). J. Davis and Sandoval (1991) suggest that such contact should "focus on the expression of sympathy on behalf of the school and, if the parents seem receptive, information about community grief support groups should be offered" (p. 84). Finally, the parent contact will be important in achieving the goals of the next crisis response task of determining what information about the suicide is to be shared.

Determine What Information to Share

The media liaison may take primary responsibility for facilitating this step. The first issue to be considered is confidentiality. Student names should not be given out unless there is prior parental consent. Additionally, there may be specific circumstances surrounding the crisis that parents may wish to remain confidential (e.g., contents of a suicide note). Following a crisis involving students, it is recommended that school staff members (ideally the crisis intervention coordinator, the media liaison, or both) discuss with the student's parents which details about the event could be shared with outsiders. Unless crisis facts are already public knowledge, rights of confidentiality must be respected (Thompson, 1990).

In determining what information to share, the media liaison or crisis response coordinator should review crisis situation facts with the crisis response team. Often the district office will need to be consulted regarding what information is to be shared. Determination of what information is shared should also take into account the rumors that proliferate quickly during crises. Thus, it is essential that the crisis response team be sensitive to rumors. The importance of doing so following a suicidal crisis has been mentioned by Davidson (1989), who points out that these rumors may predict additional suicides in such a way that it would lend significant notoriety to further suicides. She indicates that rumors of suicide pacts can be particularly problematic and that on occasion these rumors can be traced to one or two disturbed students. From these observations, Davidson concludes that it is essential that the school provide the information needed to dispel rumors.

Following most crises, it will be important to provide as much information as is possible and to do so in a clear, honest, and direct fashion (Poland & McCormick, 1999). An exception to this rule, however, would be student suicide. In these instances, it is essential to avoid presenting information that might be perceived as glorifying the act (Weinberg, 1990), while at the same time providing a timely flow of accurate and appropriate information to the public (O'Carroll, Mercy, & Steward, 1988). Garfinkel et al. (1988b) recommend that an announcement of the death be made within the first hour. As mentioned previously, before officially classifying the death as a suicide (which is done by a coroner's office), it is important to avoid classifying the student's death as such. According to Garfinkel et al. (1988a): "Because suicides sometimes are recorded as accidental deaths and because some families will go to great lengths to cover up a suicide, teachers should restrict their answers to students' questions to basic information and avoid speculation" (p. 15). Consequently, the initial announcement will typically only report that a death has occurred. Once the death is officially ruled a suicide, school staff members will need to exercise some discretion regarding the kind of information it shares with students. Garfinkel et al. (1988a) recommend avoiding the release of details such as the time of death, circumstances under which the death occurred, or contents of a suicide note. Additionally, the media liaison should work with the media to downplay the incident by placing it on an inside page or preferably by not reporting it at all. It is also advisable that a photo of the victim not be included and that the word "suicide" not be used in the caption (Rouf & Harris, 1988). Research indicates nonfictional media coverage of suicide to be associated with an increase in the reported number of suicides (J. Davis & Sandoval, 1991; Gould, 1992). Ideally, the groundwork for media relations will have been completed before the suicide. According to J. Davis and Sandoval: "Close work with reporters and editors can create positive voluntary guidelines for reporting suicides" (p. 168). For example, besides compliance with the just-mentioned reporting issues, the media might agree to include information about the community resources that are available for those with suicidal thoughts.

Determine How to Share Information

After a determination has been made regarding what to share with students, staff members, the community, and the media, the crisis response team needs to begin to consider how this information will be presented. The media liaison, in consultation with school mental health professionals, helps to determine the most effective and appropriate way to share information. Many times the district office will need to be consulted regarding how this is to be done. Options include written bulletins, letters, phone calls, classroom presentations and discussions, assemblies, and parent and community meetings. Sample letters and announcements for use following a variety of crises can be found in Appendix D. Regardless of the method, it is critical that this information be delivered as soon as possible. The longer the school delays in sharing the facts, the greater is the likelihood that harmful rumors will get started. Besides providing parents with crisis facts, it may also be productive at this point to provide families with information regarding how they can assist their child(ren) cope with the crisis event. The National Institute of Mental Health's (1985) *Helping Your Child in a Disaster* (Appendix C) is an example of a format for providing families with such information.

Informing students of a crisis is best done in small groups or homeroom discussions (Davidson, 1989). Use of public address systems should be avoided (Purvis et al., 1991). Vidal (1986) suggests that small group contact is especially important following a suicide. Following the suicidal crisis, it is critical to avoid sharing information over a school's public address system or, in most cases, in a schoolwide assembly. It is better for the announcement to be made simultaneously in classes (J. Davis & Sandoval, 1991) where a staff member can be present to handle students' concerns directly (A. Berman & Jobes, 1991; Rouf & Harris, 1988). (It may be appropriate to share information individually or in small groups with students who are particularly vulnerable or who were close to the student who committed suicide. It will be important to try to avoid casting the deceased in the role of villain or hero. Grieving and seeking to learn from the tragedy should be the focus of attention. When informing college students of a suicide, Webb (1986) suggests it to be helpful to use phrases such as "unfortunate," "ill-advised," "untimely," and "final." Assure staff members and students that blame is not an issue and that the school is committed to learning from the suicide.

When appropriate, the media liaison coordinates press interviews of school staff. Interviews with children should not occur unless there is prior parental consent. Crisis victims may have a need to have their stories told and doing so can be a helpful way of actualizing what has happened. For example, following Ms. Smith's death, her students initially expressed concern regarding the possibility of media interference. However, by the end of the day, the students were interested in using the media to tell more than the basic description of Ms. Smith that had already appeared in the press. As a result, the media was invited into the classroom to hear about Ms. Smith from the students' point of view.

INITIATE PSYCHOLOGICAL TRIAGE AND REFERRAL

The crisis intervention coordinator is primarily responsible for implementing the psychological triage procedures that will identify those students most significantly traumatized by the crisis. Following the death of Ms. Smith, for example, the coordinator was responsible for identifying and ensuring that interventions are offered to those most affected by this loss. Additional referral procedures include making referral forms available to all staff, maintaining a list of students referred, designating where the list will be maintained, and designating interview or counseling locations. A procedure for self-referral should also be operationalized. The crisis intervention coordinator should distribute a summary of referrals to the support staff.

IDENTIFY HIGH-RISK STUDENTS AND PLAN INTERVENTIONS

The crisis intervention coordinator is responsible for initiating this process. From the results of the initial referrals and interviews, a list of high-risk students should be developed. Decisions about which classrooms will need intervention and which individual students will need immediate psychological first aid, and possibly professional mental health treatment referrals, will need to be made. It is important for all those involved in the crisis response to have access to the list of students considered to be high-risk for not coping with the crisis.

Whether developed by the regional-, district-, or school site-level team, it is essential for all intervention procedures to be discussed with the school's mental health professionals. This communication is especially important in this crisis team model, which has the school crisis team eventually taking over the responsibility for all crisis interventions. Thus, intervention plans must be something that the school's designated helpers can implement and continue successfully. As was illustrated in the case of Ms. Smith's death, crisis intervention options should include but not be limited to the following: individual meetings, group crisis intervention, classroom activities or presentations, parent meetings, staff meetings, and referrals to community agencies.

In choosing intervention options it is important to keep in mind that structure and routine can be reassuring to students in the days immediately following a crisis event (Bertoia & Allan, 1988; Brock et al., 1990; Sandall, 1986). Thus, although it may be appropriate to put aside the normal academic curriculum in favor of the "crisis curriculum," doing so should not be allowed to affect the school schedule. In implementing the crisis intervention, the crisis intervenors should strive to fit into the school's bell schedule. Because structure is reassuring to children traumatized by a crisis event, it is important for children to return to school as soon as possible following the trauma. Failure to do so might lead students to believe that things were so bad that school could not be resumed. A quick return to school, on the other hand, gives the message that normalcy is within reach and that the school is capable of coping with the trauma (Sandall, 1986).

Following a suicide or suicide attempt, special attention should be given to the possibility that the event may have triggered suicidal feelings within other students. School personnel should be aware of the types of students who are likely to be affected by a suicide. In particular, they should be aware of those who are most likely to be at high-risk for suicide

Table 6.4

Factors That Place Students At-Risk Following the Suicide of a Peer

Risk Factor	Examples
Facilitated the suicide	• Were involved in a suicide pact. • Helped write the suicide note. • Provided the means of the suicide. • Knew about and did not try to stop the suicide.
Failed to recognize the suicidal intent	• Observed events that were later learned to be signs of the impending suicide. • Did not take a suicide threat seriously. • Had been too busy to talk to a person who committed suicide who asked for help.
Believe they may have caused the suicide	• Feel guilty about things said or done to the victim before the suicide. • Recently punished or threatened to punish the person who committed suicide for some misdeed.
Had a relationship or identifies with the person who committed suicide	• Were mentioned in the suicide note. • Were relatives, best friends, or self-appointed therapists of the person who committed suicide. • Identifies with the situation of the person who committed suicide. • Have life circumstances that parallel the suicide victim's.
History of prior suicidal behavior	• Have previously attempted or threatened suicide. • Have family members, acquaintances, or role models who have died by suicide.
History of psychopathology and/or behavior problems	• Have poor baseline mental health. • Have substance abuse problems. • Have a history of impulsive/violent behavior directed either toward self or others.
Symptoms of helplessness and/or hopelessness	• Are desperate and now consider suicide a viable alternative. • Feel powerless to change distressing life circumstances. • Are depressed.

Table 6.4 *(Continued)*

Risk Factor	Examples
Significant life stresses or losses	• Had family members or acquaintances who have died by accident or homicide. • Had someone they were close to die violently. • Had recently broken up with a girlfriend or boyfriend. • Have been disrupted by changes in residence, schools or parental figures.

Source: Adapted from "The School Psychologist's Role in Suicide Prevention," by J. Sandoval & S.E. Brock, 1996, *School Psychology Quarterly, 11*, p. 180, and based on Brent et al. (1989); Davidson (1989); Davidson, Rosenberg, Mercy, Franklin, & Simmons (1989); Gould, 1992; O'Carroll et al., 1988; and Rouf & Harris (1988). Copyright, 1996, by the American Psychological Association.

themselves as part of a suicide cluster (Davidson, 1989). Table 6.4 provides a list of factors that may place a student at-high risk following a suicide.

STAFF MEETING

A staff meeting (which as appropriate may include classified as well as certificated personnel) should be held as soon as possible (A. Berman & Jobes, 1991; Kneisel & Richards, 1988; Stacy, 1988). For example, following Ms. Smith's death, a staff meeting was held before school started on Monday morning. As a part of these meetings it is important to provide staff with the crisis facts and share with them the intervention plan (Thompson, 1990). It is also helpful to review suggestions for discussions during a crisis (Table 6.5), suggestions for classroom management following a crisis (Chapter 4, Table 4.6), and the possible reactions adults, as well as students, might display following a crisis event (Chapter 8, Table 8.1).

J. Davis and Sandoval (1991), citing the work of Lamb and Dunne-Maxim (1987), point out that a staff meeting serves a dual purpose. Not only should it educate staff on how they can assist their students to cope with the crisis, but it also needs to help faculty members deal with their own feelings and reactions. Davis and Sandoval suggest that it may be helpful to include an outside mental health consultant to help staff deal with these feelings. The staff meeting should help the faculty begin to deal with feelings of grief, guilt, or anger generated by the crisis event.

Table 6.5

Suggestions for Discussions during Crisis

- Make yourself available and accessible to those who want to talk. Try to be flexible and responsive to the needs of others. Exhibit and model concern, care, understanding, and acceptance.
- Give accurate information about the incident. When you do not know something, say so, offer to find (and report back) the answer for them, or explain that some things may not have an answer or ever be known.
- Emphasize the confidentiality of what is said during the discussion and that everyone should respect the feelings and rights of others.
- Be prepared for and allow others to express any and all thoughts, feelings, and perceptions, even some that may seem illogical or inexplicable, about the situation. A variety of behaviors, including laughter (often from tension) and no reaction, are likely and acceptable. Because children and adolescents frequently act out their feelings, observe their behavior.
- Expect (and address) feelings from or about previous trauma/problems that emerge in response to the current situation. The crisis reactions may be directly related or relevant to past experiences and current feelings may be symbolic of them.
- Listen and give people time to express themselves and respond to questions.
- Try to validate the feelings of others by telling them that it is all right to feel that way and by helping them see that many people feel similarly.
- Express your own feelings, thoughts, and perceptions openly and honestly as a means of encouraging discussion. However, try to maintain a relatively even and calm affect/demeanor and tone of voice.
- Encourage others to ask for clarification, information, and help when needed. Provide information about where these might be available.
- Encourage others to identify and seek out support/resources and to take action. This will foster independence, self-reliance and coping skills, and help them feel better.
- Encourage people to make themselves comfortable, relax, sit in an informal arrangement (i.e., circle), and/or break into small groups. Allow those who prefer it to find a quiet place to be alone or with a few others.
- Stress that people's feelings and problems are often temporary and encourage patience. Without being trite or using clichés, communicate that life must go on and return to some type of "normalcy," although things will never be exactly the same as they were before the incident. Display personal confidence that things will get better.

Table 6.5 *(Continued)*

- When appropriate, reassure people that they do not bear responsibility for what happened and that no one could have foreseen such a thing occurring. Discourage guilt and unrealistic expectations or demands on themselves.
- Seek help when you need it.

Things to Avoid
- Do not force crisis intervention services upon anyone, especially those who appear capable of independently coping with the crisis.
- Do not ignore individuals who are judged likely to be traumatized, but do not accept crisis intervention.
- Do not be judgmental or make value statements about the feelings, concerns, perceptions, or behaviors of others.
- Do not use the discussion as a means of meeting your own needs, discharging your own feelings, or an opportunity to make your views known. While some modeling of reactions to the event would be appropriate, avoid excessive emotion (i.e., do not agree to be a crisis intervenor if you fear you might become hysterical).
- Avoid using "should, must, never, always, everyone" types of words because of their connotations and judgmental quality. Avoid clichés and trite expressions.
- Avoid focusing on the "what's and why's" of the situation.
- Avoid negative implications or statements about individuals or the way they may have reacted to or handled a situation.
- Do not force everyone to participate or express themselves, but also do not isolate anyone who wants to participate. People may need to feel like they belong and are part of the group.
- Do not avoid making yourself available or reaching out to others in need simply because you are feeling similarly or feel unsure about doing so. However, do not force yourself to try to be therapeutic if you are so distraught or uncomfortable doing so that you would be likely to make the situation worse or cannot begin to meet the needs of others.
- Do not avoid topics or issues that others genuinely feel a need to discuss. Do not try to protect others, change the subject, force positive statements or feelings, or show a negative reaction when you become uncomfortable with an issue.
- Avoid trying to make others feel better or to "rescue" them. Each person has to resolve his/her own difficulties at their own pace. Do not expect everyone to recover within a certain time period.

(continued)

Table 6.5 *(Continued)*

- Do not assume that a person is not reacting or hurting just because they do not show it. They may be in pain now or later and may not be ready to express their feelings or seek help for a while after the crisis.
- Do not allow others to interrupt someone who is struggling to express himself/herself or has not completed what he/she has to say.
- Do not be too structured or demanding. People may not be ready to do or discuss some things or may be very distracted and unable to concentrate.
- Do not expect everyone to see things in the same way or to have the same depth of understanding. Not only do people differ, but also children and adolescents have different capacities and characteristics at different ages and developmental levels.
- Avoid acting in a condescending manner and making excessive special allowances for or granting special privileges to certain individuals.

Source: Adapted from "Parkway School District Crisis Intervention Manual," by S. Colombo and D. Oegema, 1986. (Available from Parkway School District, Pupil Personnel/Special Services, 455 N. Woods Mill Rd., Chesterfield, MO 63017.)

In fact, it might be argued that dealing with such feelings is prerequisite to effectively assisting others cope with crises. During this meeting, staff members should be given permission to feel uncomfortable about discussing the crisis with their students. Each crisis is unique and some staff members may have particular difficulty dealing with certain situations. It is important to respect these feelings of discomfort and understand that in some cases they may interfere to the point that the staff member may not be able to provide students with the support and guidance they need. These individuals should be provided with alternative opportunities for helping students cope. For example, it may be appropriate to provide the staff member with direct assistance from a crisis response team member to assist with this difficult task.

Activate a Base of Operations

This Checklist item is especially important if regional- or district-level or regional and district crisis response team assistance is brought into school grounds. This base of operations would be the location from which the crisis response team would coordinate its activities. Outside crisis response team resources should all be directed to report to the base of operations who would also help site administration to know who is on-site at any given time. Figure 6.4 provides a staffing sheet that may be used at the base of operations to keep track of crisis response team personnel. Use of ID badges facilitates identification (Figure 6.5 on page 119). It is recommended that these badges be relatively difficult to copy to minimize the chance that they could be forged. Finally, a centrally located message board to facilitate communication among support staff is helpful.

COMPUTERS, ATTENDANCE REGISTERS, AND STUDENT BELONGINGS

If there is a student death, it is important to make certain to delete the name from computers and attendance registers (Poland & McCormick, 1999). The crisis response team should make sure that an attendance clerk does not call home reporting the student absent. While removing student belongings from lockers is a relatively straightforward task, care should be exercised when removing student belongings from the classroom. With the approval of the deceased student's family, it is recommended that the crisis response team discuss with classmates how this is to be done. Priority should be given to the feelings of classmates.

DEBRIEFING

It is critical to have a debriefing on a daily basis to allow for a review of the intervention process and the status of referrals (A. Berman & Jobes, 1991). Prioritization of needs and plans for follow-up actions should also be discussed. Perhaps most important, the debriefing is an opportunity to assess how the intervenors are coping with the crisis. It is not uncommon for caretakers to deal with their grief by denying it and directing their energy to caring for others. This meeting provides an opportunity for mutual support and allows staff to deal with their own emotions and feelings. Davidson (1989) emphasizes the importance of the debriefing session:

> Provisions for the needs of teachers and other caregivers during the crisis should be planned. Those committed to meeting students' needs during a suicide crisis are under tremendous pressure. They also need opportunities to ventilate feelings, seek reassurance, get outside assistance, and exchange information. Teaching often isolates the educator from peers, and increased contact with coprofessionals during the crisis is valuable. (pp. 96–97)

Crisis Response Team Check-In Sheet

Today's Date: _____

Name	Sending Agency or School District	Phone Number	Assignment	Arrival Time	Departure Time
1.					
2.					
3.					
4.					
5.					
6.					
7.					
8.					
9.					
10.					
11.					
12.					
13.					
14.					
15.					
16.					
17.					
18.					
19.					
20.					
21.					
22.					
23.					
24.					
25.					
26.					
27.					
28.					
29.					
30.					

Figure 6.4 The Crisis Response Team Check-In Sheet is typically kept at the crisis response team's base of operations. Usually this will be a school office. All crisis response personnel need to be instructed to use this sheet whenever they arrive or depart from the school site. Use of this *Check-In Sheet* is especially important during a crisis response that involves crisis intervenors who are not permanent school staff members.

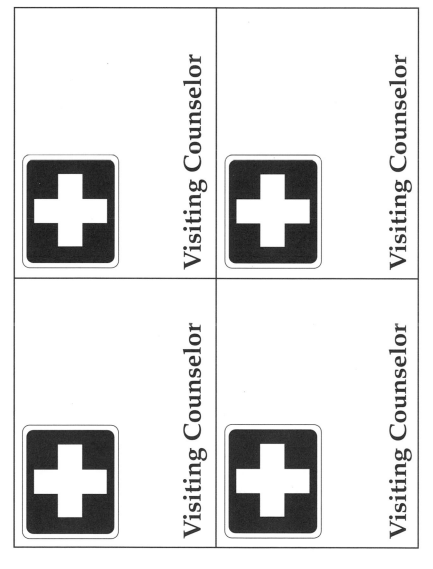

Figure 6.5 Use of the Crisis Response Team Name Badges is especially critical during a crisis response that involves personnel who are not permanent members of the school staff.

MORNING PLANNING SESSIONS

At the start of each day following the crisis, the crisis response team should hold a planning session to obtain updated information regarding the crisis, to review responsibilities, and to plan interventions.

MEMORIALS

When a crisis event results in death, many people feel the need to express their grief, say good-bye, and do something as a memorial. A funeral service is often used as a vehicle for such memorials. Whether or not students attend a funeral should be up to individual students and their parents. Recommendations from Goldman (1996) for preparing students for funerals include the following:

- Describe what is likely to happen at the funeral.
- Invite attendance, but do not insist upon it.
- Identify who will likely attend.
- Give permission to leave if it is too uncomfortable.
- Prepare students for the emotional expressions of grief that may be displayed.
- Normalize feelings and expressions of grief.
- Encourage questions.

R. Wayne Jones (McKee, Jones, & Richardson, 1991) recommends against making special arrangements to send students from school to funerals. Although he sees no problem with a student choosing to go to the funeral and doing so with parental permission, Jones feels that it is not appropriate to let school out early so all children can attend.

Following a crisis, staff members and students may also need to do something to prevent the crisis event from reoccurring. Following a suicide, for example, as mentioned earlier, staff may enlist student aid in identifying the hurts that lead to suicide and discuss ways to help other students cope with their feelings and problems. Special interest groups may grow out of students' need to do something to express their feelings. Following Ms. Smith's death in an accident with an allegedly drunk driver, her students expressed an interest in forming a Students Against Drunk Driving chapter at their school. Crisis intervenors assisted students in planning these memorials. Working together on these projects helped them focus their grief, fears, and anger constructively.

When choosing memorials following a suicide, particular care should be taken not to romanticize or stigmatize the act of suicide. Referring to the work of Gould and Shaffer (1986) and Phillips and Carstensen (1986), Kneisel and Richards (1988) point out ". . . that broadly publicizing a suicide may glorify and draw attention to the event, thereby increasing the risk of additional suicides" (p. 165). Because of such concerns, R. Wayne Jones (McKee et al., 1991) recommends avoiding memorials completely. He states that they may reinforce the message that death is a way to obtain an incredible amount of attention. Jones states: "Recognize death without glorifying it." He also indicates that if students want to develop a memorial, they should be allowed to do so on their own time. Schools should not sanction such activities.

If the school does choose to sponsor the development of a memorial, it is critical that school staff closely supervises student activities. Students may not know what would make an appropriate memorial. For example, they may include in it aspects of the deceased's life (such as drinking) which while important to the peer group, may be offensive or even hurtful to the family. Students will need to be taught what a memorial is, how it will be used, and for whom it is intended (i.e., friends and family). Appropriate models will need to be provided. Activities recommended by Poland and McCormick (1999) include the listing of the deceased's attributes, development of memory books, a balloon ceremony, and memory ribbons.

DEBRIEF AND EVALUATE

Following the crisis response, the crisis response team will need to be demobilized and the response evaluated (described in detail in Chapter 13). The daily debriefings can serve as a beginning to both of these procedures.

The primary purpose of demobilization is to allow crisis response team members to integrate the crisis intervention into their lives and to allow them to return to their regular assignments. Such demobilization can be an important part of the overall crisis response evaluation that is typically conducted by the crisis response coordinator. An important part of the crisis response evaluation is the summary report written by the crisis intervention coordinator (Table 6.6). Focusing on the direct crisis intervention services provided by the crisis response team, the summary report should be completed within two weeks of the conclusion of crisis interventions.

Table 6.6
Crisis Incident Summary Report Guidelines

To: (Staff member(s) in charge of crisis intervention)   Date:_____

From: (Name of person reporting)

       (Title of person reporting)

Subject: Crisis intervention at (Name of school) (Date(s) of incident)

Team Contact
  Include who requested crisis intervention services and how services
were obtained.

Brief Description of the Crisis and Stressors
  Include as appropriate:
    1 to 2 paragraph summary of crisis event
    Facts/events precipitating crisis
    Involvement of law enforcement, hospitals, other agencies, if applicable

Interventions
  Include:
    1. Describe first procedure in detail
    2. Describe second procedure
    3. Other procedures
  Include as appropriate:
    Triage procedures used to determine who was at risk
    Strategies used to control rumors
    Counseling interventions used (e.g., individual and/or group
    counseling)
      Classroom discussions and presentations
      How the media was involved
      Handouts used with teachers, parents, and/or students
      Planning meetings held
      Debriefing meetings held
      Assessment of the need for follow-up services

Evaluation of Effectiveness
  Include a brief summary evaluating the interventions

Recommendations
  Include list recommendations for follow-up as well as suggestions for
preventing and/or dealing with future crisis situations

Source: Adapted from "Administrative Guidelines for Crisis Intervention," by
S.E. Brock, S. Lewis, P. Slauson, and S. Yund, 1995, pp. 34–35. (Available
from Lodi Unified School District, Special Services/SELPA, 1305 E. Vine St.,
Lodi, CA 95240.)

The summary report serves at least two important purposes. First, it documents the intervention. This can be helpful if questions arise in the future about what was or was not done. Second, it can be a powerful learning tool. Each crisis response is unique and thus presents its own learning opportunities. The summary report can be a way of sharing with crisis response planners preparedness strengths and weaknesses. In addition, it can be a way to document strategies designed to prevent future crises. Finally, it can serve as a reminder or planning aid for use on the anniversary of crisis events. The importance of this planning has previously been pointed out by Dillard (1989, 1990, cited in Pitcher & Poland, 1992).

SUMMARY

This chapter focused on a procedure to follow during times of crisis. At its heart is a procedural checklist that may be used and modified locally to help a crisis team get mobilized. We recommend this strategy for school personnel, particularly when they are under stress. It is important to point out, however, that use of this checklist assumes that the crisis response team members have done a number of crisis preparedness activities before the crisis event. Although it is possible to respond to crises without such planning (see Pitcher & Poland, 1992, for suggestions on doing so), this will, at the very least, result in greater anxiety among the crisis responders. At worst, a lack of preparedness can adversely affect the quality of the crisis response services offered to students.

CHAPTER 7

Psychological Triage
and Referral

John, a sophomore with a known congenital heart defect,
collapsed during his first period science class on Thursday.
John's heart had stopped beating. The science teacher and one of
his colleagues used CPR in an attempt to revive John. They
continued these efforts on the classroom floor until the
paramedics arrived. Unfortunately, their efforts were not enough.
John was declared dead upon arrival at the hospital. Although
John was not an especially well-known student, he was active in
extracurricular activities. He had attended school in the area
since the early elementary grades. Many students considered
him a friend.

SITUATIONAL CRISES such as this one can have devastating effects on
large numbers of students and staff members (Allen et al., 1999). One
of the defining characteristics of a *situational crisis* is its potential to
affect an entire community (Slaikeu, 1990). This creates one of the more
significant dilemmas for schools as they respond to crises: with limited resources, how does a school determine which individuals to help first? In
this crisis situation, there were several dozen students affected, some more
than others were. How are decisions made about who receives assistance?
Furthermore, who makes these decisions? This chapter's section on psychological triage is designed to answer these questions. Also discussed are
strategies for identifying crisis intervention referral options.

Keeping in mind that situational crisis can affect a school's caregivers
as well as its students, it is important to develop triage and referral plans

before psychological traumas occur. Immediately following a crisis is the worst time to develop these procedures. Consequently, it is recommended that psychological triage and referral procedures be made a part of school crisis preparedness efforts.

THE CRISIS INTERVENTION COORDINATOR

As discussed in Chapters 5 and 6, the crisis response plan specifies that a crisis intervention coordinator be a member of *all* crisis response teams (Brock et al., 1995). This coordinator is the team member primarily responsible for developing crisis intervention resources and psychological triage procedures. Crisis intervention resource development includes the formation of a school-based team of crisis intervenors. Following a crisis event, with the crisis intervention coordinator taking the lead, this team is responsible for conducting psychological triage (classifying individuals according to suspected degree of psychological trauma) and ensuring that immediate assistance is provided to those most traumatized. Additionally, the crisis intervention coordinator is responsible for maintaining documentation of those identified as psychological trauma victims, and coordinating referrals to school crisis intervenors and mental health professionals.

TRIAGE DEFINED

According to Taber's *Cyclopedic Medical Dictionary* (Thomas, 1993), the word *triage* is derived from the French word for sorting. It is defined as follows:

> The screening and classification of sick, wounded, or injured persons during war or other disasters to determine priority needs for efficient use of medical and nursing manpower, equipment, and facilities. It is also done in emergency rooms and in acute care clinics to determine priority of treatment. Use of triage is essential if the maximum number of lives is to be saved during an emergency situation that produces many more sick and wounded than the available medical care facilities and personnel can possibly handle.[1] (p. 1767)

As indicated in this definition, triage is traditionally associated with medical treatment decisions. However, it is a concept also applicable to

---

[1] From *Taber's Cyclopedic Medical Dictionary*, 17th ed., by C.L. Thomas (Ed.), 1993, Philadelphia: Davis.

psychological interventions. In describing the importance of psychological triage, Cohen (1985) states: "It is essential to begin with a triage approach and attend to acute mental health needs first" (p. 12). The importance of effective triage procedures is further emphasized by Slaikeu (1990), who suggests that the effectiveness of a crisis intervention is directly related to the intervention's proximity in both time and place to the crisis event. In other words, effective crisis intervention provides immediate assistance to individuals in crisis.

The definition of triage used by the authors in the development of their crisis response plan keeps Slaikeu's comments in mind, providing individuals in need with crisis intervention assistance as soon as possible. The following definition of psychological triage was inspired by the Los Angeles Unified School District's (1994) *A Handbook for Crisis Intervention:*

> Psychological triage sorts or classifies individuals according to the degree to which they are judged to be traumatized by a situational crisis event. It is required to determine crisis intervention treatment priorities. The initial triage task classifies individuals by degree of exposure to the crisis event, relationship(s) with crisis victim(s) and unique personal vulnerability(ies). From these classifications, decisions are made regarding the provision of psychological first aid. The second triage task classifies individuals by degree of crisis reaction(s) and individual perceptions of threat. From psychological fist aid interventions and assessments of crisis reaction(s) and threat perceptions, the final triage task classifies individuals according to need for professional psychotherapeutic treatment. These referrals are made whenever an individual appears unable to cope with a crisis and/or psychological first aid is judged insufficient.

The primary triage task is to identify students and staff most significantly affected by a crisis. From these data, decisions are made regarding the provision of immediate psychological first aid assistance. Additionally, this definition of psychological triage also includes decisions regarding the need for psychotherapeutic treatment. Psychotherapy in this case refers to the range of interventions provided by mental health professionals to psychological trauma victims. Valuable information, used in the making of referral decisions, comes from initial psychological first aid contacts.

In addition to identifying those individuals in need of crisis intervention assistance, psychological triage is also a tool for identifying those individuals who may *not* require such support. It is critical for crisis response teams to acknowledge that not all individuals exposed to or affected by a crisis event will require crisis intervention assistance. Depending on the nature of the crisis and how it is perceived, a certain number will be able to adaptively cope with the crisis. This potential for dealing with crisis problems independently needs to be acknowledged by crisis teams. Not only does doing so free crisis intervention resources for those who truly need support, but also it may be counterproductive to force crisis services on these individuals. Students and staff who are capable of adaptively coping with a crisis may come to resent the directiveness that characterizes crisis intervention. Such resentment may minimize the schoolwide effectiveness of the crisis intervenors. Perhaps more damaging, however, is the possibility that such intervention may result in an individual not realizing how capable they truly are. It is possible that by providing crisis intervention in this circumstance, an individual may come to believe that they *need* crisis intervention to cope with adversity, when in fact they have the resources to do so on their own. Thus, it will be important to ensure that a psychological triage makes judgments about who is considered to be at low risk and establishes an attitude encouraging team members to intervene cautiously (if at all) with these individuals.

To the extent that crisis intervention services are made available to individuals judged to be at relatively low risk of traumatization or maladaptive coping, it is recommended that large group procedures be utilized. Groups of students, for example, can be addressed through classroom discussions of the crisis event. An example of classroom crisis intervention is discussed in Chapter 8. The classroom teacher can often help to facilitate this type of psychological first aid.

REFERRAL PLANNING PROCEDURES

Psychological triage is meaningless without carefully developed psychological first aid and psychotherapy referral options. If a school has not previously identified individuals capable of providing crisis intervention assistance, there will be a delay in the provision of this support. Thus, an effective triage will have previously developed or identified referral options (Thompson, 1995). Because of the importance of having crisis intervention referral options, this chapter examines referral planning procedures before returning to a more detailed discussion of psychological triage.

We distinguish between two types or levels of crisis intervention assistance: psychological first aid and psychotherapeutic treatment. Slaikeu (1990), in making a similar distinction, labels psychological first aid as first-order crisis intervention and psychotherapeutic treatment (or crisis therapy) as second-order crisis intervention. Typically, most initial triage classifications will result in the provision of first-order crisis intervention by school staff members. However, as a crisis intervention progresses, the need for mental health professionals and psychotherapies may become apparent. Table 7.1, adapted from Slaikeu, further clarifies this distinction between first aid and therapy.

Slaikeu (1990) points out that psychological first aid involves immediate assistance and usually takes only one session. He goes on to state: "Psychological first aid is primarily intended to provide support, reduce lethality, and link the person-in-crisis to other helping resources. Furthermore, it can and should be given by persons who first see the need, at the time and place it arises" (p. 102). In describing second-order crisis intervention, Slaikeu states that this form of intervention is ". . . a short-term therapeutic process that goes beyond restoration of immediate coping, and aims instead at crisis resolution" (p. 103). Given this perspective, school personnel would typically handle psychological first aid referrals immediately at the school site. Classroom teachers, for example, are potentially in an excellent position to provide their students with this

Table 7.1
Differences between Crisis Intervention Types (or Levels)

| | Type of Crisis Intervention | |
	Psychological First Aid	Psychotherapeutic Treatments
When?	Provided immediately	Provided when the individual is unable to work through crises on his or her own
How Long?	Minutes to hours	Weeks to months
By Whom?	Teachers, administrators, counselors, nurses, etc.	School and community mental health professional
Where?	The immediate school community	School and community mental health settings
Goals?	Reestablish immediate coping: give support; reduce lethality; link to helping resources	Resolve the crisis: manage crisis reactions; work through the crisis event; integrate the event into the fabric of life; establish openness/readiness to face the future

Source: Adapted from Karl A. Slaikeu, *Crisis intervention: A handbook for practice and research* (2nd ed., p. 102). Copyright © 1990 by Allyn and Bacon. Adapted by permission.

type of support. On the other hand, psychotherapies will require mental health professionals.

PREPARING FOR PSYCHOLOGICAL FIRST AID

Psychological first aid referral planning procedures typically involve staff development. Given that effective crisis intervention is provided immediately, it is desirable to have as many staff members as possible trained to provide psychological first aid. This training should be made a part of annual school crisis response in-services. At a minimum, every member of a response team's group of crisis intervenors should have a clear understanding of the principles, goals, and limitations of psychological first aid. For further information on how to provide psychological first aid in-service training, see Slaikeu's (1990) discussion of this topic. In addition, Appendix A is a training program for psychological first aid skill development developed by Brock.

PREPARING FOR PSYCHOTHERAPEUTIC TREATMENTS

Unlike psychological first aid, psychotherapeutic treatments are necessarily professional mental health responses. Thus, referral planning involves identifying professional resources, both within the school and in the community, capable of providing this support.

Identifying school mental health resources is typically a relatively straightforward task. Simply surveying school district psychologists, counselors, and social workers regarding their expertise may result in a number of in-house referral sources. If district resources are not available, however, a significant amount of work may be required. In these cases, crisis response planners will want to consider creating their own school psychotherapeutic treatment referral sources. This is perhaps best done through the establishment of the district and/or regional crisis response teams. In-service training of team members may ultimately result in a team of individuals capable of providing both psychological first aid and psychotherapy.

Identifying community resources may involve survey of both community mental health agencies and private practitioners. Community agencies are typically well-known to most school mental health professionals. These individuals should be able to develop a comprehensive list of local community mental health agencies. Local county mental health departments are an especially valuable resource.

Identifying private mental health practitioner referrals is typically more difficult than identifying community agencies. This is especially true in urban communities where there are many private practitioners. Although it may be profitable to survey district support personnel regarding their own private practitioner referral resources, a more detailed process is suggested. While, district personnel will be able to identify a list of practitioners who have been proven effective, it is just as likely that they will not have had experiences with other competent, well-trained practitioners.

IDENTIFYING PRIVATE MENTAL HEALTH RESOURCES

Given the importance of knowing available mental health resources (Dillard, 1989, 1990, cited in Pitcher & Poland, 1992), it is recommend that a Referral Questionnaire (Figure 7.1) be mailed to all psychologists, psychiatrists, licensed clinical social workers, and marriage, family, and child counselors listed in the local phone book(s). It is also profitable to include in this questionnaire a broad range of referral questions and issues, and not simply to limit it to crisis intervention referrals. The Referral Questionnaire has significant practical utility.

PREPARING FOR THE IDENTIFICATION OF LETHALITY

Special mention needs to be made of crisis intervention procedures with suicidal or homicidal individuals. J. Davis and Sandoval (1991) suggest that each school have a designated reporter who receives and acts on all reports of suicidal or homicidal individuals. This designated reporter is typically a school mental health professional (e.g., school counselor or psychologist) who has received special training. The Suicide Intervention Workshop (Table 3.3), developed by Ramsay, Tanney, Tierney, and Lang (1996), provides this training. It is important to have school mental health professionals take primary responsibility for crisis intervention whenever an individual's behavior or thinking involves any degree of lethality.

IDENTIFY CRISIS INTERVENTION SETTINGS

It is also important to address the logistical question of where individual and group crisis intervention assistance will be provided following a crisis. Significant crises require several locations be made available. Thus, it is important for a school to evaluate its physical resources. School offices,

Private Practitioner Referral Questionnaire

Thank you for providing us with the information that will help us to make more appropriate referrals to you and your colleagues. Please complete as much of the Questionnaire as is possible and return it in the attached, self-addressed envelope.

Name: _____   Title: _____

Office Location: _____   License(s): _____

Phone Number(s): _____   License Number(s): _____

Training and Experience

1. What degrees do you hold? _____

2. What schools did you attend? _____

3. How long have you been in practice? _____

4. What other types of special training do you have? _____

Financial Questions

5. What type of insurance do you accept? _____

6. What payment options do you offer? _____

7. Would you consider a therapeutic fee adjustment?   YES / NO

8. Do you offer a sliding fee schedule?   YES / NO

9. What are your current fees? (Attach fee schedule if available) _____

Logistics

10. Are you currently taking new referrals   YES / NO
    If no, when will you do so? _____

11. What are your work hours? _____

12. Do you work evenings?   YES / NO

13. Do you work Saturdays?   YES / NO

14. Do you have a waiting list?   YES / NO
    If yes, how long is the typical wait before the first session? _____

Therapeutic Issues

15. With which of the following populations do you feel you are best trained to work? (Circle all that apply to you.)

    Children   *Adults*   *Adolescents*   *Families*

    (continued)

Figure 7.1   The Private Practitioner Referral Questionnaire is used to identify community mental health resources. It not only identifies crisis therapy resources, but surveys local professionals regarding a variety of treatment issues.

16. Which of the following issues and/or areas do you consider to be your specialty(ies)? (Circle all that apply to you.)

substance abuse	*child abuse*	*grief processing*
eating disorders	*crisis therapy*	*attention deficit disorders*
anger issues	*suicide prevention*	*suicidal ideation*
empowerment issues	*co-dependency*	*crisis intervention*
creative divorce	*divorce mediation*	*transitional issues*
decision making	*family communication*	*self-esteem/self-concept*
depression	*behavior analysis*	*conduct disorders*

others (please list) _____

17. Which of the following therapeutic techniques do you employ? (Circle all that apply to you.)

behavior modification	*biofeedback*	*hypnosis*
EMDR	*client centered*	*cognitive-behavioral*
RET	*relaxation*	*sand tray*
play therapy	*stress inoculation training*	*cognitive therapy*
creative therapies	*psychoanalysis*	*supportive group therapy*

others (please list) _____

18. What special programs or services do you offer?_____

19. Do you conduct group therapy?   YES / NO

20. Are you bilingual?   YES / NO
    If yes, what language(s) do you speak?_____

21. Are the services of an interpreter available to you?   YES / NO
    If yes, what language(s) do your interpreters speak? _____

22. Do you have expertise working with specific ethnic/
    cultural groups?   YES / NO
    If yes, specify the group(s). _____

23. When making a referral to you, what information would you find most helpful? _____

24. What type of arrangements do you make with your clients for assistance during your non-work hours when they are experiencing a crisis?_____

25. On the average, how many times per month will you see the typical client? _____

26. How long are your sessions? _____

27. Please list any other information that may help us make appropriate referrals to you. _____
    _____
    _____

Figure 7.1   *(Continued)*

the library, resource rooms, and workrooms are all possible meeting locations. It is also advisable to obtain staff approval and suggestions for locations that would affect the workspace of staff members (e.g., teacher workrooms). Questions, comments, and concerns about the use of these areas for intervention need to be worked out *before* a crisis. The natural tension created by a crisis event may make rational discussion during these times more difficult. It would not be surprising if tempers flared if a teacher were to come to work the day after a crisis and find his or her workspace taken over by an unfamiliar crisis intervenor. The authors' crisis plan (Brock et al., 1995) mandates the designation of crisis intervention locations as one of the issues to be addressed annually by each school as they complete the Planning Checklist. (See Chapter 5 for a detailed discussion of this document.) Every year schools re-examine the changing physical resources of their campus and determine the best locations for crisis intervention to occur.

CULTURAL SENSITIVITY

The importance of cultural awareness among the team of crisis intervenors cannot be overstated. As highlighted in Chapter 5, different cultural groups may respond differently to trauma. It is essential for team members be aware of these differences (Klingman, 1986). For this reason questions regarding cultural awareness and language facility are included in the Referral Questionnaire (Figure 7.1).

THE PSYCHOLOGICAL TRIAGE CHECKLIST

The Psychological Triage Checklist (Figure 7.2) provides crisis intervention coordinators with guidelines to the process of identifying psychological victims of crisis events and in making of initial and secondary treatment decisions. Initial triage actions (Items 1, 2, and 3) classify traumatization risk according to known crisis facts and knowledge of the personal characteristics of individuals within the school's population. This includes classifying individuals according to degree of exposure to the crisis event (Item 1), familiarity with crisis victims (Item 2), and unique personal vulnerabilities (Item 3). Data from these classifications are used to help identify individuals most likely to need immediate psychological first aid. These treatment decisions are made as soon as possible following a crisis event and require knowledge of crisis facts and familiarity with the school's population.

Psychological Triage Checklist

A. Initial Risk Screening

Conducted as soon as possible following a crisis event. Designed to quickly identify those most likely to be in need of a psychological first aid response. Requires
knowledge of crisis facts and familiarity with the school's population. Complete
an *Initial Risk Screening Summary* form for all individuals from the population
judged to be potentially affected by the crisis event. Record all names on the
Psychological Triage Summary Sheet.

_____ 1. **Classify individuals according to degree of crisis exposure.**
The factors used in identifying these individuals include degree of
proximity and, if necessary, degree of exposure.

Dates/Times Updated:_____/_____   _____/_____   _____/___

_____ 2. **Classify individuals according to their relationship(s) with crisis
victim(s).**

Date/Times Updated: _____/_____   _____/_____   _____/___

_____ 3. **Classify individuals according to their unique personal vulnerabilities.**
The factors used in identifying these individuals include (a) mental
illness, (b) developmental immaturity, (c) trauma history, and (d) lack
of resources.

Dates/Times Updated:_____/_____   _____/_____   _____/___

B. Secondary Risk Screening

Conducted in conjunction with initial psychological first aid interventions. Designed
to identify those who display significant crisis reactions. If an individual's crisis reactions include any degree of lethality (i.e., suicidal/homicidal threats/thoughts),
an immediate referral to a mental health professional should be made. Requires
knowledge of reactions associated with psychological trauma, and effective
screening and referral procedures. If not already done, complete an *Initial Risk
Screening Summary* for all individuals included in the secondary risk screening.
Record all names on the *Psychological Triage Summary Sheet.*

_____ 4. **Conduct initial psychological first aid interventions.**
Document severity of crisis reactions via the *Secondary Screening of
Risk: Interview Outline.* Determine if the individual perceived the situation as threatening. If not, further psychological first aid may not be
required. If the individual judged the crisis to have been a personal
threat continued crisis intervention may be needed.

Date/Time Initiated: _____/_____

Figure 7.2 Crisis intervention coordinators can use the Psychological Triage
Checklist (PTCL) to help identify psychological first aid treatment priorities and to
begin to document which individuals may require referral to a mental health
professional.

_____ 5. **Establish referral procedures.**
Distribute referral forms to all classrooms affected by the crisis event. Make sure that attached to each packet of forms is the handout *Assessing a Child's Need for Psychological First Aid in a Crisis Situation.* Ensure that parents are informed of signs of maladaptive coping and know how to obtain crisis intervention for their children. Ensure that students are aware of how to obtain/ask for crisis intervention assistance.

Date/Time Initiated: _____/_____

_____ 6. **Mass Screening.**
If judged to be necessary, mass screening procedures may be used to survey the entire population to identify students and staff members who are displaying crisis reactions.

Date/Time Initiated: _____/_____

C. Psychotherapeutic Treatment Screening

Implemented as psychological first aid interventions are concluded. Designed to identify those who may require a professional counseling or psychotherapeutic referral. Makes use of data provided by *Secondary Screening of Risk: Interview Outline,* crisis intervention referrals and, if available, mass screenings.

_____ 7. **If possible, obtain permission from parent(s) or guardian(s) for crisis intervenor(s) to speak with identified students.**
Discuss the crisis situation, the individual student's reactions, and crisis intervenor concerns with the parent(s) or guardian(s). This contact will facilitate a psychotherapeutic treatment referral if it becomes necessary. Document parental contact(s) with the appropriate code on the *Psychological Triage Summary Sheet.*

_____ 8. **Continue psychological first aid interventions.**
Use information provided by on-going psychological first aid sessions to further document individual need for psychotherapeutic treatment referrals.

Date/Time Updated: _____/_____

_____ 9. **Identify individuals who need psychotherapeutic treatment referrals.**
These are the most severely affected individuals who, even with psychological first aid assistance, may not be able to cope with the crisis event. They may require professional counseling intervention. Document such a referral with the code "PT" on the *Psychological Triage Summary Sheet.*

Date/Time Updated: _____/_____

Figure 7.2 *(Continued)*

The next triage actions (Items 4, 5, and 6) are conducted in conjunction with the initial psychological first aid interventions and are designed to classify traumatization risk according to significance of crisis reactions. In addition to psychological first aid interventions (Item 4), classification according to degree of crisis reactions includes crisis intervention referrals (Item 5) and, when necessary, mass screening (Item 6). These triage procedures are conducted as soon as possible following initiation of psychological first aid interventions. They require knowledge of crisis reactions and procedures to assess these reactions among a school's population.

The final triage actions (Items 7, 8, and 9) are implemented as psychological first aid interventions are concluded. They are designed to identify individuals who may require professional counseling or psychotherapeutic treatment referrals. These referrals will be facilitated by parental contacts (Item 7) and are made from data provided by psychological first aid interventions (Item 8). Psychological triage concludes with the identification of those in need of a psychotherapeutic treatment (Item 9).

An effective triage requires that all the facts regarding the crisis event be obtained quickly. The initial triage procedure, identification of the students involved in the crisis, requires these facts. The crisis response coordinator, who is usually a school administrator (See Figure 6.1, Item 1), typically conducts this task. However, given that psychological triage is so dependent on this information, it would be appropriate for the crisis intervention coordinator to assist the administrator with this critical first step of any crisis response.

In addition, as has already been mentioned, an effective triage requires familiarity with the population judged to be at risk. Thus, it is critical that any psychological triage make use of staff members from the affected school(s). Ideally, the crisis intervention coordinator will be a school staff member that has intimate knowledge of the school's population.

Although the Psychological Triage Checklist is presented sequentially, it is acknowledged that the process of triage is dynamic. It is subject to change depending on the evolving nature of a given crisis situation and the individuals involved. For example, if at any time during psychological triage an individual is identified as being suicidal or homicidal, an immediate referral to a mental health professional should be made. In this case, it would not be appropriate to continue sequentially down the checklist until the point that psychotherapeutic referral decisions are made. With this caution in mind, it is recommended that this checklist be made a part of all crisis response plans.

INITIAL RISK SCREENING

Armed with knowledge of crisis facts and familiarity with the affected school's or schools' population, the crisis intervention coordinator's first task is to conduct an initial risk screening. This screening is facilitated by the use of the Initial Risk Screening Summary form (Figure 7.3). The crisis intervention coordinator should ensure this form is completed for all individuals judged to be affected by the crisis event. This population may be as small as a single classroom or grade level, or as large as an entire school. For example, following an event such as the death of a sixth-grade teacher (as described at the beginning of Chapters 5 and 6), this form would be completed for all students in the affected classroom. On the other hand, following an event such as a schoolyard shooting (as described at the beginning of Chapter 3) an Initial Risk Screening Summary would be completed for all students on the playground at the time of the shooting.

The Initial Risk Screening Summary quantifies risk of psychological traumatization. Risk ratings may range from 3 to 24, with higher ratings indicating greater risk. Individual ratings should be made relative to the specific school population judged to be potentially affected by the crisis event. This quantification is far from perfect, however, it has the potential to give the crisis intervention coordinator basic information helpful in determining initial psychological first aid intervention priorities. Using this form, the greatest intervention priorities would be those individuals who were most intimately involved in the crisis event, who had the closet relationships with crisis victims and had the most personal vulnerabilities. Conversely, those who were relatively removed from the crisis event, who had no relationship(s) with the crisis victim(s) and had no personal vulnerabilities, would be the lowest intervention priorities. While the former groups of individuals should be seen as soon as possible (if not immediately), provision of psychological first aid for the later group could be delayed (or not provided at all).

As the initial risk screening ratings are completed the Triage Checklist also directs that all ratings be recorded on the Psychological Triage Summary (Figure 7.4 on page 140). This Summary can be used to sort or rank individuals according to risk ratings. The documentation provided by this type of form is especially critical whenever a school is faced with a crisis involving large numbers of students.* Keeping in mind that such an event will

---

*Placing the columns found on Figure 7.4 in a computer spread sheet program and then directing the program to sort according to the column within which the risk rating numbers are contained can facilitate these rankings.

Initial Risk Screening Summary

Name: _____   M ____ F ____ Date: _____

Referred by: _____   Room: _____ Teacher: _____

Dominant Language: _____   Screener: _____

A. Crisis Exposure
Proximity to the Crisis Event

10	5	4	3	2	1
Crisis victim, *with* life threat and/or injury	Crisis victim, *without* life threat and/or injury	Directly exposed to the crisis event (eyewitness)	Present on the site of the crisis event	Not present on the site of the crisis event	Out of the vicinity of the crisis event

Elaborate: _____

_____

Duration of Exposure to the Crisis Event (optional)

5	4	3	2	1
Days	Hours	Minutes	Seconds	None

Elaborate: _____

_____

B. Relationship(s) with Crisis Victim(s)

5	4	3	2	1
Relative(s)	Best and/or only friend(s)	Good friend(s)	Friend(s) or acquaintance(s)	Did not know victim(s)

Elaborate: _____

_____

Figure 7.3 The Initial Risk Screening Summary (IRSS) should be completed for all individuals from the population judged to be at risk for psychological trauma. The IRSS attempts to quantify variables known to be correlated with psychological trauma. Data from this form can be used to identify psychological first aid treatment priorities. In other words, when faced with more potential crisis victims than the available resources can handle, these data help crisis intervenors determine who will be helped first.

C. Personal Vulnerability(ies)

	Yes	No	Elaborate
Known/Suspected mental illness			
Developmental immaturity			
Previous trauma or loss			
Lack or resource			□ social □ financial □ familial
Total			

Elaborate: _____

D. Initial Risk Screening Rating

Initial Risk Screening Category	Rating
Proximity to the crisis event	
Duration of exposure to the crisis event	
Relationship(s) with crisis victim(s)	
Personal vulnerability(ies)	
Total	

Figure 7.3   *(Continued)*

affect staff as well as students, the crisis intervention coordinator might expect some difficulty performing his or her duties. Memory problems are common and need to be anticipated. Thus, this documentation will help to ensure that no student is forgotten or "slips through the cracks."

ITEM 1. CLASSIFY INDIVIDUALS ACCORDING TO DEGREE OF CRISIS EXPOSURE

The first item on the Psychological Triage Checklist specifies the classification of individuals according to their proximity to the crisis event. The greater the involvement in, or exposure to, the crisis event, the greater the risk of psychological traumatization. When appropriate, or necessary, duration of exposure can also be used to further classify degree of crisis exposure. For example, duration may be used when large numbers of individuals were directly exposed to a crisis event (e.g., a schoolyard sniper attack). In such a circumstance, it is likely that some individuals will be exposed to the event longer than others will (e.g., some were caught on the schoolyard while others were able to quickly escape). These students or staff members should be given a relatively high psychological first aid

Psychological Triage Summary

(Confidential, for Crisis Response Team use only)

Date	Name	Teacher	Risk Rating[1]	Risk Category[2]	Crisis Intervenor	Parental Contact[3]	Status[4]
1.							
2.							
3.							
4.							
5.							
6.							
7.							
8.							
9.							
10.							
11.							
12.							

[1] Record initial risk screening rating from the *Initial Risk Screening Summary* form.

[2] Record the risk category(ies) that is (are) likely to have caused psychological trauma.
Category Codes: V = victim; I = directly involved; W = witness; F = familiarity with victim(s); MI = preexisting mental illness; DIM = developmental immaturity; TH = trauma history; R = lack of resources; Em = severe emotional reactions; PT = perceived threat.

[3] Record information regarding parental contact.
Parental Contact Codes: SM = school meeting; HV = home visit; Ph = phone contact.

[4] Record information regarding the current need for crisis intervention services and support.
Status Codes: A = active (currently being seen); WIC = watch and consult (not currently being seen); FU = needs follow-up; I/A = inactive (not being seen and no follow-up is judged to be needed); PT = psychotherapeutic treatment referral (psychological first aid not sufficient).

Figure 7.4 Psychological Triage Summary is designed to assist a crisis intervention coordinator document psychological triage decisions and actions. *Note:* The names of all individuals brought to the attention of crisis intervenors should be placed on this form. In addition to documenting treatment priorities, this form also allows crisis intervenors to quickly view the general psychological trauma risk factors, identifies individuals responsible for crisis intervention services, and documents the individual's current crisis intervention status. Finally, it also documents parental contacts.

intervention priority. Referring to the scenario presented at the beginning of this chapter, the teachers who performed CPR on the student who died of a heart attack should be given the highest psychological first aid intervention priority. Also, all students in the classroom at the time the victim collapsed should be identified as being directly exposed to the crisis event (i.e., eyewitnesses) and should be made psychological first aid intervention priorities.

The rationale behind this item is that the effect of a crisis event is primarily a function of the individual's physical proximity to the event. The closer one is, the greater the likelihood of being traumatized. Conversely, the greater the physical distance between an individual and the place in which the crisis event occurred, the less the likelihood of being traumatized (Bloch, Silber, & Perry, 1956; Green, Grace, & Lindy, 1983; Green et al., 1991; McFarlane, 1986; Nader et al., 1990; Newman, 1976; Shore, Tatum, & Vollmer, 1986, 1990). Pynoos et al. (1987), for example, demonstrated the overriding importance of degree of exposure to a traumatic event (a schoolyard sniper attack) in predicting the development of posttraumatic stress (PTSD) responses.

Also, from the research of Resnick et al. (1993) it is suggested that special attention be directed toward those individuals who experienced life threat or injury because of the crisis event. The Resnick et al. study found that among female crime victims rates of both current and lifetime traumatic stress reactions were a function of life threat or injury. The rate of these stress reactions among those that experienced both life threat and injury "was more than twice that observed in the subgroup [of crime victims] that had experienced neither life threat or injury" (p. 988).

ITEM 2. CLASSIFY INDIVIDUALS ACCORDING TO THEIR RELATIONSHIP(S) WITH CRISIS VICTIM(S)

The Los Angeles Unified School District's (1994) original triage definition recognized that physical proximity to a crisis event alone does not account for all individuals who enter a crisis state. Simply being out of the area of a crisis event does not necessarily prevent an individual from being affected by a crisis. This gives additional justification for the crisis intervention coordinator being someone, such as a school counselor, who knows the school's population well. The more familiar the coordinator is with the school's population, the easier it will be to identify those who are familiar with crisis victim(s).

This triage task suggests that what affects those who are close to us has an effect on us as well. No doubt if a best friend was murdered while on vacation, you would become significantly distraught. In fact, a close friend may be just as traumatized, as would those strangers who witnessed the murder. Thus, in the school setting, following a crisis event, crisis intervention coordinators must look closely at those who were emotionally close to those involved in the crisis. The stronger the relationship, the more likely it is that the individual will enter a crisis state. For example, in the case described at the beginning of the chapter, crisis intervenors would want to take a careful look at all students who considered John to be their friend as well as those who were closely involved with him in extracurricular activities.

The importance of this factor has been demonstrated by Nader et al. (1990), who found that greater acquaintance with the victim of a schoolyard shooting was significantly related to higher scores on a measure of posttraumatic stress reactions. Similarly, Milgram et al. (1988) found both acute and chronic stress reactions, following a schoolbus disaster, to be more related to friendship with disaster victims than to exposure to accident-related stressors. Bloch et al. (1956) found a significant relationship between a child's emotional disturbance following a natural disaster and injury or death of family members.

ITEM 3: CLASSIFY INDIVIDUALS ACCORDING TO THEIR UNIQUE PERSONAL VULNERABILITIES

The final initial risk screening procedure involves identifying students who might be especially vulnerable to traumatic stress due to unique personal factors. Again, as was mentioned in the discussion of Item 2, who we are can be of equal importance to where we were at the time of a crisis. Note that here again, it is important for the crisis intervention coordinator to be familiar with the school's population. The greater such familiarity, the more likely it is that the following unique personal vulnerabilities will be identified.

While the resiliency literature has identified a number of variables affecting how children respond to traumatic events (e.g., Doll & Lyon, 1998; Masten & Coatsworth, 1998), we have selected four that are especially accessible to a site-level crisis intervention coordinator.* These factors are as follows:

---

*In addition to factors discussed in this chapter, other factors shown to influence resiliency and vulnerability to environmental stress include coping style, regulation of emotion, language competence, sense of humor, locus of control, and a resilient religious belief system. The reader is referred to Brock (in press-b) for a further discussion of these factors.

1. *Mental illness.* Although entry into a crisis state alone is not a sign of mental illness (it is a normal reaction to abnormal circumstances), a history of emotional upset can lower resistance to crises. According to the American Psychiatric Association's (1994) *Diagnostic and Statistical Manual of Mental Disorders,* (4th ed.) "There is some evidence that . . . preexisting mental disorders may influence the development of Acute Stress Disorder" (p. 431). A preexisting psychopathology can also make it more difficult to work through a crisis. The family's mental health should also be considered (Lystad, 1985). For example, following a schoolbus kidnapping, Terr (1983) found ". . . relationships between the clinical severity of the children's posttraumatic conditions and their preexisting family pathology . . ." (p. 1550). Green et al. (1991) and Bloch et al. (1956) have reported similar findings. Additionally, Mike Armstrong (personal communication, April 1992) indicates that his experience working with children following a schoolyard shooting has found family psychopathology to play a significant role both in the number and intensity of crisis reactions.

2. *Developmental immaturity.* Although it is possible for developmental immaturity to be a protective factor when it comes to initial traumatization (i.e., younger children may not understand the trauma threat), once an event is judged to be threatening, the developmentally younger the crisis survivor is, the greater the traumatization (Carlson, 1997). Conversely, it would appear that resiliency is promoted by good intellectual functioning (Doll & Lyon, 1998). Thus, developmentally younger trauma victims should be given a relatively high crisis intervention service priority when compared to maturer crisis survivors. For example, special education classrooms for children with developmental delays might need special attention.

3. *Trauma history.* A history of prior traumatization increases vulnerability to future traumatization (Bremner, Southwick, Johnson, Yehuda, & Charney, 1993; Breslau, 1998; King, King, Foy, & Gudanowski, 1996; Matsakis, 1994). Thus, special attention needs to be given to students who have experienced other traumas within the past year or those who have experienced prior crises similar in nature to the current crisis event (Horowitz, 1976; Nader & Pynoos, 1993). How an individual perceives a crisis event will impact his or her frame of reference at the time of the event. If the individual has experienced numerous recent significant traumas and losses, a relatively minor or significantly removed crisis event might be sufficient to cause entry into a crisis state.

Continuing with the situational crisis caused by John's death from heart failure, crisis intervenors should take a close look at all students who previously had close friends die. Although these students may not have been in the classroom at the time of John's collapse, nor had even known him, his death might rekindle feelings associated with this previous loss. Nader et al. (1990) reported that children who have experienced previous traumas had renewed PTSD symptoms related to the previous experience, following a sniper attack at their school.

4. *Lack of resources.* This item is a risk factor because outside resources may assist individuals through difficult times. Conversely, a lack of resources can make it much more difficult for people to cope with crises. Slaikeu (1990) observes: "How an individual responds to a precipitating event and later works through the crisis experience depends on his or her material, personal, and social resources" (p. 27). For example, a lack of material resources such as money, food, housing, and transportation can turn a moderately stressful event into a crisis. Poverty is one of the most powerful predictors of vulnerability to environmental stress (Doll & Lyon, 1998).

Familial resources are also important to the individual facing a crisis event (Brock, in press-b). Specific family factors that have been shown to adversely affect the availability of such resources, and thus increase trauma risk, include the following:

- Not living with any nuclear family member
- Ineffective and uncaring parenting
- Family dysfunction (e.g., alcoholism, violence, mental illness)
- Parental posttraumatic stress disorder
- Child maltreatment

Finally, according to the American Psychiatric Association (1994), "There is some evidence that social supports . . . may influence the development of Acute Stress Disorder" (p. 431). Individuals who must face traumatic circumstances alone, have been shown to suffer more than do those who have at least one supportive relationship (Carlson, 1997). For example, in the case of John's death, crisis intervenors might expect the student who considered John to be his or her only friend to be more significantly affected than the student who saw John as one of many such relationships.

SECONDARY RISK SCREENING

Conducted in conjunction with the initial psychological first aid interventions, secondary risk screening procedures are designed to assist in the identification of individuals who display significant crisis reactions. The severity of such reactions can be used to further classify psychological trauma victims and is critical in determining the need for a psychotherapeutic treatment referral. Completing this level of psychological triage will require the ability to assess crisis reactions and effective screening and referral procedures. A potentially helpful tool in assessing crisis reactions is the Secondary Screening of Risk: Interview Outline (Figure 7.5). Inspired by a questionnaire originally developed by The Los Angeles Unified School District (1994), this interview form makes use of the Diagnostic and Statistical Manual of Mental Disorders' (American Psychiatric Association, 1994) diagnostic criteria for acute distress.

Table 7.2, on page 150, provides a summary of the symptoms of acute distress. Simply put, those who display more of these reactions will be at greater risk for traumatization (Matsakis, 1994; McFarlane & Yehuda, 1996). In particular, it would appear that there are specific crisis reactions that may indicate greater need for psychotherapeutic treatment. If insomnia, anxiety and general agitation do not subside in the first few weeks following the crisis event, there is a greater risk of PTSD (Weisaeth, 1989). Also, according to McFarlane and Yehuda, an enduring startle response, hypervigilance, increased irritability, sleep disturbance and disturbed memory and concentration" (p. 172) predicts posttraumatic stress. Conversely, the presence of intrusive trauma memories immediately following a crisis event is suggested to be much less pathological.

As the presence of significant crisis reactions are identified, they should be noted on the Psychological Triage Summary (using the risk category code of "Em" for severe emotional reactions). If not already completed an Initial Risk Screening Summary should also be filled out. It is important to note that severity of emotional reaction alone should be sufficient reason to classify individuals as being in need of psychological first aid. The importance of doing so is underscored by the research of Schwarz and Kowalski (1991). These researchers report posttraumatic stress to be more associated with emotional states recalled from a school shooting than with proximity to the event. Similarly, Ersland, Weisaeth, and Sund (1989) report that there "is a relation between stress reactions in the acute phase of the disaster and reported poor mental health 9 months after" (p. 48).

A secondary screening of risk should include an evaluation of what constitutes the individual's subjective perception of threat. Regardless of the actual threat that the event presented, if the individual viewed the event as threatening, then there is a risk for psychological trauma. Simply put, traumatized individuals will have perceived the event as extremely negative (Caplan, 1964; Carlson, 1997; Mitchell & Everly, 1996a). On the other hand,

Secondary Screening of Risk

Interview Outline

Student Name: _____   Teacher: _____

Crisis Intervenor: _____   Date: _____

What constitutes the interviewee's crisis event exposure and recollections?

1. Do you remember what happened? [*Note any aspects of the event the student is unable to remember.*] _____
   _____

2. Where were you when the event occurred? [*Note proximity to the crisis event.*]
   _____

3. What did you see/hear, what was told to you? [*Note duration of the crisis event.*] _____

4. Did you ever feel as if you were personally threatened by the event? [*Note any aspect(s) of the event that was/were perceived as involving actual or threatened death or serious injury, or a threat to physical integrity of self or others.*] _____
   _____

5. How well do you know victim(s)? [*Note how important the victim(s) were to the interviewee.*] _____
   _____

Is the event persistently reexperienced?

6. Do you have thoughts about the event that you wish you could stop? [*Note recurrent and intrusive recollections (images, thoughts, perceptions) which the interviewee finds distressing.*] _____
   _____

7. Do you have bad dreams? _____

7a. Describe these dreams. [*Note if the dreams are about the event.*]
   _____

7b. How frequently do they occur? _____
   _____

Figure 7.5 An interview outline that may be used by a crisis intervenor to help identify crisis reactions. *Note:* In addition to investigating symptoms of acute distress, the interview also explores recollections of the crisis event/experience, investigates suicidal/homicidal ideation, and determines if the crisis reactions are impacting daily functioning. Finally, the interview also explores the availability of resources, which might prove helpful in coping with the crisis circumstances. *Sources:* Adapted with permission from the Los Angeles Unified School District (1994). Also, adapted with permission from the *Diagnostic and Statistical Manual of Mental Disorders,* Fourth Edition. Copyright 1994 American Psychiatric Association.

8. Do you ever act or feel as if the event were happening to you again? [*Note reports of feeling as if reliving the experience.*] [*Note reports of illusions, hallucinations, and flashbacks.*] _____

9. How do you feel when you return to the location of the event? [*Note reports of intense psychological distress.*] _____

10. How do you feel when you are exposed to reminders of the event? [*Note reports of intense psychological distress.*] _____

11. How does your body respond when you return to the location of the event? [*Note reports of physiological reactivity.*] _____

12. How does you body respond when you are exposed to reminders of the event? [*Note reports of physiological reactivity.*] _____

Is there an avoidance of crisis event reminders?

13. Do you find yourself trying to avoid thinking, feeling, talking about the event? _____

14. Do you try to avoid activities, places, people or situations that remind you of the event? _____

Is there a numbing of general responsiveness?

15. Are there activities that were important to you before the event that are no longer of interest? _____

16. Since the event have you found yourself feeling different or separated from other people? [*Note feelings of detachment and/or estrangement.*] [*Note a reduction in awareness of environment (i.e., in a daze).*] _____

17. What emotions have you been able to feel since the event? [*Note a restricted range of affect.*] [*Note feelings of numbing, detachment, or a lack of a emotional response.*] _____

18. Do you think your life will be different now? In what way? _____

19. Are you feeling any different about your future since the event? [*Note feelings of a foreshortened future.*] _____

(continued)

Figure 7.5 *(Continued)*

Is there an increased level of arousal?

20. Are you having sleeping difficulties? [*Note difficulties falling or staying asleep.*] _____

21. Since the event, have you found that you have had difficulty controlling your temper? [*Note any reports of irritability or angry outbursts.*] _____

22. Have you had difficulty concentrating on your school work? _____

23. Do you feel that you are "hypervigilant" since the event? _____

24. Have you experienced an exaggerated startle response since the event?___

Are there feelings of survivor guilt?

25. Are you angry/guilty about what happened? _____

26. Do you think you could have done anything to prevent the incident? _____

27. Do you want to "get even" or seek revenge?

Are there any somatic complaints?

28. How have you felt physically since the event? [*Note any reports of headaches, stomach aches, bowel and bladder problems, etc.*] _____

Are there self-destructive and impulsive behaviors?

29. Do you find yourself acting without thinking?

30. Have you engaged in any behaviors that might result in self-injury?

31. Have you had thoughts of suicide/homicide? [*If yes, continue with questions 32 to 35. If no, skip to question 36. If yes, make an immediate crisis therapy referral.*] _____

32. How often have you had these thoughts? _____

33. Do you have a plan? [*Note if the interviewee knows how he or she will commit suicide/homicide.*] [*Note if the interviewee knows how soon he or she will commit suicide/homicide.*] [*Note if the interviewee has the means to c   a   r   r   y out the plan.*] _____

34. Have you ever tried to commit suicide/homicide before? _____

Figure 7.5 *(Continued)*

148

35. Is there anyone or anything that could keep you from killing (self or other)? _____

What is the effect of crisis reactions on daily functioning?

36. Have you been able to complete any work activities since the event?_____

37. Have you had any difficulty taking care of yourself since the event?_____

38. Has there been a change in your ability to relate socially to others since the event? _____

39. How long have these effects been perceived as troublesome? _____

What are some resources that are available?

40. Do you think this will affect your family? ____   _____

41. Who can you talk to in your family or friends?_____

42. What will you do when you leave school today? _____

43. Will you be in school tomorrow? _____

44. Would you like to talk again, or perhaps join a group of students to discuss the event? _____

Summary [*Is response in proportion to degree of exposure?*] [*Is the student over- or underreacting to the crisis?*]

_____

_____

_____

_____

Referral Decisions

_____ *Referral to Community Agency*
Name of Agency: _____
Telephone: (_____) _____ - _____

_____ *Referral to a Private Practitioner*
Name of Private Practitioner:_____
Telephone: (_____) _____ - _____

_____ Subsequent appointment with Crisis Team   When? _____ Who? _____

_____ Refer to local school group   When? _____ Who? _____

_____ Watch and consult

Figure 7.5   *(Continued)*

Table 7.2

Manifestations of Acute Distress

Type of Reaction	Symptoms		
	Reexperience	Avoidance and Numbing	Increased Arousal
Somatic	• Reactivity to reminders (e.g., sweating, rapid heart beat, nausea, dizziness, dry mouth, difficulty breathing)	• Sensory numbing	• Abdominal distress • Hot flashes or chills • Frequent urination • Trouble swallowing
Behavioral	• Insomnia • Increased activity • Aggression • Repetitive play • Act as if trauma were recurring	• Avoidance of trauma reminders (e.g., activities, locations, conversations, people, things) • Decrease interest in significant activities • Social withdrawal	• Insomnia • Exaggerated startle
Cognitive	• Intrusive recall • Flashbacks • Trauma nightmares	• Amnesia • Sense of foreshortened future	• Poor concentration • Hypervigilance
Emotional	• Psychological distress with exposure to reminders (e.g., anxiety, anger, guilt, shame, hopelessness)	• Emotional numbing • Impaired affect modulation	• Irritability • Outburst of anger

Source: From "Crisis theory: A foundation for the comprehensive crisis prevention and intervention team," by S.E. Brock (in press-c), in *Best Practices in Crisis Prevention and Intervention in the Schools,* Washington, DC: National Association of School Psychologists. Copyright by the National Association of School Psychologists. Reprinted with permission.

individuals who did not perceive the event as severe, regardless of how dangerous and intense it actually was, will not be as traumatized. For example, Pynoos et al. (1987) found that some children exposed to a school shooting, who were not aware that their lives were in danger, reported fewer symptoms than was typical of other similarly exposed children. From these observations, it is suggested that it is important to assess perceived threat when determining individual crisis intervention service priorities. As secondary risk screenings identify individuals who subjectively viewed the event as dangerous, this fact should also be noted on the Psychological Triage Summary (using the risk category code of "PT" for perceived threat).

In addition to gaining information about crisis reactions, secondary screening of risk should determine whether the individual is considered to be over- or underreacting to the crisis (given their degree of crisis exposure). Such a question is especially important given that denial, blocking, emotional numbing of the unpleasant reality of a crisis, or a combination of these is often part of the early reactions to a crisis event (Horowitz, 1976). Individuals, who were, for example, directly exposed to a crisis event and are not reacting to it, should be monitored closely. On the other hand, individuals whose crisis reactions are greater than might be expected (given their crisis experiences) should have their perceptions of the threat presented by the crisis carefully evaluated.

ITEM 4. CONDUCT INITIAL PSYCHOLOGICAL FIRST AID INTERVENTIONS

As initial psychological first aid interventions are conducted, this psychological triage item directs the crisis intervenor to document the severity of crisis reactions. The Secondary Screening of Risk: Interview Outline may be a helpful tool for doing so. As was just mentioned, an important part of this interview is determining whether or not the individual viewed the crisis event as threatening. If it was not viewed as such, then further psychological first aid assistance may not be needed. However, if it was viewed as a threat, then continued support and potentially a psychotherapeutic treatment referral may be needed. During the initial psychological first aid interventions it is also important to determine if the crisis reactions include any degree of lethality (i.e., suicidal and/or homicidal threats and/or thoughts). If so, it is appropriate to make an immediate referral to a mental health professional.

ITEM 5. ESTABLISH REFERRAL PROCEDURES

Referral procedures allow teachers and parents to alert the school's crisis response team to additional students in need of crisis intervention. Through this mechanism students who are not identified by initial risk screening are brought to the attention of the crisis response team. To facilitate the referral process, Item 5 specifies the distribution of referral forms to all staff members. They should also be made available to parents. Figure 7.6 provides a Crisis Intervention Referral Form. This form provides the crisis intervention coordinator with general information about the referred

Crisis Intervention Referral Form

Date: _____   Parent: _____

Student: _____   Address: _____

Birthdate: _____   Phone: H _____

Teacher: _____   W _____

Grade: _____   Primary Language: _____

                                   Student: _____

                                   Parent(s): _____

Reason for Referral: *Please state why you are concerned.*

_____

_____

_____

How close was the student to the crisis event? _____

How long was the student exposed to the crisis event? _____

How close was the student's relationship(s) to crisis victim(s)? _____

Did the students perceive a threat to self or others? _____

Has the student experienced a similar event in the past?   YES   NO

(If YES, please elaborate) _____

_____

Has the child experienced any other traumas within the
past year?   YES   NO

(If YES, please elaborate) _____

_____

Does the student have a known or suspected emotional
disturbance?   YES   NO

(If YES, please elaborate) _____

_____

Is the student in any way developmentally immature?   YES   NO

(If YES, please elaborate) _____

_____

Are there any known resources that might help the student cope? YES   NO
(If YES, please elaborate) _____

_____

Figure 7.6   The Crisis Intervention Referral Form is designed to help parents
and teachers bring students to the crisis intervention coordinator. *Sources:*
From diagnostic criteria for Posttraumatic and Acute Stress Disorders. Adapted
with permission from the *Diagnostic and Statistical Manual of Mental Disorders,*
Fourth Edition. Copyright 1994 American Psychiatric Association.

Crisis Reaction Symptom Checklist

(Check all that you believe apply to the student you are referring for crisis intervention.)

General Feelings/Behaviors Generated by the Event
_____ Fear   _____ Helplessness   _____ Horror

_____ Disorganized behavior   _____ Agitated behavior

Specific Feelings/Behaviors Generated by the Event

Dissociative Symptoms

_____ Has lost interest in previously enjoyed activities.

_____ Appears to feel separated, detached, or estranged from others.

_____ Appears to feel separated or detached from his or her body.

_____ No longer shows his or her previous range of emotions.

_____ Appears to feel guilty about having survived.

_____ Appears to feel guilty about not having been more severely affected by the event.

_____ Appears to feel that their life is unreal and/or dream like.

Symptoms That Suggest a Reexperiencing of the Event

_____ Reports recurrent, intrusive, and unwanted recollections, thoughts, images, and/or perceptions of the event.

_____ Exhibits repetitive play that may be symbolic of the event.

_____ Reports having recurrent frightening dreams.

_____ Reports having recurrent dreams about the event.

_____ Behaves as if reliving the event.

_____ Displays intense psychological distress when exposed to reminders of the event.

_____ Display physiological reactivity when exposed to reminders of the event.

Symptoms That Suggest an Avoidance of Event Reminders

_____ Avoids talking about the event.

_____ Avoids situations/locations that are associated with the event.

_____ Avoids reminders of the event.

_____ Does not remember important details of the event.

_____ Has diminished expectations for the future.

Symptoms That Suggest an Increased Level of Arousal

_____ Has difficulty falling asleep.

_____ Awakens in the middle of the night and cannot get back to sleep.

_____ Displays an exaggerated startle response.

(continued)

Figure 7.6   *(Continued)*

153

_____ Appears to have difficulty concentrating.
_____ Has difficulty completing tasks.
_____ Displays increased irritability.
_____ Displays increased aggressiveness.
_____ Appears to be hypervigilant.
_____ Reports physical problems such as stomachaches and headaches.
_____ Appears to be depressed.

Interventions Already Attempted: *Please list the things already tried to assist the student.* _____

_____
_____
_____
_____
_____
_____
_____

Services Recommended: *Please indicate how you think a crisis intervenor can help.* _____

_____
_____
_____
_____
_____
_____

Figure 7.6   *(Continued)*

student. The reason for referral statement provides issues of primary concern to the referring party. Additional information provided by this form assists in determining both the student's risk level and the presence of a variety of crisis reactions. The Crisis Reaction Symptoms Checklist included on this form is based on the diagnostic criteria for Posttraumatic and Acute Stress Disorders (American Psychiatric Association, 1994).

The crisis intervention coordinator should ensure that an Initial Risk Screening Summary form is completed for all students referred to the crisis team. In addition, all individuals so identified should have their name placed on the Psychological Triage Summary.

An effective referral mechanism should educate care providers about what reactions to look for following a crisis. It should tell them what signs suggest the need for a crisis intervention. Staff in-service both during and before a crisis event is important in this regard. School newsletter articles both before and during a crisis event serves a similar purpose for parents. Finally, the media can be very helpful, quickly and efficiently alerting parents and the community to signs, symptoms, and reactions suggesting the need for counseling and where such assistance can be obtained. Chapter 9 provides more detail on how the media can be used as an effective resource in times of crisis.

Because of the need for a referral mechanism to educate care providers, it is recommended that an informational handout be given to all staff members. For example, the handout in Appendix E, Assessing Student Need for Psychological First Aid Following a Crisis, could be attached to each packet of Crisis Intervention Referral Forms. This handout can also be modified for use with parents. Similarly, it is appropriate to provide parents, teachers, and the media with Frederick's (1985) list of signs that suggest the need for intervention. These signs are as follows:

1. Sleep disturbances that continue for more than several days, wherein actual dreams of the trauma may or may not appear
2. Separation anxiety or clinging behavior, such as a reluctance to return to school
3. Phobias about the distressing stimuli (e.g., a school building, TV scene, or person) that remind the victim of the traumatic event
4. Conduct disturbances, including problems that occur at home or at school, which serve as responses to anxiety and frustration
5. Doubts about the self, including comments about body confusion, self-worth, and desire for withdrawal (pp. 87–88)

The establishment of student self-referral procedures is an important action. This procedure is relatively straightforward. All students need to be informed about the availability of crisis intervention assistance. Especially following crises affecting large numbers of students, it is possible that crisis team members, teachers, and parents may misread signs suggesting the need for crisis intervention. Thus, students need to know where to go for assistance on their own. This information can be disseminated in a variety of ways. Intercom announcements, school assemblies, and teacher-led discussions are all options. A member of the school crisis intervention team might meet with each of the affected classrooms and present such information personally.

ITEM 6. MASS SCREENING

The final secondary risk screening procedure is to conduct a mass screening of the entire population judged to have been affected by the crisis event. Mass screening may be an especially important procedure following crises that affect large numbers of students. During these situations, it is unlikely that the initial risk screening will be able to identify all individuals significantly affected by the crisis. The Classroom Crisis Intervention procedure, to be discussed in Chapter 8, might serve as such a screening tool to help identify students who are in need of further assistance (Allen et al., 1999).

In his discussion of mass screening, Klingman (1988) points out that this triage procedure is conducted primarily by ". . . observation of signs of behavior maladaption, child paper-and-pencil products (e.g., free writing, drawing), anxiety scales administered to children, and the identification of absentees" (pp. 210–211). Milgram et al. (1988), for example, used a "posttraumatic stress reaction scale" to screen 675 seventh-graders one week following a schoolbus disaster. The Impact Event Scale (Zilberg, Weiss, & Horowitz, 1982) provided in Figure 7.7 offers an example of a scale that could be used during a mass screening.

A commercially available measure developed by Briere (1996), purported to be useful for the group screening of psychological trauma victims is the *Trauma Symptom Checklist for Children*™ (TSC-C). Developed for children ages 7 to 17, the *TSC-C* is a 54-item, self-report measure of psychological distress. For a further discussion of potential mass screening measures the reader is referred to Carlson's (1997) text *Trauma Assessments: A Clinician's Guide*. This book provides a very useful review of measures of trauma and trauma responses for children (pp. 241–262). Finally, group crisis intervention procedures, such as Classroom Crisis Intervention (discussed in Chapter 8), may also prove to be an effective mass screening tool.

PSYCHOTHERAPEUTIC TREATMENT SCREENING

The final group of psychological triage procedures, psychotherapeutic treatment screening, is conducted at the conclusion of the psychological first aid interventions. The goal of these procedures is to identify those individuals who may require additional crisis intervention. While for

Impact of Event Scale

On _____ you experienced _____
    (Date)   (Event)

Below is a list of comments made by people after stressful events. Please check each item, indicating how frequently these comments were true for you DURING THE PAST SEVEN DAYS. If they did not occur during that time, please mark the "not at all" column.

	Not at all	Rarely	Some-times	Often
1. I thought it when I didn't mean to.				
2. I avoided letting myself get upset when I thought about it or was reminded of it.				
3. I tried to remove it from memory.				
4. I had trouble falling asleep or staying asleep.				
5. I had waves of strong feelings about it.				
6. I had dreams about it.				
7. I stayed away from reminders of it.				
8. I felt as if it hadn't happened or it wasn't real.				
9. I tried not to talk about it.				
10. Pictures about it popped into my mind.				

(continued)

Figure 7.7 The Impact of Event Scale is useful when conducting a mass screening of large numbers of potential psychological trauma victims. *Source:* From Zilberg, Weiss, and Horowitz (1982, p. 409). Copyright (1982) by the American Psychological Association. Reprinted by permission.

	Not at all	Rarely	Some-times	Often
11. Other things kept making me think about it.				
12. I was aware that I still had a lot of feelings about it, but I didn't deal with them.				
13. I tried not to think about it.				
14. Any reminder brought back feelings about it.				
15. My feelings about it were kind of numb.				

Figure 7.7   *(Continued)*

many psychological trauma victims the initial psychological first aid response will be sufficient, others will find this intervention only a first step. These final classifications require data provided by the secondary risk screening procedures (i.e., Secondary Screening of Risk: Interview Outline, crisis intervention referrals, and mass screenings).

ITEM 7. OBTAIN PERMISSION FROM PARENT(S) OR GUARDIAN(S) FOR CRISIS INTERVENORS TO SPEAK WITH IDENTIFIED STUDENTS

It is always preferable to obtain parental consent for crisis intervenors to meet with students identified as being at risk. To facilitate this process, it is a good idea to have a number of crisis intervention permission slips available and to have them in whatever languages are spoken by the families at a school (Figure 7.8a and 7.8b). Parent conferences can also be helpful. At these conferences, it is important to discuss the crisis, the individual child's reactions to it, and the crisis intervenor's concerns. This contact is especially important given that the school's initial interventions may evolve into a psychotherapeutic treatment referral involving an outside agency. The student's family is more likely to be cooperative and agreeable to such referrals if they have been involved in the crisis intervention process at as early a stage as possible.

Because of the sudden and unexpected nature of situational crises, it is recognized that it is not always possible to contact a student's family right

Crisis Response Team

Crisis Intervention Permission Slip

I give permission for my child to meet with the school psychologist, school counselor or other member of the Crisis Intervention Team. I understand that they will meet and speak with my child in order to help my child with his/her feelings and reactions to tragic events.

Pupil's Name	Home Room

Signature of Parent or Guardian	Grade	Date

Figure 7.8a   The Crisis Intervention Permission Slip can be used to help document parental contacts following a crisis event. It is recommended that this form be used with those students who are seen for more than one crisis intervention session. It is especially important to obtain parental consent if it is suspected that a crisis therapy referral may need to be made.

away. Furthermore, some students will need to be seen immediately and in a crisis this is an appropriate course of action. However, if at all possible obtaining parental consent is the best practice.

ITEM 8. CONTINUE PSYCHOLOGICAL FIRST AID INTERVENTIONS

Continue to provide direct intervention to students based on the teacher, parent, and student self-referrals; the initial intervention sessions; and mass screenings. Also continue to use the Psychological Triage Summary

Equipo De Apoyo Respuesta en la Crisis

Permiso para ayudar/intervencir en la crisis

Doy permiso para que mi hijo/hija se reuna con el psicólogo de la escuela, el consejero de la escuela u otro miembro del equipo de ayuda en crisis. Entiendo que satisfarán y hablarán con mi niño para ayudar a mi niño con sus/sus sensaciones y reacciones a los acontecimientos trágicos.

Nombre del Alumno	Salon

Firma del Padre/Guarda	Grado	Fecha

Figure 7.8b   The Crisis Intervention Permission Slip in Spanish.

(Figure 7.3) and Secondary Screening of Risk (Figure 7.4) to document interventions and to assist in the process of making additional referral decisions.

ITEM 9. IDENTIFY INDIVIDUALS WHO NEED PSYCHOTHERAPEUTIC TREATMENT REFERRALS

The final psychological triage task involves identifying the individuals most severely affected by the crisis event. These are individuals, who even with psychological first aid assistance, appear to be unable to cope with the crisis event. They require professional counseling intervention. As psychotherapeutic treatment screening identifies individuals in need, this should also be noted on the Psychological Triage Summary (using the risk category code of "CT" for crisis therapy).

SUMMARY

The purpose of triage for victims of situational crises is to prioritize crisis interventions. Its goal is to provide crisis intervention services to those most in need of assistance as soon as possible. Use of triage procedures is especially important when large numbers of students are affected by a significant trauma. Under these circumstances, triage procedures help to answer the critical question of who should be provided help first. An effective triage procedure, however, is next to useless without clearly laid out referral options. Thus, it is important to identify these resources well before a crisis event.

As was mentioned at the beginning of this chapter, the triage process is dynamic and each crisis presents a unique series of challenges. As a result each triage is a learning experience; an experience, which if carefully analyzed, can help improve responses to future crisis events. Therefore, it is suggested that at the conclusion of each crisis intervention, a Detailed Crisis Incident Summary (Guidelines provided in Chapter 6, Tables 6.5) be written by the crisis intervention coordinator. This Summary would include an evaluation of triage procedures as well as an evaluation of the overall effectiveness of the crisis intervention. Such a document gives the coordinator a chance to reflect upon his or her experiences, to learn from mistakes, to make appropriate crisis plan modifications, and to determine what procedures are most valuable. When shared with school and support staffs this document can also help to improve the entire system's crisis response readiness. Evaluation of the crisis response is discussed further in Chapter 13.

CHAPTER 8

Crisis Intervention

It was a crisp, clear January afternoon as I walked across the playground, which two days earlier had witnessed one of the most violent incidents ever to occur on school grounds. I remembered thinking how difficult it was to comprehend that almost three dozen children and one teacher had been shot. "If I'm having difficulty coming to terms with this," I said to myself, "what are the children going through?" The afternoon recess bell had rung, and the primary grade children began to move onto the playground. On my way to the teacher's room, for a much-needed break, I noticed a lone second-grade girl standing in a corner just out of view of the playground. She was crying. I approached her, and after giving my name, learned her name was Lisa. I said: "You look sad. Can you tell me what's wrong?" Lisa told me that since the shooting she was scared to return to the playground. I told her I understood and placed a reassuring arm around her shoulder. I asked her to share with me her experiences during the shooting, and through her tears she did. When Lisa had finished, I said: "That was really scary. You know you're not alone. A lot of kids feel the same way you do." I then asked if she liked the playground before the shooting. She confirmed that it had been a happy place for her. With a little encouragement, I was able to get Lisa to move toward the playground and asked her to tell me what she saw. Lisa's response was brief. Softly she replied, "Kids are playing." I pointed out that there were police officers on the playground and reassured her that she was not in any danger. I asked her if she would like to try playing again. As we talked, Lisa told me that several of her friends were on the playground. After several minutes more of sharing, Lisa agreed that if her friends would

161

come and get her, and I would watch, she might like to try playing. Lisa had already pointed out several of her friends who, when asked, readily included her in their tetherball game. After recess, I reported this psychological first aid intervention to the crisis intervention coordinator. The information would be helpful in making a decision about Lisa's need for a mental health referral. For the next two days I looked for Lisa during each recess and made certain she knew I was watching. After the second day, I asked her if she still needed me on the playground and she said, "Not any more."

—Compilation of several playground conversations
following the Stockton schoolyard shooting (January 1989)

I N CHAPTERS 5 and 6, it was suggested that the crisis intervention coordinator should be the crisis response team member responsible for facilitating the identification of students and staff members in need of crisis intervention services and for developing the resources for meeting these needs. Chapter 7 provided strategies for identifying psychological trauma victims. This chapter reviews crisis intervention strategies for use with psychological trauma victims. It begins with a discussion of why crisis intervention is needed and reviews some general crisis intervention principles. Next, specific individual and group crisis psychological first aid strategies are reviewed. The chapter emphasizes discussion of these approaches because they are techniques provided in the school environment by school professionals.

As mentioned in Chapter 7, there is a difference between first- and second-order crisis intervention (Slaikeu, 1990). The former are psychological first aid strategies. They are the immediate response to the person-in-crisis, usually provided at the scene of the crisis event, by natural caregivers. For many psychological trauma victims, this initial response is sufficient. For others, however, psychological first aid will be only the first step in a longer, more involved professional mental health crisis intervention. The term *psychotherapeutic treatments* has been used to identify these professional mental health interventions. As this volume is designed for educators, not mental health professionals, discussion of these treatments will be brief and will provide only an awareness of the work mental health professionals do with psychological trauma victims. It should help to clarify where school-based interventions stop and professional mental health treatment begins.

THE NEED FOR CRISIS INTERVENTION

As mentioned earlier, situational crises are events that significantly alter the life circumstance of their victims. These are events that result in the loss of something valued or previously taken for granted. For example, a crisis might result in the loss of a loved one (due to accident, murder, or suicide), the loss of a home (following a natural disaster), or, as happened for Lisa, the loss of a feeling of safety on the playground (following a schoolyard shooting).

It is important to acknowledge that no matter what an individual does following a crisis it is typically difficult, if not impossible, to replace the losses incurred. Old coping strategies, such as seeking support from an adult, may no longer appear effective. For example, one would imagine that previously when Lisa ran into difficulty on the playground, such as a fight with a peer, she was able to cope with it independently or by asking a teacher for help. Following the schoolyard shooting, however, these old coping strategies would no longer be perceived as effective. Clearly, Lisa found it difficult to respond to being shot at on her own. Additionally, after having seen a teacher shot and wounded, the use of a teacher as a problem-solving resource was no longer perceived as powerful as it once was. As was mentioned in Chapter 2, the failure of previously established coping mechanisms to manage a problem situation is a defining characteristic of the crisis state. This failure, and the distress that accompany it, manifests itself as any one of a number of crisis reactions. Table 8.1, for example, provides a developmental list of disaster victim behavior symptoms and possible treatment options for these symptoms.

Following crises, victims are typically unable to return their life to the status quo. An unalterable change has occurred. Thus, there are really only two post-crisis options. Either grow, by developing new coping strategies and integrating the experience into your life, or allow the crisis to become overwhelming and all-consuming. In the latter case, instead of growing, the individual regresses to the point that daily functioning becomes worse than it was before the crisis. For Lisa, she will never again feel as safe on the playground as she did before the shooting. This leaves only two possible outcomes. Either fear of the playground and being shot can be allowed to overwhelm her (in which case Lisa may, for example, become school phobic), or she can develop new coping strategies for dealing with scary situations. In the former case, she gets worse and regresses, while in the latter case she gets better and grows.

Table 8.1

Summary of Behavior Symptoms Seen and Treatment Options Used Following a Disaster

| Ages | Behavior Symptoms | | | Possible Treatment Options |
	Regressive	Body	Emotions	
1–5	Resumption of bedwetting, thumb sucking, fear of darkness	Loss of appetite Indigestion Vomiting Bowel or bladder problems (e.g., diarrhea, constipation, loss of sphincter)	Nervousness Irritability Disobedience Tics (muscle spasms) Speech difficulties (e.g., appearance of stammering) Refusal to leave proximity of parents	Give additional verbal assurance and ample physical comfort (e.g., holding and caressing) Give warm milk and comforting bedtime routines Permit child to sleep in parents' room temporarily if necessary Provide opportunity and encouragement for expression of emotions through play activities (e.g., finger painting, clay modeling, physical reenactment of disaster)
5–11	Increased competition with younger siblings of parents' attention	Headaches Complaints of visual or hearing problems Persistent itching and scratching Sleep disorders	School phobia Withdrawal from play group and friends Withdrawal from family contacts Unusual social behavior (e.g., fighting with close friends or siblings)	Give attention and consideration Temporarily lessen requirements for optimum performance in school and home activities Encourage verbal expression of thoughts and feelings about the disaster

Age	Behavior	Physical symptoms	Intervention
	Loss of interest in previously preferred activities		Provide opportunity for structured but not demanding chores and responsibilities at home
	Inability to concentrate and drop in level of school achievement		Rehearse safety measures to be taken in future disasters
11–14	Competing with younger siblings of parental attention	Headaches	Give attention and consideration
	Failure to carry out chores previously completed	Complaints of vague aches and pains	Temporarily lower expectations of performance at school and home
	School phobia	Loss of appetite	Encourage verbal expression of feelings
	Reappearance of earlier speech and behavior habits	Bowel problems	Provide structure but undemanding responsibilities and rehabilitation activities
	Loss of interest in peer social activities	Sudden appearance of skin disorders	Encourage and assist child to become involved with same-age group activities
	Loss of interest in hobbies and recreations	Sleep disorders	Rehearse safety measures for future disasters
	Increased difficulty in relating with siblings and parents		
	Sharp increase in resisting parental or school authority		

(continued)

Table 8.1 *(Continued)*

Ages	Behavior Symptoms			Possible Treatment Options
	Regressive	Body	Emotions	
14–18	Resumption of earlier behaviors and attitudes	Bowel and bladder complaints	Marked increase or decline in physical activity level	Encourage discussion of disaster experiences with peers and extrafamily significant others
	Decline in previous responsible behavior	Headaches	Frequent expression of feelings of inadequacy	If adolescent chooses to discuss disaster fears within family setting such expression is to be encouraged but not insisted upon
	Decline in emancipatory struggles over parental control	Skin rash	Increased difficulties in concentration on planned activities	
	Decline in sexual interests	Sleep disorders		Reduce expectations for level of school and general performance temporarily
		Disorders of digestion		Provide opportunity for involvement in rehabilitation planning and participation to fullest extent possible
				Encourage and assist in becoming fully involved in peer social activities
				Rehearse safety measures for future disasters

Source: Institute for the Study of Destructive Behaviors and the Los Angeles Suicide Prevention Center. (1978, pp. 28–30)

This dual nature of crisis outcomes is illustrated in the Chinese symbol for the word crisis (*weiji*). This symbol is composed of two figures standing for danger and opportunity at the same time (Slaikeu, 1990; Wilhelm, 1967). Similarly, the English definition of crisis (which is based on the Greek word *Krinein* meaning to decide), refers to the turning point at which time things will either get better or worse (Lidell & Scott, 1968; Slaikeu, 1990; *Webster's New Collegiate Dictionary*, 1976). The psychological danger of a crisis event is that it can seriously interfere with the ability to function and enjoy life. The psychological opportunity of crisis is that it can foster new coping strategies that result in a more resilient individual. It is from this perspective that the need for crisis intervention becomes clear. Its purposes include avoiding danger, and realizing opportunity.

PRACTICAL PRINCIPLES OF CRISIS INTERVENTION

According to Slaikeu (1990), there are several principles that guide most crisis intervenors as they help people in crisis. Crisis intervention is generally viewed as a short-term, time-limited procedure (less than six weeks) where the goal is to assist the individual to regain a precrisis level of functioning. Helper behavior during a crisis intervention is active, directive, and goal-oriented, while at the same time encouraging crisis victims to do as much as possible for themselves. Sandoval's (1988a) summary of generic crisis intervention principles includes the following: (1) facilitate the reestablishment of a social support network, (2) engage in focused problem solving, (3) focus on self-concept, and (4) encourage self-reliance.

FIRST AID FOR PSYCHOLOGICAL TRAUMA

Psychological first aid is the response given by any caregiver who discovers an individual in psychological distress. It is administered at the time and place where the need for it arises.* The typical psychological first aid response lasts from several minutes to several hours, and is a basic problem-solving strategy with a primary goal of reestablishing immediate coping (Slaikeu, 1990). An analogy can be made between a deer frozen in the headlights of an oncoming car and a psychological crisis victim. The crisis-generated problem(s) may appear so overwhelming,

---

*While an immediate crisis intervention response is important, a crisis intervenor should keep in mind that if the crisis event involved a criminal act, law enforcement will need to interview victims, witnesses, or both. Crisis intervention should not be provided until after these interviews take place.

that the person-in-crisis is immobilized. The crisis intervenor's task is to assist the individual to move away from danger and toward adaptive coping with the crisis problems. Subgoals of psychological first aid include providing support, reducing lethality, and linking the individual to other resources.

As with medical first aid, if the injury is not severe, psychological first aid will be sufficient. However, if traumatization is severe, psychological first aid is only the first step in a crisis intervention. In such a circumstance, the goal of first aid is not to cure the underlying problem, but rather to keep victims out of danger long enough to get them to a mental health professional. The reestablishment of immediate coping helps to stop the psychological bleeding that, if not checked, could result in significant harm. As with medical first aid, if a trained clinician is available it would be most appropriate for this person to provide psychological first aid. However, there is no guarantee that a doctor or psychologist will be available when someone enters a medical or psychological crisis. Thus, just as today's educators are provided with cardiopulmonary resuscitation (CPR) training, it is appropriate also to provide them with psychological first aid training.

Psychological first aid response includes the following five steps: (1) making psychological contact, (2) examining dimensions of the problem, (3) exploring possible solutions, (4) assisting in taking concrete action, and (5) following up to check progress (Slaikeu, 1990). The mnemonic "MEETU" (read as "meet you") helps remember each of these steps (Figure 8.1). View psychological first aid as a process where

Mnemonic Device for Psychological First Aid

M	ake psychological contact
E	xplore dimensions of the problem
E	xamine possible solutions
Assist in | T | aking concrete action |
Follow- | U | p

Figure 8.1 A Mnemonic device to remember the steps involved in psychological first aid. *Note:* The word "MEETU" is to be read as "meet you" and refers to the situation where a crisis intervenor says to a crisis victim: "I'm going to MEETU to provide assistance."

a crisis intervenor says to a crisis victim: "I am going to 'MEETU' to provide assistance."

Although psychological first aid procedures are presented in a sequential order, in practice these components can be ordered and combined in many different ways. The five components, corresponding helper behaviors, and their objectives as summarized by Slaikeu (1990) are presented in Table 8.2. A sample intervention dialogue is provided in Table 8.3.

MAKING PSYCHOLOGICAL CONTACT

Making psychological contact with an individual in crisis is not necessarily a difficult task. Individuals in crisis are usually very open to connecting with someone who presents as being willing and able to help. During this phase of psychological first aid, it is critical to listen carefully, reflect both feelings and facts and, perhaps most importantly, communicate acceptance. Conversely, it is important for the crisis intervenor to avoid telling his or her own story (at least at this phase of first aid), ignore either facts or feelings, or be judgmental (Slaikeu, 1990). Key to the success of making psychological contact is what Carkhuff (1993) refers to as *responding skills*. Specifically, empathy, respect, and warmth are the vehicles that bring one into psychological contact with the person-in-crisis.

EMPATHY

This responding skill involves listening to what the individual is saying (the content or the facts) and then trying to identify the feelings associated with this information. The crisis intervenor should try to generate words that convey to the person-in-crisis an understanding of both experiences and feelings. These important active listen skills are often identified as paraphrasing, summarizing, and perception-checking. Through the use of these skills, the person-in-crisis will be made to feel less alone (Klingman, 1986). Some educators may find the use of listening skills initially awkward. With practice, however, they will become second nature. Empathy is *not* synonymous with sympathy. While empathy refers to understanding, sympathy refers to feeling. A crisis intervenor does not (and probably should not) need to feel what the person-in-crisis is feeling to be effective (Gazda et al., 1995).

RESPECT

This responding skill involves demonstrating faith in the individual's ability to overcome the crisis problem(s). Respect is communicated by

Table 8.2

Components of Psychological First Aid

Component	Helper Behavior	Objective
Make psychological contact	Invite student to talk Listen for facts and feelings Summarize/reflect facts/feelings Make empathic statements Communicate concern Physically touch/hold Bring "calm control" to an intense situation	Student feels heard, understood, accepted, supported Intensity of emotional distress reduced Problem-solving capabilities reactivated

Explore dimension of the problem	Inquire about:
	  Immediate past
	    Precipitating event
	    Precrisis functioning
	  Present functioning
	    Personal resources
	    Social resources
	    Lethality
	  Immediate future
	    Impending decisions (tonight, weekend, next several days/weeks)
		Rank order: (a) immediate needs; (b) later needs

Examine possible solutions	Ask what student has attempted so far Explore what student can do now Propose other alternatives: new student behavior, redefinition of the problem, outside (3rd party) assistance, environmental change	Identify one or more solutions to immediate needs and later needs
Assist in taking concrete action	See below	Implement immediate solutions intended to meet immediate needs

- If (a) lethality is low, and (b) student is capable of action on own behalf, then take a *facilitative stance* (i.e., we talk, you act). Contract for action is between helper and student.
- Ranges from active listening to giving advice.

- If (a) lethality is high or (b) student is not capable of acting on own behalf, then take a *directive stance* (i.e., we talk, I may act on your behalf). Contract for action might include family and other community resources.
- Ranges from actively mobilizing resources to controlling the situation.

Table 8.2 *(Continued)*

Component	Helper Behavior	Objective
Follow-up	Secure identifying information Explore possible follow-up procedures Set up contract for recontact	Secure feedback of subgoals of psychological first aid: (1) support received, (2) lethality reduced, (3) linkage to resources accomplished. Set next phase in motion. Implement later solutions. If (a) immediate needs were met by immediate solutions and concrete action taken, and if (b) linkage for later needs is made, then STOP. If not go back to Step 2 (Dimensions of Problem) and continue

Source: Adapted from Karl Slaikeu, *Crisis intervention: A handbook for practice and research* (2nd ed., pp. 108–109). Copyright © 1990 by Allyn and Bacon. Adapted by permission.

Table 8.3
A Sample Psychological First Aid Dialogue

The following dialogue expands on the psychological first aid scenario presented at the beginning of this chapter. As may be recalled, it begins with a second-grade girl, Lisa, crying in a corner of a schoolyard, just out of view of the playground. Two days earlier, Lisa had witnessed a schoolyard shooting.

Making Psychological Contact

Counselor: Hi. I'm Mr. Brock. What's your name?
Lisa: Lisa.
Counselor: Hello Lisa. You look sad, can you tell me what's wrong?
Lisa: (Through her tears Lisa says:) I'm scared.
Counselor: I think I know why, but could you tell me why you're scared?
Lisa: I'm afraid of being shot.
Counselor: It is frightening to be shot at. (The counselor places his arm around Lisa's shoulder.) I understand why you are crying. Would it be okay if we talked? I would like to help.
Lisa: (Lisa stops crying and looks at the counselor.) Okay.

(continued)

Table 8.3 *(Continued)*

Exploring Dimensions of the Problem

Counselor: Do you think you could tell me about what happened to you the other day?

Lisa: Yes. I was standing right over there (Lisa looks around the corner and points to the tetherball circle). I was waiting my turn when the shooting started. At first I didn't know what was happening. Then I saw all the kids screaming and falling to the ground. My friend Suzie was bleeding from her foot. (Lisa begins to cry again.)

Counselor: That was real scary. You know you're not alone. A lot of kids feel the same way you do. It's even hard for me to understand. Before now, have you told any one about being afraid to go out to play?

Lisa: No.

Counselor: Are their people who you can talk to?

Lisa: Yes. I would like to talk to Suzie.

Counselor: Is there anyone else who might be able to help you not be scared of the playground?

Lisa: My mom, my teacher, my other friends—(pause)—and you? (Lisa looks up at the counselor as her tears subside again.)

Counselor: Yes, I think I can help. Before the shooting what was the playground like for you?

Lisa: Fun. I was the tetherball champ. My friends and I would always play right there (Lisa again pokes her head around the corner and points to the tetherball circle.)

Counselor: Where are your friends now?

Lisa: Right there. (Lisa points to a group of five girls playing at the tetherball circle.) Except Suzie. She's at home. Her foot was bleeding. I miss her. She's my best friend. Can I talk to her?

Examining Possible Solutions

Counselor: We can look into talking to Suzie after recess. But for now what can we do about your recess time. What have you done so far about being scared to go out and play.

Lisa: I've hid here or in the restroom. Once I stayed in class with my teacher.

Counselor: Look out on the playground and tell me what you see.

Lisa: (Lisa pokes her head around the corner and looks at the playground.) Kids are playing.

Counselor: Are they having fun?

Lisa: Yes. (A tentative smile briefly flashes across Lisa's face.)

Counselor: Who are those people over there and there? (The counselor points in the direction of the two police officers that have been temporarily assigned to the school after the shooting.)

Table 8.3 *(Continued)*

Lisa:	Policemen.
Counselor:	I think that it is safe to go out on the playground today. And your friends look like they can still have fun playing tetherball. Do you think that anyone will hurt you on the playground today?
Lisa:	No.

Assisting in Taking Concrete Action

Counselor:	So if it's safe and still fun, why not try going out and playing again.
Lisa:	But I'm still scared. (Lisa's eyes become teary.)
Counselor:	Okay. Let's see what we can do to help you not be scared. What if your friends helped you go out and play? What if I stayed on the playground and watched you?
Lisa:	That might help. (Lisa's tears subside.)
Counselor:	I'll go talk to your friends and see what I can do about getting them to include you in their tetherball game. (The counselor approaches Lisa's friends and explains her problem to them. They readily agree to come over to Lisa and invite her to play.)
Friend:	Lisa, tetherball is still fun. Will you please come and play with us?
Lisa:	Okay. (Lisa's friend takes Lisa by the hand and begins to walk toward the playground.)

Following-Up

Counselor:	Before you go Lisa, can you give me your last name and your classroom. I'd like to be able to check up on you to make sure you are okay.
Lisa:	Sure. My last name is Smith, and I'm in Mrs. James classroom.
Counselor:	I'll be standing right over there Lisa. (The counselor points to an area just off the playground within view of the tetherball circle.) I'll be there during all your recesses for the next few days. When the bell rings in a few minutes come over and see me and we can look into how Suzie is doing.
Lisa:	Okay. (Lisa has stopped crying and a smile comes across her face as she walks with her friends out onto the playground.)

Source: Compilation of several playground conversations following the Stockton schoolyard shooting in January, 1989.

pausing to listen, offering to talk, indicating a willingness to enter into a relationship, and allowing the individual the space (when appropriate) to solve problems for themselves. On the other hand, it avoids being perceived as trying to smooth things over, offering lectures or explanations, being judgmental or dominating the conversation (Gazda et al., 1995).

WARMTH

This responding is demonstrated primarily by the crisis intervenor's body language (e.g., gestures, posture, tone of voice, touch, facial expression). By itself, warmth is not sufficient to establish psychological contact. However, it is a necessary element. Congruence between verbal and nonverbal messages is critical. Physical touch can be a very helpful tool for demonstrating warmth. For the person-in-crisis, it can have a calming effect. However, it is important to be aware of the level of trust and familiarity before using this tool. If the crisis event in some way involved physical touch (e.g., sexual abuse) it should be used cautiously (Gazda et al., 1995). Table 8.4 summarizes important variables in making psychological contact.

The crisis intervention with Lisa, described at the beginning of the chapter and presented in Table 8.3, illustrates many of the psychological first aid components. As the intervention began, the intervenor's first step was to make psychological contact with Lisa. After exchanging names, the intervenor invited Lisa to talk, reflected the obvious distress of this frightened little girl, and attempted to communicate his concern.

Table 8.4
Making Psychological Contact

Empathy
Understanding facts and feelings

Respect
Pausing to listen
    Not trying to smooth things over
    Not dominating the conversation

Warmth
Nonverbal communication
    Congruent with verbal communication
Touch
    Used carefully

Empathetic statements were made (i.e., "It is frightening to be shot at. I understand why you are crying."). Physical contact or warmth, in the form of a reassuring arm around her shoulder, was made and Lisa was assured that she was not alone. Further guidance on making psychological contact is offered in Table 8.5.

EXPLORE DIMENSIONS OF THE PROBLEM

The next component of psychological first aid involves assessing the dimensions of the crisis problem(s) (Table 8.6). In conducting this phase of the intervention, it is important to ask direct questions designed to assess the immediate past (crisis precursors), the present (the crisis story), and the immediate future (the crisis problem or problems). The main objective is to identify the apparently unsolvable problem(s). While it is important to ask direct questions during this phase, it is also recommended

Table 8.5
Recommendations for Establishing Rapport with Disaster Victims

Rapport means:

- Constantly checking with each other to make sure that each understands what the other is saying;
- Having genuine respect and regard for the other;
- Providing the client with a feeling that you are an informed authority, experienced and aware;
- Being nonjudgmental and accepting of another even if he is "different" or has different attitudes and feelings;
- Establishing trust by promising only what you can do, not what you would like to do or what he would want you to do that is not possible;
- Listening to an account of the disaster that may have been repeated many times, while the process of "working through" the feeling occurs; and
- Understanding that, many times, what is actually said may be a cover for vastly different feelings. Listening and being willing to understand allows getting beyond the initial surface words and lets the feelings come out; learning to discern between requests for immediate aid and the need to talk about feelings.

Source: From "Training Manual for Human Service Workers in Major Disasters," by Institute for the Study of Destructive Behaviors and Los Angeles Suicide Prevention Center, 1978, p. 16. Rockville: MD: National Institute of Mental Health.

Table 8.6
Exploring Dimensions of the Problem

Direct Inquiry About:

- *Immediate past (crisis precursors)*
- *Present (the crisis story)*
- *Immediate future (crisis problems)*

Main Objective: *Identify the apparently unsolvable problem(s)*

that relying solely on yes/no questions be avoided (Slaikeu, 1990). The telling of the crisis story in very concrete terms often yields an emotional release for which the crisis intervenor must be prepared. In addition, it may result in the psychological trauma victim gaining a greater understanding of what needs to be done to cope.

Questions regarding the immediate past should be designed to further clarify the event(s) that led up to the crisis as well as to explore pre-crisis level of functioning. If it is found that prior to the crisis event the individual in crisis demonstrated good coping skills, there would be reason to be optimistic. On the other hand, if the individual had coping difficulties before the crisis, there is reason for increased concern. Assessment of present functioning should involve clarification of the crisis story. In addition, it is important to listen for and ask about personal and social resources. The presence of such resources will be critical when it comes to developing a plan for dealing with the crisis problem(s). Also, if there are any indications of suicidal or homicidal thinking, it will be important to ask direct questions designed to assess such lethality. Finally, assessment of the immediate future will document those apparently unsolvable problems that have been generated by the crisis event and resulted in entry to the crisis state.

In the intervention with Lisa note that the crisis intervenor asks about her precrisis playground experiences. From this he learned that Lisa was a child who had many friends and who previously found the playground to be a happy place. Assessment of the present situation involved having Lisa tell her crisis story. Through this story it was learned that not only was Lisa fearful of being shot, but that her friend had been wounded. Finally, inquiry regarding Lisa's immediate future could have focused on what difficulties will arise for her if she continued to be afraid to go onto the playground.

Slaikeu (1990) points out that the main objective of this stage "... is to work toward a rank ordering of the person's needs within two categories:

(1) issues which need to be addressed immediately, and (2) issues which can be postponed until later" (p. 111). In Lisa's case, the immediate issue was what she was going to do during her recess time. She could not be permitted to stand in a corner alone outside the view of supervising adults during recess. Either she would need to move onto the playground or other recess arrangements would have to be made. Later needs such as Lisa's desire to speak to her wounded friend or her potential need for individual psychotherapeutic treatment were addressed after recess by contacting the crisis intervention coordinator.

EXAMINING POSSIBLE SOLUTIONS

The third component of psychological first aid involves identifying potential solutions for the problem(s) generated by the crisis (Slaikeu, 1990). It involves asking the person-in-crisis about coping attempts already made, facilitating exploration of additional coping strategies, and, if necessary, proposing other coping alternatives. The primary goal here is to identify solutions for the immediate and later needs that were just identified (Table 8.7).

In Lisa's case, examining possible solutions involved discussion of how to spend her recess time. This component also involved examining the pros and cons of the identified solutions. For example, it might be discussed that the pros of playing on the playground include that it can be fun and that her friends are already out there. Additionally, mentioning that police officers were on the playground further reassured Lisa that this was a safe option. For Lisa, these pros outweighed the con that it was now somewhat scary to be on the playground during recess.

In identifying possible solutions, it is essential to keep the crisis victim as involved in the process as is possible (Klingman, 1986; Slaikeu, 1990). To the extent that victims are able to generate their own solutions to the crisis-caused problems, they should be allowed to do so. This will result in the crisis victim obtaining a greater sense of control over the traumatic circumstances.

Table 8.7
Examining Possible Solutions

---
1. Ask about coping attempts already made.
2. Facilitate exploration of additional coping strategies.
3. Propose other problem-solving options.

Taking Concrete Action

The fourth step in psychological first aid requires the crisis intervenor to assist the person-in-crisis take concrete action to address the immediate needs identified (Slaikeu, 1990). If the identified needs do not involve lethality (e.g., injury, suicide, or homicide) and the individual is capable of acting independently, then the crisis intervenor would take a facilitative stance. This means the person-in-crisis would take responsibility for implementing problem solutions. On the other hand, if lethality is high or the individual is not able to act independently, then the crisis intervenor should take a directive stance. This means that the crisis intervenor will take primary responsibility for the implementation of problem solutions. These principles are summarized in Table 8.8.

For Lisa, taking concrete action meant coming to an agreement about going onto the playground. Note that although the crisis intervenor did agree to stay and watch Lisa on the playground, he did not go out on the playground with her. He allowed her to play with her friends on her own. However, if Lisa was not capable of acting on her own or if there was some danger of physical harm, the crisis intervenor would need to take a more directive stance. For example, if during a crisis intervention suicidal risk is identified, the crisis intervenor will need to take primary responsibility for the solutions to crisis problems (i.e., an immediate referral to a mental health professional).

Follow-Up

The final component of psychological first aid involves ensuring that a plan to follow up on the crisis victim be established (Slaikeu, 1990). This includes securing identifying information, specifying follow-up procedures,

Table 8.8
Taking Concrete Action

If lethality is low (i.e., little or no danger of injury, suicide, or homicide)
- *Facilitate* implementation of solutions to crisis problems.
- Person-in-crisis is primarily responsible for taking action.

If lethality is high (i.e., danger of injury, suicide, or homicide)
- *Direct* implementation of solutions to crisis problems.
- Crisis intervenor is primarily responsible for taking action.

and obtaining a contract for recontact. It will be important to ensure that the person-in-crisis feels supported, has had lethality reduced, and has been linked with other appropriate helping resources. If any of these objectives are not obtained, the crisis intervenor will need to return to assessment of problem dimensions to see if anything has been missed. (See Table 8.9).

In Lisa's intervention, follow-up involved obtaining her last name and her teacher's name. In addition, an agreement was made that the crisis intervenor would continue to be available during recess. The primary purpose of follow-up is to ensure that immediate needs (i.e., finding an appropriate recess activity) have been met and to ensure that progress has been made toward the meeting of later needs (i.e., making contact with her wounded friend or a psychotherapeutic treatment referral). If immediate needs have been met and appropriate linkages for meeting of later needs have been made (i.e., letting the crisis intervention coordinator know of her reaction to the playground), then the psychological first aid provider's responsibilities are ended. A summary of the psychological first aid process is provided in Figure 8.2.

PSYCHOLOGICAL FIRST AID AND SUICIDE

Crisis events significantly alter the life circumstances of crisis victims. Crises are events that can result in significant losses for crisis victims. Because these are losses that usually cannot be replaced and these are events over which crisis victims typically have little control, feelings of hopelessness and helplessness would not be surprising. The experience

Table 8.9
Follow-Up

Secure identifying information.
Specify follow-up procedures.
Set a contract for re-contact.
Assess attainment of goals.
Is support provided?
Is lethality reduced?
Are linkages to helping resources made?
Recycle the first aid process if necessary.

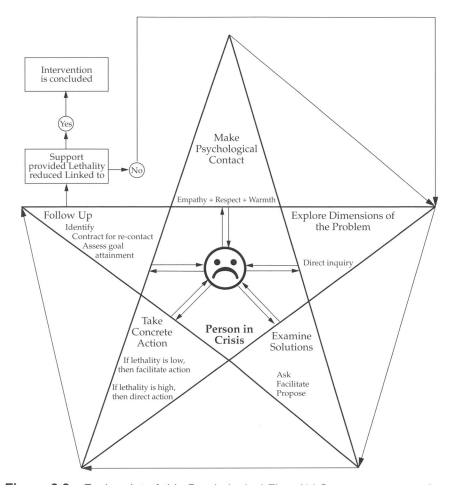

Figure 8.2 Each point of this Psychological First Aid Star represents a phase in the psychological first aid process. At the center of this star is a symbol for the person-in-crisis. The arrows represent crisis intervenor and the person-in-crisis actions. Arrows coming out from the face are person-in-crisis actions, while arrows going to the face are crisis intervenor actions. The process begins with the person-in-crisis sharing the crisis experience and the crisis intervenor using active listening to demonstrate empathy. Next, the crisis intervenor asks direct questions to clarify the dimensions of the crisis problem(s). Person-in-crisis answers to the questions will clarify what work needs to be done. The third step finds the crisis intervenor exploring possible solutions to crisis problems. Ideally the crisis intervenor facilitates the person-in-crisis' search for solutions. If necessary, however, a more direct approach is used wherein the crisis intervenor proposes possible solutions. The fourth step involves taking some concrete action to solve the crisis problem(s). Here again, ideally the crisis intervenor facilitates this action. If necessary, however, the crisis intervenor may become very directive. Finally, the crisis intervenor requests that the person-in-crisis provide information needed for follow-up. Also, note that arrows connect each point of the star. This illustrates the process followed during a psychological first aid intervention. When first aid subgoals are obtained, the process is concluded. However, if they are not obtained, then the intervention continues with further exploration of crisis problem(s).

of loss and feelings of helplessness or hopelessness are often associated with suicidal thinking (e.g., Asarnow, Carlson, & Guthrie, 1987; Beck, Steer, Kovacs, & Garrison, 1985; Fremouw, de Perczel, & Ellis, 1990; Garfinkel, Froese, & Hood, 1982; Kazdin, French, Unis, Esveldt-Dawson, & Sherick, 1983; Kazdin, Rodgers, & Colbus, 1986). Thus, if a crisis intervenor finds crisis events have generated losses perceived as significantly devaluing the victim's life, and there are corresponding feelings of helplessness and hopelessness, he or she should ask if the victim has suicidal thoughts (Ramsay et al., 1996). For example, the crisis intervenor might say: "Many times when people feel the way you do they think of suicide. Is this something that you have thought of?" It is important to note that the directness of such questioning is essential (J. Davis & Sandoval, 1991; Poland, 1989). It lets the person-in-crisis know that the crisis intervenor is truly open to talking about suicide. If, for example, the intervenor had asked, "You're not thinking of hurting yourself are you?" the individual might believe that suicide is not a topic that the crisis intervenor is comfortable discussing. This would make it more difficult for the person-in-crisis to express suicidal feelings (Ramsay et al., 1996). It is also important to note that such direct inquiry will not plant suicidal thoughts in an individual's mind (Bonner, 1987).

If, in response to direct questioning about suicide, the crisis victim indicates that there are no thoughts of suicide, the intervenor can continue the intervention and allow the victim to do as much for him- or herself as is possible (Slaikeu, 1990). If, on the other hand, there are thoughts of suicide, the intervenor will need to be relatively directive. An immediate referral to a mental health professional should be made and a suicide risk assessment conducted.

SUICIDAL BEHAVIOR

Thoughts of suicide are surprisingly frequent. For example, data from the *Youth Risk Behavior Survey* (Kann et al., 1997) found 20.5 percent of high school students sampled reported having seriously considered suicide. However, not all of these students go on to kill themselves. Although indications of suicidal thinking is in itself a reason for concern and indicates the need for assistance from a mental health professional, more information is needed to assess just how directive the crisis intervenor will need to be. Thus, a suicide risk assessment should be conducted. While this assessment is ideally conducted by a mental health professional, the possibility that such an individual may not be readily accessible needs to be acknowledged. Thus, the following discussion of essential suicide risk assessment elements is offered.

Based on the work of Litman, Wold, Farberow, and Brown (1974) and Lettieri (1974), Ramsay et al. (1996) suggest that suicidal behavior can be predicted by asking questions about a current plan, prior suicidal behavior, and available resources. Ramsay et al. recommends that these risk assessment components can be easily remembered by using the mnemonic "CPR." Whereas in medical first aid CPR refers to cardiopulmonary resuscitation, in psychological first aid it refers to **C**urrent plan, **P**rior behavior, and **R**esources.

In determining the presence of a *plan*, direct questions need to be asked regarding "how, how prepared, and how soon." For example, the intervenor will need to ask: "Have you thought about how you would kill yourself?" "Do you have access to the means of the suicide attempt (e.g., a gun)?" "Have you thought about when you will commit suicide?" The more detail provided by the crisis victim, the more severe is the suicide risk.

In determining if there has been *prior suicidal behavior,* direct questions need to be asked regarding the victim's personal history (Ramsay et al. 1996). This inquiry should include questions about whether anyone close to the person-in-crisis has modeled suicidal behavior as a solution to problems. For example, the intervenor will need to ask, "Have you ever tried to commit suicide before?" or "Has anyone close to you ever committed suicide before?" The greater the prior suicidal behavior, the more severe is the suicide risk. Ramsay et al. report the findings of several studies that have found the rate of completed suicide among individuals who had previously made suicide attempts to be 35 to 54 times greater than that found in the general population (Ettlinger, 1964; Paerregaard, 1975; Tanney & Motto, 1990; Udsen, 1966). "There is good evidence that siblings, offspring and 'survivors' of those who complete suicide, are themselves at increased risk of suicidal behaviors" (Ramsay et al., p. 159).

In determining if the person-in-crisis has *resources* that might be protective, direct questions need to be asked about the victim's reasons for living (Ramsay et al., 1996). For example, the crisis intervenor might ask: "Can you think of anyone or anything that might be able to keep you from committing suicide?" If the person-in-crisis subjectively views their situation as lacking these resources, the suicide risk will be more severe.

If the answer to any one of the three sets of CPR questions is positive for suicide risk, the crisis intervenor will need to become highly directive in conducting the crisis intervention. (See Tables 8.2 and 8.8.) If it has not already been accomplished, the intervenor should ensure that the person-in-crisis has been linked with the appropriate mental health professionals.

Until such a linkage is made, the crisis intervenor should not let the in-dividual be alone. If the answers to each of the three sets of CPR ques-tions yield information suggesting the absence of suicide risk, the chance that the person-in-crisis will act out suicidal thoughts is low. Nevertheless, the presence of these thoughts suggests the need for pro-fessional mental health intervention, but the urgency of such a referral would not be as high.

COMPLETED SUICIDE

Crisis intervention following a suicide is a topic that deserves special at-tention. Following this crisis, the intervenor not only strives to reestablish immediate coping, but also needs to minimize identification with and glorification of the suicide victim. Failure to achieve these goals creates the potential for a suicide cluster.

To avoid identification with the victim, Rouf and Harris (1988) suggest that the crisis intervenor point out how the survivors are different from the suicide victim. They state: "Don't say the death was unexplainable, for ex-ample, 'He had everything going for him'; say instead, 'There were serious things troubling him that we may never know about'" (p. 8). To avoid glo-rifying the act, Rouf and Harris also recommend that counselors should not "make the suicide itself seem exciting or the suicide victim admirable by only emphasizing his good qualities. Point out that suicide is a poor choice" (p. 8). When working with students following a suicide, it is impor-tant to help them to express their feelings about the suicide. Talk with the students about their feelings; let them know that it's normal to feel not only grief but also fear, anger, and confusion. In addition, provide opportu-nities for individual counseling for any student who appears to be having difficulties dealing with the suicide, especially youngsters who were close friends of the deceased. Davidson (1989) suggests that small group coun-seling sessions (as opposed to schoolwide assemblies) provide the appro-priate environment for addressing student needs and concerns. She indicates that during these sessions a supportive school staff can help stu-dents to understand the following important concepts:

1. Death is permanent, and the decedent will not gain satisfaction from any of the postmortem events.
2. Suicide can be portrayed as a permanent solution to temporary prob-lems for which help is available.
3. Many people have suicidal thoughts when a suicide has occurred in the community. Students should understand that having thoughts of

suicide does not mean that they are "crazy." Persistent and intrusive suicidal thoughts are a signal that something important is troubling the person and he or she should seek help. Teachers can provide information about available mental health resources.

4. The student who committed suicide can be portrayed as seriously disturbed and as someone who, sadly, had not found an avenue to effectively work on his or her problems. Students can be helped to disidentify with the decedent without abusing the victim's character. (p. 96)

CLASSROOM CRISIS INTERVENTION

According to Terr (1992), "When a community, a neighborhood, or a single group (such as a church or school) is hit by a sudden tragic event, relatively long and large group counseling sessions that are relevant to most age groups and offered early in the aftermath of the event can be extremely helpful" (p. 76). Group or classroom crisis intervention can be a critical first step in a crisis intervention. This type of intervention can be done for both students and staff members. However, when staff members are the focus of the intervention, students should not be involved.

Classroom or group crisis intervention is especially important and practical following crises that affect large numbers of students (Terr, 1989). For example, following a tragedy such as the Stockton schoolyard shooting, it will be safe to assume that most, if not all, of Lisa's classmates will need some sort of crisis intervention. However, with limited resources it may be difficult to meet all student needs through one-on-one crisis intervention. At least initially all such assistance needs to be reserved for those most directly involved in the crisis (i.e., those students who were shot). Thus, classroom or group sessions are a way to quickly meet the needs of a number of crisis victims (Weinberg, 1990).

Classroom crisis intervention is also a way to help identify children who may need an individual crisis intervention. As discussed in Chapter 7, it will not always be readily apparent who is most affected by a crisis. In some cases, students not directly involved in the crisis event will enter a crisis state and will need crisis intervention. In making these referral decisions, it may be helpful to keep in mind Weinberg's (1990) indicators, which he has found to trigger referrals following crisis group sessions (Table 8.10).

Initially, identified as *Classroom Crisis Counseling* (Brock, 1996; Brock et al., 1996), the group crisis intervention model presented here was

Table 8.10

Indicators of the Need for Individual Crisis Intervention

The following indicators may be used during or following a group crisis intervention session to help determine if a referral for individual therapy is needed.

- The absence of emotional reactions in a student who either was close to the victim or witnessed the incident
- An inability to bring emotion under control
- Excessive self-blame or intropunitive anger
- Allusions to or admissions of suicidal thoughts or intentions
- Evidence of loose associations or bizarre behavior
- Preoccupation with personal, family, or relationship problems

Source: From "Serving large numbers of adolescent victim-survivors: Group interventions following trauma at school," by R.B. Weinberg, 1990, p. 275, *Professional Psychology: Research and Practice, 21,* 271–278.

influenced by Terr's (1992) discussion of *Mini-Marathon Groups.* Subsequently, the author's training in *Critical Incident Stress Management* (Mitchell & Everly, 1996b) and participation in the *National Community Crisis Response Team Regional Training Institute* (Young, 1998) led to several significant modifications that are included in the current discussion. The most obvious modification was relabeling the model as *Classroom Crisis Intervention* (CCI). This was done to help clarify that crisis counselors are not required to implement this type of intervention (Galante & Foa, 1986). While, mental health professionals will typically play an important role in CCI, is a type of psychological first aid, not a professional psychotherapeutic treatment. As such, it is appropriate for almost any school professional to become a CCI facilitator. The discussion that follows is adapted from Brock's (1998b) article "Helping Classrooms Cope with Traumatic Events."

GENERAL CCI ISSUES AND PROCEDURES

Any group of students having difficulty coping with a common crisis event could be brought together in a CCI. As a rule, CCI groupings are relatively homogeneous (Mitchell & Everly, 1996a; Weinberg, 1990; Wollman,

1993). CCI has been found by the author to be effective with classrooms ranging in size from 15 to 30 students. Combining classrooms, or creating groups of more than 40 students is not recommended (Bell, 1995; Mitchell & Everly, 1996a). Large groups are likely to inhibit sharing and interfere with the expression of feelings (Schonfeld, 1989). The adult-led processing provided by CCI helps children move from viewing themselves as crisis victims to viewing themselves as crisis survivors. Allen et al. (1999) concluded: "communication (i.e., adult-led processing by parents or teachers) with children was extremely useful in helping children of all ages cope . . ." (p. 97).

Whenever possible, CCI should take place in the students regular classroom (Schonfeld, 1989). Traditional counseling settings should be avoided (Farrington, 1995). In this way, unnecessary labeling of students as "patients" is avoided (Klingman, 1987) and the normality of crisis reactions more easily reinforced. If the classroom is not available, the group should meet in as natural, accessible, and comfortable an environment as is possible.

It is recommended that CCI be provided first thing in the morning on the first school day after the crisis event has concluded. Besides ensuring the CCI session can be completed within the school day, waiting until the next morning has another advantage. It gives the crisis response team a chance to prepare. Facts can be verified, and the CCI process reviewed with the classroom teacher or other CCI cofacilitators.

Group crisis intervention sessions are a team effort (Farrington, 1995; Mitchell & Everly, 1996a, 1996b; Young, 1998). Thus, it is recommended that two or more staff members facilitate CCI. A ratio of one facilitator for every 10 students is recommended (Weinberg, 1990).

Ideally, at least one of the CCI facilitators is familiar to students. A CCI team composed entirely of outside crisis intervenors suggests the crisis event was so overwhelming that school staff members are themselves unable to cope. This may increase feelings of hopelessness. In addition, students may be less willing to share reactions and feelings with strangers than with familiar adults. Typically, a familiar adult can be included by having the classroom teacher in the session. Alternatively, the school counselor or psychologist could fill this role (Weinberg, 1990).

In situations where CCI team members do not include the teacher(s) of the classroom(s) affected by the crisis event, intervenors need to be sensitive to the needs and desires of the teacher whose classroom they have entered. Doing so helps to ensure that the intervention is well received. Insofar as it is possible, it is recommended that the teacher takes an active role in CCI. This recommendation comes from the observation that collaboration is facilitated if crisis intervenors do not act as "the experts" but strive to involve the teacher in planning and implementing the classroom session (Blom et al., 1991). However, when the teacher is having significant difficulty coping with the crisis, outside crisis intervenors must recognize the teacher's limitations (Klingman, 1988).

A critical issue to consider before each session is facilitator roles. Typically, the CCI leader is a crisis response team member who has experience working with people-in-crisis (Farrington, 1995; Wollman, 1993) and is familiar with CCI. The lead-facilitator is responsible for directing progress through CCI. CCI support-facilitators should say very little in the CCI session unless called upon by the lead-facilitator (Young, 1998). This is not to say, however, that they are not very active in the CCI process. These individuals assist the lead-facilitator in monitoring group reactions. Support-facilitators help identify students in need of further crisis intervention support. In addition, they intervene with individuals who are unable to participate in CCI. For example, they would gently remove and talk individually to students who become hysterical. Young further suggests that additional support-facilitator roles may include providing emotional and practical support to the lead-facilitator, recording group response on a chalkboard or flip chart, and taking over the group if for some reason the lead-facilitator is unable to continue. Finally, support-facilitators are responsible for following, and ensuring the safety of, students who leave the classroom (Mitchell & Everly, 1996a; Weinberg, 1990; Young, 1998).

CCI is effective in a variety of situations. However, Johnson (1993) indicates that group crisis counseling approaches should be avoided under the following circumstances: (1) when the class has a history of being hurtful, divisive, or nonsupportive; (2) when student needs, relative to the trauma, are polarized (e.g., some students are deeply effected while others are untouched or find the crisis beneficial); and (3) when the traumatic event is politicized (e.g., gang membership had a role in the trauma).

THE CCI MODEL

CCI has the following six steps: (1) introduction, (2) providing facts and dispelling rumors, (3) sharing stories, (4) sharing reactions, (5) empowerment, and (6) closure. Table 8.11 provides a summary of CCI. The CCI procedure aims at helping students to understand the trauma, express thoughts and feelings, and learn coping behaviors.

Table 8.11

Classroom Crisis Intervention (CCI) Summary

CCI Step	Facilitative Statements	Goal(s)	Goal Attainment Signs
Introduction	"I'm sorry this happened to your (our) school. When bad things like this happen, it is helpful to talk about it. So, we are going to spend some time today talking. From our discussion we will have a better understanding of what happened, how it has affected us, and what we can do to help each other."	Explain CCI purpose Identify facilitators Review CCI steps Review classroom rules	Questions about CCI stop
Providing facts and dispelling rumors	"We have experienced an event that was so unusual we might find it hard to understand. I would like to share with you what we know about this tragedy. Feel free to ask questions. It's important that you understand what happened."	Assist students come to a reality-based understanding of the crisis event	Questions about the crisis event stop
Sharing stories	"Each person who gets through an event, such as the one we have just experienced, has a story. We are going to tell as many of these stories as we can today. Who wants to start?" (Terr, 1992, p. 79)	Get students to talk about their experiences Help students feel less alone and more connected to classmates	Everyone has had a chance to share crisis stories

Table 8.11 *(Continued)*

CCI Step	Facilitative Statements	Goal(s)	Goal Attainment Signs
Sharing reactions	"Following an event, such as the one we've just experienced, it is not unusual for people to feel and behave differently for a while. Some common reactions are (*identify common reactions*). These are normal reactions to abnormal circumstances."	Get students to talk about crisis reactions Help students feel more connected to classmates Normalize crisis reactions	Everyone has had a chance to share crisis reactions
Empowerment	"Crises can make us feel helpless. I would like to see us take action or make plans to help us now and in the future."	Help students regain a sense of control over their lives	Concrete action is taken or planned for
Closure	"What can we do to help place this event behind us and move on with our lives?"	Help students place the crisis behind them	Completion of activities that allow students to say goodbye to that which was lost

As currently conceptualized, CCI is ideally completed in one session lasting approximately three hours. However, the length of CCI must be tailored to the developmental level of the classroom (i.e., older students will be able to participate in sessions for longer uninterrupted periods of time). For example, Johnson (1993) suggests that elementary age students can at most be expected to participate in sessions lasting up to one hour. Thus, especially when working with younger children, it will be necessary to take bathroom and recess breaks. However, once students have begun to share trauma experiences, breaks should be avoided until after the group has reviewed activities designed to help manage trauma reactions (Empowerment; Mitchell & Everly, 1996a). While it may be difficult to complete CCI in one uninterrupted session, it is recommended that all six steps be completed during the same school day.

CCI begins with an introduction (Mitchell & Everly, 1996a; Young, 1998). This step, which lasts 10 to 15 minutes, starts with introduction of

CCI support-facilitators and identification of the group leader. A facilitator familiar to the students should introduce facilitators who are not known to the classroom.

Once introductions are completed and the group leader identified, the leader explains the purpose of the meeting. In doing so it is important to be positive and offer the expectation that CCI is effective. The leader should convey that with talk and time most students will cope with the trauma. The leader states that students will be working together to understand and cope with the trauma. However, it should be acknowledged that facilitators have special information to share on how to cope. Following this preface, each CCI step is briefly described.

Next, CCI rules are reviewed. Students are reminded they are still in school and that regular classroom rules are in effect. Perhaps most importantly, students are told that they are not allowed to leave the room without permission. However, students are told that active participation is voluntary. Additional group process rules may also need to be established. Examples of the types of group process rules that should be set include speaking one at a time, encouraging and supporting the efforts of others, and that put-downs are not allowed. In concluding the introduction, it should also be mentioned that facilitators will be available to the classroom after the CCI session is completed.

Providing Facts and Dispelling Rumors

The second and perhaps most important CCI step provides students with facts about the trauma and dispels rumors (Cohen, 1988). This step lasts approximately 30 minutes. Because school-aged youth will typically have had little experience with traumatic events, they will likely be confused. In particular, young children are least likely to understand and most likely to be confused about a crisis event. Allen et al. (1999) report that following the Oklahoma City bombing younger children "were most likely to have the highest number of wrong facts about the traumatic event" (p. 97). Thus, CCI begins by making certain students have a reality-based understanding of the crisis event. This is done much more explicitly than in other forms of group crisis intervention (e.g., Young, 1998). In CCI, the lead-facilitators begins by reporting very directly the crisis facts and then attempts to answer as many questions as possible about what had happened.

When providing crisis facts it is important to be sensitive to developmental levels (J. Lord, 1990; Mitchell & Everly, 1996b; Poland & McCormick, 1999). For example, with intermediate grade students, carefully selected, well-written newspaper articles about the crisis may be helpful in clarifying for students what happened (Klingman, 1987, 1993; Terr, 1989). However, with younger students this would be an inappropriate strategy. More simplistic descriptions of the event will need to be offered. Also, it is important to remember that, because of the novelty of the situation, facts may be difficult to understand, and facilitators should be prepared to repeat them frequently (J. Lord, 1990).

Dispelling rumors is especially important given that they are typically more frightening than reality (Blom et al., 1991). For example, following the schoolyard shooting described at the beginning of this chapter, there was a persistent rumor that only one of two gunmen had been identified. This belief was fostered by the fact that the lone gunman, who had assaulted the playground and then committed suicide, had fired from two separate locations (M. Armstrong, 1990). The mistaken belief that there was still a gunman at large was frightening for students. Such mistaken information can be very distracting, and serves to make coping more difficult. Thus, making sure students have a reality-based understanding of the crisis is important to crisis resolution (J. Lord, 1990).

SHARING STORIES

When questions about trauma facts and rumors stop, the classroom is ready to continue. The sharing of student experiences during the event is the next step (Galante & Foa, 1986; Mitchell & Everly, 1996a; Terr, 1992; Young, 1998) and may last up to 45 minutes.

Keeping in mind that active participation is voluntary, in smaller classrooms facilitators will want to move around the CCI group and give each student the opportunity to share. In larger groups (i.e., 30 student classrooms) there may not be enough time to do this and facilitators may simply ask for volunteers. Specific questions to facilitate this step suggested by Young (1998) include the following: Where were you when it happened? Who were you with? What did you see, hear, smell, taste, or touch at the time? What did you do? How did you react?

All experiences and reactions should be validated by facilitators, and common themes identified (Terr, 1992). This will help students feel more connected to each other and less alone because of their common experiences. It will help give students the added strength needed to face and work through the trauma.

Besides asking students to verbalize experiences, it is also helpful to allow them to recount experiences and reactions in other ways. Art and other creative activities can be a helpful way of doing so (Farrell & Joseph,

1991; Johnson, 1993; Klingman, Koenigsfeld, & Markman, 1987; Terr, 1992) and are especially important for younger students who may have difficulty verbalizing what has happened. These activities are also a way to break-up a CCI session and may be especially helpful for students who have difficulty sitting for an entire CCI session. Johnson (1993), for example, suggests that with elementary age students activities may comprise a majority of the session. Petersen and Straub (1992) and Poland and McCormick (1999) offer excellent compilations of activities that may prove helpful in a CCI session.

SHARING REACTIONS

Common initial psychological and behavioral symptoms displayed by children following crisis events include sleep disorders, bad dreams, persistent thoughts of the crisis, belief that another crisis will occur, conduct disturbances, hyper-alertness, avoidance of crisis reminders, and somatic reactions. In younger children, regression to enuresis, thumb-sucking, and more dependent behavior may also be seen (Frederick, 1985). These reactions can be very unsettling, and it is not uncommon for survivors to fear that they are going crazy. Group sharing and facilitator anticipation of crisis reactions helps normalize these sometimes frightening symptoms (K. Armstrong, Lund, McWright, & Tichenor, 1995; Mitchell & Everly, 1996a; Terr, 1992). Terr recommends the following approach to this step: (1) stating common reactions, (2) asking those who have experienced each reaction to raise their hands, (3) asking for individual examples, (4) making summarizing comments about reactions experienced, and (5) anticipating reactions that may arise in the future. This step lasts approximately 30 minutes.

As students share feelings and reactions, facilitators should not be surprised if some students begin to cry. Students should be told that this reaction is normal and, as long as the classroom is not too distracted by these tears, crying students should remain in the classroom (J. Lord, 1990). However, students who become hysterical may need to be removed. Their presence can be so distracting that the CCI process will stop (Mitchell & Everly, 1996a).

During this step, CCI facilitators should explicitly state that initial trauma reactions are normal responses to abnormal circumstances (J. Lord, 1990). Facilitators should also let students know that with time, for most people, these reactions will go away. However, students should be informed of what to do if they feel that they are unable to manage crisis reactions. This is a natural time to ensure students are aware of self-referral procedures for obtaining individual crisis intervention. Facilitators should assure students that, if used early, crisis intervention can reduce symptoms quickly and with a minimum of pain. "If a traumatic response does not have the chance to become entrenched, it will become only a small scar on a very large life" (Terr, 1992, p. 32).

EMPOWERMENT

After students have shared trauma experiences and effects, the next step is for students to begin to participate in activities that help them regain a sense of control. During this step students learn no matter how impossible circumstances may appear, there are things they can do to improve their situation (Allan & Nairne, 1984). An important goal of this step is identifying coping strategies (K. Armstrong et al., 1995). It may last up to 60 minutes.

The importance of this step is emphasized by the observation that youth that believe that they are in control of the forces that shape their lives are more resistant to stress. Regarding this observation Luthar (1991) states:

> When people believe they are powerless to control what happens to them, they become passive and restricted in coping abilities. On the other hand, when individuals believe that events and outcomes are controllable, learned helplessness is avoided, and, instead, active attempts are made to overcome aversive situations. (p. 610)

As CCI is a form of crisis intervention, facilitators can be very directive during this step. However, students should be as active as possible in identifying coping strategies. Encouraging this independent thinking will reinforce that students are regaining control over what is happening. During this step it is important that basic stress management techniques be presented. Specifically, the importance of getting needed sleep, food, exercise, and talking to friends and family are emphasized (Mitchell & Everly, 1996a; Weinberg, 1990). Additional options for this step include having students work together on developing strategies to gradually desensitize each other to crisis related fears (Terr, 1992) and teaching them how to reply to intrusive thoughts and images (Brown, 1996). Through this discussion, students will begin to see that there are a variety of options for coping with crisis.

Another activity that may be appropriate following certain types of crises is to ask students to brainstorm strategies to prevent reoccurrence of the traumatic event. During this initial brainstorming, student ideas and suggestions are recorded and validated as ways of regaining control over circumstances. Once all ideas have been presented, facilitators can help guide students toward an evaluation of each suggestion. Especially helpful are suggestions that allow for immediate concrete action. For example, following the shooting described at the beginning of this chapter, one classroom decided to write letters to government officials regarding the need for gun control. It should be mentioned that this approach to empowerment must be used carefully. Caution must be exercised to ensure that the ideas and suggestions generated do not create guilt feelings. For example, the crisis intervenor would want to avoid reinforcing ideas that might lead students to believe they could or should have done something to prevent the trauma (e.g., we could prevent schoolyard shootings if students agree to attack gunmen). If these beliefs were validated it could foster survivor guilt that would make crisis resolution more difficult.

In closing this step, Terr (1992) suggests that facilitators review tales of heroism and survival. They should praise the courage of students in facing the trauma and looking ahead toward the future.

CLOSURE

The final step in CCI is for students to engage in activities that help bring a sense of closure to the crisis. This step may last up to 30 minutes. A natural activity for crises resulting in death is the development of memorials. A variety of creative projects could serve as memorials. Goldman (1996), for example, suggests the following as ways in which students can memorialize a loss:

- Plant a flower or a tree.
- Send a balloon.
- Blow bubbles.
- Light a candle.
- Say a prayer.
- Create a mural or collage about the life of the person who died.
- Make cookies or cake.
- Make a memory gift for the child's family.
- Write a poem, story, or song about the loved one who died.
- Talk into a tape recorder or make a video of memories (p. 71).

Ideally, these will be projects that all students can actively help to develop. It is important to mention that all memorial projects should be carefully screened before they are delivered to trauma victims and their families. Because of their own anxiety and beliefs students may create messages that are potentially hurtful. These messages should be screened out (J. Lord, 1990). In addition, if time is a problem this step may only involve the planning of memorial projects. Completion of these projects could be reserved for another day.

Other closure activity options include preparation for attending or participating in funerals (Mitchell & Everly, 1996b), and the writing of get-well cards and letters to victims. If the classroom has experienced the death of a classmate or teacher, this step should include discussion of what to do with the deceased's desk and belongings (J. Lord, 1990).

In concluding CCI, facilitators should answer any remaining questions. The CCI is then summarized and closing comments made. If time permits students may be asked to share what they have learned from the CCI session, and what empowerment ideas they are committed to implementing (Allan & Nairne, 1984). In making closing comments, facilitators should remind students that they are experiencing normal reactions to abnormal circumstances. Facilitators should be positive about the future and remind students that while memories will remain, with time and talk, the associated pain will lessen and symptoms will typically disappear. Finally, students are reassured that if needed additional crisis intervention services are available and self-referral procedures are reiterated.

POST-CCI ACTIVITIES

After the CCI has ended, at least one, but preferably all, of the facilitators should remain with the students (Mitchell & Everly, 1996a). Ideally, facilitators should be available to students throughout the remainder of the school day. This allows students additional opportunities to seek out support and to have questions answered. It also gives facilitators additional opportunities to assess how individual students are coping.

Finally, as soon as possible after the CCI, facilitators should debrief the session. This typically occurs at the end of the school day. During debriefing decisions need to be made regarding whom will need one-on-one crisis intervention. Table 8.10 provides a list of indicators suggesting the need for these referrals. In addition, facilitators should focus on their own crisis reactions and ability to cope with the trauma. In particular, special attention needs to be directed toward the classroom teacher (J. Lord, 1990). If needed, crisis intervention services should be made available to the teacher and other CCI team members.

PROFESSIONAL PSYCHOTHERAPEUTIC TREATMENT

Although most school professionals can play an important role in the provision of crisis intervention services following a situational crisis, there are limitations to what the typical school-based crisis intervenor can handle. Thus, it is essential that all school professionals be knowledgeable of the kinds of crises and symptoms that require professional mental health intervention. In line with this need, the National Institute of Mental Health (Institute for the Study of Destructive Behaviors and The Los Angeles Suicide Prevention Center, 1978) provides in its *Training Manual for Human Service Workers in Major Disasters* a list of "Help and Seek-Help Behaviors" (pp. 18–19). This list provided in Table 8.12 is intended to assist disaster workers in differentiating between victims they can help and those who may require a mental health specialist.

In general, any situation that involves threat of physical harm to self or others (e.g., suicide, homicide, child abuse) requires an immediate mental health professional referral. Additionally, Pitcher and Poland (1992) suggest that if a student is so emotional he or she cannot be involved in classroom activities, or is very withdrawn and depressed, and does not respond to comfort or support, he or she should be referred to a school mental health professional.

Besides identifying situations and symptoms that require professional mental health interventions, it is essential that all staff know how to obtain such assistance. Doing so can be as simple as informing the crisis intervention coordinator of the observed situation and symptoms. As was discussed in Chapter 7, the crisis intervention coordinator, as part of his or her crisis planning responsibilities should have already identified the professional mental health resources available in the community.

PSYCHOTHERAPEUTIC TREATMENT OPTIONS

The remainder of this chapter briefly reviews examples of the types of crisis intervention services (or psychotherapeutic treatments) mental health professionals may employ when a crisis victim is referred to them. First, crisis therapy is offered as an example of a counseling approach designed to facilitate the adaptive resolution of the crisis state. Next, several cognitive-behavioral treatments (i.e., exposure-based therapies, anxiety management, and cognitive therapy) are described to familiarize the reader with treatments commonly used by mental health professionals to treat traumatic stress.

Table 8.12

Behaviors Suggesting the Need for a Mental Health Referral

Alertness and Awareness

Consider referral to a mental health agency if the client:

- Is unable to give own name or names of people with whom he is living
- Cannot give date or state where he is or tell what he does
- Cannot recall events of the past 24 hours
- Complains of memory gaps

Actions

Consider referral if the client:

- Is depressed and shows agitation, restlessness, and paces
- Is apathetic, immobile, unable to arouse self to movement
- Is incontinent
- Mutilates self
- Uses alcohol or drugs excessively
- Is unable to care for self (e.g., doesn't eat, drink, bathe, or change clothes)
- Repeats ritualistic acts

Speech

Consider referral if the client:

- Hallucinates (hears voices, sees visions, or has unverified bodily sensations)
- States his body feels unreal and he* fears he is losing his mind
- Is excessively preoccupied with one idea or thought
- Has the delusion that someone or something is out to get him and his family
- Is afraid he will kill self or another
- Is unable to make simple decisions or carry out everyday functions
- Shows extreme pressure of speech—talk overflows

Emotions

Consider referral if the client:

- Is excessively flat, unable to be aroused, completely withdrawn
- Is excessively emotional and shows inappropriate emotional reactions

*"He or she" is implied.
Source: Adapted from "Training manual for human service workers in major disasters," by Institute for the Study of Destructive Behaviors and Los Angeles Suicide Prevention Center, 1978, pp. 18–19. Rockville, MD: National Institute of Mental Health.

CRISIS THERAPY

Slaikeu's (1990) discussion of crisis therapy asserts that crisis therapy begins where psychological first aid ends. (Table 7.1 in Chapter 7 provides a summary of the differences between these two forms of crisis intervention.) He goes on to indicate that crisis therapy goes beyond the reestablishment of immediate coping and aims at assisting the individual to resolve the trauma. The desired outcome of this form of therapy is for the person-in-crisis to be able to face the future. Through this approach, the crisis intervenor hopes to help the individual avoid becoming a psychological casualty of the trauma. In crisis therapy, treatment focus is on assisting the crisis victim to accomplish "four tasks of crisis resolution" (Slaikeu, 1990, pp. 166–177). These tasks are (1) physical survival, (2) expression of feelings, (3) cognitive mastery, and (4) behavioral and interpersonal adjustments.

Physical survival quite simply involves staying alive long enough and keeping physically well enough to take advantage of the special training and skill of the crisis therapist. Psychological first aid is the main approach used to facilitate attainment of this task. The identification and expression of feelings are important in freeing emotional energy for use in rebuilding the crisis victim's life and for focusing on the future. Obtaining cognitive mastery over the trauma involves three different activities. First, the person-in-crisis needs to come to a reality-based understanding of the crisis event (e.g., A man shot at me on the playground, some of my friends were killed or wounded, he then shot himself. He can no longer harm me). Second, the person-in-crisis needs to understand how the trauma alters his or her view of the world and their place in it (e.g., I am no longer confident in my ability to cope with the playground and am now afraid of being shot). Third, new beliefs about the world that fit with the available facts need to be developed (e.g., Sometimes the world can be dangerous and bad things can happen, the playground is not as safe as I once thought, but schoolyard shootings do not happen every day. I can cope with the fear it has caused). The last crisis resolution task is the making of behavioral and interpersonal adjustments. In his description of this task, Slaikeu states that it ". . . is based on the idea that behavioral change is the 'bottom line' for crisis resolution" (p. 174). Activities necessary to complete this task may include "ground to be recovered" (e.g., being able to return to the playground and play with friends), and "new ground to be broken" (e.g., learning to play without friends who have been killed or wounded and/or making new friends).

EXPOSURE-BASED THERAPIES

Of the cognitive-behavioral treatments (which also include anxiety management and cognitive therapy) exposure-based therapies (in particular a treatment known as Prolonged Exposure) are currently judged to be the most effective (Foa & Meadows, 1998). These treatments are based on popular principles of human learning (i.e., classical and operant conditioning). They involve asking psychological trauma victims to systematically confront their fears. Eye movement desensitization and reprocessing (EMDR) is an example of such an approach (Shapiro, 1995). Using this approach a therapist instructs the person-in-crisis to imagine the traumatizing scene. Then this scene is paired with instructions to make small rapid jerky movements of the eye.

Foa and Meadows (1998) suggest that prolonged exposure is the most efficacious treatment approach for traumatic stress reactions. Their description of this treatment indicates that it has the following five components: Information gathering, breathing retraining, psychoeducation, imaginal exposure (i.e., mentally reliving the traumatic event) and in vivo exposure (i.e., directly confronting reminders of the trauma).

In addition to providing the therapist with information about the traumatic event, information gathering demonstrates the therapist's availability to hear the often times disturbing and frightening crisis facts. It also helps to identify those experiences that need to be addressed during treatment. Breathing retraining is a relaxation technique, which when done properly, results in a sense of physical calm. In the psychoeducational phase of treatment, the person-in-crisis is given information about common reactions to traumatic stressors. This helps to normalize the sometimes frightening crisis reactions (crisis victims sometimes fear they are going crazy) and provides a focus for the remaining treatment session.

Next, in vivo exposure involves confrontation with the experiences that are causing problems and impairing functioning. It involves the construction of a list of stress producing situations or objects (related to the crisis) and ordering these from most to least stressful. These stressors are then confronted one at a time, moving from the least to the most stressful.

Finally, instructing the traumatized individual to begin to visualize the traumatic event facilitates imaginal exposure. The visualization is narrated in the present tense and the individual is instructed to provided as much detail as possible (including related thoughts, perceptions, and feelings). At the end of this visualization period, the individual is then asked to use the previously taught relaxation skills. The power of this treatment approach is thought to rest in the pairing of a sense of physical calm (resulting from use of relaxation techniques) with the traumatic stress.

ANXIETY MANAGEMENT

According to Foa and Meadows (1998), this form of treatment takes the view that traumatic stress can be addressed by teaching individuals to better manage their crisis reactions. Specific strategies taught include relaxation training, breathing retraining, biofeedback, social skills training, and distraction techniques.

COGNITIVE THERAPIES

Originally developed by Beck (1976), these therapies are often used in the treatment of depression and anxiety disorders. Its basic premise is that it is the interpretation of the crisis event, rather than the event itself, which results in traumatic stress reactions (Foa & Meadows, 1998). Such interpretations lead to the pathological thinking that is at the core of crisis reactions. Treatment involves first helping the person-in-crisis to identify the thoughts that lead to crisis reactions. Then, the individual is taught to analyze and assess the validity of these thoughts. Finally, the incorrect or harmful thinking is challenged and attempts are made to replace them with thoughts that are more functional.

SUMMARY

This chapter provided suggestions for helping the person-in-crisis cope with trauma. It has reviewed both individual and group psychological first aid interventions. These are the crisis interventions that might be offered by any school professional. If these interventions are not sufficient in meeting the needs of a person-in-crisis, then a referral to a mental health professional will be required. Although most educators are not trained to provide such psychotherapeutic treatments, it is nevertheless important that they know of their existence, and their role in determining the need for such services.

CHAPTER 9

Media Relations

The morning after the Stockton schoolyard shooting was chaotic. The media were out in force covering one of the biggest stories of the year. Vans topped with satellite dishes lined the street in front of the school. Reporters, hungry for a story, approached students, parents, and teachers for interviews. Virtually every staff member entering the school was asked to comment on the school's response to this tragedy. Having been told that the district's spokesperson would, at least initially, handle all media inquiries, reporters were referred to the school district's main office.

—Author recollection of the morning after
the shooting (January 18, 1993)

C RISIS EVENTS occurring on or near a school site, such as the Stockton shooting or the Columbine tragedy, are newsworthy. Following traumatic circumstances, electronic and print reporters will often immediately contact school personnel. Effective communication with these reporters not only keeps the community informed, but may also facilitate the school crisis response. For example, following a suicide, a newspaper article might include suicide prevention hotline phone numbers and identify other resources for suicidal individuals (thus helping to reduce the risk of a suicide cluster). Additionally, through accurate reporting, rumors can be dispelled and the likelihood of community panic minimized.

The media are motivated to report events that reporters and editors believe will be of interest to the public.* The events of a particular day and

---

*See Petersen and Straub (1992, pp. 54–58) for an interesting presentation from the media's perspective of what they are motivated by and trying to accomplish in reporting crisis stories.

their news value determine what kind of coverage the media gives to any particular event. On a slow news day, a local newspaper might place on the front page a relatively trivial event, such as the weather. On other days, when there are other significant news events, school crises such as suicide, injury, or fire may not even be reported. Other things being equal, however, school crisis response teams should expect interest from the media when a traumatic event is associated with a school. The media are giving increasing attention to school crises, particularly school violence. (For more general comments by a newspaper reporter working with schools, see Hennessey, 1992.)

Most school districts realize that public relations cannot be ignored. Increasingly, administrators have obtained training in media relations or have hired media consultants. Media relations are especially important in times of crisis. Thus, understanding of the work of the media liaison is critical.

This chapter's discussion of media relations begins with a discussion of specific media liaison duties and responsibilities. To facilitate an understanding of the media, a discussion of what the media want follows. Further preparation for working with the media is offered by reviewing how to prepare for and how to conduct the media interview. Finally, we conclude with an examination of the issue of sensationalism and media access to crisis scenes.

THE MEDIA LIAISON

Because there will be media interest in school crises and because there are constitutional protections for a free press, schools must be prepared to work with media. Someone must be prepared to assume the role of media liaison. The main objectives for the individual filling this role during times of crisis are (a) to dispel rumors, (b) to help the media honor the public's right to know the facts, (c) to set realistic expectations for the outcome of a crisis situation, and (d) to provide the public with information regarding caregiving/healing resources. As with other crisis team members, it is suggested that a liaison be appointed at both the site- and district-level.

A media liaison must learn how to schedule and hold a press conference. In preparation for a news conference, as well as other media contacts, the liaison should train and drill with the information supplied in this chapter and have simulations of media interviews. The liaison should also identify a location (or locations) that could serve as a press interview site in advance of need. Each liaison should also set up a special telephone

Press Release

This is _____ a _____
         (Name of individual)   (Individual's position)

in the _____ School District. At _____ on _____
         (District's name)   (Time)   (Date)

_____ did _____
           (Who)   (What)

to _____ . This occurred at _____ .
        (Whom)   (Location where
                                               incident occurred)

At this time
- (a) we have no confirmation of the injuries or damage.
  - OR
- (b) the following injuries or damages have been confirmed.

_____

_____

_____

_____

The prognosis for those involved is _____
                                       (Good, Poor, etc.)

Local community resources are responding in the following way: _____

_____

_____

The following community agencies and resources are assisting the school and will provide the following services to children, parents, and staff.

Name of Community Agency/Resource   Services Provided

_____   _____

_____   _____

_____   _____

The school district is responding in the following way: _____

_____

_____

_____

We will keep you updated as we learn further information.

We ask the public to avoid the area (if appropriate).

If the parents of children in the affected school (school district) need to contact us, please call the following community information telephone number: _____

_____

Figure 9.1 Press Release. The district-level media liaison and the school site-level media liaison should ensure that similar press release forms are prepared for all anticipated crisis situations.

number that can be used in times of crisis. Once such a media line is set up, an answering machine can play back a press release or make other announcements about when the press will be updated.

In many large districts, the role of district media liaison is a full-time job. These individuals may hold the title of public information officer or public relations director. They may have journalism training and/or experience working in the media. Typically, they are educators who have assumed the responsibility of school district/community communications. Eventually, they will be involved with the media following a crisis, but they may not be the first individuals contacted. Thus, part of their role is to prepare principals and the superintendent for their communications to the media and to parents.

The school media liaison should maintain contact with other media spokespersons at other school sites. The site-level liaison should receive media training and be prepared with materials and forms that are up-to-date.* In small schools, the principal will ordinarily assume this role.

MEDIA LIAISON DUTIES

The media liaison has several special crisis response responsibilities. Boldface type indicates duties typically performed only by a district-level liaison.

PRIOR TO CRISES

As a part of crisis response planning, the media liaison should complete the following tasks:

1. Know who the media spokespersons are at other school sites and maintain contact with them.
2. Prepare supporting documents and sample press releases. Figure 9.1 is a sample press release with blanks for the specifics of the crisis event. Appendix D provides additional samples of prepared statements.

---

*For more information about media training, contact the Public Relations Society of America (PRSA) at www.prsa.org and follow the links to conferences/seminars and crisis management. Resources include training programs, a video, and a home study program. PRSA can also be reached at the following address/phone number: 33 Irving Place, New York, NY 10003-2376, (212) 995-2230.

3. **Conduct training exercises with school site personnel to help them better understand how to prepare for and work with the media.**

4. Develop school policies for responding to media inquires. A sample policy is provided in Table 9.1.

5. **Coordinate with other community media liaisons and invite them to supplement district staff during emergencies, if possible. Local public health, mental health, and governmental agencies, particularly the police, may have media spokespersons and they should be identified.**

6. Establish a professional relationship with local media personnel before crisis events and create an awareness of how press coverage can affect crisis survivors (Kneisel & Richards, 1988). Determine the names of local newspaper reporters who cover the area for various newspapers and maintain a media contact list (i.e., the names of media working in the area). Figure 9.2 provides a form for doing so.

Table 9.1
Sample Policy Statement Regarding Responses to the
Media during Times of Crisis

Following a crisis event members of the press may contact staff members. Because of the need to control rumors (which can run rampant following a crisis), it is our policy not to speak to members of the press immediately following a crisis. Rather the journalist should be referred to the crisis spokesperson. The principal will identify the crisis spokesperson to all staff members.

As the given crisis situation stabilizes and the facts become clear, it may become appropriate for staff members to be interviewed. Such interviews should either be cleared through or arranged by the crisis spokesperson.

In some instances, it may be appropriate for office staff to be given prepared statements (developed by the media liaison), which they could read to journalists over the phone.

Whenever possible all staff members will be briefed on press releases before they are given to the press. However, it needs to be recognized that there may be some situations where this is not possible.

Source: Adapted from "Administrative response to crisis situations: Recommendations for the implementation of Board Policy 5141.5" by S.E. Brock, S. Lewis, and S. Yund, 1990. (Available from Lodi Unified School District, Special Services/SELPA, 1305 E. Vine St., Lodi, CA 95240.)

Media Contact List

Print Media

Name	Local Address	Frequency of Publication	Managing Editor	Telephone
Newspapers				
News Services				
Associated Press				
United Press International				

Electronic Media
Television

	Call Letters	Channel	Hours of Operation	Address	Deadline Times	Remote Vans or Aircraft?	News Director	24-Hour Newsroom Phone #
Commercial								
Cable								
Public								

Radio

	Call Letters	Channel	Hours of Operation	Address	Deadline Times	Remote Vans or Aircraft?	News Director	24-Hour Newsroom Phone #
Local								
Regional								

Figure 9.2 Media contact list for identifying and documenting the identities of local media personnel. As a part of their planning responsibilities, it is recommended that media liaisons complete this form.

7. Maintain a list of local and national resources for appropriate referral of media inquiries on various crises. Table 3.2 provides a sample of such referral sources.
8. Identify a suitable location for an emergency media center and inform others of its location and possible use during a crisis. This center should be in an area that will not allow media presence to significantly affect school operations.
9. Prepare a mobile media kit for use in the media center or at school site. Table 9.2 provides a list of items that should be included in this kit. A cell phone would be quite useful as well.

DURING CRISES

If it is a districtwide crisis or if the district-level media liaison is designated as the crisis spokesperson, the school-level liaison should be directed to refer inquiries to the district-level liaison. If the school-level liaison is designated as the crisis spokesperson, the district-level liaison would still perform the duties indicated by boldface type:

1. Ensure that the media do not disrupt school operations. While the media have the right to be in emergency areas, they do not have the right to interfere with school operations (e.g., teaching, crisis intervention).
2. Help to determine what information regarding the crisis is to be disseminated and release information to the public as necessary. The format suggested in Figure 9.1 may be used once local details have been added. Ensure that the information is accurate, can legally be released, and does not violate individual privacy rights.
3. Help determine how information is to be disseminated to the media and to the public. The media liaison helps to identify the strategy that will best get the response team's message out. For example, would a news conference be in order or individual interviews more appropriate?
4. Ensure that all staff are aware of who handles press inquires.
5. Coordinate interviews with school staff (when necessary).
6. **Release media-only telephone numbers and a public telephone number.**
7. **Respond to calls and record telephone messages for media and public hotlines and update these messages as the situation changes.**

Table 9.2
Mobile Media Kit

The district media spokesperson should have the following items in an easily accessible place for rapid transport to and use at the scene of an emergency or in the media center, if appropriate.

Contents

Maps of city and county (the county map should include maps of all major cities within the county)

Regional map (for multicounty emergencies)

Acetate map covers

Marking pens

Easel for display of map

Battery-powered PA system (lectern and microphone)

Ruled pads or steno notebooks

Pens and pencils

Scotch tape/masking tape

Scissors, stapler, paper clips—other office supplies

Easel with blank flip pad, pointer

Telephone contact list

Sign (Day-Glo) "All Media—Please Report Here"

Lighting for night operations

Cassette recorder/blank tapes (battery-operated) to record all briefings to the media.

Sign-in sheet for media

Blank press passes, if appropriate (coordinate with law enforcement authorities)

AM/FM portable radio

Local telephone book

Assembly

- Gather items already in-house (surplus equipment, office supplies, etc.).
- Scrounge around other departments for possible additions.
- Buy heavy-duty rather than low-price.

Table 9.2 *(Continued)*

- Buy reliable names rather than unknowns (easier to find replacement cords, batteries, bulbs, etc.)
- Secure rugged cases with locks.
- Secure rolling cart to make transport easy.
- Buy lots of extra batteries in all sizes.
- Buy software (videotape, audiocassettes, etc.).
- Make sure transformer, cable, and adapters are compatible.
- Find a safe, easily accessible place to store kit.
- Train other staff in kit operation and contents.
- Test it at your next emergency preparedness drill.
- Don't let others pilfer or borrow items—keep it off limits.
- Make a list of everything in the kit.

Source: Adapted from "Multihazard functional planning guidance" by California Governor's Office of Emergency Services (1985).

8. **Involve the school-level media spokespersons to the greatest extent possible.**
9. Open a media center if a number of reporters arrive. The media center should consist of an area for reporters to congregate and for hard copy of news releases to be posted, along with maps and diagrams as appropriate. Ideally, it is located off school grounds.
10. As needed, arrange media briefings and press conferences.
11. Produce news releases as required. Releases may be posted on a district Web site.
12. Provide information releases in foreign languages as required.
13. Maintain a media contact log (Figure 9.3) that summarizes the information released to reporters.
14. If necessary and appropriate, arrange for media access to emergency sites. Supply media with identification badges.
15. Release damage assessment figures when obtained.
16. Be sensitive to the possibility that some members of the media may be adversely affected by the crisis and in need of crisis intervention support.

Media Contact Log

Date	Contact Time 24-Hour Time	Media Type				Media Identification		Contact Type				Contact Person and Information Released Reporter name and a brief summary of information released
		Radio	News-paper	News Service	TV	Station Call Letter	Paper Name	Phone Report	Office Visit	Field Contact	News Release	

Figure 9.3 Media contact log for documenting the information released to the media as part of a school crisis response. *Source:* Adapted from "Multihazard functional planning guidance" by California Governor's Office of Emergency Services (1985).

Following Crises

Following stabilization of a crisis, the media liaison should perform the following tasks:

1. Continue to release status information on request.
2. Gather all records kept during the emergency and prepare a chronological summary of all events, actions taken, inquiries made, and responses given.
3. Collect newspaper clippings, radio, and television audio/video tapes if available.
4. Survey staff and local media personnel for suggestions on how to improve media response in the future.
5. Provide the crisis response coordinator with a summary report of media activities during the crisis response.
6. Debrief all of those involved in media contact and evaluate effectiveness of communications response.

Throughout All Phases of Crises

During all periods and phases of a crisis event the media liaison should:

1. Ensure that all information is clear, concise, confirmed, and approved by the appropriate school authorities before it is released to the media or public. Unconfirmed information or speculation must be avoided.
2. Monitor published and broadcast information for accuracy and attempt to correct serious misinformation as quickly as possible.
3. Provide sufficient staffing and telephones to handle incoming media and public calls efficiently.
4. Ensure that all site-level spokespersons are thoroughly briefed about all aspects of the emergency.
5. Keep the superintendent informed of all actions taken or planned.
6. Keep public information officers from other community agencies aware of the information released.

WHAT MEDIA PERSONNEL WANT

Journalists, in attempting to communicate news, usually follow the old formula of Who, What, When, Where, Why, and How. Consequently, in their contact with the schools they will wish to have this information first if they do not already have it. With respect to the "Why" and "How," the newspaper and other media are often most interested in unusual or bizarre aspects of the situation, although there may also be an attempt to tie the particular situation into a more general societal issue. A story on a student suicide, for example, might be tied into growing national trends related to drug abuse, or other societal problems.

Often reporters or talk-show hosts focus on "why" in an attempt to affix blame. As a society, we are particularly interested in determining the cause of a crisis event. On the positive side, this can lead to action that will prevent future tragedy. On the negative side, pundits may seek to tie a crisis event to a particular crusade, such as lack of parental discipline, the bad influence of television, or use of the Internet (Lazarus et al., 1999). Media spokespersons should anticipate being pressured into speculation on causes that fit a reporter or editor's agenda but which may not help the situation at the school. Table 9.3 offers additional guidance on providing the media with information.

Young (1998) has outlined a timetable for how the media responds to the aftermath of many large-scale traumatic events. She notes that in the first 12 hours following the event there is a focus on what, when, and how the crisis happened in an attempt to sort out fact from fiction. During the next 12 hours, the focus is on who was involved. During this period, reporters are more aggressive in wishing to talk to victims, eyewitnesses, or family members. Media personnel will wish to have the names of those involved as quickly as possible which may put them in conflict with school policies about the release of names. From the period 24 to 36 hours after the event, the focus shifts to why. Often the question is asked in an effort to fix blame. During the 36- to 72-hour period, there is usually a more in-depth focus on what happened and why, although often the focus shifts to funerals and memorials if there has been a death. After 72 hours, there may be more funerals or events such as the release of victims from the hospital, but generally, media interest dies until perhaps an anniversary of the event or the beginning of a new school year. Smaller scale traumatic events, such as a suicide or a fire, may not command this same attention, unless there are sensational elements involved.

Media is a very competitive business. Consequently, reporters vie with each other to learn the most about an event. There is constant pressure on journalists to gather more data or to speculate about an event. Moreover, in an attempt to gather a scoop, members of the media may become very persistent.

Table 9.3

Reporting Information to the Media

Typically, the media liaison will first report the information that has been gathered on the Crisis Intervention Fact Sheet (Figure 6.2). He or she will report the following:

Who was involved: This can be released, again using general terms and not names of individuals (unless this information is public knowledge and next of kin have been notified). A victim can be described in terms of sex and grade in school and other demographic facts of relevance, but typically not by name.

What happened: In doing so, it is important to avoid a sensational, or romantic account of what occurred and omitting precise information on methods used to create trauma if they can be easily copied by impressionable individuals. For example, following a suicide one might announce the death was a result of carbon monoxide poisoning. It might be counterproductive to go into details about how a hose acquired from a local store, was hooked between the tailpipe of a car and the driver's window, while the deceased sat in a car with its engine running in a closed garage.

How the individuals were involved: This information may also be reported in a general way. How the event happened (who did what to whom) may also be reported, although one should not indicate details that either could be imitated or that speculate as to the reasons why a particular event occurred. The media liaison is as a rule not qualified to report on a state of mind. Typically, a news release would not indicate any speculation as to why.

Where it happened: To the extent that this is relevant, "where" can be reported. However, addresses of private residences or businesses should not be released.

When it occurred: This information should be reported as precisely as known.

What the prognosis is for those involved: This should also be reported along with any other information about a victim's status, as long as it is verified. If there is injury, a hospital will often provide this information.

Other sources of information: The reporter may be referred to other sources such as local and national resources for media inquiries. A list of such resources should be maintained in advance.

Avoid "no comment" answers: These statements suggest that the spokesperson has something to hide. If the media liaison cannot make a comment he or she might respond, "I do not have enough information to

(continued)

Table 9.3   *(Continued)*

form an opinion," or "I have not had enough time to talk to others," or "we have just received the information and must study it before giving an answer." Even if the media liaison cannot comment on a particular topic, he or she should still try to give reporters something to report, even if it is only a general statement of sympathy. In this situation offer a reasonable timetable for when the school will be able to answer questions, make comments, or provide an alternative source of information.

Be honest: In some cases, the truth may hurt, but lies are much more deadly. If you do not know the answer to a question, say so. It is important to avoid "whitewashing" what is going on, that is, to claim that everything is under control, or giving other assurances that may later prove to be unwarranted. Minimizing the problem will undermine the spokesperson's credibility with the press and community at large should the problem later prove to be serious. Instead, the media liaison should attempt to discuss the positive steps being taken to address the crisis and try to get the media to help in the overall response by reporting where troubled persons or individuals involved in the crisis can go for help. After a terrorist attack, for example, the newspapers can be very useful in letting the community know that various mental health agencies are available to those who are suffering emotional distress so that they may appropriately refer themselves. The media liaison should emphasize that the primary goal of the school district is to provide assistance to students and their families so that students can get through the crisis situation and back to the normal routine as quickly as possible.

Another relevant factor is the time pressures that various media are under. Each reporter has a deadline. Some reporters may be extremely concerned about making their deadline and will not be put off in their questioning. One of the first questions a media liaison should ask is the reporter's deadline. Insofar as possible, a liaison should attempt to cooperate in helping the reporter meet the deadline.

In talking to someone, either on the telephone or on a live microphone, everything is on the record. Liaisons must not say anything to the reporter that cannot be said to potentially tens of thousands of individuals.

In addition to wishing to talk with a media liaison, reporters will also want to talk to individuals directly involved. They will wish to speak particularly to those involved in the crisis event, and possibly even with parents. While it is impossible to prevent media from talking to individuals, it is not appropriate for a school spokesperson to give out a list of teachers and students involved. It may be appropriate, given the inevitability of reporter contact, for the school's media liaison to act as a broker, introducing the reporter to both students and teachers who volunteer ahead of time to talk with the media. Before giving the reporter a student's name, the parent should also give their permission for the contact to take place and be willing to sign a release. Students should be taught they have the right to refuse to speak to media even though reporters are adults (Poland & McCormick, 1999).

Electronic media representatives particularly wish to get eyewitness accounts from individuals on the scene. Schools can insist on maintaining privacy on the school grounds, but will have little control over what happens in the community.

SPECIAL MEDIA REQUIREMENTS

Although reporters from all media wish to have the facts in a case, different media have different requirements.

TELEVISION

Television reporters usually wish to have something of visual interest to display while they are interviewing a school spokesperson. They might ask the interviewee to stand in a particular location so they may film other activity of interest in the background. The spokesperson must be sensitive to these special visual needs, at the same time judge the appropriateness of displaying activities on the screen. The spokesperson should exercise some control over where an interview is granted with the media, so that the location is mutually acceptable. In many cases, it is best to be interviewed near the scene, to show involvement, rather than behind a desk. In addition, it is important to keep in mind that television media often displays a visual over your words.

Another aspect of television reporting is the fact that reports are very brief. Consequently, it is important to have a relatively simple and clear message to give to television reporters. The average television news story is 90 seconds, with a nine-second introduction. Anticipate a few brief questions for a live report, and give succinct answers conveying clear messages. For a taped report, the interview will be longer, but only a little of what has been taped will be shown. Anticipate this by repeating important messages and giving summaries from time to time of the key issues you wish to communicate.

RADIO

Radio reporters similarly have brief reports and are interested in short phrases that can be edited and played back in hourly newscasts. On the other hand, some radio reporters will conduct interviews, either in person or over the telephone with the media liaison, that may be broadcast live.

In addition, for both audio recordings and live broadcasts, it is important to have as good sound quality as possible. Media liaisons should choose a location to talk that is free of background school noise such as air conditioning or crowds of children talking or yelling. Radio reporters prefer to record individuals with well-modulated and expressive voices.

PRINT

Print journalists generally are more able to take time with interviewing a media liaison and are somewhat less interested in direct quotations than in the substance of the information. They have time for more facts and figures than do other journalists. Because messages to newspaper reporters are often more complex, it is important to check that the reporter has understood your message. The reporter's understanding can be determined by asking the reporter to repeat back the message you have delivered. Newspaper reporters will often read back quotes to you after they have written their story, but are under no obligation to do so. In fact, many journalists view allowing outsiders to review their copy as unethical. It should be remembered that reporters do not write headlines, so cannot be blamed for the headline their story carries. News stories should be monitored for accuracy because errors can be corrected in later editions.

MEDIA INTERVIEWS

Before meeting with any representative of the media, there are a number of issues to clarify, including:

- *Identify the spokesperson.* Before meeting with the media, it is important to make sure a spokesperson has been identified. If the person to be interviewed is not the identified spokesperson, it is important to refer the reporter to another source in the school district who might better answer the reporter's questions or who has more complete information.
- *Identify the topic.* When scheduling an interview or press conference, it is important that the media liaison ask in advance for a reporter's

name, affiliation, and the topic of interest. Media liaisons have a right to prepare their response. It is possible to negotiate various aspects of an interview. A media liaison can agree in advance to talk about certain topics and not talk about others as long as you have some rational reason for doing so.

- *Determine the structure.* If the media liaison is being asked to appear on a television show other than the news, it is important to determine what the program is like and how it is structured. If it is a panel, who will the other panel members be? Media liaisons have the right to turn down an appearance on a television show whose format they do not agree with. Radio and television call-in programs are difficult to predict and may cause messages to be distorted. For this reason, media liaisons may wish to avoid this format (Lazarus et al., 1999).

- *Decide what to wear.* If a media liaison is going to appear on television or be photographed, a number of special considerations need to be given to appearance. The liaison should wear normal apparel—clothing that is appropriate to the setting of the interview. If the setting is a school, work clothing is correct. In a studio, wear what the interviewer wears. A media liaison should not wear dark or tinted glasses.

- *Identify main communication points.* Before communicating to the news media, a liaison should identify priorities among dispelling rumors, providing accurate information, creating realistic expectations, and providing information about resources. It is most important for the media liaison to determine in advance what he or she wants to communicate. A liaison should enumerate a small number of *communication points*, or ideas that should be communicated, and plan to repeat them. When being audio- or videotaped, if the media liaison feels a point was made awkwardly, it is appropriate and reasonable to restate that point more than one time. With a recorded tape, reporters will select the most lucid presentation for their broadcast. On the evening news, the average length of a recording from someone being interviewed for a story will range from 9 to 14 seconds. This is not a long time and means that only one or two sentences will be used from an interview.

Often, in addition to releasing information, the media liaison will be asked to comment on what has happened. This is an opportunity to highlight what the schools are already doing or can do to prevent traumatic events. Efforts to curb school violence or other prevention programs might be mentioned as appropriate. In addition, there is an opportunity to garner public support for efforts under-way at the school and in the community. Table 9.4 presents a

Table 9.4
Possible Comments When Asked to Editorialize
about School Violence

---

1. We must end this conspiracy of silence among teenagers.

2. We must teach our children how to resolve conflicts without violence.

3. Parents must spend time talking with their children.

4. Programs that teach effective problem solving, anger management, and conflict resolution must be in place in our schools.

5. We must have effective after care school programs that provide protection, supervision, instruction, and enrichment for our youngsters.

6. We need to monitor and mentor our youth.

7. We need to find ways to keep guns out of the hands of distraught youngsters.

8. All schools need to have programs that emphasize prevention as well as response teams that intervene to either prevent a crisis from occurring or to respond in the aftermath.

Source: From "Dealing with the Media in the Aftermath of School Shootings," by P.J. Lazarus, S.E. Brock, and T. Feinberg, 1999, *Communiqué, 28,* p. 10. Copyright 1999 by the National Association of School Psychologists. Adapted with the authors' permission.

list of key messages in single sentence form that could be communication points during a comment period on school violence (Lazarus et al., 1999).

- *Anticipate difficult questions.* The media liaison should anticipate any difficult questions that may be asked, and develop some answers should the worst case occur. If there are questions the crisis response team would like not to answer, the liaison should plan to respond as briefly as possible and then move on to a main communication point.
- *Practice.* The media liaison should practice aloud with someone aware of the issues. He or she should practice fielding questions and get feedback from a colleague as to what kind of impression they are making.

How to Communicate

Although speaking with newspaper reporters may be done in a relatively natural style, it is important to be aware of style in dealing with broadcast journalists. A media liaison should keep the following information in mind when providing an interview:

- *Display a relatively high energy level.* In speaking with members of the media, it is important to realize that television and to a certain degree radio, tend to mute or cover up many subtle communication behaviors. Nervousness is less noticeable on television than it would be in a person-to-person situation. On the other hand, broad gestures and exaggerated speech appear more normal on television than in person. Therefore, in communicating to the broadcast media, you should put more energy into the communication than you normally would.
- *Use simple language rather than technical terms.* Media liaisons should avoid the use of jargon, acronyms, or excessively complex vocabulary. Often examples help to keep things clear and simple.
- *Be brief.* Remember that broadcast journalists want answers of approximately 12 seconds in length. Most television news stories run about one minute, which is the same amount of time it takes to read 4 or 5 newspaper paragraphs.
- *Be friendly.* Smile as much as is appropriate. In many crises, more somber demeanor is more appropriate. Do not be seduced into giving flippant or humorous responses. Chances are that a joke will fall flat in the print media or be misinterpreted.
- *Be knowledgeable, sincere, and compassionate.* Audiences are impressed most with the attitudes of those involved and often these attitudes are more important than the message.
- *Use good nonverbal communications.* Use hand gestures if appropriate. Gestures often make a point clearly and show up well on television. Maintain eye contact with the reporter. Do not look into the camera unless you are very experienced in doing this. Keep as much inflection in your voice as possible.

Avoid Sensationalism

Given the current public interest in school violence, most traumatic events will be reported by the media. As television talk shows have shown, there is a particular fascination with the bizarre and the sensational. Most school personnel do not wish to contribute to this climate. Moreover, there is a concern that with violent acts, there is a danger publicity might lead to imitation. This phenomenon is well-documented in the suicide literature (J. Davis & Sandoval, 1991). Publicity about suicide, particularly information that makes the act sound romantic, leads to copycat acts. Media liaisons should be comfortable in expressing that there is a scientific basis for concern about copycat acts when approached by reporters. Lazarus et al. (1999) offer a list of things to avoid when reporting acts of school violence (Table 9.5). While a media liaison should

Table 9.5
Suggestions for Reducing Violence Contagion from the
Centers for Disease Control

Avoid:

- *Presenting simplistic explanations.* It is important to acknowledge that multiple factors will have contributed to an act of school violence.

- *Engaging in repetitive, ongoing, or excessive reporting of school violence in the news.* Alternative approaches for coverage of newsworthy acts of school violence should be considered since repetitive coverage may promote copycat acts.

- *Providing sensational coverage of school violence.* Limiting morbid details of the act can minimize sensationalism, decreasing the prominence of the news report, and avoiding the use of dramatic photographs related to the event.

- *Reporting how-to descriptions of acts of violence.* Technical details about the act of violence (e.g., how bombs were made, how weapons were purchased) is not recommended and may facilitate imitation of the event by other at-risk individuals.

- *Presenting the act of violence as a tool for accomplishing certain ends.* Violence should not be presented as an effective coping strategy because other potentially violent individuals may view it as an attractive solution.

- *Glorifying the person(s) who committed the act of violence.* News coverage is less likely to contribute to copycat acts of violence when reports do not give undue attention to the perpetrator(s).

- *Focusing on the positive characteristics of the perpetrator.* Perpetrators of school violence typically have serious problems. It would be appropriate to report the problems that may have led to the act of violence.

Source: From "Dealing with the Media in the Aftermath of School Shootings," by P.J. Lazarus, S.E. Brock, and T. Feinberg, 1999, *Communiqué, 28,* p. 7. Copyright 1999 by the National Association of School Psychologists. Adapted with the authors' permission.

not attempt to tell reporters how to do their job (it would be highly insulting to tell them what and how to report), it is appropriate to express concern when it contributes to sensationalism.

MEDIA ACCESS PRIVILEGES

In general, members of the media are permitted free movement in an area where a crisis is occurring, as long as they do not hamper, deter, or interfere with law enforcement or public service functions of the police or other personnel. Media personnel cannot hamper teachers from teaching, but it is less clear when they are impeding the work of other school personnel such as administrators, counselors, and psychologists, who do not have strict time and place responsibilities. As public employees, there is some obligation to respond to press inquiries, although reasonable constraints may be imposed to allow school personnel to do their work.

If in the opinion of an authority in charge (e.g., a principal) restrictions to the media are unavoidable, a "pool system" may be established. That is, reporters on the scene may be permitted to select one representative from each medium and one from each level of coverage (i.e., local, national, and international), who can be escorted into the area. Reporters will then share information, photographs, and video- or audiotape with other accredited reporters. If access by the media must be denied or restricted for any reason, it is important to give a complete and thorough explanation.

SUMMARY

The media should be viewed as a resource that can prove valuable during a crisis response. While there may be times when their reporting places them in adversarial situations, it is best not to treat them as the enemy. Crisis response teams need to remember that following a crisis the school will have a series of messages to get out to the public and the media can be extremely helpful in assisting in this critical task. The information provided in this chapter will help schools approach the task of collaborating with the media.

CHAPTER 10

Security and Safety Procedures

The 14-year-old student walked into his small, suburban, Midwestern junior high school at about 11:00 A.M. on a January Monday. He carried a semi-automatic rifle, a handgun, and pockets full of ammunition. The principal stepped out of his office, called him by name, and asked where he was going. When the shooting stopped, a student and two teachers lay wounded; the principal, airlifted by helicopter in full view of television cameras, was dead. The youth escaped through an adjoining elementary school building, only to be captured an hour later in a nearby field—again, in full view of television cameras. The scene has been rerun hundreds of times; an officer taking handfuls of shells from his jacket and the handcuffed boy, head down, led away to a waiting police car.

—Collison et al. (1987, p. 389)

CRIME AND violence are unfortunate realities in today's schools. For example, the National Center for Educational Statistics (Kaufman et al., 1998, 1999) reports that in 1997 there were 202,000 incidents of nonfatal serious violent crime at school (among students ages 12 through 18). In addition, during the 1996/97 school year 10 percent of public schools reported at least one serious violent crime to local law enforcement. Perhaps most disturbingly, 63 students were murdered at school during the years 1992 and 1993. Clearly, these statistics argue for the development of school security and safety procedures.

At the same time, however, it must be acknowledged that schools are relatively safe places. Further examination of the just mentioned statistics reveals that in 1996 there were 671,000 incidents of nonfatal serious violent crime against youth away from school (versus 255,000 at school). In addition, during the 1996/97 school year 90 percent of public schools did not report any serious violent crime (versus 10 percent that did so). Finally, 7,294 youth (ages 5 through 19) were murdered away from school (versus 63 at school) (Kaufman et al., 1998). Not only would it be inaccurate, but it may also weaken schools, if somehow security and safety efforts were viewed as suggesting that schools are dangerous places (Brock, 1999b). Keep the true incidence of school crime and violence in mind when making security and safety plans.

Regardless of the fact that schools are relatively safe places, one incident of crime or violence at school is one to many. In the state of California, this position was validated in 1982 by the *Victims Bill of Rights.* This initiative amended the state's Constitution [Article 1, Section 28(c)] such that it now guarantees that all students and staff members have the "inalienable" right to attend schools that are "safe, secure, and peaceful." In addition to such public calls for school safety, school districts have been found liable for failing to engage in preparedness efforts (e.g., *Kelson v. City of Springfield*, 1985). This chapter provides suggestions for school security and safety. It will include a review of general safety procedures (designed to prevent potential crisis events), as well as discussion of security strategies for responding to hazardous events.

THE SECURITY LIAISON

As mentioned in Chapters 5 and 6, it is recommended that a security liaison be a member of the crisis response team. In addition to a district-level liaison, it is also recommended that a security liaison be identified at each school site. This liaison has two primary responsibilities. The first is to facilitate general school safety planning. The second is to develop and coordinate procedures that provide for security during and/or following crisis events (such as was illustrated by the scenario at the beginning of this chapter). Security liaisons should establish relationships with school district and local law enforcement personnel. Contact with local emergency service offices may also be appropriate.

GENERAL SAFETY PLANNING

While a security liaison may take primary responsibility for general safety planning, school staff and community members may also assist in this process. Formation of a "School Safety Committee" (SSC) is recommended. When constituted, a SSC might undertake the following: (1) establishment of safety conscious rules, policies, and procedures; (2) development of a positive school climate; (3) an examination of the school's physical environment; (4) physical and personal safety; (5) school security; and (6) staff development. Before discussing each of these topics, it is important to point out the evolving nature of school safety planning. New ideas and needs should be incorporated into school safety plans as they are identified (rather than waiting for a predetermined review). Once drafted, a safety plan must not be viewed as a static document.

Establish Safety Conscious Rules, Polices, and Procedures

A critical safety planning procedure is to establish school rules, policies, and procedures that are safety conscious (National School Safety Center, 1990). Table 10.1 provides examples of issues that many SSC may need to consider. All rules, policies, and procedures (even those not typically thought to have security and/or safety implications) should be carefully

Table 10.1
Issues to Consider When Establishing Safety-
Conscious School Rules, Procedures, and Policies

- Student conduct codes
- Student searches
- Prescription medication administration
- Use of physical force with students
- Gangs
- Employee background checks
- Weapons
- Use of pagers and cellular phones
- Use of school computers
- Property control and theft prevention

- Ethnic, cultural, and linguistic diversity
- Staff misconduct investigations
- Harassment policies
- Student suspension and expulsion
- Staff and student accident reporting
- Dress code
- Responding to threats
- Responding to student fights
- Visitor sign-in and identifying strangers

Sources: Knapp (1996), National School Safety Center (1990), Poland (1993, 1994), Stephens (1994), and Trump (1998a).

examined. For instance, student transfer and enrollment request should be monitored to assess the possibility that a gang may be attempting to adopt a school as their "turf" (Trump, 1998a). If policies do not exist on issues such as "Responding to Threats," it may be useful to formulate them.

STUDENT DISCIPLINE

The *School Safety Check Book* (National School Safety Center, 1990) advocates the establishment of written discipline rules that clearly differentiate between a discipline infraction (unacceptable behavior such as lying and inappropriate language) and criminal acts (behavior that violates the law such as assault and vandalism). School rules need to state specific unacceptable behaviors and their consequences. The rules should be reasonable and should allow for due process and appeal as appropriate. Administrators are obliged to report criminal behavior in a manner consistent with state penal codes. The establishment of an ongoing working relationship between schools, law enforcement, and the judicial system is critical.*

STUDENT FIGHTS

If not already in place, policies and procedures for school fights should be developed. The benefits of doing so have been illustrated in the Houston public schools. According to Poland (1997), these schools reported a dramatic decrease in the number of fights after implementing a policy requiring students involved in fights to make a court appearance and pay a $200 fine.

When developing procedures for responding to school fights, it needs to be kept in mind that more school staff are injured while breaking up fights than during any other type of activity. Injuries occur because the person breaking up the altercation impulsively makes one of several possible mistakes. Most typically, the staff member runs up to the fight, immediately jumps into the fracas, and starts pulling the combatants apart. By jumping right into the middle of the dispute, without first analyzing the situation, the staff member does not know what is happening and also puts him or herself in harms way from a flying fist or even a weapon. Before intervening, the staff member should evaluate the situation to determine if a weapon is being used and who is the aggressor (Blauvelt, 1981).

---

*Historically there has been poor coordination among these agencies (James, 1994; Poland, 1994). For example, schools may not enforce legal consequences for criminal acts committed at school. While perhaps suspending or expelling the student(s) involved, the offense may not be reported to the police. Similarly, law enforcement may not inform schools when a student commits a crime in the community, or a student on parole is placed in a school.

Other factors to assess are the audience, resources available to the intervenor, size, strength, and energy level of combatants, and number involved. Calling for assistance is always wise. A loud blowing of a whistle is certainly safer than putting oneself between two assailants, and may be equally efficacious. These and other issues for responding to school fights are summarized in Table 10.2.

CAMPUS VISITORS

An essential safety-conscious policy involves the identification of campus visitors. Signs should be posted at all school entry points directing visitors to check-in at the school office. It is important to establish policies that ask all staff members to approach and identify unfamiliar campus visitors (Stephens, 1994; Trump, 1998a). If visitors have not already done so, they should be directed to sign-in. After having signed-in, all campus visitors should be issued identification badges (which are to be worn while on campus, and returned just before leaving). Staff should be trained in and comfortable with challenging visitors not wearing a badge.

EMPLOYEE AND STUDENT IDENTIFICATION

To further assist in the identification of campus visitors, it is also helpful if students and employees are issued their own personal identification cards. If funds are available, a system of photo-identification badges, with the district or school logo, name, and employee job title for employees should be used. Special identification badges for temporary staff members (such as crisis intervenors brought onto campus from other schools to assist following a major crisis) should also be available (Figure 6.5).

DEVELOP A POSITIVE SCHOOL CLIMATE

Together the security liaison and the SSC should also carefully examine the overall school climate. Positive school climates are both the result of, and contribute to, secure, and safe schools. Stephens (1994) advocates creating a positive school climate by building pride and ownership in the school, making the campus welcoming (by having staff greet students as they arrive and being present during class changes), and having high administrator visibility (including class visitations and attendance at special events).

Resiliency and school climate research provide important data regarding factors influencing the safety of the school. Specifically, it highlights the importance of a positive relationship with a caring adult (Masten, 1994;

Table 10.2
Intervening in School Fights and Assaults:
Recommendations for School Staff Members

1. Determine comfort level with physical intervention.
2. Do not place self in physical danger. Assess situation before intervening.
3. Identify an escape route in case the situation escalates.
4. Do whatever is possible and appropriate to stop the altercation. Options include:
   - Calling for assistance (e.g., campus security, school administration)
   - Dispersing onlookers
   - Negotiating and persuading
   - Physically separating combatants
5. When dealing with visibly agitated individuals give choices (rather than threats), maintain eye contact and respect personal space. Defer to rules rather than asserting personal authority.
6. Obtain medical assistance as needed.
7. Obtain the names of any witnesses and document observed behavior.
8. Preserve the crime scene (for those cases in which the assailant is not known and/or serious injury has occurred).
9. Call the police if a crime has been committed.
10. Notify parents of involved students.
11. Assign a staff member to remain with the victim while medical attention is being obtained.
12. Assign a staff member to remain with the assailant until police, security, or the administrator who is going to conduct an investigation arrives on the scene.
13. Obtain psychological debriefing for students and staff involved in the fight or assault. If staff is the focus of the debriefing, students should not be present.

Sources: Adapted from Blauvelt (1981), Glenn (1990), Pitcher and Poland (1992), Stephens (1994), and Trump (1998a).

Werner & Smith, 1982). Many vehicles are available for making this kind of adult-child interaction possible, including schools within schools, use of community mentors and providing sufficient numbers of school counselors. Dwyer, Osher, and Warger (1998) have reviewed the school climate literature. Their findings on the characteristics of effective schools are summarized in Table 10.3.

The SSC may also want to assist teachers in examining the climate in their individual classrooms. The characteristics of secure and safe classrooms, as noted by Striepling (1997), are summarized in Table 10.4. Students feel secure when there is a sense of community and there is sufficient routine for students to know what to expect.

Examine the School's Physical Environment

The security liaison and SSC should examine the physical environment of the school because a relationship exists between student and staff behavior, and their surroundings. Crowe (1990) describes the *Crime Prevention*

Table 10.3
Characteristics of Effective Schools

1. Focus on academic achievement.
2. Involve families in meaningful ways.
3. Develop links to the community.
4. Emphasize positive relationships among students and staff.
5. Discuss safety issues openly.
6. Treat students with equal respect.
7. Create ways for students to share their concerns.
8. Help children feel safe expressing their feelings.
9. Have in place a system for referring children who are suspected of being abused or neglected.
10. Offer extended day programs for children.
11. Promote good citizenship and character.
12. Identify problems and assess progress toward solutions.
13. Support students in making the transition to adult life and the workplace.
14. Develop and consistently enforce schoolwide rules that are clear, broad-based, and fair.

Source: Dwyer, Osher, and Wagner (1998, pp. 4–5).

Table 10.4
Characteristics of Secure and Safe Classrooms

1. Early building of a community of learners (using collaboration between students and teacher, school and home).
2. Enthusiasm for learning.
3. Teachers and students learn and use each other's names.
4. Classroom meetings are held to discuss issues and solve problems.
5. Classroom management includes firm, fair, and consistent rules and procedures.
6. Use of learning centers.
7. Opportunity for cooperative group work.
8. Leisure areas exist for discussions, downtime, and reading.
9. Books and magazines readily available.
10. Displays of students' in-progress and completed work.
11. Plants and objects that assist students in developing an identity of the classroom space as "ours."

Source: Striepling (1997).

Through Environmental Design Theory, which purports that the appropriate physical "design" and effective use of the "built environment" decreases the incidence of crime and prevalence of fear of harm or loss. Crowe identifies significant problem areas on school campuses, including parking lots and lockers, and suggests potential remedies. For example, restroom location is typically a problem area because they are often located at the end of hallways. In addition, double door entry to restrooms is a poor design for safety. They require students to first enter a small entry room and then proceed through a second door into the actual restroom. Consequently, students are unable to see what kind of situation they are entering.

Another area to consider from a school design perspective is the playground. Most accidents occur in this play setting, where adult supervision may be limited. Bowers (1989) offers a number of useful recommendations for improving playground safety by designing equipment to minimize the risk of injuries. His recommendations include placing physical barriers to discourage children from running into moving swings; providing safe clearances by placing equipment at least 20 feet from trees, fences, and so on; providing safe ground covering; inspecting equipment regularly; and increasing playground supervision. Proper lighting for the playground as well as the rest of the school also is an important factor in increasing safety.

One method for school and community participation in this planning activity is through the use of surveys. *Safe Schools: A Planning Guide for Action* (California Department of Education, 1989) is a resource containing a safe schools questionnaire for both students and adults on "The School's Physical Environment" (see Appendix F). Topics covered for evaluation include school location, school grounds, school buildings and classrooms, internal security (e.g., school alarms) and school property. Additionally, Brooks (1993) suggests evaluating patterns of student congregation, paying particular attention to shifts in clusters of students, rival groups binding together, students attending events they normally do not attend, sudden appearance of underground publications, and parents withdrawing their children from school due to a fear that something might happen.

ADDRESS PERSONAL AND PHYSICAL SAFETY ON CAMPUS

The security liaison and SSC need to address both personal and physical safety issues. Personal safety refers to "crimes against persons" or how often students and staff are exposed to assaults, substance abuse, suicide, victimization, or child abuse. Physical safety refers to "crimes against property" dealing with arson, burglary, theft, trespass, vandalism, and bombs. Gang activity on campus may affect both areas of safety.

ASSESSMENT

The first step in the assessment process is for the security liaison to collect crime data. Blauvelt (1990) describes a method for collecting such data that makes use of either index cards or a computer to record the following information: "What happened? When did it happen? Where did it happen? Who was involved? What action was taken?" (p. 5). The second step is to analyze the data by category of offense. Once patterns are identified, administrators can then determine where and when to allocate their resources to reduce vulnerability to illegal acts. Once the security liaison completes the assessment, the procedure would be to present a summary report of problem areas to the SSC, who may look for solutions. Stephens (1997) recommends identifying and tracking repeat offenders, as the majority of problems involve a small number of students. SSC involvement may also take place in assessing site personal and physical safety through development of surveys such as the one included in Appendix F. Outside consultants may be brought in to conduct an audit or assessment. However, caution is urged in selection of such a consultant as many "overnight experts" on school safety and security have recently

School Crime Assessment Tool

1.	Has your community crime rate increased over the past 12 months?	YES	NO
2.	Are more than 15 percent of your work order repairs vandalism-related?	YES	NO
3.	Do you have an open campus?	YES	NO
4.	Has there been an emergence of an underground student newspaper?	YES	NO
5.	Is your community transiency rate increasing?	YES	NO
6.	Do you have an increasing presence of graffiti in your community?	YES	NO
7.	Do you have an increased presence of gangs in your community?	YES	NO
8.	Is your truancy rate increasing?	YES	NO
9.	Are your suspension and expulsion rates increasing?	YES	NO
10.	Have you had increased conflicts relative to dress styles, food services, and types of music played at special events?	YES	NO
11.	Do you have an increasing number of students on probation at your school?	YES	NO
12.	Have you had isolated racial fights?	YES	NO
13.	Have you reduced the number of extracurricular programs and sports at your school?	YES	NO
14.	Has there been an increasing incidence of parents withdrawing students from your school due to fear?	YES	NO
15.	Has your budget for professional development opportunities and in-service training for your staff been reduced or eliminated?	YES	NO
16.	Are you discovering more weapons on your campus?	YES	NO
17.	Do you have written screening and selection guidelines for new teachers and other youth-serving professionals who work in your school?	YES	NO

(continued)

Figure 10.1 The School Crime Assessment Tool can be used by a security liaison to assess the degree to which school violence or crime is a problem in a given district or school site. *Scoring and Interpretation.* Multiply each affirmative answer by 5 and add the total. Scores of 0–20 indicate there are no significant safety problems at your school. If you have scores ranging from 25 to 45, you have an emerging school safety problem and should develop a safe school plan. Scores of 50 to 70 indicate that there is a significant potential for school safety problems. A safe school plan should be developed. Begin working on your safe school plan immediately. Get some outside help. *Source:* Reproduced with permission from the National School Safety Center, Westlake Village, CA. From R.D. Stephens (1993, Spring), School safety reality check: Assessing your situation. *School Safety,* 2 and 35.

18.	Are drugs easily available in or around your school?	YES	NO
19.	Are more than 40 percent of your students bused to school?	YES	NO
20.	Have you had a student demonstration or other signs of unrest within the past 12 months?	YES	NO
	Totals:		

Figure 10.1 *(Continued)*

emerged. These individuals may not have the knowledge or expertise needed to assess safety related to school settings but nevertheless charge exorbitant fees (Trump, 1998a).

Employee unions, if concerned about underreporting of school crime by administration, may request staff to collect their own data on incidents at sites and physical evidence, photos or videos, which may then be utilized to address safety and security concerns (Trump, 1998a). Additionally, bargaining units are increasingly addressing the issue of giving teachers the opportunity to transfer schools after being victimized by students (Stephens, 1997).

Stephens (1993) has developed another method of assessing school violence. He provides a quick (20 question) School Crime Assessment Tool to quantify the need for school safety planning (Figure 10.1). The score generated by this measure indicates severity of school safety problems and may help an SSC determine how much of a priority should be placed on safety planning. Stephens (1994) advocates the use of focus groups to discuss issues of violence and safety planning. These focus groups composed of students, school staff, parents and community members, can be used to determine perceptions of violence and then to provide input on ways to improve safety. Finally, Morrison, Furlong, and Morrison (1994) note that school psychologists, using their skills in group facilitation and consultation, are key resources in safety planning.

INTERVENTION

To assist the security liaison and the SSC improve the physical environment and personal and physical safety at school, consideration of additional security and safety interventions may be necessary. Once interventions have been implemented, the security liaison should periodically review their effectiveness. Table 10.5 provides a summary of possible interventions. Interventions are placed into categories of supervision, physical environment, transportation and parking, and collaboration.

Many of the interventions invoke the use of technology for surveillance, which is expensive. The ultimate, perhaps, is the use of metal detectors. A balance must be struck between adequate monitoring for safety and the establishment of a friendly, caring school climate.

REVIEW CAMPUS SECURITY

General safety planning should also include a review of school security. Models of campus security, described by Grant (1993), include "officer friendly" and "campus cop." In the former the police officer has a public

Table 10.5
Possible Interventions for Improving School Safety

Supervision

1. Reduce class and school size.
2. Stagger dismissal times and lunch periods.
3. Adjust scheduling and shorten passing periods to minimize time in the hallways or potentially dangerous locations and lengthen instructional periods.
4. Restrict students from entering classrooms alone and from loitering in restrooms and hallways.
5. Deal with problems while they are small. Address rumors, boyfriend/girlfriend conflicts, or matters of disrespect before these incidents escalate to violence.
6. Do not allow students to congregate in areas that are isolated (e.g., parking lots). Encourage students to get together in areas with natural surveillance opportunities (e.g., near the office).
7. Relocate school staff offices (e.g., counselor or school psychologist) to areas where problems have been occurring or throughout campus.
8. Increase supervision of access to the campus and grounds.
9. Keep security personnel moving about the campus.
10. Use mobile security patrol for nights and weekends if vandalism rate is high.
11. Monitor surrounding school grounds including landscaped areas, parking lots, and bus stops.
12. Check stairwells, restrooms, and hallways after the bell rings to ensure students have not been detained.

(continued)

Table 10.5 *(Continued)*

13. In addition to monitoring duties, encourage school security personnel to build relationships with students, including troubled ones. Development of trust may help security to be alerted before incidents escalate.

14. Staff custodial personnel to provide services to the school 24 hours per day.

15. Post, review, and practice lab safety routinely. Provide adult supervision in labs when students are present.

16. Require vendors and any workers on campus to have identification.

17. Use metal detectors at entrances to extra-curricular activities or for access to the campus on a daily basis. However, keep in mind that such detectors are not perfect. Box cutters are an example of a weapon that often passes through metal detectors unnoticed.

Physical Environment

1. Strongly define school perimeters by transition markers, such as fencing. This increases effectiveness of security by facilitating monitoring of outsiders on campus.

2. Designate one point of entry and control all access to campus through this main area.

3. Use vertical metal or small mesh (unclimbable) fencing.

4. Plant prickly bushes next to areas that need to be protected.

5. Require staff to lock their classrooms when leaving.

6. Ensure classroom doors have a window to allow someone looking in a view of most of the classroom, as well as someone looking out a view of the hallway. In the event of a lockdown, this window should be able to be quickly covered to block visibility from outside.

7. Place teachers' desks to maximize the ability to see the room, and leave space between student desks in classrooms to minimize incidental student contact.

8. Ensure doors are solid, well maintained, and lockable with a key.

9. Tightly control access to keys.

10. Lock all outside doors. Do so, however, only after installing panic bars that allow emergency exits in case there is a need for a quick evacuation.

11. Use hydraulic dampers on doors so that the harder someone pushes, the slower the door moves.

12. Install two-way intercoms in every office.

Table 10.5 *(Continued)*

13. Use parabolic (convex) mirrors in stairwells and other strategic locations.

14. Set restroom thermostats at 62 degrees Fahrenheit.

15. Ensure adequate lighting exists, especially outside at night. Make sure school maintenance personnel quickly replace burned out bulbs.

16. Keep and review maintenance records of all interior and exterior work, including doors and windows to ensure they are up-to-date.

17. Keep chemical storage areas, mechanical rooms, boiler rooms, and hazardous materials locked at all times.

18. Review the need for, and use of, intrusion detection systems (alarms and their monitoring system). Routinely check and maintain these systems.

19. Place any trees, shrubs, and bushes far enough away from buildings and windows to ensure good visibility.

20. Design hallways and classes with few hidden corners or closets.

21. Arrange furniture to allow ease of movement during transitions and to facilitate teacher's access to students.

22. Make sure classroom storage areas are visible to teacher. Do not leave potential weapons (e.g., scissors, staplers) laying around.

23. Eliminate obstacles such as trashcans and architectural barriers that block traffic flow and impede visibility and supervision.

24. Use surveillance cameras in specific problem areas. For example, a mobile surveillance camera could be used to target select campuses that are subject to vandalism. Decisions regarding placement of cameras need to keep student privacy rights in mind.

25. Use camcorders to tape fights, criminal or disruptive behavior, and trespassers. Such documentation provides a record of the inappropriate or illegal action and disarms parents who may deny their child's involvement.

26. Install toughened glass.

27. Place grillwork over windows if broken frequently in schools with high vandalism.

28. Use graffiti-resistant wall surfaces such as Teflon, plastic laminate, fiberglass, or melamine covering.

29. Post warning signs that trespassers and vandals will be prosecuted.

(continued)

Table 10.5 *(Continued)*

30. Eliminate use of lockers and book bags by providing one set of books to be kept at students' homes and a second set for use in class, or allow for book bags only if they are see through mesh or plastic.

Transportation and Parking

1. Employ a vehicle identification system.
2. Restrict student access to parking and bus loading areas.
3. Restrict vehicle access to play areas when students are present.
4. Assign staff to student parking areas during arrival and dismissal times.
5. Ensure that there are regular safety checks of district vehicles including buses, vans, and cars.
6. For all bus routes (including field trips) maintain passenger lists and route descriptions at the school site.
7. Require students and staff to carry identification with them on field trips. Check staff and students back into school once they return.
8. Use surveillance cameras on buses. Use two-way radios to facilitate communication between bus drivers and the district transportation department to improve bus safety.
9. Install slash-proof seat coverings on school vehicles.

Collaboration

1. Work with law enforcement to provide staff with information on current trends in drug use and trafficking.
2. Ask city and/or county governments to install crosswalks and crossing lights near schools and on routes students use to travel to and from schools.
3. Collaborate with neighbors to encourage them to monitor school after hours and report suspicious activity.
4. Encourage local emergency response teams to train on school buses.
5. Use the campus as much as possible. Coordinate the use of facilities for after school programs and evening use by the community.
6. Set up a hotline or anonymous phone tip line to report crime and school safety concerns.

Sources: Brooks (1993), Cornell (1998), Crowe (1990), Goldstein (1997), Goldstein and Conoley (1997), Haller (1992), James (1994), Nelson (1996), McDaniel (n.d.), McGiboney (1998), Muir (1988), Poland (1994), Striepling (1997), Stephens (1994, 1997), Steward & Knapp (1997), and Trump (1998a, 1998b).

relations role; educates children on safety, gangs, and substance abuse; and is viewed as a positive role model. In the later model, the officer's role is to enforce laws. Combining both models Grant also describes the development of the *School Liaison Officer Program* in Richmond, British Columbia. In this program, police officers attend sporting events, dances, field trips; have casual conversations with students; investigate school-based crimes; follow-up on disclosures; and provide enforcement. Table 10.6 summarizes Blauvelt's (1990) description of the types of security available to schools and advantages and disadvantages of each type. Cost is weighed against control and against sensitivity to educational needs and traditions.

ADDRESS STAFF DEVELOPMENT NEEDS

It is important for the security liaison to assess the need for in-service training. Staff development may cover a wide range of topics. Examples include suicide prevention; behavior management; CPR/first aid; how to contact emergency personnel; issues affecting gay, lesbian, and bisexual youth; multicultural awareness; conflict management; and gangs. Staff development planning should identify topics most appropriate for given employees groups. For example, while bus drivers may require staff development in managing accidents, school administrators may benefit from staff development in legal issues (e.g., how to conduct student searches). Failure to provide staff with certain types of staff development may generate a certain degree of liability. For example, James (1993) reports that schools may be sued if teachers are not provided training on how to respond to threatened or suspected disruptions (e.g., gang fights).

One recommended staff development program is behavior management. Effective behavior management skills help to better ensure safety at a school site (Glenn, 1990). Training for teachers and other staff, including bus drivers and noon duty aides, in this area is essential. When staff have the skills to handle disruptive students many potential problems are avoided. A specific program recommended by the authors is the *Nonviolent Crisis Intervention Workshop* (Steiger, 1987) developed by the National Crisis Prevention Institute. (See Table 3.3.) This Workshop is designed to teach school personnel techniques in managing disruptive, assaultive, out-of-control behavior, and to resolve conflicts before they become violent. Another recommended staff development topic is personal safety (Glenn, 1990). Reminding staff to avoid situations that place them in isolation is important. Large campuses with isolated areas would particularly need to address this issue.

Table 10.6
Types of School Security: Advantages and Disadvantages

School Security Type	Advantages	Disadvantages
1. No formal security program, call law enforcement as needed	No cost	Works only if number of crimes is low and local law enforcement can respond quickly
2. Employ local police	Trained, screened, uniformed, armed highly visible personnel Radio communication and reporting procedures established Size of the force can be increased or decreased as needs dictate Police power extends beyond school boundaries	Officers responsible to authority other than Board of Education; lack of commitment to educational philosophy Lack of flexibility in dealing with delinquent acts; possible violation of student rights No input in selection of assigned personnel; high turnover rate; dissatisfaction with school assignment School may become overly dependent on police to solve all their problems; costly if schools must pay for their services
3. Contract with guard service	Low cost Size of force can be increased or decreased as needs dictate School assignments, deployment, and dismissal of unsatisfactory personnel is at the discretion of school authorities School authorities decide how guards are dressed and whether they carry weapons	Personnel likely to be poorly trained, less educated, and not prescreened by a background investigation Lack commitment to educational philosophy; lack of insight into student problems Contractor may inadequately supervise personnel; school personnel may have difficult time supervising and controlling the guards High turnover rate; general disrespect for "Rent-a-Cops" Degree of school liability for guard error may be uncertain

Table 10.6 *(Continued)*

School Security Type	Advantages	Disadvantages
4. Hire security professionals	Personnel screened, hired by, and responsible to school authorities	Program must be budgeted a year in advance; difficult to increase force size quickly
	Flexible duty assignments; school system control over entire program	Dismissal of personnel must follow established procedures (i.e., "with cause")
	School system decides role, mode of dress, and whether weapons will be carried	High cost
		Training program must be implemented
	Incident reporting system can be designed to meet specific needs	Schools often become overly dependent on security personnel and tend to involve them in administrative issues rather than just security issues
	In-house response unit available for crises	
5. Combination of 2, 3, and 4	See above	See above

Source: Adapted with permission from the National School Safety Center, Westlake Village, CA. From P.D. Blauvelt (1990, Fall), School security: Who you gonna call? *School Safety*, 4–8.

DEVELOP A SCHOOL SAFETY PLAN

The result of general safety planning should be the development of a comprehensive school safety plan. The publication, *Safe Schools: A Planning Guide for Action* illustrates the process of developing such a plan (California Department of Education, 1989). This guide focuses on four components that contribute to the overall school environment: personal characteristics of students and staff, physical environment, social environment, and cultural environment. Another valuable resource is the *School Safety Check Book* (National School Safety Center, 1990). This document not only assists in assessing safety on campus, but also helps in the development of prevention and response strategies. Descriptions of model programs are also provided. Additional models for safe schools planning that may prove helpful have been authored by Stephens (1994), Furlong, Morrison, and Clontz (1991, 1993), and Kandel and Follman (1993a, 1993b).

PREPARING FOR AND RESPONDING
TO SCHOOL CRISES

In addition to general safety planning, the security liaison is also responsible for school security during and immediately following a crisis event.

Crisis Communication

Within-School Communication

The security liaison should make sure that there are ways for staff members to communicate with each other throughout the school day. Clear and effective communication among all staff members (including crossing guards and parking attendants) is essential for ensuring student security and safety in times of crisis. Basic tools to ensure such communication at a school site include school intercoms, walkie-talkies, cell phones, and other similar devices. Alternative message delivery systems need to be available should primary communication mechanisms break down (California Department of Education, 2000; Oregon School Boards Association, 1999).

Crisis Response Team Communication

It is essential for the security liaison to make sure that there exist immediate and redundant communication mechanisms linking crisis response team members to each other, and to school and district offices. Use of beepers, cellular telephones, battery operated two-way radios, e-mail, fax machines, and ham radios are all possible communication options. Among the more elaborate communication options is the establishment of a district-wide emergency operations center (School Safety Update, 1991). Using modern technologies, such a center is capable of linking administration with individual schools, district security, transportation, maintenance, and local law enforcement.

The need for redundant communication mechanisms is emphasized by the authors' crisis response experiences that have found that following major events it is not unusual for traditional communication devices (e.g., phones) to be quickly overwhelmed. In addition, it is typical that natural disasters disrupt or destroy some communication links. Regarding the need for additional phone lines in times of crisis, it is interesting to note that some crisis response plans list a phone number for phone company representatives who can quickly obtain additional dedicated phone lines for a school in times of crisis (e.g., Nettleton Public School District, 1998).

When sending crisis communications by alternative communication means (e.g., fax machines), it will be important to include in the message instructions for replying immediately. This way the sender will be sure that the message has been received. If a reply is not obtained within a few minutes, the sender will know that there is a need to try another communication strategy (e.g., e-mail).

A caution regarding use of cellular phones needs to be offered. While this communication device can be very helpful during a crisis response, it is important to note that such communications may not be secure. Poland and McCormick (1999) have pointed out that the media has the capacity to monitor cell phones. Thus, communication regarding confidential information should be avoided when talking on a cellular phone.

COMMUNICATION BETWEEN THE SCHOOL AND THE COMMUNITY

It is also important to establish communication links between the school and the community (Oregon School Boards Association, 1999). Although in the current model of school crisis response the media liaison (see Chapter 9) would be primarily responsible for this activity, the security liaison may help to craft the message from the school to the community about the crisis and ensure that appropriate communication linkages are available.

DANGER SIGNALS

Among the many recommendations for improving school communications reported by Poland (1994) is the need for clear "danger" signals. These signals or code words can be used in different ways. For example, they can be used by school staff members to notify school administration of a potentially hazardous situation. One possible system for doing so is to state over the school's intercom a previously established code. A code 1, for example, could mean that there is an incident on campus (such as a fight between two students) that requires immediate assistance from the school office. A code 2 could mean that an incident has occurred (such as a fight with major injuries) that will require emergency medical assistance. And a code 3 could mean that an incident is occurring (such as a student with a gun) that will require immediate police assistance. Use of such codes communicate the need for assistance without alerting individuals, who might be making threats, to the staffs' intended actions.

Another danger signal procedure that needs to be established is one that can alert an entire school's staff of a hazardous situation (California Department of Education, 2000). An example of a situation necessitating such a response would be the scenario described at the beginning of this chapter. This danger signal (which could make use of a code word or specific bell sequence) would communicate to school staff members that a crisis situation is in progress, and that all students are to be moved to a secured (locked) location. Such a procedure is often referred to as a "lockdown."

It is essential that all school staff members be frequently drilled regarding the meaning of the different danger signals. To ensure that substitute personnel will know the danger signals, this (and other important crisis response information) should be placed inside student attendance registers and/or lesson plan books. In addition, it is recommend that selected codes be changed on a regular basis. Doing so will lessen the likelihood of perpetrators becoming aware of school actions. Finally, it is important to note that in addition to danger signals, an "all clear" signal will also need to be established. Such a signal would communicate that the crisis has passed (California Department of Education, 2000).

Danger Procedures

Complementary to training in the danger signals, school staffs need to be trained regarding exactly what to do when a danger signal is broadcast. During a lockdown, for example, staff must know that students are to be directed to a secure room, doors locked, cover taken underneath tables or desks, windows closed, and curtains drawn (California Department of Education, 2000). Drills will be helpful in reinforcing these instructions. Again, to ensure that substitutes are aware of these procedures, this information should be placed inside student attendance registers or lesson plan books, and substitute teachers should be oriented to school safety procedures.

Involving Law Enforcement

The California Department of Education (2000) recommends obtaining a written agreement regarding coordination of the law enforcement response to school crisis events. This document should detail the point at which responsibility for a situation would be assumed by law enforcement. Also, when preparing for the involvement of law enforcement in school crisis events (such as school shootings) it is important to provide them with a detailed floor plan of the school (showing entrances, windows, roof latches, ventilation systems, etc.) and current estimates of the number and identities of staff and students in each class area (Petersen & Straub, 1992; Trump, 1998a). Often school yearbooks or class pictures become handy tools for helping law enforcement to identify students. Police should also have a master key to the school and know if there are parking permits used to identify student and staff cars (Neal, 1999).

RESPONDING TO BOMBS AND BOMB THREATS

Fortunately, school bombings are an extremely rare occurrence (Goldstein & Conoly, 1997). However, bomb threats are not unusual. For example, it has been estimated that there are 500 to 1,000 threats for every bomb actually found (Poland & McCormick, 1999). This fact, combined with the observation that many schools handle bomb threats poorly, argues strongly for developing explicit procedures for responding to bomb threats. Training in these procedures should be provided to all school staff members, including support personnel such as bus drivers, custodians, cafeteria workers and secretaries (National School Safety and Security Services, 1999). Poland and McCormick recommend that law enforcement be involved in this training and provide school staff members with information about what a bomb might look like and where they are likely to be found.

The development of school bomb threat procedures would be a security liaison responsibility. A first step of any bomb threat procedure should be to immediately notify local law enforcement and to then evaluate the threat. Bomb threat evaluation should also include the following: (1) documenting as precisely as possible the exact words of the person making the threat, (2) attempting to identify characteristics of the person making the threat, and (3) obtaining as many details as possible regarding the specifics of the threat (National School Safety Center, 1990). A specific bomb and bomb threat checklist is offered in Figure 10.2.

EMERGENCY EVACUATIONS

A variety of crisis events may necessitate the evacuation of students from one location to another (e.g., fire, plane crash, toxic waste or chemical spills, bomb threats). These crisis response procedures have the potential to save lives. In fact, the principal of one school that had suffered a particularly devastating shooting reported that the drill that required her students to evacuate an area protected a number of children during the event (National School Safety Center, 1991).

The first step in developing an evacuation plan is to identify potential safe areas that students could be moved to in the event that their school and/or their classrooms are no longer safe. Ideally, the area chosen would

Checklist for Bomb Threats, Suspicious Devices, and Explosions

Bomb Threat

_____ Document the nature of the threat as precisely as possible.

☐ Note the exact words of the person making the threat. _____
_____
_____
_____
_____

☐ Identify characteristics of the person making the threat.

   (a) Gender   ☐ Male   ☐ Female

   (b) Tone of voice _____

   (c) Age of person making the threat _____

   (d) Presence of an accent ☐ Yes   ☐ No   Type _____

☐ Write down any familiar and/or unfamiliar background sounds. _____
_____

☐ Obtain as many details as possible regarding the specifics of the threat.

   (a) Where the bomb is to explode? _____

   (b) Where the bomb is right now? _____

   (c) What kind of bomb it is? _____

   (d) What the bomb looks like? _____

   (e) Why is the bomb being placed? _____

_____ Consult with local law enforcement and evaluate the credibility of the threat. Information used to assess credibility includes both evidence and experience.

☐ Evidence:

   1. What is the nature of the threat?   (see above)

   2. Are there signs of illegal entry into the school? ☐ Yes ☐ No

   3. Are there reports of missing chemicals? ☐ Yes ☐ No

☐ Experience:

   1. Have all other bomb threats proven to be hoaxes? ☐ Yes ☐ No

   2. Are tests scheduled for today? ☐ Yes ☐ No

   3. Is it the first warm day of spring? ☐ Yes ☐ No

   4. Is today "Senior Skip Day"? ☐ Yes ☐ No

   5. Is the school playing its rival school in an athletic event? ☐ Yes ☐ No

   6. Was the caller obviously a youngster? ☐ Yes ☐ No

   7. Was there giggling in the background when call was received? ☐ Yes ☐ No

Figure 10.2 The Checklist for Bomb Threats, Suspicious Devices, and Explosions can be used by a security liaison to help guide the response to bomb threat situations. It is important to note that it will likely need to be modified for local use.

244

8. Is there unexplained student unrest? ☐ Yes ☐ No

9. Is there employee unrest? ☐ Yes ☐ No

_____ If the threat is judged to be credible, then . . .

☐ Make a decision regarding the need to evacuate. This decision would be made only if it is judged that students will be safer in another location. (Previously established evacuation procedures are prerequisite to this step.)

☐ Notify school staff. Ideally, this is done by prearranged signals. These signals would communicate the following:

☐ A bomb threat has been made.

☐ Staff needs to look for suspicious devices.

☐ Students need to be evacuated to safe locations (i.e., away from areas where the bomb is suspected to be).

_____ Conduct a limited search of the building. This may be done with the assistance of local law enforcement. However, school staff are most likely to identify objects that are out of place.

☐ If students are not evacuated, teachers should inspect their classrooms without alarming students.

☐ School staff not assigned to supervise students should begin to search the school for suspicious devices. The most common locations for bombs include the following:

☐ Boys' restrooms   ☐ Student lockers   ☐ Principal's offices

☐ Parking lots   ☐ Hallways   ☐ Windows/Skylights

☐ Trophy cases   ☐ Planters   ☐ Stairwells

☐ Water fountains   ☐ Trash cans   ☐ Dumpsters

☐ If a suspicious device is found, then the following procedures should be implemented:

Suspicious Device Found

_____ Do not touch the device.

_____ Immediately report the device to the school office and local law enforcement.

_____ Isolate the area.

_____ Carefully evacuate the students from affected area(s). Evacuate those closest to the device first.

_____ Use the fire alarm as an evacuation signal only if it is determined that prearranged evacuation routes do not result in students and staff walking directly near the device.

_____ Re-enter affected areas only after being advised to do so by appropriate law enforcement officials.

(continued)

Figure 10.2 *(Continued)*

_____ If a bomb explodes, then the following procedures should be implemented:

Bomb Explosion

_____ Call 911.

_____ Pending arrival of emergency equipment and additional help, evacuate the school. Get students and staff to a safe location and maintain control of the students.

_____ Identify and care for injured students and staff.

_____ Develop a list of casualties.

_____ Whether or not the building will be reoccupied will be a decision made by the fire department and/or the police department. In either case, the following will need to be done:

☐ Notify the superintendent.

☐ Establish an information center. (Staffed by senior officials who will be able to handle all inquiries about injured persons and the status of the school.)

☐ Arrange transportation for the students, should the school be closed.

_____ Call the school's legal counsel. (This is particularly important in those cases in which a bomb threat has been received and you made the decision not to evacuate the school.)

Sources: Adapted with permission from *Effective Strategies for School Security*, published by the National Association of Secondary School Principals, Reston, VA, and authored by P.E. Blauvelt (1981). Other sources for this Checklist include the National School Safety Center (1990) and Poland and McCormick (1999). For more information about NASSP programs and services, call (703) 860-0200.

Figure 10.2   *(Continued)*

be large enough to accommodate the entire student body. Examples of such locations include shopping centers, community recreation facilities, business offices, and churches. It is important to note that before an area is selected, the personnel who operate the facility should be consulted. In addition to making certain their willingness to have their building serve such a purpose, it is also to ensure that they know what to expect should an evacuation be required.

The direction of the prevailing winds might also be taken into account in planning an evacuation route. Winds can carry smoke and flames as well as toxic chemicals released into the atmosphere. Children should be led up-wind from sources of pollution.

The next step is to consult with local law enforcement and fire departments regarding evacuation plan proposals. In some situations, it will be the police and/or fire department themselves who will make the decision regarding whether and when to evacuate (Petersen & Straub, 1992). Thus, it may prove beneficial if they participate in the development of evacuation procedures.

Additional considerations for evacuation plans include ensuring that basic needs such as water, food, blankets, sunscreen, insect spray, and activities to fill the student's time are available (Poland, 1994). Poland and McCormick (1999) recommend developing a portable emergency supply box that can be used during an evacuation. Suggested supply box items include staff and student emergency phone cards, flashlights, bullhorns, portable phone, pencil and paper, and staff identification badges or attire.

The final step is to document the evacuation plan. For a sample evacuation procedure, the reader is referred to Table 10.7. In most cases, existing fire drill evacuation routes can be adapted to other potential emergencies requiring evacuation. However, the evacuation procedure should contain alternative evacuation routes in the event that the primary evacuation routes and/or safe areas are affected by the crisis event.

ACCOUNTING FOR STUDENTS AND STAFF

It is also important that the security liaison facilitate the development of plans and procedures that will allow the school to quickly and efficiently account for students and staff members following crisis events. Reporting methods may include the use of alphabetical listings of all students and staff and/or class lists. Again, a method needs to be developed to ensure that substitutes are aware of a school's student and staff accounting procedures. For a sample of such a procedure, refer to Table 10.8.

REUNITING STUDENTS WITH PARENTS

Facilitating the development of procedures for reuniting students with their families following crisis events is yet another security liaison task. Literally hundreds of parents arriving simultaneously to locate their children following a school crisis event emphasizes the importance of these procedures. At elementary schools, it is recommended that these procedures give priority to reuniting younger students with their families first. These plans also need to specify where reunification will take place. When possible the child's regular classroom is ideal, since parents are likely to know where it is. However, when faced with large numbers of parents, or when the classroom is either damaged or otherwise unavailable, alternative locations will need to be identified.

Table 10.7

Sample Crisis Evacuation Procedures

1. The security liaison and/or local law enforcement will be in charge of evacuations during times of crisis. The crisis response plan has designated (<u>Liaison's name and title</u>) as this liaison.

2. Depending upon the crisis circumstances the security liaison may consult with law enforcement and/or the fire department to determine whether an evacuation is appropriate and how the evacuation should proceed.

3. The following signal indicates the need to evacuate the school:

   _____

4. Typically, evacuation procedures will follow the same procedures as those used during fire drills. When the entire school needs to be evacuated, classes will proceed as directed by the security liaison or firemen/police officers, to the following location:

   a. _____

5. Alternate evacuation areas to be used in the event that the designated area is not accessible or poses a danger to staff and students are as follows:

   b. _____

   c. _____

6. The evacuation should be conducted as quietly as possible so that instructions can be heard.

7. Teachers should ensure that all students have left the room before closing the door.

8. All teachers should bring class lists with them and roll should be taken as soon as possible after evacuating to a safe area.

9. Appropriate instructional materials should be brought with the classroom so that instruction can continue once students are in a safe area.

10. If buses are needed for transportation during the evacuation, the security liaison is responsible for contacting (<u>Name and title of district transportation contact</u>) at the district transportation department (<u>Phone number or alternate cellular phone number</u>) to make immediate arrangements.

11. The following "all clear" signal indicates that the hazardous situation has passed and it is safe to return to classrooms: _____

    _____

Source: Adapted from Brock, Lewis, and Yund (1990), and Poland and McCormick (1999).

Table 10.8
Sample Student Body Accounting Procedures

1. The security liaison is in charge of student accounting procedures during times of crisis. The Crisis Response Plan has designated (<u>Liaison's name and title</u>) as this liaison. Procedures include the following:

2. Following a crisis situation, when it is safe, the following "all-clear" signal will be given: _____

   _____

   At this time, all students are to return to their regular classrooms. An adult must accompany students who were not in their rooms (e.g., at recess, PE, or in pullout programs) back to their classrooms.

3. Once students have returned to their rooms, the teacher will take roll.

4. Over the "all-call," the principal will next ask all teachers to report their enrollment. At this time, only those teachers who *cannot* account for all of their students will call the office. When reporting a student as unaccounted, teachers will do so by student identification number only.

5. The security liaison will help determine the location of all unaccounted for students. The security liaison will obtain the names of injured students and the locations that they have been transported to for medical treatment. This information should be provided to the medical liaison at the earliest opportunity.

6. At least once per year a drill will be conducted to ensure that this student body accounting procedure is viable.

An important component of this procedure is a method of documenting the release of children to specific family members. It is possible, for example, for both of a student's parents to arrive independently at the school to retrieve their child, particularly when an event has been publicized in the media. This documentation ensures that such a child is not mistakenly thought to be missing when, in fact, they were sent home with the other parent. A sample release form that can be used for this purpose is provided in Figure 10.3.

Student and parent reunion procedures also need to include strategies for identifying who is authorized to pick-up a child from school. This information may be collected when a child registers for school, but should be updated quarterly.

A sample reunion procedure is provided in Table 10.9 on page 251. There is a plan A, when small numbers are involved, and plan B for when large

Student Release Form

Student's Name:	Teacher's Name:
Birthdate:	Parent's Name:
Address:	Phone Number:

Date and time of departure:

Signatures

Administrator/Designee:
Parent/Guardian:

Figure 10.3 The Student Release Form can be distributed by the security liaison to parents as part of a student checkout procedure during times of school crisis. Use of this form will help to document when and to whom each student has been released.

numbers of children are involved. Note that the plan specifies location and includes the use of a release form.

CROWD CONTROL

Crowd control procedures complement student and parent reunion procedures. In advance of a crisis, areas need to be designated where parents can wait until they can be reunited with their children. Possible location may include school cafeterias, multipurpose rooms, playground areas, and libraries. Additionally, however, these procedures will also need to include strategies to manage the media. In the current model of school crisis response, the media liaison would be responsible for managing the media. However, the security liaison may play a planning role in helping to determine where the emergency media center (described in Chapter 9) will be located.

Another part of crowd control procedures is ensuring that the crisis response team is able to communicate with large groups of people at one time. This will mean making sure that bullhorns and/or public address systems are available.

Table 10.9
Sample Parent/Child Reunion Procedure

Only after all students in a given classroom have been accounted for can the students within that room be released to their parents or guardian. Reunification procedures will vary depending upon the number of parents coming to school. The security liaison will indicate which of the following two plans will be utilized in the given situation by announcing Plan A or Plan B over the "all call."

Plan A: Assuming that a relatively small number of parents come to school, individual children will be called out of their classroom by the office. Parents will sign-out their children and be reunified with them in the office.

Plan B: If a great number of parents come to school, sign-out and reunification will take place in three separate areas: the cafeteria, outdoor stage, and the library (and adjacent classrooms if needed). Teachers will bring their students to their designated area when notified to do so by the office. This will be done by grade level beginning with Kindergarten and ending with 6th grade. Teachers will not release their students until a release form has been filled out and signed by the parent and an administrator or designee has released the child to his or her parent.

Note: If Plan B is utilized it will cause delays in releasing children to their parents. To avoid unnecessary parental anxiety the office staff will post class lists of those classes where all students are accounted for as soon as possible. In situations where some students are not accounted for and /or are injured, such notification will have to be postponed until the parents of these children are notified.

Source: Adapted from Brock et al. (1990).

TRAFFIC MANAGEMENT

Traffic management issues include the importance of keeping driveways clear to allow emergency response vehicle access to school grounds. The location of an emergency medical helicopter landing site may also play a role in traffic management procedures (i.e., if the landing zone is identified as being on a parking or traffic area). As a rule, traffic management procedures should encourage school visitors to park on side streets during times of crisis. This will help to ensure that the front of the school is free for emergency vehicle access. Ideally, nearby parking areas such as shopping centers and specific side streets would be designated as parking areas during the crisis. As is the case with many of the other procedures

Table 10.10

Traffic Management Procedures during Times of Crisis

---

1. The security liaison is in charge of traffic management during times of crisis. The crisis intervention plan has designated (Liaison's name and title) as this liaison.

2. Keep driveways clear at all times.

3. Always be sure that there are ways for emergency vehicles to get to classrooms and onto the playground.

4. If site resources are not sufficient to manage traffic control, the security liaison will be responsible for calling district security and/or the police.

5. Encourage parents to park on side streets, not in the parking lot.

6. The center of the grass playground has been identified as an area for a medical helicopter landing site.

Source: Adapted from Brock et al. (1990).

discussed in this section, consultation with local law enforcement and fire department personnel may prove beneficial when developing traffic management procedures. Table 10.10 contains a sample traffic management procedure. It includes locations for emergency vehicles, including helicopters, to arrive and emphasizes the need for traffic flow to the school.

SUMMARY

Security and safety planning before a crisis will help to prevent and/or minimize crisis events. Having these procedures in place may also help schools avoid litigation. The security liaison is responsible for coordinating the development of security and safety procedures for use during and immediately following a crisis and for assisting the crisis response coordinator in general safety planning. It is recommended that a School Safety Committee be developed to assist in safety planning. Collaboration with district and/or local law enforcement agencies in review and development of security and safety procedures is a necessity. Good communications are a key to safety and security before, during, and after a traumatic event.

CHAPTER 11

Working with Potentially
Violent Students

For some of the families of the dead children of Columbine, the
very idea of "closure" is an insult and a hoax. There can never be
closure for them. "To say that we want to move on and put this
behind us, that's not true," says Brian Rohrbough, whose son
Daniel was among the first to die. There is still too much pain and
too many questions, and even if the answers come, their children
will never come back, and nothing will be the same again.
—Goldstein (1999, p. 53)

I N REACTION to school shootings, such as the Columbine tragedy, communities across the country are trying to come to grips with the question of why such horrifying acts of violence are committed. We look
for new insights in the hope that this knowledge will help to prevent future tragedies. A great deal is known about anger in children and the behavioral signs of future violence. Nevertheless, there are many issues,
both ethical and practical, making this topic particularly complicated.

In Chapter 10 suggestions were provided for security and safety planning, not only to minimize harm during a crisis, but also to prevent crises
from happening in the first place. This chapter offers a further discussion
of violence prevention. Specifically, it explores procedures for identifying
and assisting troubled students.

IDENTIFYING TROUBLED STUDENTS

An important first step in the prevention of student violence is to recognize the warning signs of students who may be a danger to others or themselves. This section provides information regarding the warning signs of both other- and self-directed aggression.

WARNING SIGNS OF OTHER-DIRECTED VIOLENCE

School staff, students, and parents should be trained to recognize the early warning signs of potentially violent students. Several resources could be used to guide such training. One of the best resources is *Early Warning, Timely Response: A Guide to Safe Schools* (Dwyer et al., 1998). This document can be viewed on line via the U.S. Department of Education's Internet Web page (http://www.ed.gov). Developed at the request of President Clinton, and mailed to every school in the nation, this document was produced by the Center for Effective Collaboration and Practice in collaboration with the National Association of School Psychologists. It reflects the views of experts in the fields of education, psychology, mental health, criminal justice, and law enforcement. One helpful resource is the materials developed by the American Psychological Association (1999). This document can be viewed online via the American Psychological Association's Internet Web page (http://www.apa.org). Another resource is the National School Safety Center (1998). This document can be viewed online via the National School Safety Center's Internet Web page (http://www.nssc1.org). Both of these organizations provide documents that were developed from analysis of school-associated violent deaths. For a summary of warning signs provided by these and other sources, see Figure 11.1. Most of these signs seem obvious indicators of problems with anger control, but unfortunately they are often dismissed as normal adolescent behaviors, especially in males. A history of displaying signs and the existence of several signs should be taken more seriously than a single behavior in isolation.

When publicizing these warning signs, professionals or training programs emphasize they be attended to with great caution. Students who display these warning signs might, or might not, commit a violent act. Warning signs should *only* be used to identify students who may require further assessment to evaluate risk and to guide interventions. They should not be viewed as perfect predictors of violent behavior, nor should they be used to exclude students from school (Brock, 1999b). Dwyer et al. (1998, pp. 6–7) provide several principles designed to help schools avoid the

Early Warning Signs of Potential Violence

Warning Signs	Sources																							
---	a	b	c	d	e	f	g	h	i	j	k	l	m	n	o	p	q	r	s	t	u	v	w	x
Physical expressions of anger/aggression (e.g., impulsive hitting, tantrums, animal cruelty, fighting, intimidating, and bullying).	✓		✓		✓						✓	✓	✓			✓	✓	✓		✓				✓
Rejection (e.g., excessive feelings of rejection, has been bullied, picked-on, teased, humiliated).			✓								✓	✓	✓								✓	✓		
Other antisocial behavior (e.g., gang activity, substance abuse, on fringe of peer group acceptance).	✓	✓	✓	✓					✓	✓	✓						✓	✓						
Withdrawal/depression (e.g., social withdrawal, mood swings, excessive feelings of isolation, and being alone).		✓	✓								✓				✓	✓	✓	✓						
Preoccupation with violence (e.g., reading materials, entertainment choices, writings, drawings).	✓	✓	✓				✓				✓						✓	✓						
Witness to or victim of violence; victim of bullying, abuse, and/or neglect.						✓		✓											✓					
Weapon interest/access (e.g., has brought weapon to school; preoccupation of, possession with, use of firearms and explosives).		✓									✓						✓	✓						
School failure (e.g., discipline problems, lack of interest, poor achievement, truancy, suspension, and expulsion).			✓								✓						✓	✓					✓	
Verbal expressions of anger/aggression (e.g., threats of violence, verbally abusive language, sweaing, name-calling).											✓				✓		✓	✓						
Intolerance (e.g., prejudicial attitudes, failure to acknowledge others' feelings or rights).		✓									✓							✓	✓					
Little of no supervision or support from parents or a caring adult.											✓							✓	✓					
Threatened or attempted suicide.		✓																✓	✓					

Figure 11.1 Early Warning Signs of Potential Violence Checklist. *Sources:* (a) American Academy of Child and Adolescent Psychiatry (1996); (b) American Psychological Association (1993); (c) American Psychological Association (1999); (d) Arthur and Erickson (1992); (e) Batsch and Knoff (1994); (f) Berman and Jobes (1991); (g) Berndt (1984); (h) Browne and Finkelhor (1986); (i) Coie, Dodge, and Kupersmidt (1990); (j) Cook (1991); (k) Dwyer, Osher, and Warger (1998); (l) Elliot, Huizinga, and Moise (1986); (m) Floyd (1985); (n) Greenbaum (1988); (o) Keller and Tapasak (1997); (p) McConaughy and Skiba (1993); (q) National Crime Prevention Council (n.d.); (r) National School Safety Center (1998); (s) Prothrow-Stith (1987); (t) Rothbart, Posner, and Hershey (1995); (u) Rubin, Hymel, Lemare, and Rowden (1989); (v) Saarni (1990); (w) Shields, Cicchetti, and Ryan (1994); and (x) Walker, Colvin, and Ramsey (1995). *Note:* Warning signs are listed according to the number of sources found.

misuse or misinterpretation of warning signs. These principles include the following:

- *Do no harm.* The intention of early warning sign checklists should be to facilitate the identification of students who are troubled and in need of supportive interventions. They should not be used to label, exclude, punish, or isolate. In addition, information about early warning signs must be kept confidential.
- *Avoid stereotypes.* It is essential not to use stereotypes (e.g., race, socioeconomic status, learning ability, appearance) to identify students. Even if the purpose of the identification is to provide "helpful" interventions, such labeling can do harm.
- *View warning signs within a developmental context.* It is important to place the student's behavior within the appropriate developmental context. Developmentally typical behavior should not be interpreted as a warning sign.
- *Understand that children typically exhibit multiple warning signs.* Troubled students typically display many warning signs, repeatedly, and with increasing intensity over time. Thus, it is important not to overreact to a single sign.

WARNING SIGNS OF SELF-DIRECTED VIOLENCE

School staff, students, and parents should also be trained to recognize the early warning signs of potentially suicidal students. Suicides rarely occur without some sort of warning (Margolin & Teicher, 1968; Peck, 1985). Specific warning signs of potential violence against self include those provided in Table 11.1. The first six signs are the most significant predictors of suicide, but the remaining signs have also been empirically validated. An excellent training resource to facilitate identification of students at risk of self-directed violence is the *Suicide Intervention Workshop* (Ramsay et al., 1996, see Table 3.3 in this volume).

REFERRAL AND ASSESSMENT

As part of school safety planning, it is recommended that schools develop referral procedures to assist in the assessment of potentially violent students. Any procedures developed should be sensitive to the level and intensity of the warning signs being observed. Specifically, at least two levels of referrals need to be in place, one for "at-risk" and another for "high-risk" students.

Table 11.1
Suicide Warning Signs

1. The medical seriousness of previous suicide attempts
2. A personal and/or family history of suicide attempts
3. Acute suicidal ideation
4. Communicating thoughts of suicide, death, dying or the afterlife (i.e., attraction to death)
5. Acute substance abuse
6. Stress resulting from significant losses
7. Giving away important possessions
8. Saying goodbye, hinting at not being around in the future, indicating problems will soon end
9. Sudden increase in moodiness
10. Drastic changes in behavior
11. Feelings of anger, guilt, worthlessness, loneliness, sadness, and especially helplessness and hopelessness
12. Self-destructive and/or reckless behavior
13. Withdrawal or isolation
14. Drastic changes in appetite and/or sleep patterns
15. Impulsive and/or aggressive behavior
16. Drastic drop in quality of school performance or interest
17. Lack of interest in usual activities, appearance, and sex
18. Getting in trouble with authority figures
19. Perfectionism

Note: The first six items have been suggested to be the most important predictors of suicidal behavior.
Sources: Adapted from American Psychological Association (1999); Peruzzi and Bongar (1999); and Ramsay, Tanney, Tierney, and Lang (1996).

AT-RISK REFERRAL PROCEDURES

The first level of referral procedures should be designed to facilitate the assessment of students who display relatively low intensity and short duration early warning signs. Vehicles for these referrals may include traditional school resources such as student study teams or student assistance programs. A standard format for these programs is to first identify both student strengths and areas of concern. Then discussion of interventions already attempted takes place. Finally, from all of the

Table 11.2

Imminent Warning Signs of Violence

---

1. Serious physical fighting with peers or family members
2. Severe destruction of property
3. Severe rage for seemingly minor reasons
4. Detailed threats of lethal violence
5. Possession and/or use of firearms and other weapons
6. Other self-injurious behaviors or threats of suicide

Source: From "Early Warning, Timely Response: A Guide to Safe Schools," by K. Dwyer, D. Osher, and C. Warger, 1998, p. 11. This document is in the public domain.

available information an action plan to address areas of concern is developed. Parent participation in this process is highly recommended. Depending on the student's developmental level, he or she may also be made a part of such a referral meeting. Once an action plan has been initiated, a method needs to be in place to monitor progress. One such method is use of weekly school "staffings." During these meetings, the appropriate school staff members (e.g., administration, school mental health staff, other support staff, teachers) consult briefly about the status and progress of the at-risk students.

High-Risk Referral Procedures

The second level of referral procedures should be designed to facilitate the assessment of students who display imminent warning signs of violence (see Table 11.2).

A school's response to these signs must be immediate. School procedures must specify that when any of these behaviors are noted, the observer should make an immediate referral to a school administrator, to a school mental health professional, or both. An initial assessment procedure should be to determine the nature of the suspected violence and to determine if the means for such behavior are available (e.g., does the student have a weapon). If the means are at hand, responsible and trusted adults should remove them as soon as possible. If the student refuses to relinquish the means of threatened violence, school staff will need to discretely call for assistance from local law enforcement. Next, once immediate safety is assured; a mental health professional should conduct a careful risk assessment. While waiting for this evaluation, a responsible and trained adult should keep the student under close supervision. Under no circumstances should a high-risk student be left alone.

Assessing the Risk of Violence

It should not be taken for granted that school personnel (even school psychologists and counselors) have had training in suicide and/or homicide risk assessment. Thus, as part of comprehensive school safety planning, it is important for school districts to assess the readiness of their staff to conduct risk assessments and, if necessary, facilitate professional development in this area.

Behavior Profiling

Two types of behavior profiling methods may be utilized by schools to identify the risk of violence toward others, one of which is inductive and the other deductive (R. Nelson, Roberts, Smith, & Irwin, 2000). Inductive profiling involves looking for patterns in student behavior to predict school violence before a crime is committed. In contrast, deductive profiling involves interpreting evidence after a crime has been committed to reconstruct behavioral patterns, characteristics, and motivations of perpetrators. One inductive behavioral profiling tool, *MOSAIC-2000,* is based on a computer program designed to evaluate threats (de Becker, 1999). Development and piloting of *MOSAIC-2000* originated through partnerships with the offices of the Los Angeles District Attorney, the State's Attorney of Cook County Illinois, the Los Angeles County Office of Education, and Gavin de Becker, Inc. (http://www.mosaic2000.com). Additionally, experts from varied fields including education, law enforcement, and mental health were consultants to the development.* The tool is to be used by site administrators when a student makes a threat or other action causing concern. de Becker cites objectivity as an advantage of this system, which addresses potential charges of lack of due process.

DeBernardo and McGee (1999) have applied a deductive profiling method to school shootings. From the FBI's profile of the "Workplace Avenger," they reviewed 14 school shootings to reconstruct behavior

---

*While educators (in particular school administrators) were represented on *MOSAIC-2000*'s "expert" Advisory Panel, it is important to note that there appear to have been no school-based mental health professionals involved in the development of this tool. Further, the Development Team was primarily composed of Gavin de Becker, Inc. staff members.

patterns, characteristics, and motivations of adolescent school shooters. From this review, they developed a "Classroom Avenger" profile. Included in this profile are exclusionary characteristics that are not associated with the Classroom Avenger (i.e., which reduce the probability that someone is a Classroom Avenger). These include gender (i.e., female), peer popularity, and extracurricular activity participation (e.g., drama, sports). Inclusionary characteristics that are purported to be associated with the Classroom Avenger include gender (i.e., male), community (i.e., small or rural), region (i.e., south or northwest), motives (i.e., vengeance to achieve power or status), and violent fantasies.

CONCERNS REGARDING USE OF BEHAVIOR PROFILING

Criticism of behavior profiling has been expressed by several sources (Brock, 1999b; M. Lord, 1999; R. Nelson et al., 2000). National Association of School Psychologists President Kevin Dwyer suggests that while deductive profiling is useful for law enforcement, he feels that it is dangerous to use inductive profiling in schools. He states: "If you're dealing with a serial killer and have 25 suspects and you can see a pattern, that might be something useful. But when you're talking about 53 million children and putting this in the hands of people who don't understand the material . . . you're going to do irreparable harm" (M. Lord, 1999, p. 57).

Labeling students as dangerous and then suspending or expelling them from school, rather than providing them treatment, represents one of the greatest concerns about the use of behavior profiling. Brock (1999b) suggests that while such exclusion "may have a short-term benefit . . . in the long run it may have devastating consequences. By removing the protective resources of the school . . . we may increase the likelihood of violence." R. Nelson et al. (2000) also fear that profiling will facilitate a reactive mode and result in the development of "alternative programs" that make it easier to remove students from general education settings. The principal of an alternative school for assaultive and violent youth notes: "It has been far too easy for educators to label or otherwise identify 'problem' students and assume someone else is responsible for them" (Braaten, 1997, p. 48). He further cautions, "Schools can no longer simply remove or refer and forget troubled and troubling students" (p. 48).

Another area of potential misuse is invasion of privacy and discrimination by over identifying certain groups of children (R. Nelson et al., 2000). Biased school staff may consciously or unconsciously target individuals from a particular group. Nelson et al. also express concern over the possibility that students labeled as dangerous might be denied access to after school programs. Such exclusion would be especially problematic given that after school programs are important elements of safe school environments.

All of these areas of potential misuse and abuse may set schools up for costly litigation. The authors urge careful consideration of the pros and cons before using profiling to identify potentially violent students.

SUICIDE RISK ASSESSMENT

As discussed in Chapter 9, in the area of suicide risk assessment, the *Suicide Intervention Workshop* (Ramsay et al., 1996) is an excellent program for training school personnel to assess and intervene with suicidal individuals. In addition, assessment tools are available to assist in suicide risk assessment (Lester, 1974). Examples of measures include the Mental Status Examination (Tishler, McKenry, & Morgan, 1981) and the *Suicidal Ideation Questionnaire* (W. Reynolds, 1988). For additional information on these and other tools, the reader may refer to J. Davis and Sandoval (1991) and Lewinshon, Garrison, Langhinrichson, and Marsteller (1988).

INTERVENTION

This section explores specific interventions designed to prevent the risk of student violence. It reviews strategies at the individual, small group (or classroom), school, and community levels. Most of these strategies will complement the safety strategies previously discussed in Chapter 10.

INDIVIDUAL STRATEGIES

A variety of strategies at the individual level may help the student at-risk for violence. These include recreation programs (Schwartz, 1999), and the use of tutors for academic difficulties. In addition, positive adult role models, or mentors, may prove beneficial. Such mentors may be obtained from service clubs, senior citizen organization, colleges or universities, and organizations such as Boys and Girls Club or Big Brothers/Big Sisters (Drug Strategies, 1998; B. Reynolds 1993). Additionally, a school may find that employment improves self-esteem, provides job skills and money, and keep troubled students occupied. All of these interventions have in common the pairing of an isolated individual with a caring adult, a strategy that has been validated indirectly in the study of resilience.

COUNSELING

One of the most important interventions for troubled children is counseling. This support may be provided by a school mental health professional.

Depending on specific student needs, a referral might also be made to an outside agency or a private practitioner. Counseling with potentially violent youth may focus on teaching skills such as anger management (e.g., Goldstein & Glick, in press) and social skills (e.g., Elliot, McKevitt, & DiPerna, in press) rather than traditional psychotherapy. As with all counseling interventions, a plan should be developed that is unique to the individual. With the student at risk for violence, however, this plan will necessarily need to include provision for immediate assistance when needed (e.g., to deescalate the student who is on the verge of losing control).

Positive Behavioral Programming

A second type of individual intervention is the development of positive behavior plans. The positive behavior model involves identifying an undesirable behavior and determining its function or purpose (Browning-Wright, Gurman, California Association of School Psychologists, & Diagnostic Center, Southern California Positive Intervention Task Force, 1998). Once the purpose of the behavior has been identified, the next step is to identify a replacement behavior. Ideally, this replacement behavior is not only more socially adaptive, but also provides an alternative way for the student to achieve his or her behavioral goal. Take for example a student who is aggressive in order to obtain the behavioral goal of control (i.e., getting his or her own way). In this situation, a positive behavior plan would first try to ensure that aggression does not result in control. Second, it would focus significant effort and energy on teaching the student that a replacement behavior (e.g., talking out a problem) did result in a degree of control or choice. The use of punishment should be used with great care as it may have unintended outcomes (Braaten, 1997). Positive behavior planning also includes a careful assessment of the environment within which the problem behavior takes place. For example, an ecological analysis of a student's behavior may reveal that aggression frequently occurs during math instruction. This finding would signal the need to carefully assess the student's math ability. It may be that a lack of skill in this subject area, and the resulting frustration, act as an antecedent for aggression. In this instance, a curriculum adjustment (i.e., a more appropriate math class) may by itself result in a significant reduction in aggression.

Responding to the Acutely Agitated Student

In addition to counseling and behavior interventions, it is also important for schools to have the resources necessary to respond to the acutely agitated student. One such resource is nonviolent crisis prevention/ intervention. Developed by the National Crisis Prevention Institute (Steiger, 1987, see Table 3.3), this program employs two strategies for the responding to disruptive, assaultive, or out-of-control behavior. The first strategy makes use of verbal and nonverbal deescalation techniques. The second makes use of physical control or restraint techniques. According to this program, the latter strategy is used only as a last resort, and only when required to ensure staff and/or student safety. Other similar programs include *Therapeutic Crisis Intervention* (Budlong, Holden, & Mooney, 1993) and *Managing Assaultive Behavior* (B-Safe Seminars, 1994).

If a program is chosen that does not include a verbal deescalation component, this component should be added to supplement the intervention. Effective communication skills used by school staff can deescalate verbally aggressive situations (Goldstein, Palumbo, Striepling, & Voutsinas, 1995). Oestman and Walker (1997) note physical intervention should not be attempted if it does not appear that it can be carried out safely. Some students may be too large or muscular and it would be inappropriate to use with students with a history of severe physical/sexual abuse. Oestman and Walker also emphasize physical intervention is not a solution to the crisis; solutions to crises involve discussion and agreement on an equitable outcome for all parties.

CLASSROOM AND SMALL GROUP STRATEGIES

At the classroom or group level, there are a variety of strategies that address student violence. Among them are group counseling approaches. Additionally, the development of a positive classroom climate is important. This might be achieved through a number of different methods. Among them are the following: (1) use of classroom meetings; (2) use of interactive teaching strategies; (3) high academic and behavioral expectations; (4) fair, firm, and consistent behavior standards; (5) small class size; (6) team planning and coteaching; and (7) group work such as cooperative learning (Gagnon & Conoley, 1997).

SCHOOLWIDE STRATEGIES

This section will discuss schoolwide strategies that may address the problem of student violence. Strategies to be discussed are conflict management and resolution, social skills and anger management, life skills training, gang prevention and intervention, and bully prevention. An excellent resource for these and other programs is *Safe Schools, Safe Students: A Guide to Violence Prevention Strategies* (Drug Strategies, 1998). In addition to the strategies discussed in this section, other schoolwide prevention and intervention approaches are found in Table 11.3.

CONFLICT RESOLUTION AND MANAGEMENT

Training of students and staff in conflict resolution and management can decrease violence and provide alternative methods of solving problems (Petersen & Straub, 1992; Stephens, 1991). Conflict resolution programs, when implemented well, help students to develop empathy and to control their own emotions. They also facilitate the development of communication and problem-solving skills. Conflict management, simply put, trains students how to settle disputes. Program graduates, called conflict managers, may be used by schools to help resolve student conflicts. It has been suggested that conflict management is helpful both for the students in conflict and the mediators. Not only do students in conflict receive assistance resolving their problem, but also the mediators will feel empowered to independently (without adult assistance) resolve difference (Schwartz, 1999). Kreidler (1984) has developed a specific program the authors have seen successfully implemented.

SOCIAL SKILLS AND ANGER MANAGEMENT

Social skills training (problem-solving and communication skills) and anger management are also effective as methods of violence prevention (Batsche & Knoff, 1994; Larson, 1994). Larson has reviewed several social skill and anger management programs. Among them is "Second Step: A Violence Prevention Curriculum" (Committee for Children, 1992). This curriculum is designed to decrease aggressive behavior and increase social competence of young children by direct instruction in empathy, impulse control, and anger management.

Another program is the "Violence Prevention Curriculum for Adolescents" (Prothrow-Stith, 1987). This curriculum reviews statistics on violence, presents anger as a normal emotion, discusses antecedents and alternatives to fighting, practices to use in avoiding fights, and how to create a nonviolent environment.

"Anger Coping Intervention with Aggressive Children" (Lockman & Curry, 1986) is currently used in the Milwaukee and Long Beach public schools. This program uses a cognitive behavioral approach for group sessions with boys in grades 4 to 6. Larson (1994) reports there is substantial research support for this program. Elements include self-instruction,

Table 11.3

1. Attractive extracurricular programs, extended school hours, and after school programs (to increase supervision and provide challenging positive activities).

2. Utilize school personnel resources (psychologist, counselor, nurse, social worker, community liaison, child welfare and attendance workers, campus supervisor, school resource officer, hall monitors) to establish relationships and work with troubled youth.

3. Referrals to protective service agencies to investigate and intervene in child abuse and neglect.

4. Parent involvement:
   - Home/school collaboration in safety planning
   - Parent training in behavior management, gang awareness, and gun safety
   - Counseling for parents of troubled youths
   - Opportunity for GED and vocational training

5. Student involvement:
   - Participation in safety planning
   - Creating a climate of ownership and school pride
   - Students Against Drunk Driving (SADD), Alcoholics Anonymous, Al-Anon, and Ala-Teen
   - Peer counseling programs that train students to assist their classmates

6. Teach gun safety.

7. Direct assistance to victims of school violence through victim support programs.

8. Character education curriculum.

9. Tolerance curriculum.

10. Multicultural awareness and education provided to both students and staff.

11. Support formation of Gay/Straight Alliances.

12. Academic programs to individualize instruction and provide remediation.

13. Early intervention programs.

(continued)

Table 11.3 *(Continued)*

14. School dropout prevention programs.

15. Anonymous hotline to report crime and safety concerns.

16. Teach difference between "tattling" to get your own way or get someone in trouble and "telling" to keep someone from hurting themselves or others.

17. Teach personal safety and assertiveness to students and staff.

18. Set up a violence in the workplace prevention program.

Sources: American Psychological Association (1993); Batsche and Knoff (1994); Braaten (1997); Desena (1991); Gagnon and Conoley (1997); Gun Safety Institute (1995); Kodluboy (1997); Larson (1994); National Association of School Psychologists (1999); National School Board Association (1993); Poland (1994); Poland and McCormick (1999); Rosen (1993); Soriano, Soriano, and Jimenez, (1994); Stephens (1994); and Stephens (1997).

perspective-taking, physiological cues to anger, social problem solving, and goal setting.

Dayton, Ohio's "Dealing with Anger: A Violence Prevention Program for African-American Youth" (Hammond, 1991) focuses on expressing anger, accepting criticism, and learning negotiation. Additional programs reviewed by Larson (1994) include "Adolescent Anger Control: Cognitive Behavioral Techniques" (Feindler & Ecton, 1986), "Aggression Replacement Training: A Comprehensive Intervention for Aggressive Youth" (Goldstein, Glick, Reiner, Zimmerman, & Coultry, 1985), and "Think First: Anger and Aggression Management for Secondary Level Students" (Larson, 1990, 1992). Refer to Larson's excellent review article for additional information on these training programs.

Life Skills Education

While these programs may not directly focus on student violence, they can help youth learn how to avoid dangerous situations. Programs typically explore how to form friendships, resist peer pressure, and have good adult relationships (Schwartz, 1999). These curriculums also focus on good decision making, being a responsible citizen, and conflict resolution (Stephens, 1994).

Gun Safety Education

Given the ready access to guns in our society, it might be argued that gun safety education is another essential to reduce violence and prevent injury. These programs teach youth about how to use guns safely and educate them about the dangers of guns. It includes storing them properly to keep them out of reach of young children, and how to render guns inactive. Including gun safety courses or units on gun safety within courses in schools is controversial. However, it has been suggested that helping young people to understand weapons and the consequences of their use is valuable and serves to prevent accident and injury (Schwartz, 1999).

As a part of gun safety education, it may also be useful to help students and staff understand common reasons why weapons are brought to school. Trump (1998a) noted students bring weapons to school for protection, for power or status, as a tool of the trade for gangs or drug dealers, and as a response to shame or embarrassment. Trump (1998a) suggests three common factors that escalate or incite students to violence are the following: (1) he said/she said rumors; (2) changes, rumors, and disputes involving girlfriends/boyfriends; and (3) real and perceived disrespect.

GANG PREVENTION AND INTERVENTION

Schools must work closely with local law enforcement (Poland, 1994) which may provide information on how to identify gangs, which gangs are currently active in the community, and what support and protection is available to those who report gang activity. Strategies developed by the National School Safety Center (1990) and reported in the publication *Gangs in Schools: Breaking Up Is Hard to Do* include the following: (1) photographing and then promptly removing gang graffiti, (2) enforcing behavior codes, (3) keeping schools as neutral territory, (4) increasing security personnel, (5) sharing information with local law enforcement, and (6) identifying gang members and involving them in violence prevention programs. Other gang prevention program resources that may prove useful include the "Paramount Program" (Kodluboy & Ervinrud, 1993) and "Gang Resistance Education and Training" (Humphrey & Baker, 1994).

BULLY PREVENTION

Bullying is defined as "a form of aggression in which one or more students physically and/or psychologically (and more recently sexually) harass another student repeatedly over a period of time" (Batsche & Knoff, 1994, p. 165). Bullying, often ignored by school staff, may have a significant impact on schools. It may affect attendance, school climate, perception of safety, and cause victims to withdraw or retaliate (National School Safety Center, 1999). Batsche and Knoff provide a comprehensive plan to control bullying, as do Porter, Garrity, Jens, and Stoker (in press). Additional bully prevention programs are reviewed in *Safe Schools, Safe Students: A Guide to Violence Prevention Strategies* (Drug Strategies, 1998). In addition, the *Maine Project Against Bullying* (1999) provides a review of extensive bully prevention materials (books, games, videos, curriculum, and programs).

COMMUNITY STRATEGIES

A variety of family and community factors are associated with school and community violence (see Table 11.4). Most of these factors may be found in schools in the inner city or in rural and suburban communities serving low-income populations. The complexity and interrelatedness of

Table 11.4

Causal Factors Associated with School and Community Violence

---

1. Poverty; unemployment; lack of affordable housing and health care
2. Child abuse; substance abuse; domestic violence
3. Ineffective parenting; punitive discipline style in the home; lack of positive involvement in child's school
4. Prejudice; discrimination; racial stereotypes
5. Violence at home; violence in the media; proviolence values
6. Gun accessibility
7. Excusing violence under intoxication
8. Transient student population
9. Overcrowding; large school size; rapid growth enrollment
10. Lack of resources (funding, materials and personnel)
11. Lack of cooperation between faculty and administration; teacher silence
12. Lack of alternative education; lack of career preparation
13. Inconsistency in rule enforcement
14. Apathy about education; low expectations
15. Family stress
16. Bicultural stress (differing rates of assimilation for the children and adults within a family)

Sources: American Psychological Association (1993); Petersen and Straub (1992); Rosen (1993); and Soriano, Soriano, and Jimenez (1994).

these factors, suggests that safe schools require a significant commitment not only from schools, but also from the community at large.

To address the problem of student violence, the community must address the problems listed in Table 11.4. Doing so will require interagency collaboration, for the schools cannot do it alone.

A summary of communitywide violence prevention and intervention strategies is offered in Table 11.5. Schools must be willing to play their part in community development. They can offer space for meetings, can open their campus after hours for needed programs, and can form partnerships with other institutions to become full-services schools. Many schools have community liaison workers assigned to the school. Their services can be

Table 11.5
Societal Violence Prevention/Intervention Strategies

1. Establish partnerships between schools, law enforcement, health/ human services, juvenile courts, probation, district attorney, department of parks and recreation, business, parent leaders and community leaders.

2. Develop community programs offering children alternatives to gangs.

3. Encourage cooperation with the media to avoid sensationalizing acts of violence committed in schools.

4. Establish prevention programs that promote safe weapon storage and deny youth access to weapons.

5. Lobby for legislation on issues related to violence (e.g., increased penalties for crimes committed at schools, gun control, media).

6. Establish community groups to sponsor anti-violence initiatives.

7. Place probation officers within schools.

8. Increase adult supervision of youth and promote childcare programs.

9. Establish truancy sweeps involving collaboration between schools, law enforcement, district attorney's office, human service departments, and the courts.

10. Establish a restitution and community service program at schools as a consequence for vandalism and other crimes.

11. Institute a nuisance abatement and/or community cleanup programs that work closely with community leaders, local law enforcement, and other city and county officials.

Sources: Muir (1988), National Association School Psychologists (1996), Rosen (1993), Stephens (1994, 1997), and Trump (1998).

invaluable in helping the school become part of the solution rather than one of the problems in the community.

SUMMARY

Identification, assessment of violence risk, and prevention and intervention efforts will help to prevent and/or minimize student violence events. Early identification of troubled students and use of prevention and intervention efforts before problems escalate to violence is critical. Prevention and intervention strategies with troubled youth may be implemented at the individual, group, classroom, schoolwide, and community levels. Collaboration among community agencies serving children is essential.

CHAPTER 12

Emergency Medical and Health Procedures

When the shooting stopped, the Cleveland Elementary School playground resembled a war zone. Almost three dozen children had been shot, five of them fatally. Without doubt, however, the emergency medical response of the Stockton community saved lives. This was due in large part to the fact that emergency medical personnel were on the scene within minutes. Further, the paramedics and fire department had routinely rehearsed their response to medical emergencies. While it was initially feared that 10 of the wounded would not survive, all did. Within the hour, all of the shooting victims were transported to one of eight local hospitals.

—M. Armstrong, personal communication

SCHOOLS NEED emergency medical and health procedures to help deal with issues generated by injuries to students and staff members when a crisis occurs. For example, the Cleveland Elementary School shooting resulted in 29 students and one teacher being wounded, treated, and transported to eight different area hospitals. One slightly injured student returned to school the second day after the shooting while several of the more seriously injured never returned for various reasons (M. Armstrong, personal communication, April 23, 1992). This chapter reviews emergency medical and general health procedures that need to be in place during and immediately following crises involving physical injuries. These procedures are also designed to provide follow-up care in the aftermath of a crisis.

THE MEDICAL LIAISON

As mentioned in Chapters 5 and 6, it is recommend that a medical liaison be a member of the Crisis Response Team. This individual, often a school nurse or a district health services administrator, would be responsible for developing district or school emergency medical and health procedures or both. These procedures would be used during and in the aftermath of a crisis. The medical liaison's responsibilities may include conducting or assisting with medical triage, and providing first aid to students and staff with minor injuries. Initially, it is important for the medical liaison to check in with the crisis response coordinator and then offer assistance to emergency medical personnel. This assistance may include medical triage and providing first aid and/or cardiopulmonary resuscitation (CPR). Perhaps most importantly, the medical liaison facilitates communication between emergency medical personnel and the crisis response coordinator. The liaison may also assist in communicating to parents, in lay terminology, the medical status of their injured children.

Before a crisis, the medical liaison addresses general medical emergency and health planning issues and carries out specific tasks resulting from such planning. Additionally, in conjunction with the site or district crisis response coordinator, the medical liaison should contact the local hospital authorities in charge of disaster planning in the area. It is appropriate to exchange information regarding district and site crisis planning and local disaster planning efforts in the medical community.

In the days and weeks following the crisis event, the medical liaison's responsibilities include facilitating communication between the school district and hospitals or other health care providers. The medical liaison also provides health counseling and debriefing to students, parents, and teachers, assist site administrators with arrangements for the home instruction of injured students, and facilitate the reentry of students and staff after an injury.

MEDICAL LIAISON DUTIES

The medical liaison has many crisis response responsibilities. This section details the liaison's planning, intervention, and follow-up duties.

PRIOR TO CRISES

The medical liaison is responsible for the planning and development of emergency medical and health procedures to be followed during a crisis.

These procedures need initially to focus on providing assistance to the crisis response coordinator and emergency response personnel to stabilize the situation, ensure provision of medical treatment, and assist in determining crisis facts (such as the number and condition of injured). In planning emergency medical and health procedures, several specific issues and tasks need to be addressed.

ENSURE THE PROVISION OF MEDICAL FIRST AID TRAINING

A primary preparedness activity is the formation of a site medical first aid team to provide immediate, in-house assistance. If the team decides that this is an appropriate role for school personnel, it will be important to ensure that those on-site have the level of training required to fill this role. There may be legal liability if casualties are inaccurately identified and treated. A list of staff members currently trained in first aid and CPR should be developed and updated as changes occur (Figure 12.1). Included in this list should be the type of American Red Cross or American Heart Association certification and date of expiration. Those certified should get refresher courses periodically. If an in-house first aid team is formed, training in addition to first aid and CPR certification could consist of simulation or practice drills. The topic of planning a drill or simulation is discussed further in Chapter 13. If practical, the medical liaison might arrange for or even teach CPR and first aid for the school staff.

ENSURE THE AVAILABILITY OF FIRST AID SUPPLIES

Another task is to ensure that supplies needed to comprise a standardized medical kit are available. Table 12.1, on page 275, provides a sample list of such supplies. The quantity of each item is dependent on the size of the school and individualized site needs. Ideally, the standardized medical kit should include trauma bandages and dressings. For example, Bergeron (1994) describes types of dressings and bandages. These types include bulky dressings, multitrauma dressings that are thick and large enough to cover large wounds to assist in the control of serious bleeding, and occlusive dressings used to create an airtight seal or close an open wound of a body cavity. In addition, it is recommended that a list of supplies for a field trip first aid kit be developed (S. Macauley, personal communication, September 1, 1994). These supplies need to be gathered and a procedure developed to ensure the kit is brought on all field trips. The field trip first aid kit should contain the same types of items as the standardized site medical kit but with a smaller quantity of each item. When multiple field trips are planned for the same day to different destinations, multiple field trip first

School Personnel Trained in First Aid/CPR

Name	Type and Expiration Date of First Aid Certification	Type and Expiration Date of CPR Certification

Figure 12.1 The School Personnel First Aid Training Form could be used by a medical liaison to help document the first aid skills and training possessed by school staff members. *Source:* Adapted from *Health Manual for School Sites* (Lodi Unified School District, 1994. (Available from Lodi Unified School District, Special Services/SELPA, Student health, 1305 E. Vine Street, Lodi, CA 95240.)

Table 12.1
Site Medical Kit Supplies

First Aid Flip Chart

Plastic Adhesive Bandages (assorted sizes, i.e., $^3/_4'' \times 3''$, $1'' \times 3''$, $2'' \times 4^1/_2''$)

Oval Eye Patches

Butterfly Bandages

Insect Sting Foil Packs

Bactine Aerosol Spray

Tubes of First Aid Cream

Tubes of Burn Cream

Bottle Eye Aid Ophthalmic Irrigating Solution

CPR Devices (disposable pocket face masks)

Rolls of Adhesive or Dermiclear Tape

Rolls of Bandage Gauze ($2'' \times 10$ yards and $3'' \times 10$ yards)

Boxes of Steri-Pads (assorted sizes, i.e., $2'' \times 2''$, $3'' \times 3''$, $4'' \times 4''$)

Triangular Bandages (with Velcro or safety pins)

Latex Disposable Gloves

Reusable Ice Packs

Disposable Rigid Splints (assorted sizes, i.e., 12″, 18″, and 24″)

Boxes of Antiseptic Towelettes

Pump Antiseptic Soap

Blankets

Bandage Scissors

Digital Thermometer (with disposable oral sheaths) or Fever Strips

Bulky Dressings

Multitrauma Dressings

Occlusive Dressings

Source: Adapted from *Health Manual for School Sites* (1994). (Available from Lodi Unified School District, Special Services/SELPA, Health Services, 1305 E. Vine Street, Lodi, CA 95240.)

aid kits are needed. All kits need to be periodically checked, to replace used supplies, and to renew any items where the shelf life has expired.

Prepare for Possible Health Crises

An initial health planning issue is to consider the crisis response to crises that involve medical issues. Plans need to be made for health procedures in the event of an acute injury or death of student(s) or staff, likely requiring mobilization of the entire site crisis team, and depending on the site impact, perhaps the district or regional crisis team. However, there also exists the potential for a crisis to be primarily medical in nature. In such instances, the medical liaison should assist the crisis response coordinator in crisis management and interventions, and depending on the impact, call in other site, or district crisis team members as needed. An outbreak of food poisoning, for example, might overwhelm a single school. Other examples of crises that are primarily medical in nature include contagious diseases and environmental events such as nearby chemical/refinery spills or explosions (S. Macauley, personal communication, September 1, 1994). The largest human caused disaster ever, Chernobyl, had incredible health-related implications for children (Kronik, Akhmerov, & Speckhard, 1999).

Identify Medical Assessment and Treatment Resources

A second health planning issue is to identify medical assessment and treatment resources available in the community. This may, for example, include establishing relationships with local doctors, hospitals, and emergency response personnel. Establishing such relationships in advance of a crisis event will greatly facilitate the response to crises with medical issues.

Another issue to be addressed, as a medical liaison identified assessment and treatment resources, is whether school personnel should conduct triage or provide first aid, CPR, or both to the injured. Medical triage refers to the sorting of casualties in order to prioritize medical treatment and has evolved to include the immediate life-saving care of patients (Klinghoffer, 1985). Because many lives may be saved if appropriate medical care is administered within the first few minutes following injury, several methods of field triage to assess casualties rapidly have been developed (Klinghoffer, 1985; Rund & Rausch, 1981). Field triage is conducted at the scene using the professional judgment of the most experienced person available (Rund & Rausch, 1981). Typically, the triage decision maker is an emergency medical technician (EMT) or paramedic. However, in some cases, a school nurse or the medical liaison may initiate and manage a medical triage. They may assume this role if they have the appropriate training and if they arrive on campus before emergency medical personnel. An example of the level of training necessary to initiate or manage a medical triage is completion of emergency response course work on procedures for first responders (typically fire service, law enforcement, and emergency medical personnel have such training). Bergeron (1994) has written a book covering immediate life-saving medical care procedures that is used as the basis for First Response course work. Their book also addresses rescuer safety (including protection from infectious diseases) and legal issues of consent and confidentiality related to patient care.

Finally, consultation with local emergency medical workers may include discussion of potential areas on campus where triage may be conducted. Ideally, this location would have water and toileting facilities available.

DOCUMENT PROCEDURES IN A HEALTH MANUAL

Preventative emergency medical and health planning efforts may focus on the development or revision of a site or district health manual. This manual can provide school personnel with guidelines for dealing with a number of issues. For example, it may cover universal health precautions, indicators of the need to call 911 and recommendations on how to handle medical incidents. Common and less common events are bee stings and anaphylactic shock, playground injuries (abrasions, lacerations, fractures, dislocations, possible back injury, head injury), seizures, convulsions, emergency care for a diabetic, poisoning, dental emergencies, communicable diseases, human bites, and needle sticks. In addition it should cover emergency medical and health procedures including administration of medication at school and recommendations for physical education during hot weather (Lodi Unified School District, 1994). Providing school personnel with specific guidelines to follow in case of a medical incident may assist staff in remaining calm and enabling effective intervention, resulting in prevention of further injury, death, or escalation of the medical crisis from an isolated incident to a schoolwide impact. Additionally, preventative efforts may take place in the provision of staff development. Besides the availability of a health manual as a resource, school secretaries, who often act as a substitute when the school nurse is not on campus, may need training in how to respond to specific medical incidents. Also, as previously indicated, staff training in first aid and CPR may be a valuable preventative measure.

DURING CRISES

FACILITATE MEDICAL TRIAGE AND FIRST AID

The first responsibility of the medical liaison during a crisis event is to ensure that medical triage and first aid are provided to injured students and staff. In some instances, this may mean actually providing emergency medical services. Most typically, however, this responsibility means making sure that emergency response personnel are available and that nothing gets in the way of their most essential activities.

MINIMIZE STUDENT EXPOSURE TO DEATH AND INJURY

Another important and often overlooked health planning issue is development of a procedure to minimize student exposure to injury and death. When possible, during the acute response phase of a crisis, the medical liaison should communicate to emergency response personnel the importance of minimizing student exposure to injured persons, dead bodies, and accident or disaster scenes. The importance of doing so is highlighted by research conducted by Nader et al. (1990), who report a link between children who witness injury and death and the degree of their posttraumatic stress reactions and rate of recovery. If possible, when injured or deceased persons are removed, they should be brought to a location away from uninjured students. Similarly, during the initial treatment of crisis victims, it is important that uninjured students' view of the crisis scene be blocked (Mitchell & Resnik, 1981). Both Nader et al. (1990) and Petersen and Straub (1992) note the importance of protecting students from images of the crisis incident, including secondary exposure through media videotapes or photos of the injured or of the crime scene prior to clean up. Mental images or memories of trauma scene are retained by witnesses for a long time and are difficult to extinguish. A sample procedural statement designed to document a school's desire to minimize exposure to the scene of a trauma is provided in Table 12.2.

IDENTIFY INJURED STUDENTS AND STAFF

Once the immediate medical needs of students and staff have been attended to, the medical liaison works closely with the security liaison to obtain a list of injured students. If any of these individuals has been transported to a hospital, the liaison should note the name and address of the hospital to which each has been sent. This practice is especially critical following a significant incident involving a large number of injuries. In

Table 12.2

Minimizing Exposure to Injury and Death Procedures

In the event that it becomes necessary to move injured students and/or the deceased to another location on the school campus, whenever safety and time factors allow, the new location should be away from those who were not injured. To the extent possible, students should not be witnesses to injury and death. They should also be protected from reminders of the incident. This shielding includes denying access to the physical site of the incident before clean-up, and secondary exposure to the trauma scene by the media reports. The location where the incident occurred should be cleaned and repaired by custodial staff as soon as police authorization allows.

such cases, it is not uncommon for injured parties to be sent to several different hospitals, and parents will need to know where their child is being treated. As soon as possible, the medical liaison should note the medical status of each injured student or staff member. It may be appropriate for the medical liaison to assist the crisis response coordinator in communicating the medical condition to the parents of injured students in terms that parents may easily understand. Klinghoffer (1985) notes the importance of notifying next of kin as soon as possible whether or not their relative is injured and if so, the medical condition of the victim. He indicates that not knowing places great emotional stress on families. For a summary of health procedures to be implemented during and immediately following a crisis event, see Table 12.3.

FOLLOWING CRISES

The medical liaison is also responsible for a variety of health procedures following a crisis. These responsibilities may include the following.

COMMUNICATION

Following crisis events the medical liaison is responsible for maintaining communication links between the school and medical personnel (e.g., hospitals, public health department, and other health-care providers). From such communication, the liaison will be able to maintain and update a list detailing the status of injured students and staff. Figure 12.2 provides a sample form that might be used for this purpose.

Table 12.3

Health Procedures during and Immediately Following a Crisis

The crisis response plan has designated (Liaison's name and title) as the medical liaison. The medical liaison checks in with the crisis response coordinator upon arriving at school during a crisis. Next, the medical liaison offers assistance to the emergency response personnel in the form of medical triage and providing first aid/CPR to injured students and staff or those in shock. When possible, the medical liaison should communicate to emergency medical personnel the need to minimize exposure of students to injury and death. School staff with current Red Cross certification in first aid and CPR may provide assistance to the medical liaison and emergency medical personnel. Once immediate medical needs of students and staff have been attended to, the medical liaison works closely with the security liaison to obtain a list of injured students and where they were taken for additional medical treatment. The medical liaison is responsible for keeping track of the medical status of each injured student or staff. These facts are then communicated by the medical liaison to the crisis coordinator. Next, it may be appropriate for the medical liaison to assist the crisis coordinator in communicating the medical condition to the parents of injured students. The crisis coordinator may assign additional responsibilities as needed.

CONSULTATION AND DEBRIEFING

The medical liaison should also be available to consult with the families of the injured. This consultation should focus on providing support, answering questions, and ensuring that the family understands the injured student's medical condition. Consulting with teachers and other staff members regarding the injured student's medical condition would also be a critical medical liaison responsibility. For example, in case of a death on campus due to chronic or terminal illness, such as a heart condition, the medical liaison will play a critical role in explaining to students and staff the medical facts.

AFTERCARE

As required the medical liaison would be responsible for assisting site administrators arrange for home instruction for seriously injured students. As these students return to school, the medical liaison will continue to play an important role. The liaison will work closely with the crisis intervention coordinator when consulting with families and

Student and Staff Injury List

Date/Time	Name	Room	Grade	Doctor	Hospital	Type of Injury/ Current Condition

Figure 12.2 The Student and Staff Injury List can be used by a medical liaison to document the injuries suffered by students and staff members. Documentation is especially critical following major disasters that have resulted in many injuries.

during planning for student reentry. Both the physical and mental health of recovery from a traumatic injury will overlap in the adjustment of an injured student.

Regarding the issue of home instruction, school psychologist Mike Armstrong (personal communication, April 23, 1992) has reported that students with history of prior family dysfunction tend to prolong such instruction. From the observation that socialization with others sharing a traumatic experience facilitates healing (Gillis, 1992), it is recommended that students return to school as soon as possible. Therefore, medical liaisons should not automatically grant parent requests for home instruction, but rather offer a return to an alternate school, or combine home instruction with a treatment component (such as desensitization).

SUMMARY

The development of emergency medical and health procedures before a crisis will help coordinate medical interventions during a crisis. These procedures will assist the crisis response coordinator and other crisis intervenors effectively deal with the crisis at hand. The medical liaison is responsible for the development of these procedures, which are used during and immediately following a crisis, as well as procedures to provide follow-up care in the aftermath of a crisis. Prior collaboration with local medical and emergency response personnel is essential.

CHAPTER 13

Evaluating and Debriefing
the Crisis Response

The crisis response team was called to a local high school
following a car accident that left one student dead and another
critically injured. As the intervention progressed, the team
began to notice that they were displaying many of the crisis
reactions that distraught students had been reporting to them.
Sleep difficulties, headaches, and digestive troubles were
common complaints from the crisis team. Although team
members did not know the student who had died in this tragic
car accident, it was apparent that in helping students cope with
this tragedy, they too were becoming crisis victims.
                                —Author recollection of a conversation
                        during a crisis intervention demobilization

EVEN AFTER every step possible has been taken to train and place crisis response teams, the process is not complete. Evaluation is a vital
part of the process of assuring that any program delivers high-
quality services. Crisis response teams should plan to gather information
regularly and systematically to find out how the crisis response might be
improved. Evaluation techniques include interviews, questionnaires, and
reviews of products (portfolios) or formal measures of outcome. Evaluations may take place before a crisis event, afterward, or both. When they
occur before a crisis these activities may be termed *drills* or *readiness
checks.* When they come afterward, evaluation efforts may be called *demobilization* and *debriefing.* Debriefing and demobilization have other important functions as well. For example, as will be discussed later, debriefing

activities are a strategy through which crisis response team members can be helped to cope with their own potential crisis reactions (resulting from helping in a stressful situation).

THE CRISIS RESPONSE EVALUATOR

Someone on the crisis team must be given the explicit task of evaluator. Typically, this individual is the crisis response coordinator, although there is some virtue in having this role assigned to a neutral outsider. The evaluator's role is to conduct drills and readiness checks, to design questionnaires and structured interviews, and to collect the needed data on crisis intervention outcome and crisis team performance. Because of natural resistance to evaluation and particularly to drills and simulations, it is advisable for the school board to declare that evaluation efforts are part of district policy (e.g., Table 4.3). The same person who does the evaluation can do debriefing, or the two roles may be separated. The latter option is often a good idea because the two roles will call for different skills—skills in program evaluation in the first instance and skills in active listening and responding to emotional distress in the second.

The evaluator must be familiar with the program, interested in evaluation, and have the sanction to conduct drills, readiness checks, and other data collection activities. This individual should have a budget, and some level of autonomy to "tell it like it is" rather than to simply make everyone look and feel good. It would be helpful for the evaluator to have received some special training, such as that offered by many universities in courses on program evaluation. The evaluator might also consult classic texts on evaluation such as those by Berk and Rossi (1990), Guba and Lincoln (1989), Patton (1990), Popham (1975), Posavac and Raymond (1989), and Rossi and Freeman (1993).

Normally the first step of evaluation is to define program goals and objectives. These revolve around the successful implementation of the crisis intervention program. If goals have not been established, work should be undertaken to make the goals and objectives operational and measurable.

DRILLS AND READINESS CHECKS

The purpose of drills and readiness checks is to make sure procedures are in place and to determine if the crisis team is up to the task of responding effectively. The prototype is the school fire drill. A fire drill determines if teachers, administrators, and children know what to do in case of fire and how well and quickly they are able to perform. In addition, the practice of desired behaviors during the drill enables personnel to better execute the plan if needed. In the example of the fire drill, learning to walk, not run, and proceeding through a doorway single file without pushing are important things for children to learn if they are to evacuate a building safely.

As important as practicing or simulating correct behavior is, a major benefit of drills is discovering which procedures and practices do *not* work as anticipated. The mark of a professional is carefully studying and learning from mistakes. Observers should watch and note difficulties in performance during a drill. Soon after the drill, the crisis team should make alterations in the crisis plan to address the problems noted. The team should not assume that the alteration will address the problem until another drill takes place because "cures" may be worse than "illnesses."

A readiness check is similar to a drill, in that the object is to detect problems in a crisis management plan and then to remediate the difficulties detected. However, it differs from a drill in that its focus is on knowledge rather than skill. To determine if the crisis team is ready, the individual members can be tested on knowledge of role responsibilities and questioned regarding level of comfort in performing these tasks. The authors suggest that tests and questionnaires should follow all training activities. The results of the tests should be to identify which concepts have been successfully taught and which should be retaught or taught differently in future training sessions. In addition to knowledge, participants in training should be asked if they are confident and ready to apply their knowledge. If not, trainers should consider whether or not more practice and supervised experience might be necessary for some individuals. Personnel lacking confidence might be given opportunities to observe or shadow others doing the task.

PLANNING A DRILL OR SIMULATION

Creating and running a crisis response drill is not difficult but does require more planning than a fire or earthquake drill. The circumstances of each drill should be unique so that there will always be some need for improvisation. The following eight steps can be used in the operation of a crisis simulation:

1. *Pick a situation or scenario.* The situation should be one that is likely to occur in a school. The scenario should be elaborate enough to involve virtually all crisis team members. Table 13.1 lists some examples of scenarios.

Table 13.1

Sample Scenarios for Simulation and Drill

---

1. A group of children are on a field trip to a distant location and the school bus is involved in an accident. There are injuries and fatalities (Klingman, 1987; Toubiana, Milgram, Strich, & Edelstein, 1988).

2. A chemical spill occurs near a district school and a large number of people are injured including children. Several homes in the area are severely contaminated.

3. A pair of students in the high school form a suicide pact. One successfully kills himself, the other is severely injured.

4. One of the teachers in an elementary school is beaten, raped, and murdered in her classroom after school.

5. A student brings a gun to school and accidentally discharges it on the playground, injuring two other children. Alternately, a deranged gunman (a baby-sitter, a misfit, a parent) invades the playground and starts shooting (Armstrong, 1990; Klingman & Ben Eli, 1981).

6. A popular second grade teacher at the school contracts cancer and dies suddenly during the school year.

7. A student comes to a member of the school staff and begins to talk about suicidal thoughts and feelings.

8. A student or group of students at the school is kidnapped and held for ransom by an unknown group seeking publicity as well as money (Terr, 1981).

9. A dam breaks (nuclear power plant leaks, etc.) killing students and family members of students and severely disrupting the functioning of the community (Erikson, 1976).

10. An airplane crashes into a school yard during recess killing the pilot and the passengers (Wright, Ursano, Bartone, & Ingraham, 1990).

Additional possibilities are found in Table 4.5. These scenarios should be added to or altered with local detail, such as the name of the school, to make the situation realistic.

2. *Schedule a drill.* Drills must be scheduled in advance. The first time a drill is attempted, it should be announced to all and come as no surprise. Enough will go wrong that the element of surprise will not add to the usefulness of the data collected. Rather, the team should be tested in situations that give them every opportunity to be successful, since the practice is such an important part of the drill. In time, when bugs have been

worked out of the system and confidence has been built, it may be possible to conduct a surprise drill. However, even in this instance, the school should be on notice that a drill is possible within a given period.

3. *Select a format for the drill.* The drill may be directed at the entire crisis team at one time, or it may be directed at individuals serially. Everyone may watch the performance of, for example, the media spokesperson executing the role, or this role may be observed at the same time that others, such as the crisis managers, do what is needed. By focusing on the individual, one may be more thorough in assessing the individual's skills. By focusing on the team, the evaluator can monitor the interpersonal relations and interactions. A compromise format would have small, related parts of a team act out the scenario.

4. *Arrange for observers.* Although participants will evaluate themselves, it will also be useful to have observers present to render impressions that are more objective. Observers might even videotape what occurs to provide the crisis team with useful feedback (Poland & Pitcher, 1990b). At a minimum, observers should be provided with checklists derived from the role responsibilities of each team member and space for open-ended comments and impressions. There may need to be as many observers as team members, although some observers will be able to do double duty. Observers should try to be unobtrusive during the simulation and should not make suggestions until the drill is over and a comment session begins. There should be a written record of each drill for comparison purposes.

5. *Arrange for those participating to be relieved of normal duties.* It may be necessary to line up substitute personnel to take over the tasks of the participants, particularly when a drill is held by surprise. One way to conduct the drill is to disguise it. The administration could announce an in-service day on a topic such as "literature across the curriculum," but when personnel arrive for the program, they could be asked to act out a simulation.

6. *Try to make the simulation real.* It is not a good idea to trick the crisis team into thinking that a simulation is the real thing; they should know it is a drill. On the other hand, it will be useful to make the simulation as accurate as possible so that the team will get used to some of the physical aspects of the problem. Use props if necessary to make it seem as if the crisis is actually happening and give accurate instructions to role players who will interact with the crisis team. For example, if the simulation involves a disaster, it will be a help in the long run if actors are placed on the ground pretending to be hurt, and fake reporters barrage the crisis team members with questions, since they must get used to such distractions.

7. *Keep the tone serious.* Many participants in simulation exercises cope with anxiety with humor. Although humor is usually a good strategy for coping, and although learning experiences should be pleasant, if possible, it is best if the role-playing participants make a strong effort to stay in their crisis team roles and the victim role players also "play it straight."

8. *Plan time for comments on performance.* It is usually a good idea to plan a separate session to deliver comments after a simulation. A separate session gives the evaluator time to integrate the information gathered and to prepare a written report. The report is useful in assessing progress over time, and in making sure all of the comments are remembered later. If possible, the discussion should take place within three days of the drill. The comment session should emphasize what went right as well as what went wrong. When problems are noted, the whole group can brainstorm and problem solve together so the team can be strengthened. In general the comments should let each member of the crisis team know how well he or she is doing the job.

If a particular behavior has been found to be ineffective and an alternative behavior has been identified through the evaluation process, it is often a good idea to role play this alternative to test it on the spot. In addition to the test, practicing the new behavior will increase the chance that it will be remembered and practiced the next time.

9. *Publicize the drill.* If it is anticipated that the crisis drill will be visible to the public, Poland and Pitcher (1990b) recommend that the drill be publicized both before and after it is held. During the drill, the observers might display a sign indicating that a drill is in progress, particularly if the public is likely to observe the drill and wonder what is happening. After a drill has been conducted, because children may bring home reports of unusual activities at school, it would be wise to inform parents of what took place. Table 13.2 is a note that could be sent home to parents on the day of a drill.

EVALUATING READINESS

Perhaps a more traditional form of evaluation before a crisis is the test or questionnaire (survey). Tests can be designed to assess the level of the participant's knowledge on a subject and questionnaires are used to assess attitudes toward self or others.

THE WRITTEN TEST

A test is often administered following training of some sort, although pretests can be used to establish a baseline of information and motivate

Table 13.2
Parental Notification of a Crisis Drill

It is our responsibility to have children prepared for any type of emergency. We have two fire drills a month and an occasional weather drill. Our district recognizes that there are other types of emergencies that can occur in our society today. We must also prepare students for these situations.

Today we had a drill that simulated an angry stranger entering the building and confronting our school psychologist. The drill gave us the opportunity to practice removing children from a potentially dangerous situation. The students responded very well.

The drill also reinforces the importance of all visitors signing in and obtaining a visitor's pass before proceeding on campus. Please cooperate with us in helping to ensure the safety of our children. Please call if you have any questions regarding today's drill.

Source: Adapted from "Expect the Unexpected," by S. Poland and G. Pitcher, 1990, *School Safety, Fall,* p. 16. Copyright 1990 by the National School Safety Center. Reprinted with permission.

learners to look for the "right" answer. Tests can be written in a variety of formats, although objective tests are most popular. An example of a test used by the first author to evaluate the training program described in Appendix A is offered in Figure 13.1

THE QUESTIONNAIRE OR SURVEY

Evaluation should not just look at knowledge attained by participants during training. Attitudes are also important. Questions such as "How comfortable are you in handling _____ problem?" "How confident are you in using your _____ skills?" "How important is _____ in _____ situation?" may yield good insights into how well crisis team members and others are prepared to function. The evaluator might also ask "How well is the district or the school prepared to deal with _____ (a specific crisis) _____?" since a respondent might be prepared but believe that others are not. In using both tests and questionnaires, be sure to provide opportunities for some open-ended responding. Although it might be efficient to use multiple choice tests and Likert-type scales on evaluation measures, it is also a good idea to give people a chance to write down their concerns and questions on topics that may or may not have come to mind.

EVALUATION DESIGNS

Traditional evaluation designs are of two types. The evaluator either compares the responses of those trained before and after training, or the

School Crisis Intervention: An In-Service for Educators

Post-Test

Name (Optional): _____ Date: _____

Occupation: _____ Affiliation: _____

Attitudes toward Crisis Intervention
*Circle the response that describes how you feel about
working with an individual in crisis.*

1. How confident are you in your ability to conduct a crisis intervention?

Extremely Confident	Very Confident	Confident	Just a Little Confident	Not at All Confident

2. How fearful are you that you might make a mistake when conducting a crisis intervention?

Extremely Fearful	Very Fearful	Fearful	Just a Little Fearful	Not at All Fearful

Knowledge about Crisis Intervention
*Please answer the following questions. If you are unsure of
an answer feel free to guess.*

3. Rank order the following events from 1 (most traumatic) to 4 (least traumatic) in terms of their potential to cause psychological trauma.
   _____ Natural disaster
   _____ Student/unexpected death
   _____ Nonfatal accident
   _____ Man-made disaster

4. What are the components of a Classroom Crisis Intervention response?
   _____
   _____
   _____

5. What are the components of an individual psychological first aid response?
   _____
   _____
   _____

6. The defining characteristics of the crisis state is:
   a. Acute distress generated by an inability to cope
   b. Acute distress generated by a stressful event
   c. An apparently unsolvable problem and mental illness
   d. Symptoms of a Posttraumatic Stress Disorder

7. The *primary* goal of psychological first aid is to:
   a. Resolve the crisis problems
   b. Reestablish immediate coping or problem solving
   c. Prevent Posttraumatic Stress Disorder
   d. All of the above

Figure 13.1 School Crisis Intervention: In-Service Post-Test.

8. A directive approach to psychological first aid should be employed when:
   a. The individual in crisis is suicidal
   b. The individual is homicidal
   c. The individual in crisis is unable to act on his or her own
   d. All of the above

9. Which of the following events typically has the lowest potential to be psychologically traumatizing:
   a. Learning about the violent assault of a significant other
   b. Events which involve personal threat or injury
   c. Natural disasters
   d. Human caused acts of assaultive violence

10. Which of the following variables is the *most* powerful predictor of initial psychological traumatization among those exposed to a crisis event:
    a. Individual vulnerability (i.e., internal/external resources)
    b. Proximity to the crisis event
    c. Friendship with crisis victims
    d. Preexisting mental illness

11. Posttraumatic stress disorder includes which of the following groups of symptoms:
    a. Reexperiencing, sleep disturbance, hypervigilance
    b. Distressing dreams, substance abuse, increased arousal
    c. Reexperiencing, avoidance of reminders/numbing, increased arousal
    d. Avoidance of reminders/numbing, distressing dreams, substance abuse

12. Strengths of group approaches to crisis intervention include which of the following:
    a. Cost effectiveness
    b. Helps survivors feel less alone
    c. A tool to identify the severely traumatized
    d. All of the above

13. Which of the following statements regarding the crisis state are true:
    a. A normal reaction to an abnormal circumstance
    b. A sign of mental illness
    c. Very much like a "stress" reaction
    d. A chronic condition

14. Which of the following statements regarding psychological first aid are true:
    a. Attempts to resolve the crisis problem
    b. Allows the individual in crisis to do as much for him- or herself as possible
    c. Requires professional counseling training
    d. Should be offered in school counseling offices

15. In the space below, please write any comments you have regarding your individual preparedness to respond to a crisis situation.

_____

16. In the space below, please write any comments you have regarding your school and/or district preparedness to respond to a crisis situation.

_____

Figure 13.1 *(Continued)*

responses of those who have undergone training and those who have not. Although these designs are useful in documenting change in participants, it is also desirable to compare responses obtained against a desired standard. Presumably, it is more important that a crisis team member knows what to do than that he or she is less ignorant than is the average school employee. Program designers should also use tests, questionnaires, and drills to determine that crisis team members have reached a mastery level of preparation.

IMPROVING READINESS

The results of evaluation should be used in improving readiness. A good readiness check will identify holes in training that can be addressed in teaching the next cohort or in providing refresher courses. Refresher courses act as "booster" shots to renew enthusiasm and commitment from team members. In any case, the review or repetition of training is pedagogically quite sound. Even if the second training is not totally new to the crisis team member, knowing what to do will make him or her more confident.

Besides didactic training, readiness can be improved by a system of mentorships whereby novice team members or members lacking particular skills can be paired with an experienced, skilled team member (even someone from the community or from another district) for the purpose of observing and modeling. Such a shadowing system has been done in the schools for some time and is usually rated by teachers as their preferred way to learn a new skill.

A key to the success of any program is effective supervision. A supervisor (or peer) can be helpful by dispassionately but sympathetically reviewing the work of the crisis team member, asking questions and clarifying additional options. Supervision usually occurs after the individual has been practicing, which brings us to other evaluative functions, debriefing, and demobilization.

DEMOBILIZATION AND DEBRIEFING

After a crisis response has concluded, it is also important to conduct demobilization and debriefing. Doing so will strengthen future crisis responses and will also serve to relieve team member stress brought on by responding to a crisis (such as was illustrated at the beginning of this chapter). We call the evaluative information-gathering strategies *demobilization* while stress-relieving activities are referred to as *debriefing*. Other authors who use the terms interchangeably do not draw this distinction. Debriefing is particularly important for identifying those members of the crisis team who will need extra time and help returning to a precrisis level of functioning, since crises affect the helper as well as the victim. The evaluator might conduct both debriefings and demobilizations. However, it should be remembered that, as will be seen, debriefing involves some therapeutic skill. Consequently, a district might wish to give this task to someone other than the crisis response coordinator (who is typically a school administrator) who has these therapeutic skills (e.g., the crisis intervention coordinator) or to bring in an outside consultant to conduct debriefing (cf. Weinberg, 1989). Often a county mental health agency will be willing to provide one of their personnel following an emergency.

STEPS IN A DEMOBILIZATION

Demobilization has as its main purpose learning how things went as various individuals responded to the crisis. The purpose is not to evaluate the individual per se, but to generate information to improve the team's functioning. Demobilization is post hoc evaluation. The following are some of the steps in planning a demobilization:

1. *Make time for the demobilization.* The demobilization should take place in a quiet, comfortable location free from interruption and where privacy can be assured so that confidential issues may be discussed. The authors suggest that this demobilization take place more than 24 hours following the event, to provide an opportunity for rest and reflection, but not more than a week afterward because memories begin to fade.

2. *Select format.* A number of formats are available for demobilization. Demobilization can consist of written or oral responses to questionnaires or as interviews. Each participant can describe his or her own functioning, or can comment on the performance of others. Evaluations of performance may be quantified or not, but they should always include a section on what should be done differently. Finally, a demobilization can be done primarily as a group process or may be done individually by someone responsible for the collection of information. Because of busy schedules, it is not always possible to reassemble a team, so the individual option needs to be retained.

3. *Refer to crisis logs.* Many individuals in the crisis response team will have kept logs during the crisis response. These logs should be considered central records for writing reports and should serve to remind team

members of their functioning during the event. They should be at hand during the demobilization.

4. *Suggested questions.* A demobilization can use a survey with written responses, or be conducted as a structured interview with oral responses. The second method generates information that is more useful because topics can be explored at length and spontaneously, but the first is faster and can be done without physical proximity. Table 13.3 presents a series of questions for a structured interview that can be modified for local use.

5. *Report writing.* There is a need to translate the results of the information gathering into a report and plan for follow-up action. Writing reports is time consuming, but institutional and personal memories are short, and it is best to have things on paper for future reference. At least one section of each follow-up report should include a section on identified strengths of the crisis management team's response and its identified weaknesses. Each of the weaknesses should be accompanied by a proposal for modification of plans and procedures, including staff training needs. Table 13.4 presents a format for a demobilization report. It is important to note that the crisis intervention coordinator's *Detailed Crisis Incident Summary* (Table 6.6) would be an important document used to

Table 13.3
Sample Structured Interview to Be Used in Demobilization

1. What do you think were the benefits of planning and implementing a crisis management team in the district now that _____ has occurred?

2. How prepared, confident, knowledgeable were you prior to this event?
   Did training help in your response?
   Which training?

3. How well did others function during the crisis?
   What would you suggest would help them function more effectively?

4. How were you successful in responding to the recent crisis?

5. How were you not effective in your role and what would have helped?

6. What made your job more effective during the crisis and what hindered you?

7. How could impediments to your and other's functioning be removed?

8. What costs or liabilities resulted to the district because of responding to this crisis?

Table 13.4

Outline for Demobilization Report

---

1. Introduction: What occurred (Who, What, When, Where, How, Why)?
2. Who was demobilized?
3. By role, how effectively did the team respond to this event?
4. What in the crisis plan seems to be working as anticipated?
5. What problems or weaknesses were detected in planning or personnel?
6. Based on identified weaknesses, by role, make recommendations for modification.

---

complete this evaluative demobilization report. The summary will provide information on the actual crisis intervention work done with students and staff members.

6. *Planning for follow-up.* After sufficient time has past for emotional regulation to take place, but before the event disappears from memory, the crisis team leaders should meet, discuss the demobilization report, and take steps to modify policies and procedures, and to secure needed new resources. Some priorities should be set, because some needs will be seen to be very important, and others will be less clear. Some changes will need to be made immediately, others come later, possibly after seeing how the crisis team responds to an additional crisis.

DEBRIEFING

Disaster workers are adversely affected by responding to a crisis (Mitchell, 1986, 1987; Mitchell & Everly, 1996a). Those responding to airline disasters seem to have a particularly difficult time, but all emergency workers are subject to the same reactions as the victims of the crisis. They too will exhibit symptoms of stress. Responses are individual and may not be apparent to an observer or supervisor. Often witnessing the aftermath of a traumatic event can recall a crisis worker's own past experience of trauma and loss (e.g., Carroll, 1998). Training and supervision permits the avoidance or diminution of counter-transference while serving as a helper during a crisis. Nevertheless, it should be anticipated that every member of the crisis team will be adversely (as well as positively) affected by participating on a crisis response team. Team members might anticipate symptoms as severe as those associated with Posttraumatic Stress Disorder, even though they are the helpers and not the direct victims of the crisis. Being close to a crisis stimulates thoughts of our own mortality and fallibility.

It is possible that participating as a member of a crisis response team will hasten the development of burnout. Burnout (Maslach, 1982) consists of *emotional exhaustion,* feelings of being overwhelmed by job demands, *depersonalization,* negative feelings and attitudes toward clients, and *reduced sense of personal accomplishment,* negative feelings about one's effectiveness and accomplishments. It can result from interpersonal factors (i.e., relations with peers and supervisors), intrapersonal factors (adequacy of training and personality adjustment), and organizational factors (role ambiguity, role conflict, and role overload) (Huebner, 1993). During a crisis, role overload may come into play, or the emotionally laden activities of crisis intervention add to the other sources of burnout, leading to high stress.

Interventions for burnout include relaxation techniques, time management training, recreational outlets (vacations), continuing education, and problem-focused stress management, although these strategies have not been carefully evaluated in the literature (Huebner, 1993). Poland and Mc-Cormick (1999) suggest that the crisis caregivers may help themselves and others cope in the aftermath of a crisis by knowing themselves and respecting their own limitations; by asking for special support from their family; by taking care of themselves physically; by supporting other members of that team; by using humor; by recognizing that crisis response team members will be impacted by the crisis; and by talking to others. The goal of debriefing, however, is to detect burnout among crisis workers and move toward an individualized stress management intervention (as recommended by Huebner and others) when it is detected. The debriefing itself can provide emotion-focused coping, in that it permits the expression of ideas and emotions in a psychologically safe environment.

Debriefing Procedures

Debriefing can begin while the crisis is in progress in the sense that a supervisor (in our model, the crisis response coordinator or the crisis intervention coordinator) should spend some time evaluating the functioning of the team members. Mitchell (1983) terms this form of debriefing "on-scene or near-scene debriefing" and recommends it take place between 24 and 72 hours after the incident (Mitchell, 1986; Mitchell & Everly, 1996a). He recommends that the evaluator, preferably a mental health professional, watch crisis intervenors for the development of symptoms of acute stress reactions. A checklist, such as the Crisis Reaction Symptom Checklist provided in Figure 7.6 may be modified for such a purpose.

The debriefer also offers encouragement and support to intervenors, never criticism. As time permits, he or she allows ventilation of feelings and reactions. In general, the debriefer uses simple active listening skills. As a result of the information obtained from listening and observing, the debriefer makes recommendations to the coordinator concerning which individual helpers need a break or a change in responsibilities (Mitchell, 1983).

Weinberg (1989) suggests that debriefing be done at monthly meetings under the direction of an outside consultant. Such meetings would be appropriate for crisis teams, which see frequent action. He has described his own work at such group meetings:

- First, members are asked to describe any particularly stressful encounters they have had with students, teachers, or others. The debriefer asks for details to make the crisis team member relive the experience and so that the others on the team might form a clear picture of what happened. Reflective listening focusing on affect, can bring the feelings to the surface so they can be discussed.

- Next the leader and the group dispel irrational beliefs about failure. Often feelings of failure will result from high expectations about what can be done and a wish for perfection. Helpers do not appreciate the disorienting nature of a crisis and are angry with themselves for impulsive acts, missed opportunities, and other errors of judgment. Others in the group should be encouraged to offer support and encouragement and the leader should continue to try to reframe the event in a positive and acceptable way.

- Finally the leader should work toward facilitating pride and acknowledge how difficult it is to respond under the pressure of an emergency. The debriefer hopes to use the debriefing process to help the crisis team recover from the trauma of the crisis response process.

The process itself may not be enough, and the debriefer must assess each individual's recovery from helping during the crisis. All individuals should receive compensatory time off after a crisis. They are at least entitled to recover the "after hours" and weekend time they have spent responding to the crisis. Administrators should consider other ways of relieving stressed team members with reduced duties following the end of the crisis.

Some members of the crisis team will need more time for recovery and some professional help. The district's health program might be examined for its disability provisions and strengthened to cover this contingency.

PRODUCT OR OUTCOME EVALUATION

In addition to the aforementioned, more subjective evaluations of what occurred during a crisis event or operation of the crisis response team, it is useful to collect other evidence about the products and long-term outcomes of having an active and effective crisis management process on line in the district. Some of the possible outcomes that may be suggestive of an effective crisis response program are as follows:

1. Crises will be resolved more quickly and will not have as great an impact on children. The school will return to normal more rapidly and less time will be lost from academic learning.
2. Information collected from debriefing and demobilization will be less dramatic and suggest fewer modifications to the crisis plan.
3. There may even be fewer crises. Some crises breed others. If there is no effective intervention with a suicide, for example, another may result. Suicide clusters can be avoided with a well-functioning crisis response team executing a good plan.
4. Improved morale. When a crisis response team has been brought into play and has known what to do, the staff should feel justifiably proud that they have contributed substantially to the well-being of the school and the community.

THE NEED FOR SYSTEMATIC RESEARCH

In addition to providing a crisis response team with information designed to improve its effectiveness, evaluation activities also might include systematic research or study. Research may, for example, add to our still evolving understanding of the child's crisis reactions (Terr, 1989) and how school systems can help children cope with trauma. In other words, such study may serve to make something positive come from tragedy. When published, research results have the potential to improve the crisis response of large numbers of crisis intervenors.

Unfortunately, as Rosenfield (1992) notes ". . . the school culture does not find research a meaningful use of its precious resources of time and personnel" (p. 43). One might expect such reactions to be particularly acute following a school crisis when staff is busy and experiencing high stress. And, in fact, following such an event this attitude may be a legitimate concern. School resources may be such that research activities will have to be given a low priority. Consequently, it may be beneficial to obtain resources from outside the school district to facilitate this task. For example, following school crises, it would not be surprising to find university researchers to be more than willing to provide their crisis intervention resources to the school in exchange for the opportunity to systematically study crisis reactions and the crisis response. Thus, not only could the research institution's needs be meet, but it is also likely that resources available to intervene directly with staff and students would be increased. Finally, to avoid the negative reactions sometimes given researchers attempting to study school crisis interventions (e.g., Blom, 1986), it may be productive to include selection of such outside resources as a component of the crisis preparedness plan. It is in everyone's interest that competent researchers be involved, not simply the first person who asks to study the situation. Schools, particularly those in low-income community are sensitive to being exploited by researchers and will want service in return for cooperation.

Since most crisis events are not easily foreseen, it is difficult to apply carefully controlled research designs to the study of school crises. If members of the crisis response team happen to be trained in ethnography, however, they may be able to contribute to case study research. Given the nature of a crisis, it will be very difficult to be a participant observer and still fulfill your role as a crisis team member. Nevertheless, much of the information collected during demobilization and debriefing can contribute significantly to case study, and over time, enough cases may occur to permit valid generalizations based on correlational methods.

SUMMARY

This chapter provided a review of the evaluative activities that could help to improve school crisis response programs. It has examined the drills and readiness checks that may be implemented before a crisis event in order to improve the crisis response. Demobilization activities, which would occur following a crisis event, were also examined. Demobilization identifies the strengths and weakness of a given crisis response and thereby improve the team's ability to respond to future traumas. Debriefing activities were suggested to be a critical component of the crisis response program. Discussions of such evaluative activities provide ideas for helping crisis intervenors cope with their own crisis reactions, which are generated by helping crisis victims. Finally, the chapter concluded with a discussion of the importance of systematic research or study.

School Crisis Intervention: An In-Service for Educators

THE NEED FOR CRISIS INTERVENTION SKILL DEVELOPMENT

THE PAST 15 years have seen an increasing interest in school crisis preparedness and response. Recently, it has been observed that an expectation for school crisis intervention services following traumatic events has begun to emerge (Brock, in press-c). This expectation is seen in a number of initiatives considered by state and federal legislators. For example, both Alaska and Virginia have passed legislation requiring their public schools to develop crisis response plans.

With these increasing expectations for crisis preparedness come the need for programs designed to provide educators with crisis response skills. Unfortunately, however, in the past many school professionals felt they had inadequate training for the crisis intervenor role (Wise et al., 1987). Thus, it would appear that there is a need for in-service programs designed to train school professionals to participate in the crisis response. This in-service training is designed to provide school-based professionals the knowledge and skills needed to provide crisis intervention services following traumatic events.

Written by S.E. Brock for the San Joaquin County Office of Education and the California Association of School Psychologists.

IN-SERVICE INFLUENCES

The origins of this in-service can be found in the author's crisis intervention training programs and in experiences facilitating other training programs. For the past five years, the author and fellow school psychologist Sharon Lewis have offered trainings to educators through the San Joaquin County Office of Education, which is located in Stockton, California. However, perhaps most significantly, the current in-service has been influenced by Ramsay et al.'s (1996) *Suicide Intervention Workshop.* From the author's experiences as a facilitator of this workshop, the current training program emphasizes the attitudes, knowledge, and skill required to provide crisis intervention services.

IN-SERVICE OVERVIEW

This training program is designed to be offered as an intensive two-day in-service program. An outline for the training is provided in Table A.1. The author has also adapted this in-service for use as a course meeting for six two-hour sessions.

This training program is designed for two or more facilitators and a facilitator/participant ratio of no more than 1:15 and no less than 1:7 (Ramsay et al., 1996). In addition to introductory and concluding activities, this training program has four learning modules. Building on introductory activities, the first section of the training program focuses on the experiences, reactions, and motivations of crisis intervenors. The goals of this section include helping to prepare participants for the reactions they might experience during and following crisis interventions. In addition, this section will assist participants understand the range of possible motivations for participating in a crisis intervention. The second learning module provides the knowledge needed to appropriately apply crisis intervention skills. This includes a review of crisis theory, an examination of the traumatizing potential of various crisis events, and exploration of the factors that place individuals at risk following crises. The third and fourth learning modules facilitate the development of participants' group and individual crisis intervention skills.

The physical requirements for the workshop include a large group meeting area or classroom; plus additional breakout rooms for each small group.* Comfortable chairs are a favorable feature. During large group

---

*The large group meeting area will typically serve as the breakout room for one of the small groups.

Table A.1

School Crisis Intervention: An In-Service for Educators

Two Day In-Service Outline

Time	Learning Module	Activities
Day 1		
8:30 to 9:00		Registration, Introduction, and Workshop Overview
9:00 to 9:30	1	Discussion of participant crisis intervention experiences/expectations
9:30 to 10:00	1	Discussion of participant reactions to crisis intervention participation
10:00 to 10:15		Morning Break
10:15 to 10:30	1	Lecture on care for the caregiver
10:30 to 11:00	1	Discussion of the possible motivations for crisis intervention work
11:00 to 11:30	2	Lecture on crisis theory
11:30 to 12:30		Lunch Break
12:30 to 1:00	2	Lecture on determining the appropriate crisis intervention response level
1:00 to 2:00	2	Video: "PTSD in Children: Moving to the Rhythm of the Child"
2:00 to 2:30	2	Lecture on the factors that influence psychological traumatization
2:30 to 2:45		Afternoon Break
2:45 to 4:00	2	Practice identifying risk of psychological traumatization
Day 2		
8:30 to 9:15	3	Lecture on group crisis intervention
9:15 to 10:00	3	Role play of a group crisis intervention
10:00 to 10:15		Morning Break
10:15 to 11:00	4	Lecture on psychological first aid
11:00 to 11:30	4	Demonstration of psychological first aid
11:30 to 12:00	4	Large group role-play of psychological first aid components
12:00 to 1:00		Lunch Break
1:00 to 2:15	4	Small group role-plays of the entire psychological first aid model
2:15 to 2:30		Afternoon Break
2:30 to 3:30	4	Continue small group role-plays of the psychological first aid model
3:30 to 4:00		Concluding activities

work, seating should be in the typical classroom arrangement. During most small group work, a circle is the recommended seating pattern.

Necessary materials include name tags, the video described next, VCR and monitor, the handouts and overhead transparencies described next, an overhead projector for each small group, and flip charts with markers (or chalkboard with chalk) for each small group room.

INTRODUCTORY ACTIVITIES

REGISTRATION

It is recommended that in-service facilitators complete all presentation preparations before the beginning of workshop registration. Doing so will allow facilitators to personally greet all workshop participants and begin developing relationships. Any training program that expects participants to practice new skills requires a certain sense of trust. By greeting participants as they arrive and engaging them in "small talk," facilitators can help them feel more comfortable in the learning environment. It is strongly recommended that name tags be worn by all participants and facilitators throughout the workshop. This allows participants to identify each other by name, which helps all to feel more connected.

INTRODUCTIONS

The workshop begins with a brief introduction of the facilitators. During this introduction, it is important to emphasize the special training(s) and experiences of the facilitators. At the same time, however, it is important to acknowledge that the participants have special knowledge and experiences that make them valuable in-service resources, as well. Facilitators should next ask the participants to briefly introduce themselves to the group. Specifically, they should be asked to give their name, professional affiliation, and what led to their attendance at the in-service. In groups of 30 or more participants, these introductions can be delayed until the start of small group activities. Finally, small group assignment should be accomplished during these activities.

PROGRAM OVERVIEW

Using Table A.1 as both a handout and overhead transparency, facilitators should next review the components of the workshop. During this overview, it will be important to emphasize the necessity of active participation and to prepare participants for the fact that the workshop is emotionally hard work.

INTRODUCTORY STATEMENT

Because this in-service aims at providing you with new skills in crisis intervention, we need to emphasize the importance of active participation. To fully benefit from this learning opportunity, you need to actively engage in a variety of activities. Passive participation will not allow you to obtain the full benefits of this program. The learning activities you are about to experience is summarized in the handout (Table A.1) and transparency (Table A.1). [Review workshop outline.]

■　■　■

CONCLUDING STATEMENT

The in-service you are about to experience is emotionally hard work. Not only will we be asking you to learn and demonstrate new skills, but for some of us the topics raised during the next two days will be disturbing. We understand that some of you may need time out from our activities. However, we ask that you let us know if you are okay, or not, and whether or not you will be able to return. If you leave the workshop, suddenly and without explanation, we will worry about you. Our first set of activities will take place in the small group setting and will require that we divide our group in two. [Divide the large group into two small groups by having participants count "one," "two," and so on. Then assign each group to a small group meeting room.]

LEARNING MODULE 1: EXPERIENCES, REACTIONS, AND MOTIVATIONS

This first set of training program activities is designed to address the unique crisis intervention experiences, reactions, and motivations that exist for all crisis intervenors. It begins with a discussion of prior crisis intervention experiences and/or expectancies, moves on to an exploration of common reactions to crisis intervention work, and concludes with an examination of possible motivations for participating in a crisis intervention. These activities all take place in a small group setting.

DISCUSSION: PRIOR CRISIS INTERVENTION EXPERIENCES

After breaking into smaller groups (each group no larger that 15 and no smaller than 7), the real work of this in-service begins with a discussion of participants' prior crisis intervention experiences. When training groups of professional educators, it is likely that they will have had prior exposure to a school crisis response. In fact, for many, such experiences will be the reason for their in-service attendance. This will be their chance to tell their stories. If participants have not had any prior experiences dealing with crises, ask them to share what their expectations are for crisis intervention work. Goals of this workshop activity include the validation of prior crisis intervention experiences and expertise, and an awareness that school crisis events are not unusual.

INTRODUCTORY STATEMENT:

Some of us have already been asked to participate in a crisis response. At the very least, all of us have likely had the opportunity to observe a school's response to a traumatic event (either in person or via media reports). I would like us to take some time now and share these prior experiences and observations.

■   ■   ■

CONCLUDING STATEMENT:

As we have just discovered, several of us have already had significant experiences dealing with traumatic circumstances. All crises are unique. Thus, all of us have special expertise. In addition, we have found that crisis experiences are not uncommon. Our experiences emphasize the importance of being prepared to respond to crisis events.

DISCUSSION: EXPERIENCED OR ANTICIPATED REACTIONS TO CRISIS INTERVENTION

As most participants will be aware, crisis intervention is emotionally draining and hard work. This workshop activity is designed to ensure that potential crisis intervenors have a basic understanding of what they are getting into when they agree to participate in a crisis response. A flip chart and marking pens can be used to document the reactions identified during this discussion.

INTRODUCTORY STATEMENT

As most of you are probably already aware, crisis intervention is hard work. A crisis event not only affects those individuals who are victims, but also those who agree to become crisis intervenors. I would like us to now take a few moments to consider what possible reactions we might expect in ourselves because of participation in a crisis intervention. From either your own personal experiences, or your anticipation of crisis work, what reactions might you expect as a result of agreeing to provide crisis intervention. [Write reactions on a flip chart.]

■ ■ ■

Concluding Statement

As you can see from the notes I have written, there are a number of common reactions to crisis intervention work that need to be anticipated. Jeffrey Mitchell and George Everly (nationally recognized experts in the development of crisis intervention teams) have taken this a step further and identified those variables that they feel signal the need for a time out from crisis intervention work. These factors are summarized in the following handout. [Distribute and review the handout titled "Warning Signs of an Overextended Crisis Intervention Worker" found in Table A.2.]

Lecture: Care for the Caregiver

It has previously been suggested that self-care should be emphasized in a training program designed for those intending to work with the survivors of trauma (Brady, Guy, Poelstra, & Brokaw, 1999). This self-care for the caregiver will involve many of the same activities designed for crisis victims. This brief lecture is designed to give workshop participants important information on how to take care of themselves and each other during and following crisis intervention work.

Lecture Introduction

Taking care of ourselves and each other during and following a crisis intervention will involve "practicing what we preach." Many of the same things we will be advising crisis victims to do, we will want to do as well. Some of these suggestions are summarized in the following handout. [Distribute and review the handout titled "Taking Care of Yourself" found in Table A.3.]

Discussion: Motivations of the Crisis Intervenor

This section of the workshop concludes with an examination of why an individual might agree to fill the role of crisis intervenor. Perhaps most importantly, it aims at helping participants identify the assets and the liabilities of different crisis intervention motivations.

Table A.2

Warning Signs of an Overextended Crisis Intervention Worker

- Excessive worry about the crisis victims. This worry goes far beyond what is necessary to achieve adequate follow-up.
- Intense irritability when a fellow team member attempts to advise a crisis intervenor about something they believe they already know.
- Obsessive thinking about the debriefing experience.
- Constant replays of the incident described in the crisis intervention even though the crisis intervenor was not present at the actual incident.
- Unfounded anger at one's fellow workers or one's loved ones after a crisis intervention.
- Loss of interest in one's own work after crisis interventions.
- Chronic feelings of fatigue for long periods after crisis interventions.
- Doing far more for individuals from a particular crisis intervention than one would do for any other person under similar circumstances.
- Maintaining a high degree of follow-up contacts when they are not necessary.
- Attempts to work independently of the team without appropriate supervision from team professional support staff.
- Frequent, unexplained loss of emotional control after crisis interventions.
- Sleeplessness after crisis interventions.
- Agitation, restlessness after crisis interventions.
- Excessive withdrawal from contact with others after going through a crisis intervention.
- Excessive volunteering to take on more and more crisis interventions.
- Feeling upset and jealous whenever others are doing a crisis intervention in which the overextended person is not involved.
- Excessive belief that no one else could provide the proper debriefing within the school(s) serviced by the team.

Source: *Critical Incident Stress Debriefing,* by J.T. Mitchell and G.S. Everly (1996), Ellicott City, MD: Chevron (pp. 257–258). Adapted with permission.

Table A.3
Taking Care of Yourself

- Maintain typical exercise routine.
- Be sure to get plenty of rest (i.e., stick to normal bedtime).
- Avoid drugs and alcohol.
- Maintain as normal a schedule as possible.
- Spend time with other crisis intervenors.
- Help your fellow crisis intervenors as much as possible by sharing feelings and check out how they are doing.
- Do things that feel good to you.
- Realize those around you are under stress.
- Eat well-balanced and regular meals (even if you don't feel like it).

Source: Adapted from *Critical Incident Stress Management: The Basic Course Workbook* (2nd ed.), by J.T. Mitchell and G.S. Everly (1998), Ellicott City, MD: International Critical Incident Stress Foundation (pp. 79–80). Adapted with permission.

INTRODUCTORY STATEMENT

Given that it is such hard work, one might wonder why an individual would agree to fill the role of crisis intervenor. In the discussion that follows, I would like for us to address the following questions:

1. Why do individuals agree to take on the role of crisis intervenor?
2. How might these motivations help and how might they hinder a person's work as a crisis intervenor?

As crisis intervention motivations are identified, they should be written on a flip chart or chalkboard. Beneath each motivation a plus (+) and a minus (–) sign should be placed and the assets and liabilities of each motivation identified.

CONCLUDING STATEMENT

A variety of reasons for agreeing to become a crisis intervenor has been identified. [Summarize identified motivations.] Each of these has their own assets and liabilities. [Summarize identified assets and liabilities.] It is important that all of us identify the motivations that are likely to result in us agreeing to take on the role of crisis intervenor. With such an awareness, it is much more likely that we will be able to maximize assets and minimize liabilities.

LEARNING MODULE 2: CRISIS INTERVENTION THEORY AND RESEARCH

Initial activities should take place in a small group setting. However, showing the video used during this learning module (*PTSD in Children*) may require that the large group be reformed. While lecture comprises the majority of this module's activities, facilitators should strive to keep participants as actively involved as possible. The goal of this module is to provide the background knowledge needed to be a crisis intervenor.

LECTURE: CRISIS THEORY

The goal of this lecture is to ensure that participants have an understanding of the terms *crisis event, crisis state,* and *crisis intervention.* Material for this lecture can be found in Chapter 2. Handouts and/or overhead transparencies for this lecture might include the information provided in Table 2.1 and Table 7.2. Additional materials that can be used as overhead transparencies are found in Tables A.4, A.5, A.6, and A.7.

INTRODUCTORY STATEMENT

Before proceeding any further, it is essential that we come to a basic understanding of what we mean by the terms *crisis event, crisis state,* and *crisis intervention.* The term *crisis* is used in a number of different contexts in our society.

■ ■ ■

CONCLUDING STATEMENT

Now that we have reached some agreement on basic terminology, we are ready to move on to an exploration of identifying trauma victims.

Table A.4
Basic Concepts: Questions Answered by Crisis Theory

What events may require a crisis intervention?

Who may require crisis intervention?

What is crisis intervention?

Table A.5

DSM IV: "Extreme Traumatic Stressor"

"*. . . direct personal experience of an event that involves actual or threatened death or serious injury, or other threat to one's physical integrity; or witnessing an event that involves death, injury, or a threat to the physical integrity of another person; or learning about unexpected or violent death, serious harm, or threat of death or injury experienced by a family member of other close associate."* (p. 424)

Source: From *DSM IV*, the American Psychiatric Association (1994), Washington, DC: Author.

LECTURE: CRISIS RESPONSE

The goal of this lecture is to help participants better understand the traumatizing potential of a given crisis event. Simply put, some crisis events are more traumatic than others. This knowledge will be helpful when it comes to determining the level of crisis response that may be required. In other words, how many crisis intervenors will be required to meet crisis intervention needs. Material for this lecture can be found in Chapter 6. Specifically, in-service facilitators are directed to the discussion of "Item 2: Assess Degree of Impact on the School." Handouts and/or overhead transparencies for this lecture might include Figure 6.3. Additional material that will facilitate the presentation of this information is found in Table A.8.

Table A.6

The Crisis State

• A problem that is viewed as unsolvable

• Acute distress

Other Characteristics:

   Positive or negative outcome

   Time limited (6 weeks)

   More than stress

   Not necessarily mental illness

Table A.7

Goals of Crisis Intervention

Reestablish Immediate Coping

- Assist in taking concrete steps to cope
- Assist in managing feelings and perceptions
- Begin problem-solving process

Provide Support

- Help to feel less alone
- Provide opportunity to talk
- Express warmth and concern

Reduce Lethality

- Remove weapons
- Ensure supervision
- Ensure hospitalization if needed

Link to Helping Resources

- Help find resources (e.g., mental health, social services, legal services)

Table A.8

Crisis Response Options

Response Option	Event Circumstances
No response	The event is not traumatic or traditional school resources can manage crisis reactions.
Site-level response	The event is traumatic, however, student crisis reactions can be managed by school site-level crisis intervention services.
District-level response	The event is traumatic and the severity of crisis reactions may overwhelm school site-level crisis intervention services.
Mutual-aid response	The event is traumatic and the severity of crisis reactions not only overwhelms school site-level crisis intervention services, but also district-level resources.

Source: From "Estimating the Crisis Response," by S.E. Brock (in press-a), in *Best Practices in School Crisis Prevention and Intervention,* Bethesda, MD: National Association of School Psychologists. Copyright by the National Association of School Psychologists. Reprinted with permission.

Introductory Statement

Before providing crisis intervention services, it is important to make an initial judgment regarding the traumatizing potential of a given crisis event. Because the crisis response is stressful, costly, and time consuming, it is important that the level of response match as closely as possible the event's traumatizing potential. Simply put, some crisis events are more traumatic than others and will require more crisis intervention services. From a review of the Posttraumatic Stress Disorder literature, this discussion will offer some generalizations regarding the level of crisis response required following specific crisis events.

■ ■ ■

Concluding Statement

Now that we have an understanding of the type of events that are most likely to result in psychological traumatization, we are ready to focus on the factors that result in an individual being traumatized. We will begin our work in this area with the viewing of a video.

Video: "PTSD in Children: Moving to the Rhythm of the Child"

Exploration of individual psychological traumatization begins with this video. Available from Gift From Within (One Lily Pond Drive, Camden, Maine 04843, 207-236-8506, cost $95), this video introduces concepts related to traumatization and begins to explore the topic of crisis intervention treatments. While the entire video may prove valuable to the in-service program, we recommend that all participants view the first 27 minutes. If possible, it is ideal for the video to be viewed in the small group setting. However, if local resources are not sufficient (i.e., two videos, two monitors, and two VCRs), then this can be viewed in the large group setting. If returning to the large group is necessary, facilitators must make sure to coordinate the ending time of the crisis response lecture.

Introductory Statement

The video "PTSD in Children: Moving to the Rhythm of the Child," is produced by the nonprofit organization Gift From Within. It does an excellent job of exploring traumatic stress and treatment. At the conclusion of the video, we hope to have some time for discussion. As you watch this production, we encourage you to take notes and try to identify those issues that your experience tells you are most critical. During our discussion, we will be asking you to share your observations.

DISCUSSION OF VIDEO

At the conclusion of the video, create an opportunity to discuss what was seen. To the extent possible, this discussion should be unstructured and allow for personal connections to the material. As participants identify important points or comments, they should be recorded on a chalkboard or flip chart.

It will also be important to attempt to emphasize some of the more significant points made by this video. Specifically, Table A.9 presents some of the more important issues raised by this presentation. Included are the running time locations (in minutes and seconds) of each identified issue. In concluding this discussion, the facilitator should summarize the points made by participants and add additional thoughts the group might have missed.

INTRODUCTORY STATEMENT

What are some of your observations? What points made in the video were suggested by your own experiences to be especially relevant? Who would like to start? [Using Table A.9 as a guide, the facilitator should make sure that the group has identified the important points.]

■   ■   ■

CONCLUDING STATEMENT

This video has helped lay the foundation for the work that follows. Next, we will further explore the topic of psychological traumatization.

LECTURE: PSYCHOLOGICAL TRAUMATIZATION

The goal of this lecture is to help participants better understand the factors that might result in psychological trauma. A given traumatic event will be more traumatic for some individuals than it will be for others. This knowledge will be helpful when it comes to determining crisis intervention service priorities—which individuals are most likely to be in need of crisis intervention and should be seen first. Material for this lecture can be found in Chapter 7. Handouts and/or overhead transparencies for this lecture would include Figure 7.2, Figure 7.3, Figure 7.4, Figure 7.5, and Figure 7.6.

Table A.9
Discussion Issues for "PTSD in Children:
Moving to the Rhythm of the Child"

Discussion Issue	Run Time
Anyone can develop PTSD.	1:00
A traumatic event combined with fear, helplessness, and horror may lead to PTSD.	2:05
Developmentally young children are more vulnerable to traumatization.	3:50
Symptoms of PTSD include:	
Re-experiencing the traumatic event	4:45
Avoidance and numbing	8:40
Arousal	10:30
Psychological first aid aims at re-establishing immediate coping.	12:40
Providing facts and normalizing crisis reactions are critical.	12:40
Maladaptive coping can have devastating consequences.	12:56
Prepare parents. Children use caregiver reactions to gauge trauma magnitude.	15:08
Trauma history affects vulnerability.	18:20
Duration of trauma exposure affects the risk of developing PTSD.	20:20
Brief or crisis therapy aims at resolving the crisis.	21:56
Severity of trauma + pre-crisis history + developmental level + personal vulnerabilities are important factors in determining the need for long-term treatment.	24:14
Behavioral approaches have been proven to be effective treatments for PTSD.	27:20

INTRODUCTORY STATEMENT

Research on posttraumatic stress has identified a number of factors that are key in determining whether a given crisis event will traumatize a given individual. The factors that will be discussed include crisis exposure, familiarity with crisis victims, and unique personal vulnerabilities.

■ ■ ■

CONCLUDING STATEMENT

Our work this afternoon has provided the knowledge needed to estimate the likelihood that an event will result in traumatization and to identify those individuals who should be made crisis intervention service priorities. We are now ready to practice applying this knowledge.

ACTIVITY: IDENTIFYING PSYCHOLOGICAL TRAUMA VICTIMS

Typically, this activity begins immediately following the afternoon break. It is designed to help participants apply the knowledge just learned. It is recommended that the crisis scenarios presented in Table 4.5 be used as prompts for this activity. Working either individually or in groups of two to three, participants are asked to read a scenario and then identify what level of crisis response might be required and who they think might be crisis intervention treatment priorities. Participants should also be asked to justify their responses. It is anticipated that in doing so participants will be required to apply the knowledge they have just gained. Table A.10 provides an example of a worksheet that can be used to facilitate this activity. After all participants have had a chance to respond to each of the scenarios, their responses should be reviewed in the large group setting.

INTRODUCTORY STATEMENT

I would next like to give you an opportunity to apply the knowledge that you have learned this afternoon. Working either individually or in small groups, please take the next 30 to 40 minutes to read each of the crisis scenarios in this handout [Table A.10] and write in your responses. After everyone has had a chance to make his or her own responses, we will discuss each scenario in the large group setting.

■ ■ ■

CONCLUDING STATEMENT

From this activity, you have demonstrated the ability to identify both the traumatizing potential of a crisis situation as well as those individuals most likely to have been traumatized by a crisis event. Today we have laid the foundation for the work that follows. Tomorrow will provide you with training in both individual and group crisis intervention skills. [Remind participants the importance of being on time and let them know group crisis intervention skill development will begin promptly at the time stated on the in-service outline sheet.]

Table A.10

Risk Assessment Practice

Crisis Situation 1: A local gang, in response to the physical beating of a fellow gang member by a student at your high school, has come on campus. A fight breaks out in the student parking lot between the gang and the student's friends. A 15-year-old gang member is hospitalized with a stab wound, and one of your students is killed by a gunshot wound to the head. The principal was in the immediate area and tried to intervene; she was hospitalized with serious stab wounds and is not expected to live.

Level of response required:

No response	Site-level response	District-level response	Mutual-aid response

Justification: _____

_____

_____

_____

Crisis Intervention Treatment Priorities:

Which students and/or staff members will need to be seen immediately?

_____

_____

Justification: _____

_____

_____

_____

Which students and/or staff members will need to be seen as soon as possible, but not right away?

Justification: _____

_____

_____

_____

Which students and/or staff may not need to be provided crisis intervention at all?

Justification: _____

_____

_____

_____

(continued)

Crisis Situation 2: A very popular sixth-grade teacher at an elementary school was supervising his students on a field trip to a local lake. He tragically drowns after hitting his head on a rock while trying to rescue one of the students who had fallen into the lake.

Level of response required:

No response	Site-level response	District-level response	Mutual-aid response

Justification: _____
_____
_____
_____

Crisis Intervention Treatment Priorities:

Which students and/or staff members will need to be seen immediately?
_____
_____

Justification: _____
_____
_____
_____
_____

Which students and/or staff members will need to be seen as soon as possible, but not right away?

Justification: _____
_____
_____
_____

Which students and/or staff may not need to be provided crisis intervention at all?

Justification: _____
_____
_____
_____
_____

Crisis Situation 3: An irate father has come on to your elementary school site at 8:30 A.M., a half hour after school has started. He heads to his kindergarten-age daughter's classroom without checking in with the office. The father enters the classroom and begins to hit his daughter. As the astounded class and the teacher watch, he severely beats her. Leaving the girl unconscious, he storms out the door and drives off in his pickup truck. The event took place in less than 5 minutes.

Level of response required:

No response	Site-level response	District-level response	Mutual-aid response

Justification: _____
_____
_____
_____

Crisis Intervention Treatment Priorities:

Which students and/or staff members will need to be seen immediately?
_____
_____
_____

Justification: _____
_____
_____
_____

Which students and/or staff members will need to be seen as soon as possible, but not right away?

Justification: _____
_____
_____

Which students and/or staff may not need to be provided crisis intervention at all?

Justification: _____
_____
_____
_____

(continued)

Crisis Situation 4: A third-grade teacher is presenting a lesson to her students. She has just soundly reprimanded students for continuing to talk out; in fact, she is still very upset. Suddenly, she turns pale, clutches her chest, and keels over in front of 29 horrified children. Two frightened children run to the office, sobbing the news. The teacher is taken by ambulance to the nearest hospital, where it is discovered that she has suffered a massive heart attack. She never regains consciousness and succumbs the next morning.

Level of response required:

No response	Site-level response	District-level response	Mutual-aid response

Justification: _____

_____

_____

_____

Crisis Intervention Treatment Priorities:

Which students and/or staff members will need to be seen immediately?

_____

_____

Justification: _____

_____

_____

_____

Which students and/or staff members will need to be seen as soon as possible, but not right away?

Justification: _____

_____

_____

_____

Which students and/or staff may not need to be provided crisis intervention at all?

Justification: _____

_____

_____

_____

Table A.10 *(Continued)*

Crisis Situation 5: A special education school bus filled with severely handicapped students was fired at while on its way to school. The bullet passed through one window and out another. No students were injured. Realizing what had happened, the bus driver headed immediately for the school where police, the school principal, and the school counselor met him.

Level of response required:

No response	Site-level response	District-level response	Mutual-aid response

Justification: _____

_____

_____

Crisis Intervention Treatment Priorities:

Which students and/or staff members will need to be seen immediately?

_____

Justification: _____

_____

_____

Which students and/or staff members will need to be seen as soon as possible, but not right away?

Justification: _____

_____

_____

Which students and/or staff may not need to be provided crisis intervention at all?

Justification: _____

_____

_____

LEARNING MODULE 3: GROUP CRISIS INTERVENTION

This learning module will take place in the morning on the second day. All activities should take place in a large group setting. While lecture will comprise a substantial portion of this module's activities, facilitators should strive to keep participants as actively involved as possible.

Lecture: Classroom Crisis Intervention

The goal of this lecture is to ensure that participants have an understanding of the issues and procedures of Classroom Crisis Intervention (CCI) (Brock, 1998a). Material for this lecture can be found in Chapter 8. Handouts and/or overhead transparencies for this lecture might include Table 7.2 and Table 8.11. Additional materials that can be used as overhead transparencies are found in Tables A.11, A.12, A.13, A.14, A.15, A.16, A.17, A.18, and A.19.

Introductory Statement

Good morning and welcome to day 2. Yesterday we provided instruction designed to give the background knowledge we feel is necessary for filling the role of crisis intervenor. Today we will focus on the development of crisis intervention skills. We begin with a look at a group approach to crisis intervention. This approach is known as Classroom Crisis Intervention or CCI.

■ ■ ■

Concluding Statement

Next, we will create a role play demonstration that will make our understanding of CCI more concrete.

Table A.11
Classroom Crisis Intervention (CCI) Issues

1. Who should participate in CCI?
2. What is the optimal size of the CCI?
3. Where should CCI be offered?
4. When should CCI be offered?
5. Who are CCI facilitators?
6. What is the role of the teacher?
7. CCI contraindications:

Table A.12

Steps in Classroom Crisis Intervention

1. Introduction
2. Providing facts and dispelling rumors
3. Sharing stories
4. Sharing reactions
5. Empowerment
6. Closure

Table A.13

CCI Introduction

- Approximate duration: 15 minutes
- Goals:
  1. Explain the purpose of CCI
  2. Identify facilitators
  3. Introduce CCI process and steps
  4. Review and/or establish rules

Table A.14

Providing Facts and Dispelling Rumors

- Approximate duration: 30 minutes
- Goals:
  1. Provide an understanding of crisis facts
  2. Stop the spread of rumors
- Strategies:
  1. Discussion
  2. Newspapers
  3. Repetition
- Caution:

  Information transmission of PTSD

Table A.15
Sharing Stories

- Approximate duration: 45 minutes
- Goals:
    1. Facilitate expression of experiences
    2. Identify common experiences
- Strategies:
    1. Ask for volunteers
    2. Move around the classroom
    3. Art activities
    4. Validate experiences
    5. Identify commonalties

Table A.16
Sharing Reactions

- Approximate duration: 30 minutes
- Goals:
    1. Facilitate expression of reactions
    2. Identify common reactions
    3. Normalize crisis reactions
- Strategies:
    1. Identify common crisis reactions
    2. Ask survivors to share reactions
    3. Point out commonalties
    4. Teach the normality of crisis reactions
    5. Mention self-referral procedures

Table A.17
Empowerment

- Approximate duration: 60 minutes
- Goals:
  1. Move from sharing to solving
  2. Identify coping strategies
  3. Take some kind of action
- Strategies:
  1. Teach stress management
  2. Identify accessible supports
  3. Brainstorm prevention strategies

Table A.18
Closure

- Approximate duration: 30 minutes
- Goals:
  1. Place the crisis in the past
  2. Begin to look forward
- Strategies:
  1. Prepare for funeral attendance
  2. Supervised memorial development
  3. Creating cards and writing letters
  4. Deciding what to do with belongings
  5. Be positive about acquiring the ability to cope
  6. Summarize what has been learned
  7. Reiterate self-referral procedures

Table A.19

Post-CCI Activities

- Communicate with families about:
  How to help their children cope
  How to make referrals

- Continue to be visible:
  Spend time on the playground
  Drop in on the class

- Continue psychological triage:
  Who needs individual crisis intervention?

- Support each other:
  Crisis intervenors are affected

LARGE GROUP ROLE PLAY: A CLASSROOM CRISIS INTERVENTION

Immediately following the lecture, facilitators should create a large group role play that will make the CCI model more concrete. It is recommended that as many in-service participants as possible take part in this activity. In-service facilitators would take on the role of CCI leaders while in-service participants take on the role of students in a classroom that has just experienced a significant crisis event. Table A.20, which can be used

Table A.20

CCI Role Play

Crisis Situation: A school community has just experienced a crisis event. On Friday evening a flash flood devastated the area surrounding the school. While the flood waters quickly receded, significant property damage was done. While the school was undamaged and there were no fatalities, there were several injuries. One of the injured was a student in the sixth grade. It is Monday morning and the classroom teacher and a district crisis intervention team member enter the room as school is about to start.

Crisis Role: Name tags will be used to specify whom you will be playing. On the back of the name tag is a description of the crisis experiences and reactions the student is supposed to be experiencing.

Note: Time may not permit us to complete an entire CCI session. Thus, the facilitators may jump ahead in the CCI model.

as an overhead transparency, is designed to facilitate the introduction of this activity.

Roles will be assigned by passing out name tags. On the back of each name tag is a brief description of the student's crisis experiences and crisis reactions. These name tags are provided in Figure A.1 and should be placed in 4″ × 3″ string name badge holders. In-services participants should be told to try to stick to their assigned roles. As the role play unfolds, participants should be directed to try to keep track of where they are in the CCI model. To facilitate this, Table A.12 should be displayed during the session. Participants should be directed to keep the handout produced from Table 8.11 and/or wallet-sized cue cards (Figure A.2) available.

INTRODUCTORY STATEMENT

To make our understanding of CCI more concrete, we will now have role play. In this role play, we (the in-service facilitators) will take on the role of CCI facilitators and you (the in-service participants) will take on the role of CCI participants. The name tags we are about to pass out have important information on the back. Please read this information and let us know if you have any questions.

■   ■   ■

CONCLUDING STATEMENT

Now that we have an understanding of a group crisis intervention technique, let's move on to a discussion of individual crisis intervention.

LEARNING MODULE 4: INDIVIDUAL CRISIS INTERVENTION

LECTURE: PSYCHOLOGICAL FIRST AID

Introduction of the individual crisis intervention technique, known as psychological first aid is provided in a lecture. The information provided in Chapter 8 lists the material needed for this lecture. During this learning module, the following tables and figures will be useful as overhead transparencies: Table 8.4, Table 8.6, Table 8.7, Table 8.8, Table 8.9, Figure 8.1, and Figure 8.2. This last figure may also be used as a handout. Other material that may help to facilitate this lecture is provided in Table A.21 on page 337. Slaikeu (1990) who also offers training suggestions has previously described psychological first aid. The reader is referred to his text for additional training activity ideas.

Juan

Juan:

Crisis Experience: Flood waters stopped just short of his house.

Crisis Reactions: Having difficulty sleeping, not hungry, can't stop thinking about the flood.

Special Issues:

Maria

Maria:

Crisis Experience: Saw damage. Her home was never threatened.

Crisis Reactions: Having bad dreams, stomachaches, can't stop thinking about the flood.

Special Issues: Best friend of Susie, who was injured during the flood.

Figure A.1 Name Tags with Role Descriptions

Jose

Jose:

Crisis Experience: Home severely damaged by the flood. Threatened injury.

Crisis Reactions: Can't concentrate, can't stop thinking about the flood.

Special Issues: Jose's sibling was injured during the flood.

Viet

Viet:

Crisis Experience: Home incurred slight damage.

Crisis Reactions: Can't sleep, can't stop thinking about the flood.

Special Issues:

Figure A.1 *(Continued)*

Steve

Steve:

Crisis Experience: Home never threatened by the flood.

Crisis Reactions: No reactions.

Special Issues:

Barbara

Barbara:

Crisis Experience: Saw flood coming, home severely damaged, father injured.

Crisis Reactions: Having difficulty sleeping, not hungry, can't stop thinking about the flood.

Special Issues: Barbara has heard a rumor that a new flash flood warning has been issued. Ask a question about this rumor when asked if there are any questions about the flood (do so even if other role players have already done so).

Figure A.1 *(Continued)*

David

David:

Crisis Experience: Saw flood damage, home threatened but not damaged.

Crisis Reactions: Having bad dreams, angry all the time, can't stop thinking about the flood.

Special Issues:

Dawn

Dawn:

Crisis Experience: Saw flood coming, home slightly damaged, family able to escape without injury.

Crisis Reactions: Having headaches/stomachaches, can't concentrate, can't stop thinking about the flood.

Special Issues: Dawn has heard a rumor that a new flash flood warning has been issued. Ask a question about this rumor when asked if there are any questions about the flood (do so even if other role players have already done so).

Figure A.1 (Continued)

Bao

Bao:

Crisis Experience: Saw flood coming, home sustained moderate damage, family able to escape with only minor injuries.

Crisis Reactions: Can't stop thinking about the flood, bad dreams, difficulty sleeping.

Special Issues: At some point Bao needs to get up and leave the "classroom." Do so unannounced. Simply get up and leave. This will be done to illustrate why it is important not to do this intervention on your own. One of the facilitators will come and get "Bao" who as it turns out just had to go to the bathroom.

Pat

Pat:

Crisis Experience: Saw flood coming, home sustained minor damage, family able to escape without injury.

Crisis Reactions: Having difficulty sleeping, not hungry, headaches.

Special Issues:

Figure A.1 (*Continued*)

Carol

Carol:

Crisis Experience: Home was unaffected by the flood, saw damage to neighboring home, family never threatened.

Crisis Reactions: Having difficulty sleeping.

Special Issues: Early on in the role play Carol needs to interrupt a classmate. After having been reminded to give everyone their turn, Carol no longer speaks out without having first raised her hand.

Sharon

Sharon:

Crisis Experience: Saw flood coming, flood waters damaged her home, family escaped with only minor injuries.

Crisis Reactions: Having bad dreams, can't stop thinking about the flood, angry.

Special Issues:

Figure A.1 *(Continued)*

Diana

Diana:

Crisis Experience: Home never threatened, saw flood damage to neighboring homes.

Crisis Reactions: Can't get mind off flood.

Special Issues:

Frank

Frank:

Crisis Experience: Saw flood coming, home severely damaged, family escaped without injury.

Crisis Reactions: Having difficulty sleeping, can't concentrate on school work.

Special Issues: Neighbor is the classmate who was injured.

Figure A.1 (Continued)

Psychological First Aid
(MEET U)

1. **M**ake psychological contact.
   Empathy, Respect & Warmth.
2. **E**xplore the problem.
   Refer to mental health professional if there is any lethality.
3. **E**xamine possible solutions.
   Identify ways to cope with/solve crisis problems.
4. Assist in **T**aking concrete action.
   If necessary, be very directive.
5. Follow-**Up**.

Psychological First Aid
(MEET U)

1. **M**ake psychological contact.
   Empathy, Respect & Warmth.
2. **E**xplore the problem.
   Refer to mental health professional if there is any lethality.
3. **E**xamine possible solutions.
   Identify ways to cope with/solve crisis problems.
4. Assist in **T**aking concrete action.
   If necessary, be very directive.
5. Follow-**Up**.

Psychological First Aid
(MEET U)

1. **M**ake psychological contact.
   Empathy, Respect & Warmth.
2. **E**xplore the problem.
   Refer to mental health professional if there is any lethality.
3. **E**xamine possible solutions.
   Identify ways to cope with/solve crisis problems.
4. Assist in **T**aking concrete action.
   If necessary, be very directive.
5. Follow-**Up**.

Psychological First Aid
(MEET U)

1. **M**ake psychological contact.
   Empathy, Respect & Warmth.
2. **E**xplore the problem.
   Refer to mental health professional if there is any lethality.
3. **E**xamine possible solutions.
   Identify ways to cope with/solve crisis problems.
4. Assist in **T**aking concrete action.
   If necessary, be very directive.
5. Follow-**Up**.

Figure A.2 Wallet-Sized Psychological First Aid and Classroom Crisis Intervention Cards. These can be used by in-service participants to help cue them to remember the steps involved in psychological first aid and classroom crisis counseling.

335

Classroom Crisis Intervention

1. Introduction
   Review process/rules. Introduce facilitators.
2. Provide facts and dispel rumors.
   Answer questions.
3. Share crisis stories.
   What happened?
4. Share crisis reactions.
   How do students feel?
5. Empower.
   Identify ways to cope with/solve crisis problems.
6. Closure.

Classroom Crisis Intervention

1. Introduction
   Review process/rules. Introduce facilitators.
2. Provide facts and dispel rumors.
   Answer questions.
3. Share crisis stories.
   What happened?
4. Share crisis reactions.
   How do students feel?
5. Empower.
   Identify ways to cope with/solve crisis problems.
6. Closure.

Classroom Crisis Intervention

1. Introduction
   Review process/rules. Introduce facilitators.
2. Provide facts and dispel rumors.
   Answer questions.
3. Share crisis stories.
   What happened?
4. Share crisis reactions.
   How do students feel?
5. Empower.
   Identify ways to cope with/solve crisis problems.
6. Closure.

Classroom Crisis Intervention

1. Introduction
   Review process/rules. Introduce facilitators.
2. Provide facts and dispel rumors.
   Answer questions.
3. Share crisis stories.
   What happened?
4. Share crisis reactions.
   How do students feel?
5. Empower.
   Identify ways to cope with/solve crisis problems.
6. Closure.

Figure A.2 *(Continued)*

Table A.21

Psychological First Aid

1. Make psychological contact
2. Explore dimensions of the problem
3. Examine possible solutions
4. Assist in taking concrete action
5. Follow-up

INTRODUCTORY STATEMENT

Next, we will explore an individual approach to crisis intervention. Developed by Karl Slaikeu, this approach is known as Psychological First Aid. The primary goal of psychological first aid is to help the person-in-crisis re-establish immediate coping.

■ ■ ■

CONCLUDING STATEMENT

Now that we understand the psychological first aid model, let's watch a demonstration of it to make our understanding more concrete.

DEMONSTRATION: PSYCHOLOGICAL FIRST AID

After having reviewed the psychological first aid model, provide a demonstration of this crisis intervention approach. Table 8.3 provides a sample dialogue that can be used to facilitate such a demonstration. It is recommended that the facilitators solicit participants to read the different roles offered in this dialogue. At its conclusion, facilitators should review how the dialogue illustrated the components of psychological first aid.

INTRODUCTORY STATEMENT

To help us with this demonstration of psychological first aid, we will need some volunteers to read a dialogue. [Obtain at least three volunteers and give them the sample dialogue provided in Table 8.3.] As you listen to these volunteers read this dialogue, try to identify the various components of psychological first aid.

■ ■ ■

CONCLUDING STATEMENT

This dialogue has provided a demonstration of psychological first aid. Next, we will engage in some large group role plays to further explore the components of this crisis intervention technique.

The large group role plays should be the last activity offered during the morning session. At their conclusion, take a lunch break. During most of these role plays, the facilitator(s) will take on the role of a person-in-crisis, and the participants will take on the role of crisis intervenor. Tables A.22, A.23, A.24, and A.25 provide directions for role plays that are designed to illustrate individual components of psychological first aid. Table A.26 offers directions for the concluding role play, which is designed to illustrate use of the entire psychological first aid model.

Table A.22
Large Group Practice: Making Psychological Contact

Goals:	To help participants examine ways to make psychological contact, and to illustrate that there are a number of ways to make such contact.
Situation:	A drive-by shooting occurred at one of your middle schools. Three students have been shot, one fatally. You are now counseling an eighth grade boy (Steve) who was best friends with the student who died. It is the day after the shooting and Steve is refusing to come to school.
Task:	How might you make psychological contact with this student? As a group, brainstorm ways to do so.
Procedure:	Display the overhead transparency made from Table 8.4 (Making Psychological Contact). The facilitator should encourage and reinforce all attempts to make psychological contact. It is recommended that all suggestions be written down on a flip chart or chalk board. As participants offer suggestions, they should be directed to phrase their responses as if they were talking directly to the student. When participants have exhausted all their ideas, move on to debriefing.
Debriefing:	Point out that there is no "right answer" to this activity. Any one of the initial responses may have worked. There are a variety of ways to make psychological contact. Ask the group to identify the next step in the psychological first aid process. Once they have identified that it is to explore the dimensions of crisis generated problems, move on to the next role play.

Table A.23

Large Group Practice: Examining Dimensions of the Problem

Goal:	To give participants a chance to practice identifying crisis problems.
Situation:	A drive-by shooting occurred at one of your middle schools. Three students have been shot, one fatally. You are now counseling an eighth grade boy (Steve) who was best friends with the student who died. It is the day after the shooting and Steve is refusing to come to school. You have made psychological contact with Steve and he is willing to talk to you.
Task:	Explore the dimensions of the problem. Determine if there are any problems that are viewed by Steve as "unsolvable." Try to identify both immediate and later concerns.
Procedure:	Display the overhead transparency made from Table 8.6 (Exploring Dimensions of the Problem). Participants should be instructed to continue to phrase their questions as if they were talking directly to the student. The facilitator should encourage and reinforce all possible attempts to identify the crisis problems. When participants identify the immediate problem is "fear" of walking to school, and the later concern of "being alone at school" (there is no one at school to be with, the student who was killed was Steve's only friend), then move on to the debriefing.
Debriefing:	Point out that Steve's immediate problem is fear of being shot himself. In addition, he is feeling very alone. Steve believes that there is no one else in the world that could be his friend. He has no other friends and perceives his family as nonsupportive. Ask the group to identify the next step in the psychological first aid process. Once they have identified that it is to help identify solutions to the crisis problems, move on to the next role play.

Table A.24

Large Group Practice: Examining Possible Solutions

Goal:	To give participants a chance to practice identifying solutions to crisis problems.
Situation:	A drive-by shooting occurred at one of your middle schools. Three students have been shot, one fatally. You are now counseling an eighth grade boy (Steve) who was best friends with the student who died. It is the day after the shooting and Steve is refusing to come to school. You have made psychological contact with Steve and he is willing to talk to you. You have also identified that he is fearful of walking to school and that he is feeling very alone. Even if he were not afraid, with his friend shot, Steve sees no reason to go to school.
Task:	How can we help Steve identify solutions to the crisis problems?
Procedure:	Display the overhead transparency made from Table 8.7 (Examining Possible Solutions). The facilitator should encourage and reinforce all possible attempts to solve the crisis problems. However, stepping into the role of the student, the facilitator should reject all proposals. In this situation everything is headed toward another murder. When participants identify that Steve is so upset that he is considering killing the person he suspects of murdering his friend move on to the debriefing.
Debriefing:	Point out that the solutions offered were all well thought out and that with just about any other student they would have worked. However, Steve is very disturbed. Ask the group to identify the next step in the psychological first aid process. Once they have identified that it is to assist in taking some concrete action, ask how directive they will need to be. Once it is clear that Steve's crisis intervenor will need to be very directive, move on to the next role play.

Table A.25

Large Group Practice: Taking Concrete
Action—Use of a Directive Approach

Goals:	To give participants a chance to practice taking action to solve crisis problems. This role play is also designed to help participants recognize when a directive approach is needed and to understand the limitations of psychological first aid.
Situation:	A drive-by shooting occurred at one of your middle schools. Three students have been shot, one fatally. You are now counseling an eighth grade boy (Steve) who was best friends with the student who died. It is the day after the shooting and Steve is refusing to come to school. You have made psychological contact with Steve and he is willing to talk to you. You have also identified that he is fearful of walking to school and that he is feeling very alone. Even if he was not afraid, with his friend shot, Steve sees no reason to go to school. Steve's initial strategy to cope with being afraid of going to school is to kill the person whom he thought murdered his friend. We will need to be very directive with Steve.
Task:	How can we help Steve take concrete action to solve the crisis problems? As a group find ways to do so.
Procedure:	Display the overhead transparency made from Table 8.8 (Taking Concrete Action). The facilitator should encourage and reinforce all possible attempts to help Steve take concrete action. However, stepping into the role of the student, the facilitator should reject all proposals. Murder is the only coping strategy that this student recognizes. The facilitator should especially reinforce responses indicating the crisis intervenor is taking a very directive role in helping Steve cope. A facilitative approach would not be appropriate.
Debriefing:	Point out the limitations of psychological first aid. For minor injuries, this may be all the attention that is needed. For example, it is possible that the individual's crisis reactions are such that he or she needs only limited attention (the crisis problems may just be a scratch). For major injuries, however, this is only a first step (the crisis problems may be a major injury). It might be thought of as the strategy that keeps the individual out of danger long enough to get professional help. An analogy between psychological and medical first aid can be made. Finally, ask participants to identify the last step in the psychological first aid process. Once they have identified that it is follow-up, display the transparency made from Table 8.9 (Follow-Up). The facilitator should discuss this step as it relates to the current role play. Once this is done, move on to the next role play.

Table A.26
Large Group Practice: Use of the Entire
Psychological First Aid Model

Goal:	To help participants see what it is like to use the entire psychological first aid model with a student who is in crisis.
Situation:	A drive-by shooting has occurred at your school during recess. The next day, as a part of the school's crisis response team, you are assigned to work with a fifth grade classroom. The recess bell rings and the students file out of the room for recess. One student, however, stays behind. She is sitting at her desk pretending to work.
Task:	Using the psychological first aid model what would you do?
Procedure:	Display the overhead transparency made from Figure 8.2 (Psychological First Aid), and remind participants to refer to their crisis intervention cue cards (Figure A.1). In this scenario, participants are one collective crisis intervenor. Each in turn builds upon the contributions of the others. One presenter will facilitate this activity, another fills the role of the student being offered psychological first aid. As participants attempt to assist the student, they should be reinforced. The facilitator should point out where they are in the model (Figure 8.2). As a step in the psychological first aid process is accomplished, the facilitator steps in and asks the group what needs to be done next.
Debriefing:	Each crisis counselor, in order of participation, will be given the opportunity of responding to the following questions: (a) How did it go? (b) What were you trying to do? and (c) How did it feel? After each crisis counselor responds, the facilitator who played the student gives brief feedback. Finally, the rest of the group is given an opportunity to respond to the role play.

INTRODUCTORY STATEMENT

Next we will engage in a series of large group role plays that are designed to further illustrate the specific components of the psychological first aid process. Throughout each of these role plays, you [the participants] will be in the role of crisis intervenor and we [the facilitators] will be in the role of person-in-crisis.

■ ■ ■

CONCLUDING STATEMENT

Now that we have had several demonstrations of the psychological first aid process, it is time for us to begin to practice this technique on our own. To do so, we will return to our small groups.

SMALL GROUP ROLE PLAYS: PSYCHOLOGICAL FIRST AID

This activity takes place in the small group setting and should take up most of the afternoon session. Table A.27 (which can be used as an

Table A.27
Small Group Practice: Use of the Entire
Psychological First Aid Model

Goal:	To help participants experience what it is like to use the entire psychological first aid model with a student who is in crisis.
Situation:	In the small group setting participants will develop their own crisis situations.
Task:	Use the psychological first aid model to help an individual in crisis.
Procedure:	Divide participants into pairs. Next, each pair decides on whom will fill the role of person-in-crisis and crisis intervenor. The person-in-crisis and the crisis intervenor will work together to create a crisis situation. It is recommended that the situation chosen not be a worst case scenario. The situation chosen should be one that role players feel will allow them to demonstrate (or teach) the entire psychological first aid model. As each pair presents their role play all other members of the small group document the psychological first aid actions that were observed. This is a no-fault activity. The crisis intervenor can stop the role play at any time and ask the group for help. We are still learning. Mistakes will be valuable.
Debriefing:	After the person in crisis has been helped, the crisis intervenor should share what they were trying to accomplish. Then the person-in-crisis should share what they experienced. Finally, other members of the small group are encouraged to share the aspects of the psychological first aid model they observed.
Continue:	As time permits roles should be rotated.

overhead transparency and/or handout) offers directions for these role plays, which are designed to give participants practice using the psychological first aid model. Figure A.2 offers wallet-sized cards that participants can use to help cue their role play efforts. Figure A.3 provides an observation sheet handout that participants can use to note what they have seen during the role plays.

INTRODUCTORY STATEMENT

The role plays we are about to engage in are designed to give us practice providing psychological first aid to a person-in-crisis. They are also designed to give us several different examples of this process. With your partner, spend the next five minutes deciding on a crisis situation. Decide who will play the person-in-crisis and who will play the crisis intervenor. In selecting a crisis situation, try to pick one that will allow you to demonstrate the entire psychological first aid model. Do not pick a worst case scenario. Try to set yourselves up for success. Also, please keep in mind that this is a "no fault" activity. If at any point in a role play you become stuck, you can ask for a time out and the rest of the group can offer suggestions on what to do next. However, the group may offer comments only when asked. At the end of each role play, we will briefly discuss what has been observed in terms of the psychological first aid model.

■   ■   ■

CONCLUDING STATEMENT

The role plays have provided us with several excellent examples of psychological first aid. I truly appreciate all the effort that you put into these role plays. I know that such an activity can be threatening, but it is an effective way to practice new skills. Next, we will conclude our in-service program in the large group meeting room.

NETWORKING AND CONCLUDING ACTIVITIES

The workshop is concluded in the large group setting. Here participants are asked to complete any evaluation the workshop sponsors may have. In addition, this is a chance for the group to identify additional local, state, and national crisis intervention resources. Along these lines, the facilitators may offer the information provided in Tables 3.2, 3.3, and 3.4 as handouts. In addition, it will be important to identify for the group that with this training the participants themselves have become important local crisis intervention resources.

Psychological First Aid Observation Sheet

Use this form to note aspects of the psychological first aid model you observed during the role plays.

Role Players: _____

Make Psychological Contact: _____

_____

_____

_____

_____

_____

Exploring Dimensions of the Problem: _____

_____

_____

_____

_____

Examining Possible Solutions: _____

_____

_____

_____

_____

Taking Concrete Action: _____

_____

_____

_____

_____

Follow-Up: _____

_____

_____

_____

_____

Figure A.3   Psychological First Aid Observation Sheet.

INTRODUCTORY STATEMENT

We have come to the end of our time together. In the few moments remaining we would like us to identify additional resources that might further our training in crisis intervention.

■ ■ ■

CONCLUDING STATEMENT

Thank you for participating in our in-service program. We hope that you have found it helpful. Please feel free to contact us if you have any questions in the future. [If appropriate, the facilitators should offer the group information on how to contact them if there are any questions.] We hope that you will never have to use the skills you have developed. However, we recognize that it is likely that you will have to do so and are confident that you will be effective crisis intervenors.

APPENDIX B

Tips for Teachers in Times of Disaster: Taking Care of Yourselves and Each Other

As TEACHERS, you are in the "front lines" in dealing with our children's reactions to crises. By virtue of working or living in the area, you may be a crisis victim yourself. It is extremely important to recognize that you, too, are under particular stress and vulnerable to "burnout." Burnout reactions include:

- Depression, irritability, anxiety, hyperexcitability, excessive rage
- Physical exhaustion, loss of energy, gastrointestinal distress, appetite disturbances, hypochondria, sleep disorders, tremors
- Hyperactivity, excessive fatigue, inability to express self verbally or in writing
- Slowness of thought, inability to make decisions, loss of objectivity in evaluating own functioning, external confusion

It is important to recognize these symptoms and find ways to relieve the stress causing them. You can use one another as support systems, by allowing one another to vent his or her experiences. Time might be set aside in staff meetings to discuss your personal responses to the crisis event, as well as to share ideas on dealing with and assisting the students.

Adapted from the Marin County Community Mental Health Services and Santa Cruz County Mental Health (1985). This work is in the public domain.

Teaching is a high-stress job under the best of circumstances. Dealing with your own responses to crisis and your students' reactions could easily feel overwhelming at times. To recognize this fact and take care of yourselves and one another can help keep the stress to a more manageable level.

REACTIONS OF CHILDREN TO DISASTER

Although many feelings and reactions are shared by people of all ages in response to the direct or indirect effects of a crisis, special attention is required to meet the needs of children.

Typical reactions for children of all ages include fears of future crises; loss of interest in school; regressive behaviors; sleep disturbance and night terrors; fears of activities, events, and/or locations associated with the crisis.

SPECIFIC AGE GROUPS

Different age groups of children tend to be vulnerable to the stress of crisis in unique ways. We next summarize typical responses for different age groups and suggested responses to them.

PRESCHOOL (1 TO 5 YEARS)

Typical responses in this age group include thumb sucking, bed-wetting, fears of the darkness or animals, clinging to parents, night terrors, loss of bladder or bowel control, constipation, speech difficulties (e.g., stammering), loss or increase of appetite.

Children in this age group are particularly vulnerable to disruption of their previously secure world. Because they generally lack the verbal and conceptual skills necessary to cope effectively with sudden stress by themselves, they look to family members for comfort. They are often strongly affected by reactions of parents and other family members. Abandonment is a major fear in this age group; children who have lost family members or even pets or toys will need special reassurance.

The following suggestions help the child integrate his or her experiences and reestablish a sense of security and mastery: encourage expression through play reenactment; provide verbal reassurance and physical comforting; give frequent attention; encourage expression regarding loss of pets or toys; provide comforting bedtime routines; allow to sleep in same room with parents (with the understanding that this is for a limited period of time).

EARLY CHILDHOOD (5 TO 11 YEARS)

Common responses in this age group include irritability, whining, clinging, aggressive behavior at home or school, overt competition with younger siblings for parents' attention, night terrors, nightmares, fear of darkness, school avoidance, withdrawal from peers, loss of interest, and poor concentration in school.

Regressive behavior is most typical of this group. Loss of pets or prized objects is particularly difficult for this group to handle.

The following responses may be helpful: patience and tolerance, play sessions with adults and peers, discussions with adults and peers, relaxation of expectations in school or at home (with the clear understanding that this is temporary and the normal routine will be resumed after a suitable period), opportunities for structured but not demanding chores and responsibilities at home, rehearsal of safety measures to be taken in future disasters.

PREADOLESCENT (11 TO 14 YEARS)

Common responses in this age group are sleep disturbance, appetite disturbance, rebellion in the home, refusal to do chores, school problems (e.g., fighting, withdrawal, loss of interest, attention-seeking behavior), physical problems (e.g., headaches, vague aches and pains, skin eruptions, bowel problems, psychosomatic complaints), loss of interest in peer social activities.

Peer reactions are especially significant in this age group. The child needs to feel that his or her fears are both appropriate and shared by others. Responses should be aimed at lessening tensions and anxieties and possible guilt feelings.

The following may be helpful: group activities geared toward the resumption of routines, involvement in same-age group activities, group discussion geared toward reliving the disaster and rehearsing appropriate behavior in future disasters, structured undemanding responsibilities, temporarily relaxed expectations of performance at school and home, additional individual attention and consideration.

ADOLESCENT (14 TO 18 YEARS)

Common responses in this age group include psychosomatic symptoms (e.g., rashes, bowel problems, asthma), headaches and tension, appetite and sleep disturbance, hypochondriasis, agitation or decrease in energy level, apathy, decline in interest in the opposite sex, irresponsible and/or delinquent behavior, decline in emancipatory struggles over parental control, poor concentration.

Most of these activities and interests of the adolescent are focused in his or her own-age peers. They tend to be especially distressed by the disruption of their peer group activities and the lack of access to full adult responsibilities in community efforts.

The following responses are recommended: encourage participation in the community rehabilitation or reclamation work; encourage resumption of social activities, athletics, clubs, and so on; encourage discussion of disaster experiences with peers, extra-family, significant others; temporarily reduce expectations for level of school and general performance; encourage but do not insist upon discussion of disaster fears within the family setting.

WHEN TO REFER TO MENTAL HEALTH PROFESSIONALS

There is a wide range of normal reactions following a disaster. Usually the reactions can be dealt with by support at home and at school. However, this isn't always the case, and you may need to recommend professional help. In making such a referral, it is important to stress that it is not a sign of failure for parents if they find they are not able to help their child by themselves. It is also important to note that early action will help the child return to normal and avoid more severe problems later.

Students who have lost family members or friends, who were physically injured, or felt that they were in extreme danger are at special risk. Individuals who have experienced previous crises or who were involved in individual or family crises in addition to the current trauma, may have more difficulty dealing with the additional stress. Counseling may be recommended as a preventive measure in cases when these circumstances are known to exist.

If symptoms that are considered normal reactions following a crisis persist for several months and/or are disruptive to the student's social, emotional, or physical functioning, referral is recommended.

PRESCHOOL AND ELEMENTARY SCHOOL

Consider referring the family for professional help if the child:

- Seems excessively withdrawn and depressed; does not respond to special attention and attempts to draw him or her out.

- Is disoriented, that is, if he or she is unable to give own name, town, and the date.
- Complains of significant memory gaps.
- Is despondent and shows agitation, restlessness, and pacing.
- Is severely depressed and withdrawn.
- Uses drugs or alcohol excessively.
- Is unable to care for self (e.g., doesn't eat, drink, bathe, or change clothes).
- Repeats ritualistic acts.
- Hallucinates—hears voices, sees visions.
- States his or her body feels "unreal" and expresses fears that she or he is "going crazy."
- Is excessively preoccupied with one idea or thought.
- Has the delusion that someone or something is out to get him and his family.
- Is afraid he or she will kill self or another.
- Is unable to make simple decisions or carry out everyday functions.
- Shows extreme pressure of speech—talk overflows.

CLASSROOM ACTIVITIES

Many teachers have responded to crises with creative classroom activities to assist their students in ventilating and integrating their experiences. We have compiled some of these activities appropriate to the specific age groups. They are meant to be vehicles for expression and discussion for your students, important steps in the healing process. These are examples of what can be done. They can be used to stimulate your own ideas and can be adapted to meet your students' needs and your teaching styles.

Preschool Activities

1. Availability of toys that encourage play reenactment of children's experiences and observations during the crisis can be helpful to them in integrating these experiences. These might include fire trucks, dump trucks, rescue trucks, ambulances, police cars, media vans, building blocks, or playing with puppets or dolls as ways for the child to ventilate his or her own feelings about what has occurred.
2. Children need much physical contact during times of stress to help them reestablish a sense of security. Games that involve physical touching among children within a structured environment are

helpful in this regard. Some examples might be: (a) Ring Around the
Rosie, (b) London Bridge, or (c) Duck, Duck, Goose.

3. Providing extra amounts of finger foods, in small portions, and flu-
ids is a concrete way of supplying the emotional and physical nour-
ishment that children need in times of stress. Oral satisfaction is
especially necessary as children tend to revert to more regressive
behavior in response to feeling that their survival or security is
threatened.

4. Have the children do a mural on butcher paper with topics such as
"What happened in your house (school or neighborhood) when the
big storm hit (earthquake, shooting, etc.)." This is recommended for
small groups with discussion afterward facilitated by an adult.

5. Have the children draw pictures about the crisis event and then discuss the pictures in small groups. This activity allows them to vent
their experiences and to discover that others share their fears.

6. Do a group collage.

Primary School Activities

1. For the younger children, availability of toys that encourage play
reenactment of their experiences and observations during the crisis
can be helpful in their integrating these experiences. These might
include ambulances, dump trucks, fire trucks, police cars, media
vans, building blocks, dolls, and so on. Play with puppets can provide ways for the older children, as well, to ventilate their feelings.

2. Help or encourage the children to develop skits or puppet shows
about what happened in the crisis. Encourage them to include anything positive about the experience as well as those aspects that were
frightening or disconcerting.

3. Do a group mural on butcher paper with topics such as "What happened in your neighborhood (school or home) when the crisis event
occurred." This is recommended for small groups with discussion
afterward, facilitated by an adult. It can help them feel less isolated
with their fears and provide the opportunity to vent their feelings.

4. Have the children create short stories (written or dictated to an
adult, depending on their ages) about their experience during the
crisis event.

5. Have the children draw pictures and then talk about them in small
groups on such topics as (a) What happened when the crisis event
occurred? (b) How did you help your family during the crisis event?

(c) How could you help your parents if you were in another crisis event? How can we be prepared for a similar crisis? (d) Did anything good happen during the crisis event? or (e) What did you, or anyone you know, lose during the crisis event? It is important in the large group discussion to end on a positive note (e.g., a feeling of mastery or preparedness), noting that the community or family pulled together to deal with the crisis, as well as to provide a vehicle for expressing their feelings about what took place.

6. Stimulate group discussion about the crisis experiences by showing your own feelings, fears, or experiences during the crisis event. It is very important to legitimize their feelings and to help them feel less isolated.

7. Have the children brainstorm on their own classroom or family disaster plan. What would they do? What would they take if they had to evacuate? How would they contact parents? How should the family be prepared? How could they help the family? Encourage them to discuss these things with their families.

8. Encourage class activities in which children can organize or build projects (scrapbooks, replicas, etc.), thus giving them a sense of mastery and ability to organize what seem like chaotic and confusing events.

JUNIOR HIGH AND HIGH SCHOOL ACTIVITIES

1. Group discussion of their experiences during the crisis is particularly important among adolescents. They need the opportunity to vent as well as to normalize the extreme emotions that come up for them. A good way to stimulate such a discussion is for the teacher to share his or her own reactions to the crisis event. They may need considerable reassurance that even extreme emotions and "crazy thoughts" are normal in a disaster. It is important to end such discussions on a positive note (e.g., What heroic acts were observed? How can we be of help at home or in the community? How could we be more prepared for a similar crisis in the future?). Such discussion is appropriate for any course of study because it can facilitate a return to more normal functioning.

2. Break the class into small groups and have them develop a crisis response plan of their own for their home, school, or community. This can be helpful in repairing a sense of mastery and security, as well as having practical merit. The small groups might then share their

plans in a discussion with the entire class. Encourage students to share their plans with their families.

3. Conduct a class discussion and/or support a class project on how the students might help the community repair the damage done by the crisis event. It is important to help them develop concrete and realistic ways to be of assistance. This helps them to overcome the feelings of helplessness, frustration, and "survivor's guilt" that are common following crisis events.

4. Classroom activities that relate the crisis event to course study can be a good way to help the students integrate their own experience or observation while providing specific learning experiences. In implementing the following suggestions (or similar ideas of your own), it is very important to allow time for the students to discuss feelings that are stimulated by the projects or issues covered.

Journalism: Have the students write stories that cover different aspects of the crisis. These might include community impact, lawsuits that result from the crisis, human interest stories from fellow students, geological impact, and so on. Issues such as accurate reporting of catastrophic events as sensationalism might be discussed. The stories might be compiled into a special student publication.

Science: Cover scientific aspects of the crisis event. For example, a project about stress might investigate the physiological responses to stress and methods of dealing with it. Discuss how flocks of birds, herds of animals, and so on, band together and work in a threatening or emergency situation. What can be learned from their instinctive actions?

English Composition: Have the students write about their own experiences during the crisis event. Such issues as the problems that arise in conveying heavy emotional tone without being overly dramatic might be discussed.

Literature: Have students report on crisis events or natural disasters in Greek mythology, American and British literature, in poetry.

Psychology: Have the students apply what they have learned in the course to the emotions, behaviors, and stress reactions they felt or observed during the crisis event. Cover posttraumatic stress syndrome. Have a guest speaker from the mental health professions who is involved in disaster work with victims speak to the class. Have students discuss (from their own experience) what things have been most helpful in dealing with crisis-related stress. Have students develop a mental health education brochure discussing emotional and behavioral reactions to disaster and things that are helpful in coping with disaster-related stress. Have students conduct a survey among their parents or friends regarding what is the most dangerous situation in which you ever found yourself? How did you react psychologically?

Peer Counseling: Provide special information on common responses to crises; encourage the students help each other integrate their own experiences.

Health: Discuss emotional reactions to crises, the importance of taking care of one's own emotional and physical well-being, and so on. Discuss the effects of adrenaline on the body during stress and danger. A guest speaker from the public health and/or mental health sector might be invited to the class.

Art: Have the students portray their experiences during the crisis event in various art media. This may be done individually or as a group effort (e.g., making a mural).

Speech/Drama: Have the students portray the catastrophic emotions that come up in response to a crisis event. Have them develop a skit or play on some aspects of the event.

Civics/Government: Study governmental agencies responsible for aid to victims, how they work, how effective they are, the political implications within a community. Examine the community systems and how the stress of the crisis event may have affected them. Have students invite a local governmental official to class to discuss crisis precautions, warning systems, and so on. Visit local Emergency Centers and learn about their functions.

History: Have students report on similar crisis events that have occurred in your community or geographic area and what lessons were learned that can be useful in preparing for future disasters.

Helping Your Child in a Disaster

C HILDREN'S REACTIONS to disasters have both short- and long-term effects in respect to duration, immediate or delayed appearance after the disaster, or both. A basic principle in working with children in disasters is relating to them as essentially normal children who have experienced great stress. Most of the problems that appear are likely, therefore, to be directly related to the disaster and transitory in nature. Relief from stress and passage of time reestablish equilibrium and functioning for most of them without outside help. The family is the first-line resource for helping children.

COMMON FEELINGS AND BEHAVIORS

- *Fears and Anxieties.* Fear is a normal reaction to disaster, frequently expressed through continuing anxieties about recurrence of the disaster, injury, death, separation, and loss. Because children's fears and anxieties after a disaster often seem strange and unconnected to anything specific in their lives, their relationship to the disaster may be difficult to determine. In dealing with children's fears and anxieties, it is best to accept them as being very real to the children. Parents' reactions to their children make a great difference in their recovery from the shock of the disaster. The intensity and duration of a child's

---

Adapted from the National Institute of Mental Health (1985, pp. 61–66). This work is in the public domain.

symptoms decrease more rapidly when his or her family are able to indicate that they understands his or her feelings.

Children are most fearful when they do not understand what is happening around them. Every effort should be made to keep them accurately informed, thereby relieving their anxieties. Children are developing storehouses of all kinds of information and responding to scientific facts and figures, new language, technical terms, and predictions. The children learn new words relating to disaster through the media and incorporate them readily, using them in their play and in talking to each other.

- *Sleep Disturbances.* Sleep disturbances are among the most common problems for children after a disaster. Their behavior is likely to take the form of resistance to bedtime, wakefulness, unwillingness to sleep in their own rooms or bed, refusal to sleep in their own rooms or bed, refusal to sleep by themselves, desire to be in a parent's bed or to sleep with a light, and insistence that the parent stay in the room until they fall asleep. Such behaviors are disruptive to a child's well-being. They also increase stress for the parents. More persistent bedtime problems, such as night terrors, nightmares, and refusal to fall asleep, may point to deep-seated fears and anxieties which may require professional intervention.

  It is helpful to explore the family's sleep arrangements. The family may need to develop a familiar bedtime routine, such as reinstating a specific time for going to bed; they may find it helpful to plan calming, prebedtime activities to reduce chaos in the evening. Developing a quiet recreational activity in which the whole family participates is also helpful.

- *School Avoidance and School Phobias.* It is important for children and teenagers to attend school because, for the most part, school is the center of life with peers. School becomes the major source of activity, guidance, direction, and structure for the child. When a youngster avoids school, it may generally be assumed that a serious problem exists. One of the reasons for not going to school may be fear of leaving the family and being separated from loved ones.

  Parents should encourage children to return to school and should talk to their teachers regarding any problems evident either at home or in school. Parent-teacher meetings and programs may assist in integrating family and school efforts to reassure and encourage the child to understand his or her feelings and to cope with loss and the need to get on with his or her life.

AGE-RELATED REACTIONS OF CHILDREN AND ADOLESCENTS TO DISASTERS

Common reactions of children and adolescents in response to a disaster can be listed by specific age groups. These symptoms of stress may appear immediately after the disaster or after the passage of days or weeks; they are not all inclusive.

Pre-school

Crying   Irritability
Thumbsucking   Confusion
Loss of bowel/bladder control   Clinging
Fear of being left alone, of strangers Immobility

Latency (6 to 11 years)

Headaches, other physical complaints Loss of ability to concentrate
Depression   Poor performance
Fears about weather, safety   Fighting
Confusion   Withdrawal from peers

Pre-adolescence and Adolescence (12 to 17 years)

Headaches, other physical complaints Poor performance
Depression   Aggressive behaviors
Confusion   Withdrawal and isolation

HELP FOR YOUR CHILD

- Talk with your child about his or her feelings and your feelings about the emergency.
- Talk with your child about what happened, providing information to him or her that he or she can understand.
- Reassure your child that you are together. Repeat this reassurance as often as necessary.
- Hold the child. Touching is important.
- Spend extra time with your child at bedtime.
- Provide play experiences for your child. Large muscle activities, such as playing ball or riding a bike, can help.

- Allow your child to mourn and grieve over a lost toy, a lost blanket, a lost home.
- Talk to your child's teacher if you feel he or she is having problems at school, so that you and the teacher can work together to help him or her.
- If you need added help for your child or any member of your family, contact a human service agency or your church.

APPENDIX D

Strategies for Informing Others of Crisis Events: Sample Letters and Announcements

CONTENTS

---

* Adapted from Colombo and Oegema (1986).

OPTION 1: OUTLINE FOR A LETTER TO PARENTS

Paragraph 1   Expression of sympathy

Paragraph 2   Discussion of verified facts

Paragraph 3   Statements regarding possible crisis reactions

Paragraph 4   Statements regarding the school's crisis response plan

Paragraph 5   Information regarding indications of the need for crisis intervention assistance

Paragraph 6   Information about how to obtain crisis intervention assistance

Paragraph 7   Expression of optimism

OPTION 2: OUTLINE FOR A COMMUNITY MEETING PRESENTATION

1. *Identify self and express sympathy.*

2. *Express optimism.*

   "It's not a question of if we will recover, it is a question of when."

3. *Identify and normalize common crisis reactions* including sleep difficulties, headaches, stomach aches, irritability, displaced anger, emotional numbing, and inattention.

   "These are all normal reactions to abnormal circumstances."

4. *Point out the source of crisis reactions.* The crisis event may have created problems that some children may find difficult to solve. Identify possible crisis problems. Point out that the crisis reactions are the result of having a problem that is judged unsolvable.

   "This crisis event presents us with challenges that we need to overcome."

5. *Discuss the course of crisis reactions.* Point out that the crisis state does not last for ever. For most crisis victims, crisis reactions last no more than six weeks.

   "Crisis reactions will not last indefinitely."

6. *Discuss how to help children cope with crisis problems/reactions.* Talk generally about how to help children through these difficult times.

   "There are some very concrete things we can do to help our children cope." Specific recommendations that should be put forth include (Mitchell & Everly, 1996b): Listening to and spending time with your child, let children know you are available to talk, do not force talk, reassuring children that they are safe, offering to help them with everyday tasks and chores, respecting their privacy, not taking anger or other feelings personally.

7. *Identify stress reduction techniques.* Specific techniques that should be put forth include the following: getting plenty of sleep/rest, keeping to a normal schedule, getting plenty of exercise, eating a normal diet. Be sure to mention that the use of drugs and alcohol are poor stress management choices.

8. *Identify factors likely to play a role in psychological traumatization.* Physical proximity to the crisis event and/or a relationship with those who were involved in the crisis may cause psychological trauma. Especially vulnerable are those who have a history of prior psychological traumatization.

9. *Point out the importance of giving children the facts.* It is important to give children as much detail as they ask for. However, it is advisable to avoid offering unasked for details (especially, frightening facts). Learning about something happening to a relative, close friend or associate can cause psychological trauma.

10. *Offer crisis intervention referral information.* Discuss the signs that might indicate the need for crisis intervention assistance. Signs of extreme distress and/or any indication of lethality (e.g., suicidal thinking) indicate the need for a referral. Let the community know where they can go for assistance if it is needed.

    "If someone is extremely upset they should receive crisis intervention support."

11. *Conclude with a statement of optimism.*

    "With time and talk, this crisis will become a small scare on a large life."

OPTION 3. GENERIC SAMPLE LETTER/ANNOUNCEMENT TO PARENTS

Dear Parents:

As you may or may not have heard, our [*district/school*] has experienced a [*crisis/tragedy/event*] that has affected us deeply. Let me briefly review the facts of the situation.

Describe incident and give known facts.

Students and staff react in different ways to these types of events. We, therefore, should expect, try to understand, and accept a variety of emotions and behaviors. The most important thing we can do is to be supportive and encourage discussion about the event, the feelings it gives rise to, and ways of responding.

We have implemented a plan for responding to this situation and helping our students and their families. This plan has evolved from our district's experiences with crises. Our staff has [*been/will*] be briefed on our plans and guidelines both for discussing the incident and understanding reactions to it. Our school's staff [*and other district personnel*] will be available to the students who need special attention and support, and we can obtain outside help or consultation if it is needed. We will try to maintain as normal a routine and structure as the situation allows, however, and encourage you to do the same. If you feel that your child[*ren*] or family needs assistance or anything else, please contact us and we will do everything we can to help.

If you have any questions or needs, please contact us by calling the school office [*Parent/Community information line*]. We will try to keep you informed of the situation as it progresses, any specific actions that we will take [*i.e., parent/community meetings, memorial funds, funeral arrangements*], and any other information that we feel you should have or that will be of help to you and your child[*ren*].

We know that you will join us in our concern, support, and sympathy for those involved in, and affected by, this incident. We also greatly appreciate your cooperation and assistance.

Sincerely,

School Principal

Option 4: Generic Sample Announcement to Students

[*I/we*] have had a difficult time deciding what to say to you today about the recent [*incident(s)/tragedy*]. As adults, we are expected to have all the answers and control our feelings. Let me tell you, however, that [*I/we*] have no real understanding of the reasons for this [*tragedy/incident*] and that we are deeply affected by it, just as many of you are. You will hear lots of reasons for and discussions about it from your friends, teachers, families, and the media, but no one will have all the right answers.

Even though [*I/we*] do not know why it happened, [*I/we*] do know many of the details of the incident and how our staff and students have acted.

Briefly review the known facts, the brave/good things that staff and students did (i.e., to help, to minimize the crisis), actions that are going to be taken, arrangements that have/are being made, and any other positive information that seems relevant and important.

Another thing [*I/we*] know is that all of us will need each other for a time and will need to pull together as a family. To help us with this, [*I/we*] would like to make some suggestions:

1. We need to respect each other's emotions, no matter how differently we feel or act. Each of us has our own way of seeing, feeling about, reacting to, and coping with problems. It's okay to cry, laugh, be angry, or even do nothing.

2. If you are having problems and feeling confused or upset, please ask for help. You do this when you have physical pain and problems, and should do this when you have emotional pain. To do so contact either your teacher or counselor. [*Mention any other self-referral procedures.*]

3. It frequently helps to talk about your feelings, even if they seem weird or embarrassing. Someone else probably feels this way, too. That's why we will give you a chance to talk.

4. It's normal to be afraid. All of us are afraid at different times and to different degrees. We have to learn to accept this. There is no way to predict or guarantee the future.

5. If you are having problems, they will probably be temporary and then will fade away. You will always remember what happened, but it will not always be as painful as it is today.

6. Again, for those of you who need more help, it will be available.

Insert the name, address, and phone number of the individual from whom crisis intervention support can be requested here.

Your parents will be made aware of this incident [*or you will be given a letter to take home to your parents*]. You and your families should ask for help or information if you need it.

Mention parent/community meetings if they have been scheduled.

---

7. Life will and must go on. Although things are difficult now they will return to normal. After time for discussion and help, classes will be held as usual. [*If necessary, report any temporary schedule changes.*]

Closing Remarks

Although it is important to be optimistic and encouraging, be careful not to give false reassurances.

Option 5. Outline for a Letter Informing Parents of the Decision Not to Provide an Immediate Crisis Intervention Response Following a Potentially Traumatic Event.

Dear Parents,

I have written this letter to inform you of an incident that has the potential to affect our school.

Insert a brief description of crisis facts here.

I have asked our school [*counselor/psychologist*] to monitor this situation carefully. [*She/He/They*] will continue to consult with your child's teacher and to observe student reactions. However, because it appears that . . .

Insert reasons for not providing a crisis intervention here, for example,

1. Children did not perceive this situation as dangerous or threatening.
2. So few children were involved in (or affected by) the incident that our school counselor and psychologist will be able to assist affected students individually. Crisis response team support is not necessary.

Thus, we have decided not to mobilize our crisis response team.

If our assessment of student reactions changes, and we feel crisis response team assistance is necessary, I will inform parents of affected students immediately. Similarly, I would like to encourage you to contact me if you perceive your child as being in need of assistance. In the mean time, I would like to recommend that you let your child know that you are available to talk about the incident, and answer any questions they might have.

Insert the following caution, if appropriate, here: In doing so, however, I caution you not to give your child unnecessary and/or unasked for details. It is important to keep in mind that we do not believe that children were traumatized by this incident. Children, especially developmentally young ones, look to adult reactions to gauge how threatening and scary crisis events are. In other words, if we behave as if an event was highly traumatic, children are likely to become traumatized even though they did not initially feel threatened.

Below find a list of common signs of traumatization. These are the behaviors that our [school counselor/psychologist] are looking for to determine if any supportive crisis intervention assistance is needed. Please let us know as soon as possible if you are observing any of these reactions in your children at home. If needed we are available to provide counseling support. If you have any questions or concerns please feel free to contact me at [*phone number*].

Sincerely,

School Principal

Signs of Traumatization

- Reactivity to reminders (e.g., sweating, rapid heart beat, nausea, dizziness, dry mouth, difficulty breathing)
- Sensory numbing
- Abdominal distress
- Hot flashes or chills
- Frequent urination
- Trouble swallowing
- Insomnia
- Increased activity
- Aggression
- Repetitive play
- Act as if trauma were recurring
- Avoidance of trauma reminders (e.g., activities, locations, conversations, people, things)
- Decrease interest in significant activities
- Social withdrawal
- Exaggerated startle response
- Intrusive recall
- Flashbacks
- Trauma nightmares
- Amnesia
- Sense of foreshortened future
- Poor concentration
- Hypervigilance
- Psychological distress with exposure to reminders (e.g., anxiety, anger, guilt, shame)
- Emotional numbing
- Impaired affect modulation
- Irritability
- Outburst of anger

Option 6: Letter/Announcement Regarding a Suicide: Before a Cause-of-Death Ruling

Dear [name of school] Family,

It is with great sadness that I write this letter to inform you that a member of our school family has died.

Insert here the identity and a brief description of the deceased.

As I write these words, a determination regarding the cause of this death has not yet been made. However, I do know that this death is currently being investigated by the Coroner's Office. As more information becomes available, I will share it with you.

This loss will create a void in our school that I would like to see filled with caring and mutual support. During times such as this it is critical that we look to family and friends for guidance. For many of us, the process of grieving this loss will be difficult and time consuming. At the same time, however, I would like us to keep in mind that with time and talk the pain associated with it will lessen.

If there is anything that school personnel can do to assist you cope with this death please let us know. This is perhaps best done by contacting your school counselor.

Insert the name, address, and phone number of the individual from whom crisis intervention support can be requested here.

At the present time information regarding the funeral is not available. As I learn of these arrangements, I will share them with you. In the meantime, I am sure that all of you join me in expressing our sympathy to the family.

If appropriate, identify any actions being taken to assist and/or support the family of the deceased.

Sincerely,

School Principal

Option 7. Letter/Announcement Regarding a Suicide: After a Cause-of-Death Ruling

Dear [name of school] Family,

It is with a heavy heart that I write this letter to you today. I have some very sad news to share. I have just learned that the death of a member of our school family has been ruled a suicide by the Coroner's Office.

Identify the victim, the general location of the suicide and briefly state the method of suicide, for example, "John Doe killed himself yesterday in a private residence by a drug overdose" or "John Doe killed himself yesterday in his home by carbon monoxide poisoning," or "John Doe killed himself at school today by a gunshot." *Do not provide excessive details about the death.*

Our school staff has made the choice not to speculate on what it was that may have led to the suicide. Rather our focus will be on what we can do to prevent other such losses.

Part of what makes this death especially tragic is that it did not have to happen. Clearly, this act was a permanent solution to problems that could have been dealt with in other ways. Perhaps some good can come from this great loss if it generates a greater awareness of the signs of possible suicidal thinking and of school and community resources available to help people cope with their problems. To this end I would like to share with you some of the signals or warning signs suggesting the need for counseling support. These warning signs include the following:

- Writing of suicide notes
- Making direct and/or indirect suicide threats
- Giving away prized possessions
- Making final arrangements
- Talking about death
- Reading or writing, and/or creating art work about death
- Hopelessness or helplessness
- Social withdrawal and isolation
- Loss of involvement in interests and activities

- Increased risk-taking
- Heavy use of alcohol or drugs
- Abrupt changes in appearance
- Sudden weight or appetite change
- Sudden changes in personality or attitude
- Inability to concentrate or think rationally
- Sudden unexpected happiness
- Sleeplessness or sleepiness
- Increased irritability or crying easily
- Abrupt changes in school attendance
- Dwindling academic performance
- Lack of interest and withdrawal

Behaviors such as these suggest the need for assistance and support coping with life difficulties. Resources available that provide such assistance include the following:

Identify local community and school resources that are available help people cope with problems.

This loss will create a void in our school that I would like to see filled with support and caring. During times such as this it is critical that we look to family and friends for guidance and support. For many of us, the process of grieving this loss will be difficult and time consuming. At the same time, however, I would like us to keep in mind that with time and talk the pain associated with this loss will lessen.

Information about the funeral includes the following:

Insert all available funeral information here.

With parental permission, we will allow students to attend the funeral as an excused absence. However, we will not be stopping school for this service.

If there is anything that school personnel can do to assist you and/or your children cope with this death please let us know. This is perhaps best done by contacting your school counselor.

Insert the name, address, and phone number of the individual from whom crisis intervention support can be requested here.

I am sure that all of you join me in expressing our sympathy to the family.

If appropriate, identify any actions being taken to assist and/or support the family of the deceased.

Sincerely,

School Principal

OPTION 8: LETTER INFORMING PARENTS OF A "LOCK DOWN."

Dear Parents,

As many of you have already heard, yesterday our school experienced a very unusual event.

Insert a description of the threatening event.

When a dangerous situation of this type occurs, our school has procedures in place to ensure student safety. Following this event we initiated these procedures. Specifically, all students were directed to go to a secure room (such as their classroom) and the doors were locked.

Insert at statement regarding the effectiveness of the Lock Down.

I would like to take this opportunity to compliment students and staff for their cooperation during this "Lock Down" procedure. Their actions help to reinforce my belief that even when frightening events occur, we are able to make our school a safe place.

Some students may be upset by this event. To provide the needed emotional support we have mobilized our crisis response team. This team will be available to students, teachers, and parents. If you feel that your child was disturbed by this event, please contact the crisis response team.

Insert the name, address, and phone number of the individual from whom crisis intervention support can be requested here.

While this event was frightening, it is important to acknowledge that it is a very rare occurrence. Our school is and will remain a safe place. If you have any questions or concerns please feel free to contact me.

Sincerely,

School Principal

OPTION 9: MEMO FROM A CRISIS RESPONSE TEAM TO
SCHOOL STAFF MEMBERS

The crisis team would like to thank all of you for your support and assistance during this difficult time. We hope that we have been able to help you and your children cope with this tragic event. All of you have certainly made our work easier. We respect and admire your personal strength and professional skill.

As of this morning, we have identified [*number*] children who may need counseling support (this number does not count children who we may have worked with during classroom counseling sessions). [*Number*] of these children have been seen and are judged to be adequately coping with the crisis. We are still seeing [or plan to see] another [*number*] students. We will eventually reach the point where your school counselor will be able to meet the counseling needs of the remaining students affected by this tragedy. At this point, the crisis intervention team will return to their regular assignments.

As this crisis intervention concludes, it would be appropriate for you to consider if you and your class would benefit from some type of memorial activity. Such an activity is a way to say good-bye and move on. [*School Principal*] has mentioned to parents that these activities will be taking place, in individual classrooms. In this way there is a greater likelihood that children can personally participate in the memorial. Many of you have already engaged in this activity. If you would like assistance with a memorial activity, members of the crisis intervention team are available. Ideas for memorials include the following:

- Creating a book of stories and drawings
- Planting a tree or other plant in memory
- Creating condolence cards for parents
- Creating condolence cards for siblings
- Any art activity that can be collected and given to the family
- Buying books dealing with loss for the school library

These are, of course, only suggestions. You and your students may have other great ideas.

Please feel free to continue to refer children to us if you feel there is a need for counseling. The crisis intervention team will remain at school as long as needed.

OPTION 10: LETTER INFORMING PARENTS OF THE DEATH OF A STUDENT

Dear Parents,

It is with great sadness that I sit down to write this letter to you. I have just received some very tragic news. A member of our school family was killed [*describe circumstances of the death*].

This may be difficult time for your child[ren], as it is for all of us. Our school counselor will be with our classroom tomorrow to help us get through this tragic time. I do not believe that it is possible to protect your child from the pain of this loss. However, I would like to suggest that it would be helpful if you let your child know that you are available to answer questions and to talk about this tragedy. Sometimes it is helpful to do something in the way of a memorial. For example, your child could draw a picture or write a story.

If you find that your child is having difficulty coping with this loss, please feel free to make use of our school counseling services. Our class is very close, we are like family here at school. I know the loss of this child will be felt most profoundly.

With deepest regards,

Classroom Teacher

OPTION 11: ANNOUNCEMENT INFORMING STUDENTS OF THE
DEATH OF A CLASSMATE

TO: Teachers
FROM: Principal
RE: Student Death

Please read the following to your students first thing this morning:
Sometimes it is hard to talk about this sort of thing. But I have some sad news to share with you about one of the students at our school. In [*grade level of deceased*], there was a student by the name of [*deceased student's name*].

Insert facts of the death here.

Please use the following as a guide for further discussion:

1. Point out that even as adults we find this kind of news difficult to understand. If it feels right, relate a personal story that would show how this can be hard to deal with.
2. Encourage questions about this loss.
3. Encourage discussion about this loss and other related events (i.e., other crises that this loss may remind students of).
4. Let students know that a variety of emotional responses would be appropriate (e.g., feeling numb, scared, or worried).
5. For most people these feelings will go away with time. However, let students know that if they find their reactions to this tragedy difficult to cope with they can talk to you (their teacher) the school counselor, their parents, and/or their friends.

Memo Requesting Teacher Assistance in Assessing Student Need for Psychological First Aid Following a Crisis

TO: Classroom Teachers   DATE:

FROM: Crisis Intervention Team

RE: Crisis Intervention Referrals

The crisis event we have just experienced has affected us all deeply. It is expected that several of your students will require crisis intervention assistance. We have already begun to identify some of these students based on their crisis event exposure and on the presence of other factors that may have made them vulnerable to this event. However, because you know your students better than most support staff, we would also like to ask for your help in identifying students in need of crisis intervention. Please read the following information on what signs to look for in making crisis intervention referrals and complete one of the attached crisis intervention referral forms for each student you would like us to see. Please let us know if we can assist you in any way.

Adapted with permission from Los Angeles Unified School District (1994).

ASSESSING A STUDENT'S NEED
FOR PSYCHOLOGICAL FIRST AID

For some of your students this event may cause entry into a crisis state. This means that they are having difficulty coping with (or solving) crisis-generated problems. Consequently, these students will feel out of control and unable to adapt or adjust. Youth who lack the perspective of adults and have yet to develop a broad array of coping strategies are particularly vulnerable to a crisis event. Because of not being able to cope with crisis-generated problems, the student in crisis will display signs of acute distress. Manifestations of this distress are variable. In fact, there will probably be as many different crisis reactions as there are students who will enter the crisis state. There are, however, several general symptoms. They include emotional, somatic, and behavioral reactions. If you feel that any of your students are displaying a significant number of these reactions, please refer them to the crisis intervention team. Specific examples of these reactions are:

Somatic	Emotional	Behavioral
Loss of energy/weakness	Exaggerated startle response	Avoidance of crisis reminders
Rashes/ persistent itching	Guilt about surviving	Unable to concentrate
Nightmares/night terrors	Irritability/frustration	Rapid/halting speech
Bowel/bladder problems	Diminished affect	Short attention span
Change in eating habits	Discouragement	Reliving the event
Sleep disturbances	Hopelessness	Poor achievement
Skin eruptions	Helplessness	Repetitive play
Headaches	Fear/anxiety	School phobia
Amnesia	Confusion	Hyperactivity
	Despair	Disobedience
	Excited	Poor memory
	Crying	Restlessness
	Anger	Aggression
		Regression
		Agitation

In addition to these crisis reactions, a crisis intervention referral may be considered if the student exhibits some of the following symptoms:

1. Doubts regarding the ability to recover
2. Denies problems or states she or he can take care of everything him- or herself
3. Blames problems on others, is vague in planning, and is bitter

4. Continuous retelling of the disaster
5. Has blunted emotions, little reaction to what is going on around self right now
6. Shows high spirits, laughs excessively
7. Complains of significant memory gaps
8. Talks about feeling detached from body
9. Shows uncharacteristic signs of self-neglect
10. Repeats ritualistic acts
11. Is unable to make simple decisions or carry out everyday functions
12. Uses drugs and alcohol excessively
13. Has an unreasonable fear that someone or something is out to get their family
14. Demonstrates a drastic change of personality or temperament
15. Hallucinates, is disoriented, or otherwise shows obvious signs of disturbed mental process
16. Evidences, for a month or longer, symptoms that are considered normal but have become disruptive to the student's social, mental, or physical functioning

Finally, the following crisis reactions are suggestive of the need for an *immediate* crisis intervention referral:

1. Suicidal thinking
2. Talks about feeling like killing self or others
3. Obviously self-destructive behavior (e.g., intentionally hurting self; or has repeated "accidents" that result in injury)
4. Directly involved in the crisis event
5. Close physical proximity to the crisis event
6. Considered self to be in extreme danger during the event
7. Familiar with victim(s) of the crisis event
8. Victim(s) were/are family members
9. Experienced significant stressors before the crisis event occurred
10. Previous trauma or loss within the last year
11. Previous trauma or loss similar in nature to the current crisis event
12. History of student mental illness or within the student's family
13. Student is worried about the safety of a family member or a significant other
14. Absence or unavailability of resources, such as family and friends, both at home and at school that might otherwise assist the student in coping with the crisis event

APPENDIX F

Safe Schools Questionnaire

Our School's Safety
(Student Version)

Grade:_____

Directions: The safe school committee needs to determine how safe you feel on campus. We also want to hear about the things at school you feel are unsafe and how they can be made safer. Do not put your name on this form, but do put your grade level.

Please show your opinions by circling one number for each statement that best shows your feelings about this school.

	Strongly Disagree	Disagree	Not Sure	Agree	Strongly Agree
1. I am not afraid of any places around my school.					
2. They take good care of the schoolyard.					
3. There is a lot of space in the classrooms at this school.					
4. There are law enforcement officers who work here on campus.					

Reprinted, by permission, from, *Safe Schools: A Planning Guide for Action,* © 1989 by the California Department of Education.

	Strongly Disagree	Disagree	Not Sure	Agree	Strongly Agree
5. When students at this school have an emergency, someone is there to help.					
6. Teachers at this school let me do projects and assignments with other students in the class.					
7. I really want this school to be "the best."					
8. I feel that I belong at this school.					
9. I work very hard in all my classes.					
10. When students break rules, they all receive the same treatment.					
11. I feel safe at this school.					
12. The buildings at this school look good.					
13. Strangers do not come and go from school easily.					
14. The principal asks students about their ideas at this school.					
15. We do not waste time in our classes at this school.					

	Strongly Disagree	Disagree	Not Sure	Agree	Strongly Agree
16. You can trust people at this school.					
17. Everyone is expected to be their best at this school.					
18. Students at this school really want to learn.					
19. Teachers go out of their way to let me know I am doing a good job.					
20. Only a few students get hurt in accidents at this school.					
21. Very few accidents happen inside the buildings at this school.					
22. Students are given many choices at this school.					
23. My parents are involved at this school.					
24. African-Americans, Hispanics, Asians, Whites, and all other students are respected at this school.					
25. The school rules are listed in the classrooms and around the school and students know what they are.					
26. I can be a success in school.					

	Strongly Disagree	Disagree	Not Sure	Agree	Strongly Agree
27. It pays to follow the rules and do well at this school.					
28. Writing on walls is cleaned or painted over quickly at this school.					
29. The classrooms at this school look very nice.					
30. I am in some classes with students of different abilities and talents.					
31. Most students get involved in school activities.					
32. People care for each other at this school.					
33. The rules at this school are fair.					
34. Teachers at this school look out for trouble makers.					
35. We learn things about ourselves, about "life," and other things in addition to regular subjects.					
36. Parents often serve as hall and playground monitors at this school.					

37. Which of these things happened to you in the past month.

	(Circle one)	
(a) I was pushed around by someone who was just being mean.	YES	NO
(b) I was in a fist fight with another student.	YES	NO
(c) I was robbed or had something stolen.	YES	NO
(d) I saw a student with a knife.	YES	NO
(e) I saw a student with a gun.	YES	NO
(f) I saw a students use drugs or alcohol on campus.	YES	NO
(g) I saw students steal from the library, a classroom, or the cafeteria.	YES	NO
(h) I saw someone destroy or mark-up school equipment or buildings (walls).	YES	NO
(i) I was afraid of being beat up on the way to or from school.	YES	NO
(j) I was afraid of gang activity at school.	YES	NO
(k) I was threatened by someone with a knife or gun.	YES	NO
(l) I was called names or put down by other students.	YES	NO
(m) I felt rejected by other students.	YES	NO
(n) I saw students smoking or chewing tobacco on campus.	YES	NO
(o) I know students who came to school high on drugs or alcohol.	YES	NO

38. You probably have other ideas about how to make our school safer. Please write your ideas in the space below.

_____

_____

_____

_____

_____

Source: Reprinted by permission, from *Safe Schools: A Planning Guide for Action*, © 1989 by the California Department of Education.

References

Adami, R., & Norton, M. (1996). Not in my school you don't. Preventing violence in the middle school level. *NASSP Bulletin, 80,* 19–23.

Adams, C.M. (1996). Adolescent suicide: One school's response. *Journal of Secondary Gifted Education, 7,* 410–417.

Aguilera, D.C. (1998). *Crisis intervention: Theory and methodology* (8th ed.). St. Louis, MO: Mosby.

Allan, J.A.B., & Nairne, J. (1984). *Class discussions for teachers and counsellors in elementary school.* Toronto, Canada: University of Toronto.

Allen, S.F., Dlugokinski, E.L., Cohen, L.A., & Walker, J.L. (1999). Assessing the impact of a traumatic community event on children and assisting with their healing. *Psychiatric Annals, 29,* 93–98.

American Academy of Child and Adolescent Psychiatry. (1996). *Understanding violent behavior in children and adolescents* [On-line]. Available: http://www.aacap .org/publications/factsfam/behavior.htm

American Association of Suicidology, Public Information Committee. (1987). Preliminary guidelines for media developed. *Newslink, 13*(2), 10.

American Psychiatric Association. (1994). *Diagnostic and statistical manual of mental disorders* (4th ed.). Washington, DC: Author.

American Psychological Association. (1993). *Violence and youth: Psychology's response.* Washington, DC: Author.

American Psychological Association. (1999). *Warning signs.* Washington, DC: Author.

Arena, C., Hermann, J., & Hoffman, T. (1984). Helping children deal with the death of a classmate: A crisis intervention model. *Elementary School Guidance and Counseling, 19,* 107–115.

Armstrong, K.R., Lund, P.E., McWright, L.T., & Tichenor, V. (1995). Multiple stress debriefing and the American Red Cross: The East Bay Hills fire experience. *Social Work, 40,* 83–90.

Armstrong, M. (1990, April). Emotional reactions to Stockton. In F. Busher (Chair), *Tragedy in Stockton schoolyard.* Symposium conducted at the meeting of the National Association of School Psychologists, San Francisco.

Arthur, R., & Erickson, E. (1992). *Gangs and schools.* Holmes Beach, FL: Learning Publications.

Asarnow, J.R., Carlson, G.A., & Guthrie, D. (1987). Coping strategies, self-perceptions, hopelessness, and perceived family environments in depressed and suicidal children. *Journal of Consulting and Clinical Psychology, 55,* 361–366.

B-Safe Seminars. (1994). *Management of assaultive behavior: Instructor's manual.* Elk Grove, CA: Author.

Batsche, G.M., & Knoff, H.M. (1994). Bullies and their victims: Understanding a pervasive problem in the schools. *School Psychology Review, 23,* 165–175.

Beck, A.T. (1976). *Cognitive therapy and emotional disorders.* New York: International University Press.

Beck, A.T., Steer, R.A., Kovacs, M., & Garrison, B. (1985). Hopelessness and eventual suicide: A 10-year prospective study of patients hospitalized with suicidal ideation. *American Journal of Psychiatry, 142,* 559–563.

Bell, J.L. (1995). Traumatic event debriefing: Service delivery designs and the role of social work. *Social Work, 40,* 36–43.

Bergeron, J.D. (1994). *First responder* (3rd ed.). Englewood Cliffs, NJ: Prentice Hall.

Berk, R.A., & Rossi, P.H. (1990). *Thinking about program evaluation.* Newbury Park, CA: Sage.

Berman, A.L., & Jobes, D.A. (1991). *Adolescent suicide: Assessment and intervention.* Washington, DC: American Psychological Association.

Berman, P., & McLaughlin, M.W. (1980). Factors affecting the process of change. In M.M. Milstein (Ed.), *Schools, conflict, and change* (pp. 57–71). New York: Teachers College Press.

Berndt, T.J. (1984). Sociometric, socio-cognitive and behavioral measures for the study of friendship and popularity. In T. Field, J.L. Roopnarine, & M. Segal (Eds.), *Friendship in normal and handicapped children* (pp. 31–45). Norwood, NJ: Ablex.

Bertoia, J., & Allan, J. (1988). School management of the bereaved child. *Elementary School Guidance and Counseling, 23,* 30–38.

Blauvelt, P.D. (1981). *Effective strategies for school security.* Reston, VA: National Association of Secondary School Principals.

Blauvelt, P.D. (1990, Fall). School security: Who you gonna call? *School Safety,* pp. 4–8.

Bloch, D.A., Silber, E., & Perry, S.E. (1956). Some factors in the emotional reactions of children to disaster. *American Journal of Psychiatry, 113,* 416–422.

Blom, G.E. (1982). Psychological reactions of a school population to a skywalk accident. In C.D. Spielberger, I.G. Sarason (Series Eds.), & N.A. Milgram (Vol. Ed.), *Stress and anxiety* (Vol. 8, pp. 361–370). New York: Hemisphere.

Blom, G.E. (1986). A school disaster: Intervention and research aspects. *Journal of the American Academy of Child Psychiatry, 25,* 336–345.

Blom, G.E., Etkind, S.L., & Carr, W.J. (1991). Psychological intervention after child and adolescent disasters in the community. *Child Psychiatry and Human Development, 21,* 257–266.

Bonner, R.L. (1987). Everyone knows asking people about thoughts of suicide won't put the idea in their heads—don't they? *Newslink, 13,* 8–12.

Bowers, L. (1989). Follow these guidelines for better and safer playgrounds. *Executive Educator, 11,* 27–29.

Boylan, S. (1987). Handling the tough ones: Case studies in crisis management. *THRUST, 16,* 20–21.

Braaten, S. (1997). Creating safe schools: A principal's perspective. In A.P. Gold-stein & J.C. Conoley (Eds.), *School violence intervention: A practical handbook* (pp. 46–57). New York: Guilford Press.

Brady, J.L., Guy, J.D., Poelstra, P.L., & Brokaw, B.R. (1999). Vicarious traumatiza-tion, spirituality, and the treatment of sexually abused survivors: A national survey of women psychotherapist. *Professional Psychology: Research and Prac-tice, 30,* 383–393.

Bremner, J.D., Southwick, S.M., Johnson, D.R., Yehuda, R., & Charney, D.S. (1993). Childhood physical abuse and combat-related posttraumatic stress disorder in Vietnam veterans. *American Journal of Psychiatry, 150,* 235–239.

Brent, D.A., Kerr, M.M., Goldstein, C., Bozigar, J., Wartella, M., & Allan, M.J. (1989). An outbreak of suicide and suicidal behavior in a high school. *Journal of the American Academy of Child and Adolescent Psychiatry, 28,* 918–924.

Breslau, N. (1998). Epidemiology of trauma and posttraumatic stress disorder. In R. Yehuda (Ed.), *Psychological trauma* (pp. 1–29). Washington, DC: American Psychiatric Press.

Briere, J. (1996). *Trauma Symptom Checklist for Children.* Odessa, FL: Psychological Assessment Resources.

Brock, S.E. (1994, June). Crisis preparedness: Strategies for the development of a crisis intervention policy. *Communiqué, 22,* 24–25.

Brock, S.E. (1996, Summer). Classroom crisis counseling. *Communiqué, 24,* 4–6.

Brock, S.E. (1998a, November). School crisis intervention mutual aid: A county-level response plan. *Communiqué, 27,* 4–5.

Brock, S.E. (1998b). Helping classrooms cope with traumatic events. *Professional School Counseling, 2,* 110–116.

Brock, S.E. (1999a, April). *Crisis theory and research: A blueprint for school crisis in-tervention.* Paper presented at the annual meeting of National Association of School Psychologists, Las Vegas, NV.

Brock, S.E. (1999b, Summer). The crisis of youth violence: Dangers and opportu-nities. *CASP Today: A quarterly magazine of the California Association of School Psychologists, 48,* 18–20.

Brock, S.E. (in press-a). Estimating the crisis response. In P. Lazarus & S.E. Brock (Eds.), *Best practices in crisis prevention and intervention in the schools.* Bethesda, MD: National Association of School Psychologists.

Brock, S.E. (in press-b). Identifying psychological trauma victims. In P. Lazarus & S.E. Brock (Eds.), *Best practices in crisis prevention and intervention in the schools.* Bethesda, MD: National Association of School Psychologists.

Brock, S.E. (in press-c). Crisis theory: A foundation for the comprehensive crisis prevention and intervention team. In P. Lazarus & S.E. Brock, *Best practices in crisis prevention and intervention in the schools.* Bethesda, MD: National Associ-ation of School Psychologists.

Brock, S.E., Lewis, S., & Sandoval, J. (1991, March). *The school psychologist's role in developing and implementing a crisis intervention plan.* Paper presented at the meeting of National Association of School Psychologists, Dallas, TX.

Brock, S.E., Lewis, S., Slauson, P., & Yund, S. (1990). *Administrative guidelines for crisis intervention.* (Available from Lodi Unified School District, Special Ser-vices/SELPA, 1305 East Vine Street, Lodi, CA 95240)

Brock, S.E., Lewis, S., Slauson, P., & Yund, S. (1995). *Administrative guidelines for crisis intervention* (Rev. ed.). (Available from Lodi Unified School District, Special Services/SELPA, 1305 East Vine Street, Lodi, CA 95240)

Brock, S.E., Lewis, S., & Yund, S. (1990). *Administrative response to crisis situations: Recommendations for the implementation of Board Policy 5141.5.* (Available from Lodi Unified School District, Special Services/SELPA, 1305 East Vine Street, Lodi, CA 95240)

Brock, S.E., & Sandoval, J. (1997, Fall). Thoughts on a school crisis response course. *Trainers Forum, 16,* 1, 6–7.

Brock, S.E., Sandoval, J., & Lewis, S. (1996). *Preparing for crises in the schools: A manual for building school crisis response teams.* Brandon, VT: Clinical Psychology.

Brooks, B.D. (1993, Winter). Signs of the times. *School Safety,* pp. 4–7.

Brooks, B., & Siegel, P.M. (1996). *The scared child: Helping kids overcome traumatic events.* New York: Wiley.

Brooks, B., Silverman, G., & Hass, R.G. (1985). When a teacher dies. A school-based intervention with latency children. *American Journal of Orthopsychiatry, 55,* 405–410.

Browne, A., & Finkelhor, D. (1986). Impact of child sexual abuse: A review of the research. *Psychological Bulletin, 99,* 66–77.

Brown, D. (1996). Counseling the victims of violence who develop posttraumatic stress disorder. *Elementary School Guidance and Counseling, 30,* 218–227.

Browning-Wright, D., Gurman, G., California Association of School Psychologists, & Diagnostic Center, Southern California Positive Intervention Task Force. (1998). *Positive intervention for serious behavior problems: Best practices in implementing the Hughes Bill [Assembly Bill 2586] and the positive behavioral intervention regulations.* Sacramento, CA: California Department of Education.

Budlong, M.J., Holden, M.J., & Mooney, A.J. (1993). *Therapeutic crisis intervention.* Ithaca, NY: Cornell University, Family Life Development Center.

Burgess, A.W., & Baldwin, B.A. (1981). *Crisis intervention theory and practice: A clinical handbook.* Englewood Cliffs, NJ: Prentice-Hall.

Busher, F. (Chair). (1990, April). *Tragedy in Stockton schoolyard.* Symposium conducted at the meeting of the National Association of School Psychologists, San Francisco.

California Department of Education. (1989). *Safe schools: A planning guide for action.* Sacramento, CA: Author.

California Department of Education. (2000). *Crisis management and response* [Online]. Available: http://www.cde.ca.gov/spbranch/safety/crisis.html

California Governor's Office of Emergency Services. (1985). *Multihazard functional planning guidance.* Sacramento, CA: Author.

California School Boards Association. (1987, September). *Policy reference updating service: Suicide prevention.* Sacramento, CA: Author.

Canter, A.S., & Carroll, S.A. (Eds.). (1999). *Crisis prevention and response: A collection of NASP resources.* Bethesda, MD: National Association of School Psychologists.

Caplan, G. (1961). *An approach to community mental health.* New York: Grune & Stratton.

Caplan, G. (1964). *Principles of preventive psychiatry.* New York: Basic Books.

Caplan, G. (1974). *Support systems and community mental health: Lectures on concept development.* New York: Behavioral.

Carkhuff, R.R. (1993). *The art of helping* (7th ed.). Amherst, MA: Human Resources Development Press.

Carlson, E.B. (1997). *Trauma assessments: A clinician's guide.* New York: Guilford Press.

Carroll, S. (1998, November). Crisis and counter-transference: Caretaking the caretaker. *Communiqué, 27,* 28–29.

Catone, W.V., & Schatz, M.T. (1991). The crisis moment: A school's response to the event of suicide. *School Psychology International, 12,* 17–23.

Cohen, R.E. (1985). Crisis counseling principles and services. In M. Lystad (Ed.), *Innovations in mental health services to disaster victims* (DHHS Publication No. ADM 85 1390, pp. 8–17). Rockville, MD: National Institute of Mental Health.

Cohen, R.E. (1988). Intervention programs for children. In M. Lystad (Ed.), *Mental health response to mass emergencies: Theory and practice* (pp. 245–252). New York: Brunner/Mazel.

Cohen, R.E., & Ahearn, F.L. (1980). *Handbook for mental health care of disaster victims.* Baltimore: Johns Hopkins University Press.

Coie, J.D., Dodge, K.A., & Kupersmidt, J. (1990). Peer group behavior and social status. In S.R. Asher & J.D. Coie (Eds.), *Peer rejection in childhood* (pp. 178–201). New York: Cambridge University Press.

Collison, B.B., Bowden, S., Patterson, M., Snyder, J., Sandall, S., & Wellman, P. (1987). After the shooting stops. *Journal of Counseling and Development, 65,* 389–390.

Colombo, S., & Oegema, D. (1986). *Parkway school district crisis intervention manual.* (Available from Parkway School District, Pupil Personnel/Special Services, 455 N. Woods Mill Rd., Chesterfield MO 63017)

Cook, P.J. (1991). The technology of personal violence. In M. Toney (Ed.), *Crime and justice: An annual review of research* (Vol. 14, pp. 235–280). Chicago: Chicago University Press.

Committee for Children. (1992). *Second step: A violence prevention curriculum* [preschool-kindergarten teacher's guide]. Seattle, WA: Author.

Cornell, D.G. (1998). *Designing safer schools for Virginia: A guide to keeping students safe from violence.* Charlottesville: University of Virginia, Thomas Jefferson Center for Educational Design.

Cornell, D.G., & Sheras, P.L. (1998). Common errors in school crisis response: Learning from our mistakes. *Psychology in the Schools, 35,* 297–307.

Cowen, E.L., & Hightower, A.D. (1986). Stressful life events and young children's school adjustment. In S.M. Auerbach & A.L. Stolberg (Eds.), *Crisis intervention with children and families* (pp. 87–103). Washington, DC: Hemisphere.

Cox, J.D., & Grieve, T. (1989, January 18). Schoolyard slaughter—5 killed, 30 injured. Stockton rampage ends with suicide. *Sacramento Bee,* p. 1.

Crime and Violence Prevention Center. (2000). *Crisis response box: A guide to help every school assemble the tools and resources needed for a critical incident response.* [On-line]. Available: http://www.caag.stage.ca.us/cvpc/crisisresponse.pdf (Hardcopy available Crime and Violence Prevention Center. Office of the Attorney General, P.O. Box 944255, Sacramento, CA 94244-2550.

Crowe, T.D. (1990, Fall). Designing safer schools. *School Safety*, pp. 9–13.

Cultice, W.W. (1992). Establishing an affective crisis intervention program. *NASSP Bulletin, 76*, 68–72.

Dallas, D. (1978). Savagery, show and tell. *American Psychologist, 33,* 388–390.

Davidson, L.E. (1989). Suicide clusters and youth. In C.R. Pfeffer (Ed.), *Suicide among youth: Perspectives on risk and prevention* (pp. 83–99). Washington, DC: American Psychiatric Association.

Davidson, L.E., Rosenberg, M.L., Mercy, J.A., Franklin, J., & Simmons, J.T. (1989). An epidemiologic study of risk factors in two teenage suicide clusters. *Journal of the American Medical Association, 262,* 2687–2692.

Davis, H.T., & Salasin, S.E. (1975). The utilization of evaluation. In E.L. Struening & M. Guttentag (Eds.), *Handbook of evaluation research* (Vol. 1, pp. 621–666). Beverly Hills, CA: Sage.

Davis, J.M., & Sandoval, J. (1991). *Suicidal youth: School-based intervention and prevention.* San Francisco: Jossey-Bass.

Davis, J.M., Sandoval, J., & Wilson, M.P. (1988). Strategies for the primary prevention of adolescent suicide. *School Psychology Review, 17,* 559–569.

de Becker, G. (1999). *MOSAIC-2000* [On-line]. Available: http://www.gdbinc.com /mosaic2000.htm

DeBernardo, C.R., & McGee, J.P. (1999, Summer/Fall). Preventing the classroom avenger's next attack: Safeguarding against school shootings. *CSMHA on the Move with School-Based Mental Health, 4,* 1, 5.

Desena, R.J. (1991, Fall). United we stand. *School Safety*, pp. 8–9.

Doll, B. (1999). Reflections from Littleton. *School Psychologist, 53,* 66, 97.

Doll, B., & Lyon, M.A. (1998). Risk and resilience: Implications for the delivery of educational and mental health services in schools. *School Psychology Review, 27,* 348–363.

Drug Strategies. (1998). *Safe schools, safe students: A guide to violence prevention strategies.* Washington, DC: Author.

Dwyer, K., Osher, D., & Warger, C. (1998). *Early warning, timely response: A guide to safe schools.* Washington, DC: U.S. Department of Education.

Elliot, D.S., Huizinga, D., & Moise, B. (1986). Self-reported violent offending: A descriptive analysis of juvenile violent offenders and their offending careers. *Journal of Interpersonal Violence, 4,* 472–514.

Elliot, S.N., McKevitt, B.C., & DiPerna, J.C. (in press). Promoting social skills and the development of socially supportive learning environments. In P.J. Lazarus & S.E. Brock (Eds.), *Best practices in school crisis prevention and intervention.* Bethesda, MD: National Association of School Psychologists.

Erikson, E.H. (1963). *Childhood and society* (2nd ed.). New York: Norton.

Erikson, K.T. (1976). *Everything in its path.* New York: Simon & Schuster.

Ersland, S., Weisaeth, L., & Sund, A. (1989). The stress upon rescuers involved in an oil rig disaster. "Alexander L. Kielland" 1980. *Acta Psychiatrica Scandinavica, 80*(Suppl. 355), 38–49.

Ettlinger, R.W. (1964). Suicide in a group of patients who have previously attempted suicide. *Acta Psychiatrica Scandinavica, 40,* 363–378.

Fairchild, T.N. (Ed.). (1997). *Crisis intervention strategies for school-based helpers* (2nd ed.). Springfield, IL: Thomas.

Farrell, J., & Joseph, A. (1991). Expressive therapies in a crisis intervention service. *Arts in Psychotherapy, 18,* 131–137.

Farrington, A. (1995). Suicide and psychological debriefing. *British Journal of Nursing, 4,* 209–211.

Federal Emergency Management Agency. (Producer). (1992). *Children and trauma: The school's response* [Videotape]. Washington, DC: Author.

Feindler, E.L., & Ecton, R.B. (1986). *Adolescent anger control: Cognitive-behavioral techniques.* New York: Pergamon Press.

Floyd, N.M. (1985). "Pick on somebody your own size?" Controlling victimization. *Pointer, 29,* 9–17.

Foa, E.B., & Meadows, E.A. (1998). Psychosocial treatments for posttraumatic stress disorder. In R. Yehuda (Ed.), *Psychological trauma* (pp. 179–204). Washington, DC: American Psychiatric Press.

Foley, C.F. (1986). Dealing with crises: One principal's experiences. *NASSP Bulletin, 70,* 46–51.

Frederick, C.J. (1985). Children traumatized by catastrophic situations. In S. Eth & R.S. Pynoos (Eds.), *Posttraumatic stress disorder in children* (pp. 71–100). Washington, DC: American Psychiatric Press.

Fremouw, W.J., de Perczel, M., & Ellis, T.F. (1990). *Suicide risk: Assessment and response guidelines.* New York: Pergamon Press.

Fullan, M.G. (1991). *The new meaning of educational change.* New York: Teachers College Press.

Furlong, M.J., Morrison, R., & Clontz, D. (1991, Spring). Broadening the scope of school safety. *School Safety,* pp. 8–11.

Furlong, M.J., Morrison, R., & Clontz, D. (1993, Spring). Planning principles for safe schools. *School Safety,* pp. 23–27.

Gagnon, W.A., & Conoley, J.C. (1997). Academic and curriculum interventions with aggressive youths. In A.P. Goldstein & J.C. Conoley (Eds.), *School violence intervention: A practical handbook* (pp. 217–235). New York: Guilford Press.

Galante, R.G., & Foa, D. (1986). An epidemiological study of psychic trauma and treatment effectiveness for children after a natural disaster. *Journal of the American Academy of Child Psychiatry, 25,* 357–363.

Garfinkel, B.D., Crosby, E., Herbert, M.R., Matus, A.L., Pfeifer, J.K., & Sheras, P.L. (1988a). *Responding to adolescent suicide.* Bloomington, IN: Phi Delta Kappa Task Force on Adolescent Suicide.

Garfinkel, B.D., Crosby, E., Herbert, M.R., Matus, A.L., Pfeifer, J.K., & Sheras, P.L. (1988b). Responding to adolescent suicide: The first 48 hours. *News, Notes, and Quotes,* 12–13.

Garfinkel, B.D., Froese, A., & Hood, J. (1982). Suicide attempts in children and adolescents. *American Journal of Psychiatry, 139,* 1257–1261.

Gazda, G.M., Asbury, F.R., Balzer, F.J., Childers, W.C., Phelps, R.E., & Walters, R.P. (1995). *Human relations development: A manual for educators.* Boston: Allyn & Bacon.

Gibbs, N. (1999, May 3). Special report: The Littleton massacre. *Time, 153,* 20–36.

Gift from Within. (Producer). (1995). *PTSD in children: Move in the rhythm of the child.* Camden, ME: Author.

Gillis, H. (1992, April 23). *Report on data collected following the Stockton schoolyard shooting.* Stockton, CA: San Joaquin County Office of Education.

Glenn, J. (1990, Fall). Training teachers for troubled times. *School Safety,* pp. 20–21.

Goldman, L.E. (1996, September). We can help children grieve: A child-oriented model for memorializing. *Young Children, 51,* 69–73.

Goldstein, A. (1999, December 20). The victims: Never again. *Time, 154,* 52–57.

Goldstein, A.P. (1997). Controlling vandalism: The person-environment duet. In A.P. Goldstein & J.C. Conoly (Eds.), *School violence intervention: A practical handbook* (pp. 290–321). New York: Guilford Press.

Goldstein, A.P., & Conoly, J.C. (1997). Student aggression: Current status. In A.P. Goldstein & J.C. Conoly (Eds.), *School violence intervention: A practical handbook* (pp. 3–19). New York: Guilford Press.

Goldstein, A.P., & Glick, B. (in press). Aggression replacement training. In P.J. Lazarus & S.E. Brock (Eds.), *Best practices in school crisis prevention and intervention.* Bethesda, MD: National Association of School Psychologists.

Goldstein, A.P., Glick, B., Reiner, S., Zimmerman, D., & Coultry, T.M. (1985). *Aggression replacement training: A comprehensive intervention for aggressive youth.* Champaign, IL: Research Press.

Goldstein, A.P., Palumbo, J., Striepling, S., & Voutsinas, A.M. (1995). *Break it up: A teacher's guide to managing student aggression.* Champaign, IL: Research Press.

Gould, M.S. (1992). Suicide contagion. *Lifesavers, 4*(2), 4.

Gould, M.S., & Shaffer, D. (1986). The impact of suicide in television movies: Evidence of imitation. *New England Journal of Medicine, 315,* 690–694.

Grant, S.A. (1993, Winter). Students respond to "campus cops." *School Safety,* pp. 15–17.

Green, B.L. (1993). Identifying survivors at risk: Trauma and stressors across events. In J.P. Wilson & B. Raphael (Eds.), *International handbook of traumatic stress syndromes* (pp. 135–144). New York: Plenum Press.

Green, B.L., Grace, M., & Lindy, J.D. (1983). Levels of functional impairment following a civilian disaster: The Beverly Hills Supper Club fire. *Journal of Consulting Clinical Psychology, 51,* 573–586.

Green, B.L., Korol, M., Grace, M.C., Vary, M.G., Leonard, A.C., Gleser, G.C., & Smitson-Cohen, S. (1991). Children and disaster: Age, gender, and parental effects on PTSD symptoms. *Journal of the American Academy of Child and Adolescent Psychiatry, 30,* 945–951.

Greenbaum, S. (1988). *School bullying and victimization.* Malibu, CA: National School Safety Center.

Guba, E.G., & Lincoln, Y.S. (1989). *Fourth generation evaluation.* Newbury Park, CA: Sage.

Gullatt, D.E., & Long, D. (1996). What are the attributes and duties of the school crisis intervention team? *NASSP Bulletin, 80,* 104–113.

Gun Safety Institute. (1995). *Solutions without guns: A curriculum guide.* Cleveland, OH: Author.

Haller, E.J. (1992). High school size and student discipline: Another aspect of the school consolidation issue? *Educational Evaluation and Policy Analysis, 14,* 145–156.

Halpern, H.A. (1973). Crisis theory: A definitional study. *Community Mental Health Journal, 9,* 342–349.

Hammond, W.R. (1991). *Dealing with anger: A violence prevention program for African-American youth.* Champaign, IL: Research Press.

Hansell, N., Wodarczyk, M., & Handlon-Lathrop, B. (1970). Decision counseling methods: Expanding coping in crisis-in-transit. *Archives of General Psychiatry, 22,* 462–467.

Hennessey, A. (1992, September). Getting the word out: Working with your local school reporter. *Phi Delta Kappan,* 82–84.

Hornblower, M. (1998, June 1). The boy who loved bombs. *Time, 151,* 42–44.

Horowitz, M.J. (1976). Diagnosis and treatment of stress response syndromes: General principles. In H.J. Parad, H.L.P. Resnik, & L.G. Parad (Eds.), *Emergency and disaster management: A mental health source book* (pp. 259–270). Bowie, MD: Charles Press.

Huebner, E.S. (1993). Professionals under stress: A review of burnout among the helping professions with implications for school psychologists. *Psychology in the Schools, 30,* 40–49.

Humphrey, K.R., & Baker, P.R. (1994, September). GREAT program: Gang resistance education and training. *FBI Law Enforcement Bulletin, 63,* 1–4.

Institute for the Study of Destructive Behaviors and the Los Angeles Suicide Prevention Center. (1978). *Training manual for human service workers in major disasters* (DHEW Publication No. ADM 77–538). Rockville, MD: National Institute of Mental Health.

James, B. (1993, Spring). Legal update: No policy may be the worst policy. *School Safety,* p. 33.

James, B. (1994). School violence and the law: The search for suitable tools. *School Psychology Review, 23,* 190–203.

Johnson, K. (1993). *School crisis management: A hands-on guide to training crisis response teams.* Alameda, CA: Hunter House.

Kandel, S., & Follman, J. (1993a). *Reducing school violence in Florida.* Tallahassee: Florida Department of Education.

Kandel, S., & Follman, J. (1993b). *Reducing school violence.* Greensboro, NC: Southeastern Regional Vision for Education.

Kann, L., Kinchen, S.A., Williams, B.I., Ross, J.G., Lowry, R., Hill, C.V., Grunbaum, J., Blumson, D.S., Collins, J.L., & Kolbe, L.J. (1997). Youth risk behavior surveillance: United States, 1997. *Morbidity and Mortality Weekly Report, 47*(SS–33), 1–89.

Kaufman, P., Chen, X., Choy, S.P., Chapman, C.D., Rand, M.R., & Ringle, C. (1998, October). *Indicators of school crime and safety, 1998.* Washington, DC: U.S. Departments of Education and Justice.

Kaufman, P., Chen, X., Choy, S.P., Ruddy, S.A., Miller, A.K., Chandler, K.A., Chapman, C.D., Rand, M.R., & Klaus, P. (1999, September). *Indicators of school crime and safety, 1999.* Washington, DC: U.S. Department of Education and Justice.

Kazdin, A.E., French, N.H., Unis, A.S., Esveldt-Dawson, K., & Sherick, R.B. (1983). Hopelessness, depression and suicidal intent among psychiatrically disturbed inpatient children. *Journal of Consulting and Clinical Psychology, 51,* 504–510.

Kazdin, A.E., Rodgers, A., & Colbus, D. (1986). The hopelessness scale for children: Psychometric characteristics and concurrent validity. *Journal of Consulting and Clinical Psychology, 54,* 241–245.

Keller, H.R., & Tapasak, R.C. (1997). Classroom management. In A. Goldstein & J.C. Conoley (Eds.), *School violence intervention: A practical handbook* (pp. 107–126). New York: Guilford Press.

Kelson v. City of Springfield, 767 F.2d 651 (10th Cir. Ct. App. 1985).

Kilpatrick, D.G., & Resnick, H.S. (1993). PTSD associated with exposure to criminal victimization in clinical and community populations. In J.R.T. Davidson & E.B. Foa (Eds.), *Posttraumatic stress disorder: DSM-IV and beyond* (pp. 113–143). Washington, DC: American Psychiatric Press.

King, D.W., King, L.A., Foy, D.W., & Gudanowski, D.M. (1996). Pre-war factors in combat-related posttraumatic stress disorder: Structural equation modeling with a national sample of female and male Vietnam veterans. *Journal of Consulting and Clinical Psychology, 64,* 520–531.

Kline, M., Schonfeld, D.J., & Lichtenstein, R. (1995). Benefits and challenges of school-based crisis response teams. *Journal of School Health, 65,* 245–247.

Klinghoffer, M. (1985). *Triage emergency care handbook.* Lancaster, PA: Technomic.

Klingman, A. (1986). Emotional first aid during the impact phase of a mass disaster. *Emotional First Aid, 3,* 51–57.

Klingman, A. (1987). A school-based emergency crisis intervention in a mass school disaster. *Professional Psychology: Research and Practice, 18,* 604–612.

Klingman, A. (1988). School community in disaster: Planning for intervention. *Journal of Community Psychology, 16,* 205–216.

Klingman, A. (1989). School-based emergency intervention following an adolescent's suicide. *Death Studies, 13,* 263–274.

Klingman, A. (1993). School-based interventions following a disaster. In C.F. Saylor (Ed.), *Children and disasters* (pp. 187–210). New York: Plenum Press.

Klingman, A., & Ben Eli, Z. (1981). A school community in disaster: Primary and secondary prevention in situational crisis. *Professional Psychology, 12,* 523–533.

Klingman, A., Koenigsfeld, A., & Markman, D. (1987). Art activity with children following a disaster: A prevention-oriented crisis intervention modality. *Arts in Psychotherapy, 14,* 153–166.

Knapp, M.J. (1996). *Violence prevention strategy use and perceived effectiveness in Kansas schools.* Unpublished doctoral dissertation, Kansas State University, College of Education, Manhattan.

Kneisel, P.J., & Richards, G.P. (1988). Crisis intervention after the suicide of a teacher. *Professional Psychology: Research and Practice, 19,* 165–169.

Kodluboy, D. (1997). Gang-oriented interventions. In A.P. Goldstein & J.C. Conoley (Eds.), *School violence intervention: A practical handbook* (pp. 189–214). New York: Guilford Press.

Kodluboy, D., & Ervinrud, L. (1993). School-based interventions: Best practice and critical issues. In A.P. Goldstein & C.R. Huff (Eds.), *The gang intervention handbook* (pp. 257–300). Champaign, IL: Research Press.

Kreidler, W.J. (1984). *Creative conflict resolution: More than 200 activities for keeping peace in the classroom.* Glenview, IL: Scott, Foresman.

Kronik, A.A., Akhmerov, R.A., & Speckhard, A. (1999). Trauma and disaster as life disrupters: A model of computer-assisted psychotherapy applied to adolescent victims of the Chernobyl disaster. *Professional Psychology: Research and Practice, 30,* 586–599.

Kulka, R.A., Schlenger, W.E., Fairbank, J.A., Hough, R.L., Jordan, B.K., Marmar, C.R., & Weiss, D.S. (1990). *Trauma and the Vietnam War generation.* New York: Brunner/Maze.

Labi, N. (1998, April 6). The hunter and the choirboy. *Time, 151,* 28–36.

Lamb, R., & Dunne-Maxim, K. (1987). Postvention in schools: Policy and process. In E.J. Dunne, J.L. McIntosh, & K. Dunne-Maxim (Eds.), *Suicide and its aftermath: Understanding and counseling the survivors* (pp. 245–260). New York: Norton.

Larson, J.D. (1990). *Think first: Anger and aggression management for secondary level students* [Videotape]. Milwaukee, WI: Milwaukee Board of School Directors.

Larson, J.D. (1992). *Think first: Anger and aggression management for secondary level students* [Treatment manual]. Whitewater, WI: Author.

Larson, J.D. (1994). Violence prevention in the schools: A review of selected programs and procedures. *School Psychology Review, 23,* 151–164.

Lazarus, P.J., Brock, S., & Feinberg, T. (1999, September). Dealing with the media in the aftermath of school shootings. *Communiqué, 28,* 1, 6–7, 10.

Lester, D. (1974). Demographic versus clinical predictors of suicidal behaviors. In A.T. Beck, H.P. Resnick, & D.J. Lettieri (Eds.), *The prediction of suicide* (pp. 71–84). Bowie, MD: Charles Press.

Lettieri, D.J. (1974). *Los Angeles suicide prevention center.* Unpublished manuscript.

Lewinshon, P.M., Garrison, C.Z., Langhinrichson, J., & Marsteller, F. (1988). *The assessment of suicidal behavior in adolescents: A review of scales suitable for epidemiologic and clinical research.* Rockville, MD: National Institute of Mental Health.

Lewis, M.S., Gottesman, D., & Gutstein, S. (1979). The course and duration of crisis. *Journal of Consulting and Clinical Psychology, 47,* 128–134.

Lewis, O. (1970). *A death in the Sanchez family.* New York: Vintage.

Lidell, H.G., & Scott, R. (1968). *The Greek–English lexicon.* Oxford, England: Clarendon Press.

Lindemann, E. (1944). The symptomatology and management of acute grief. *American Journal of Psychiatry, 101,* 141–149.

Lindemann, E. (1979). *Beyond grief: Studies in crisis intervention.* New York: Aronson.

Litman, R.E., Wold, C.I., Farberow, N.L., & Brown, T.R. (1974). Prediction models of suicidal behaviors. In A.T. Beck, H.L. Resnik, & D.J. Lettieri (Eds.), *The prediction of suicide* (pp. 141–162). Bowie, MD: Charles Press.

Lockman, J.E., & Curry, J.F. (1986). Effects of social problem-solving training and of self-instruction training with aggressive boys. *Journal of Clinical Child Psychology, 15,* 159–164.

Lodi Unified School District. (1989). *Governing Board Policy 5141.5: Administrative response to crisis situations.* (Available from Lodi Unified School District, 1305 East Vine Street, Lodi, Ca. 95240)

Lodi Unified School District. (1994). *Health manual for school sites.* (Available from Lodi Unified School District, Special Services/SELPA, Student Health, 1305 East Vine Street, Lodi, CA 95240)

Lord, J.H. (1990). *Death at school: A guide for teachers, school nurses, counselors, and administrators.* Dallas, TX: Mothers Against Drunk Driving.

Lord, M. (1999, October 11). The violent-kid profile: A controversial new technique for beating violence. *US News & World Report, 127,* 56–57.

Los Angeles Unified School District. (1994, Spring). *A handbook for crisis intervention* (Rev. ed.). (Available from the Los Angeles Unified School District, Mental Health Services, 6520 Newcastle Ave., Reseda, CA 91335-6230)

Luthar, S.S. (1991). Vulnerability and resilience: A study of high-risk adolescents. *Child Development, 62,* 600–616.

Lystad, M. (1985). Special programs for children. In M. Lystad (Ed.), *Innovations in mental health services to disaster victims* (DHHS Publication No. ADM 85–1390, pp. 151–160). Rockville, MD: National Institute of Mental Health.

Maher, C.A., & Illback, R.J. (1985). Implementing school psychological service programs: Description and application of the DURABLE approach. *Journal of School Psychology, 23,* 81–89.

Maine Project Against Bullying. (1999). *Materials database* [On-line]. Available: http://lincoln.midcoast.com/%7ewps/against/bullying.html

Margolin, N., & Teicher, J. (1968). Thirteen adolescent suicide attempts: Dynamic considerations. *Journal of the American Academy of Child Psychiatry, 7,* 296–315.

Marin County Community Mental Health Services & Santa Cruz County Mental Health. (1985). Tips for teachers in time of disaster. In M. Lystad (Ed.), *Innovations in mental health services to disaster victims* (DHHS Publication No. ADM 85–1390, pp. 101–116). Rockville, MA: National Institute of Mental Health.

Maslach, C.M. (1982). *Burnout: The cost of caring.* Englewood Cliffs, NJ: Prentice Hall.

Masten, A.S. (1994). Resilience in individual development: Successful adaptation despite risk and adversity. In M.C. Wang & E.W. Gordon (Eds.), *Educational resilience in inner-city America: Challenges and prospects* (pp. 3–25). Hillsdale, NJ: Erlbaum.

Masten, A.S., & Coatsworth, J.D. (1998). The development of competence in favorable and unfavorable environments: Lessons from research on successful children. *American Psychologist, 53,* 205–220.

Mathers, K. (1996). Never again would we be the same: The Oklahoma City bombing. *NASSP Bulletin, 80,* 38–43.

Matsakis, A. (1994). *Post-traumatic stress disorder: A complete treatment guide.* Oakland, CA: New Harbinger.

McConaughy, S.H., & Skiba, R.J. (1993). Comorbidity of externalizing and internalizing problems. *School Psychology Review, 22,* 421–436.

McDaniel, J. (n.d.). *Communicating about school safety* [On-line]. Available: http://www.keepschoolssafe.org/wssd.htm

McFarlane, A.C. (1986). Long-term psychiatric morbidity after a natural disaster: Implications for disaster planners and emergency services. *Medical Journal of Australia, 145,* 561–563.

McFarlane, A.C., & De Girolamo, G. (1996). The nature of traumatic stressors and the epidemiology of posttraumatic reactions. In B.A. van der Kolk, A.C. McFarlane, & L. Weisaeth (Eds.), *Traumatic stress: The effects of overwhelming experience on mind, body, and society* (pp. 129–153). New York: Guilford Press.

McFarlane, A.C., & Yehuda, R. (1996). Resilience, vulnerability, and the course of posttraumatic reactions. In B.A. van der Kolk, A.C. McFarlane, & L. Weisaeth (Eds.), *Traumatic stress: The effects of overwhelming experience on mind, body, and society* (pp. 155–181). New York: Guilford Press.

McGiboney, G. (1998, Fall). School safety is more than just student discipline. *School Safety,* pp. 13–17.

McKee, P., Jones, R.W., & Richardson, J.A. (1991). *Students suicide: Educational, psychological, and legal issues for the schools.* Alexandria, VA: LRP Publications.

Meyers, J., & Pitt, N. (1976). A consultation approach to help a school cope with the bereavement process. *Professional Psychology, 7,* 559–564.

Milgram, N.A., Toubiana, Y.H., Klingman, A., Raviv, A., & Goldstein, R. (1988). Situational exposure and personal loss in children's acute and chronic stress reactions to a school bus disaster. *Journal of Traumatic Stress, 1,* 339–352.

Mitchell, J.T. (1983). When disaster strikes: The critical incident stress debriefing process. *Journal of Emergency Medical Services, 8,* 36–39.

Mitchell, J.T. (1986, September/October). Critical incident stress management. *Response!* pp. 24–25.

Mitchell, J.T. (1987). Effective stress control at major incidents. *Maryland Fire and Rescue Bulletin,* pp. 3, 6.

Mitchell, J.T., & Everly, G.S. (1996a). *Critical incident stress debriefing: An operations manual for the prevention of traumatic stress among emergency services and disaster workers* (2nd ed., rev.). Ellicott City, MD: Chevron.

Mitchell, J.T., & Everly, G.S. (1996b). *Critical incident stress management: The basic course workbook.* Ellicott City, MD: International Critical Incident Stress Foundation.

Mitchell, J.T., & Everly, G.S. (1998). *Critical incident stress management: The basic course workbook* (2nd ed.). Ellicott City, MD: International Critical Incident Stress Foundation.

Mitchell, J.T., & Resnik, H.L.P. (1981). *Emergency response to crisis: A crisis intervention guidebook for emergency service personnel.* Bowie, MD: Brady.

Monahan, C. (1997). *Children and trauma: A guide for parents and professionals.* San Francisco: Jossey-Bass.

Morrison, G.M., Furlong, M.J., & Morrison, R.L. (1994). School violence to school safety: Reframing the issue for school psychologists. *School Psychology Review, 23,* 236–256.

Muir, E. (1988, Fall). The Blackboard jungle revisited. *National School Safety Journal,* pp. 25–27.

Murray, B. (2000, February). Crisis-induced stress undermines group cooperation. *Monitor on Psychology, 31,* 18–19.

Nader, K., & Pynoos, R. (1993). School disaster: Planning and initial interventions. *Journal of Social Behavior and Personality, 8,* 1–22.

Nader, K., Pynoos, R., Fairbanks, L., & Frederick, C. (1990). Children's posttraumatic stress disorder reactions one year after a sniper attack at their school. *American Journal of Psychiatry, 147,* 1526–1530.

National Association of School Psychologists. (1996). *Position statement: School violence.* Bethesda, MD: Author.

National Association of School Psychologists. (1999). Strategies to increase student involvement in violence prevention. In A.S. Canter & S.A. Carroll (Eds.), *Crisis prevention and response: A collection of NASP resources* (p. 57). Bethesda, MD: Author.

National Crime Prevention Council. *Stopping school violence* [On-line]. Available: http://www.ncpc.org/2schvio.htm#signs

National Institute of Mental Health. (1985). Helping your child in a disaster. In M. Lystad (Ed.), *Innovations in mental health services to disaster victims* (DHHS Publication No. ADM 85–1390, pp. 61–66). Rockville, MD: Author.

National School Board Association. (1993). *Violence in the schools: How America's school boards are safeguarding our children.* Alexandria, VA: Author.

National School Safety Center. (1990). *School safety check book.* Westlake Village, CA: Author.

National School Safety Center. (Producer). (1991). *School crisis: Under control* [Videotape]. Westlake Village, CA: Author.

National School Safety Center. (1998). *Checklist of characteristics of youth who have caused school-associated violent deaths.* Malibu, CA: Author.

National School Safety Center. (1999, July). *School bullying and victimization.* Westlake Village, CA: Author.

National School Safety and Security Services. (1999). *Bombs and school security: Are your schools prepared for the explosion of bomb threats and bombs?* [On-line]. Available: http://www.schoolsecurity.org/trends/school-bombs.html

Neal, C. (1999, September). *Keynote speaker: First responding officer, Columbine High School.* Keynote speech presented at the Western Regional Hate Crimes Symposium, Sacramento, CA.

Nelson, R., Roberts, M., Smith, D., & Irwin, G. (2000, February). The trouble with profiling youth at-risk for violence. *Communiqué, 28,* 10.

Nelson, E.R., & Slaikeu, K.A. (1990). Crisis intervention in the schools. In K.A. Slaikeu (Ed.), *Crisis intervention: A handbook for practice and research* (2nd ed., pp. 329–347). Needham Heights, MA: Allyn & Bacon.

Nelson, J.R. (1996). Designing schools to meet the needs of students who exhibit disruptive behavior. *Journal of Emotional and Behavioral Disorders, 4,* 147–161.

Nettleton Public School District. (1998). *Crisis response plan, 1998* [On-line]. Available: http://www.nettelton.crsc.k12.ar.us/crisis.htm

Newgrass, S., & Schonfeld, D.J. (1996, Spring). A crisis in the classroom: Anticipating and responding to student needs. *Educational Horizons, 74,* 124–129.

Newman, C.J. (1976). Children of disaster: Clinical observations at Buffalo Creek. *American Journal of Psychiatry, 133,* 306–312.

Nye, K.P. (1997). He's got a gun! *American School Board Journal, 18,* 43–45.

O'Carroll, P.W., Mercy, J.A., & Steward, J.A. (1988). CDC recommendations for a community plan for the prevention and containment of suicide clusters. *Morbidity and Mortality Weekly Report, 37*(Suppl. 6), 1–12.

Oestman, J., & Walker, M.B. (1997). Interventions for aggressive students in a public-school-based day treatment program. In A.P. Goldstein & J.C. Conoley (Eds.), *School violence intervention: A practical handbook* (pp. 160–188). New York: Guilford Press.

Oklahoma State Department of Education. (1995). *Administrator's guide for managing crisis.* Oklahoma City, OK: Author.

Oregon School Boards Association. (1999). *Never say never* [On-line]. Available: http://www.osba.org/hotopics/crismgmt/nspra.htm

Paerregaard, G. (1975). Suicide among attempted suicides: A 10-year follow-up. *Suicide, 5,* 140–144.

Paine, C.K. (1998a, November). Tragedy, response and healing: Springfield unites. *Communiqué, 27,* 16–17.

Paine, C.K. (1998b, November). Memorials: Guidelines for educators and communities. *Communiqué, 27,* 25.

Paine, C.K. (1999, June). Reflections on a tragedy: A school shooting in Springfield. *Communiqué, 27,* 6.

Paine, C.K. (2000, February). Reflections on a tragedy: A school shooting in Springfield, Oregon. *Communiqué, 28*(5), 11.

Palmo, A.J., Langlois, D.E., & Bender, I. (1988). Development of a policy and procedural statement for crisis situations in the schools. *The School Counselor, 36,* 94–102.

Parad, H.J. (Ed.). (1965). *Crisis intervention: Selected readings.* New York: Family Service Association of America.

Patton, M.Q. (1990). *Qualitative evaluation and research methods* (2nd ed.). Newbury Park, CA: Sage.

Peck, M.L. (1985). Crisis intervention treatment with chronically and acutely suicidal adolescents. In M.L. Peck, N.L. Farberow, & R.E. Litman (Eds.), *Youth suicide* (pp. 112–122). New York: Springer.

Peruzzi, N., & Bongar, B. (1999). Assessing risk for completed suicide in patients with major depression: Psychologists' views of critical factors. *Professional Psychology: Research and Practice, 30,* 576–580.

Petersen, S., & Straub, R.L. (1992). *School crisis survival guide: Management techniques and materials for counselors and administrators.* West Nyack, NY: Center for Applied Research in Education.

Phillips, D.P., & Carstensen, L.L. (1986). Clustering of teenage suicides after television news stories about suicide. *New England Journal of Medicine, 315,* 685–689.

Pitcher, G.D., & Poland, S. (1992). *Crisis intervention in the schools.* New York: Guilford Press.

Poland, S. (1989). *Suicide intervention in the schools.* New York: Guilford Press.

Poland, S. (1993). *Crisis manual for the Alaska schools.* Juneau, AK: State Department of Education.

Poland, S. (1994). The role of school crisis intervention teams to prevent and reduce school violence and trauma. *School Psychology Review, 23,* 175–189.

Poland, S. (1997). School crisis teams. In A.P. Goldstein & J.C. Conoly (Eds.), *School violence intervention: A practical handbook* (pp. 127–159). New York: Guilford Press.

Poland, S. (1998, June). Jonesboro turns to school psychologists for leadership. *Communiqué, 26,* 4–5.

Poland, S., & McCormick, J.S. (1999). *Coping with crisis: Lessons learned.* Longmont, CO: Sopris West.

Poland, S., & Pitcher, G. (1990a). Best practices in crisis intervention. In A. Thomas & J. Grimes (Eds.), *Best practices in school psychology: II* (pp. 259–274). Bethesda, MD: National Association of School Psychologists.

Poland, S., & Pitcher, G. (1990b, Fall). Expect the unexpected. *School Safety,* pp. 14–17.

Ponton, L.E., & Bryant, E.C. (1991). After the earthquake: Organizing to respond to children and adolescents. *Psychiatric Annals, 21,* 539–546.

Popham, W.J. (1975). *Educational evaluation.* Englewood Cliffs, NJ: Prentice Hall.

Porter, W., Garrity, C., Jens, K., & Stoker, S. (in press). Bully proofing your school: Violence prevention through skill development and the creation of caring community. In P.J. Lazarus & S.E. Brock (Eds.), *Best practices in school crisis prevention and intervention.* Bethesda, MD: National Association of School Psychologists.

Posavac, E.J., & Raymond, G.C. (1989). *Program evaluation: Methods and case studies* (3rd ed.). Englewood Cliffs, NJ: Prentice Hall.

Prothrow-Stith, D. (1987). *Violence prevention curriculum for adolescents.* Newton, MA: Education Development Center.

Purvis, J.R., Porter, R.L., Authement, C.C., & Boren, L.C. (1991). Crisis intervention teams in the schools. *Psychology in the Schools, 28,* 331–339.

Pynoos, R.S., Frederick, C., Nader, K., Steinberg, A., Eth, S., Nune, F., & Fairbanks, L. (1987). Life threat and post traumatic stress in school-age children. *Archives of General Psychiatry, 44,* 1057–1063.

Pynoos, R.S., Goenjian, A., Tashjain, M., Karakashian, M., Manjikian, R., Manoukian, G., Steinberg, A.M., & Fairbanks, L.A. (1993). Post-traumatic stress reactions in children after the 1988 Armenian earthquake. *British Journal of Psychiatry, 163,* 239–247.

Ramsay, R.F., Tanney, B.L., Tierney, R.J., & Lang, W.A. (1996). *Suicide intervention workshop.* Calgary, Canada: LivingWorks Education.

Rapoport, L. (1965). The state of crisis: Some theoretical considerations. In H.J. Parad (Ed.), *Crisis intervention: Selected readings* (pp. 22–31). New York: Family Service Association of America.

Resnick, H.S., Kilpatrick, D.G., Dansky, B.S., Saunders, B.E., & Best, C.L. (1993). Prevalence of civilian trauma and posttraumatic stress disorders in a representative national sample of women. *Journal of Consulting and Clinical Psychology, 61,* 984–991.

Reynolds, B. (1993, Spring). Helping one student to succeed. *School Safety,* pp. 13–14.

Reynolds, W.M. (1988). *Suicidal Ideation Questionnaire: Professional manual.* Odessa, FL: Psychological Assessment Resources.

Roberts, A.R. (1990). An overview of crisis theory and crisis intervention. In A.R. Roberts (Ed.), *Crisis intervention handbook: Assessment, treatment and research* (pp. 1–15). Belmont, CA: Wadsworth.

Rohrer, J.C. (1996). We interrupt this program to show you a bombing: Children and schools respond to war. *Childhood Education, 72,* 201–205.

Rosen, L. (1993, Spring). Violence prevention: School's newest challenge. *School Safety,* pp. 9–12.

Rosenfield, S. (1992). Developing school-based consultation teams: A design for organizational change. *School Psychology Quarterly, 7,* 27–46.

Rossi, P.H., & Freeman, H.E. (1993). *Evaluation: A systematic approach* (5th ed.). Newbury Park, CA: Sage.

Rothbart, M.K., Posner, M.I., & Hershey, K.L. (1995). Temperament, attention, and developmental psychopathology. In D. Cicchetti & D. Cohen (Eds.), *Manual of developmental psychopathology* (pp. 315–340). New York: Wiley.

Rouf, S.R., & Harris, J.M. (1988, May). Suicide contagion: Guilt and modeling. *Communiqué, 16,* 8.

Rubin, K.H., Hymel, S., Lemare, L., & Rowden, L. (1989). Children experiencing social difficulties: Sociometric neglect reconsidered. *Canadian Journal of Behavioural Science, 21,* 94–111.

Rund, D.A., & Rausch, T.S. (1981). *Triage.* St. Louis, MO: Mosby.

Saarni, C. (1990). Emotional competence: How emotions and relationships become integrated. In R.A. Thompson (Ed.), *Socio-emotional development* (pp. 115–182). Lincoln: University of Nebraska Press.

Sacramento City Unified School District, Psychological Services. (n.d.). *Situational problems.* Unpublished manuscript.

Sandall, G.N. (1986, October). Early intervention in a disaster: The Cokeville hostage/bombing crisis. *Communiqué, 15,* 1–2.

Sandoval, J. (1985a). Editor's comments: Crisis counseling in the schools. *School Psychology Review, 14,* 255–256.

Sandoval, J. (1985b). Crisis counseling: Conceptualizations and general principles. *School Psychology Review, 14,* 257–265.

Sandoval, J. (1987). Crisis intervention. In C.A. Maher & J.E. Zins (Eds.), *Psychoeducational interventions in schools* (pp. 177–192). Elmsford, NY: Pergamon Press.

Sandoval, J. (1988a). Conceptualizations and general principles of crisis counseling, intervention, and prevention. In J. Sandoval (Ed.), *Crisis counseling, intervention, and prevention in the schools* (pp. 3–20). Hillsdale, NJ: Erlbaum.

Sandoval, J. (Ed.). (1988b). *Crisis counseling, intervention, and prevention in the schools*. Hillsdale, NJ: Erlbaum.

Sandoval, J. (1989). The school-based prevention of childhood crises. *Special Services in the Schools, 5*, 241–259.

Sandoval, J. (Ed.). (in press-a). *Crisis counseling, intervention and prevention in the schools* (2nd ed.). Hillsdale, NJ: Erlbaum.

Sandoval, J. (in press-b). Conceptualizations and general principles of crisis counseling, intervention, and prevention. In J. Sandoval (Ed.), *Crisis counseling, intervention, and prevention in the schools* (2nd ed.). Hillsdale, NJ: Erlbaum.

Sandoval, J. (in press-c). Moves and transitions. In J. Sandoval (Ed.), *Crisis counseling, intervention, and prevention in the schools* (2nd ed.). Hillsdale, NJ: Erlbaum.

Sandoval, J., & Brock, S.E. (1996). The school psychologist's role in suicide prevention *School Psychology Quarterly, 11*, 169–185.

Sandoval, J., Davis, J.M., & Wilson, M.P. (1987). An overview of the school-based prevention of adolescent suicide. *Special Services in the Schools, 3*, 103–120.

Sandoval, J., London, M.D., & Rey, T. (1994). The status of suicide prevention in California schools. *Death Studies, 18*, 595–608.

Saylor, C.F. (1993). *Children and disasters*. New York: Plenum.

Schonfeld, D.J. (1989). Crisis intervention for bereavement support: A model of intervention in the children's school. *Clinical Pediatrics, 28*, 27–33.

School Safety Update. (1991, October). Rascon sets pace with innovations for school safety. *National School Safety Center News Service*, p. 4.

Schwarz, E.D., & Kowalski, J.M. (1991). Malignant memories: PTSD in children and adults after a school shooting. *Journal of the American Academy of Child and Adolescent Psychiatry, 30*, 936–944.

Schwartz, W. (1999, October 12). *A guide to community programs to prevent youth violence* [On-line]. Available: http://eric-web.tc.columbia.edu/guides/pg9.html

Shalev, A.Y. (1996). Stress versus traumatic stress: From acute homeostatic reactions to chronic psychopathology. In B.A. van der Kolk, A.C. McFarlane, & L. Weisaeth (Eds.), *Traumatic stress: The effects of overwhelming experience on mind, body, and society* (pp. 77–101). New York: Guilford Press.

Shapiro, F. (1995). *Eye movement desensitization and reprocessing: Basic principles, protocols and procedures*. New York: Guilford Press.

Shields, A.M., Cicchetti, D., & Ryan, R.M. (1994). The development of emotional and behavioral self-regulation and social competence among maltreated school-age children. *Development and Psychopathology, 6*, 57–75.

Shore, J.H., Tatum, E.L., & Vollmer, W.M. (1986). Psychiatric reactions to disaster: The Mount St. Helens' experience. *American Journal of Psychiatry, 143*, 590–595.

Shore, J.H., Tatum, E.L., & Vollmer, W.M. (1990). The Mount St. Helens' stress response syndrome. In J.H. Shore (Ed.), *Disaster stress studies: New methods and findings* (pp. 78–97). Washington, DC: American Psychiatric Press.

Silverman, W.H. (1977). Planning for crisis intervention with community mental health concepts. *Psychotherapy: Theory, Research and Practice, 14,* 293–297.

Slaikeu, K.A. (1990). *Crisis intervention: A handbook for practice and research* (2nd ed.). Needham Heights, MA: Allyn & Bacon.

Smith, L.L. (1990). Crisis intervention: Theory and practice. In J.E. Mezzich & B. Zimmer (Eds.), *Emergency psychiatry* (pp. 305–331). Madison, CT: International University Press.

Sorensen, J.R. (1989). Responding to teacher or student death: Preplanning crisis intervention. *Journal of Counseling and Development, 67,* 426–427.

Soriano, M., Soriano, F., & Jimenez, E. (1994). School violence among culturally diverse populations: Sociocultural and institutional considerations. *School Psychology Review, 23,* 216–235.

Stack, C. (1974). *All our kin: Strategies for survival in a Black community.* New York: Harper.

Stacy, M. (1988, March). Tragic accident tests professional resources. *Communiqué, 16,* 5.

Steiger, L.K. (1987). *Participant workbook. Nonviolent crisis intervention: A program focusing on management of disruptive, assaultive, or out-of-control behavior.* Brookfield, WI: National Crisis Prevention Institute.

Stephens, R.D. (1991, July). *National School Safety Center.* Testimony to House Subcommittee on Crime and Criminal Justice. (Available from National School Safety Center, 141 Duesenberg Drive, Suite 11, Westlake Village, CA 91362)

Stephens, R.D. (1993, Spring). School safety reality check: Assessing your situation. *School Safety,* pp. 2, 35.

Stephens, R.D. (1994). Planning for safer and better schools: School violence prevention and intervention strategies. *School Psychology Review, 23,* 204–215.

Stephens, R.D. (1997). National trends in school violence: Statistics and prevention strategies. In A.P. Goldstein & J.C. Conoly (Eds.), *School violence intervention: A practical handbook* (pp. 72–90). New York: Guilford Press.

Steward, G.K., & Knap, M.J. (1997). How to modify your facilities to minimize violence and vandalism. *School Business Affairs, 63,* 43–46.

Striepling, S.H. (1997). The low-aggression classroom: A teacher's view. In A.P. Goldstein & J.C. Conoly (Eds.), *School violence intervention: A practical handbook* (pp. 23–45). New York: Guilford Press.

Tanney, B.L., & Motto, G. (1990). *Long-term follow-up of 1570 attempted suicides.* Proceedings of the twenty-third annual conference of the American Association of Suicidology, New Orleans, LA.

Taplin, J.R. (1971). Crisis theory: Critique and reformulation. *Community Mental Health Journal, 7,* 13–23.

Terr, L.C. (1979). Children of Chowchilla: A study of psychic trauma. *Psychoanalytic Study of the Child, 34,* 547–623.

Terr, L.C. (1981). Psychic trauma in children: Observations following the Chowchilla school-bus kidnapping. *American Journal of Psychiatry, 138,* 14–19.

Terr, L.C. (1983). Chowchilla revisited: The effects of psychic trauma four years after a school-bus kidnapping. *American Journal of Psychiatry, 140,* 1543–1555.

Terr, L.C. (1989). Treating psychic trauma in children: A preliminary discussion. *Journal of Traumatic Stress, 2,* 3–20.

Terr, L.C. (1992). Mini-marathon groups: Psychological "first aid" following disasters. *Bulletin of the Menninger Clinic, 56,* 76–86.

Thomas, C.L. (Ed.). (1993). *Taber's encyclopedic medical dictionary* (17th ed.). Philadelphia: F.A. Davis.

Thompson, R. (1990). Suicide and sudden loss: Crisis management in the schools. In *Highlights: An ERIC/CAPS Digest.* Ann Arbor, MI: Counseling and Personnel Services Clearinghouse.

Thompson, R.A. (1995). Being prepared for suicide or sudden death in schools: Strategies to restore equilibrium. *Journal of Mental Health Counseling, 17,* 264–277.

Tishler, C., McHenry, P., & Morgan, K. (1981). Adolescent suicide attempts: Some significant factors. *Suicide and Life-Threatening Behavior, 11,* 86–92.

Toubiana, Y.H., Milgram, N.A., Strich, Y., & Edelstein, A. (1988). Crisis intervention in a school community disaster: Principles and practices. *Journal of Community Psychology, 16,* 228–240.

Trump, K.S. (1998a). *Practical school security: Basic guidelines for safe and secure schools.* Thousand Oaks, CA: Corwin Press.

Trump, K.S. (1998b, June/July). Crisis in the classroom: Can your schools' security pass the exam? *Updating, 29*(3), 1–4.

Vidal, J.A. (1986). Establishing a suicide prevention program. *NASSP Bulletin, 70,* 68–71.

Walker, H.M., Colvin, G., & Ramsey, E. (1995). *Antisocial behavior in school: Strategies and best practices.* Pacific Grove, CA: Brooks/Cole.

Weatherley, R., & Lipsky, M. (1977). Street-level bureaucrats and institutional innovation: Implementing special education reform. *Harvard Educational Review, 47,* 171–197.

Webb, N.B. (1986). Before and after suicide: A preventative outreach program for colleges. *Suicide and Life-Threatening Behavior, 16,* 469–480.

Webster's new collegiate dictionary. (1976). Springfield, MA: Merriam.

Weinberg, R.B. (1989). Consultation and training with school-based crisis teams. *Professional Psychology: Research and Practice, 20,* 305–308.

Weinberg, R.B. (1990). Serving large numbers of adolescent victim-survivors: Group interventions following trauma at school. *Professional Psychology: Research and Practice, 21,* 271–278.

Weisaeth, L. (1989). A study of behavioural responses to an industrial disaster. *Acta Psychiatrica Scandinavica, 80*(Suppl. 355), 13–24.

Werner, E.E., & Smith, R.S. (1982). *Vulnerable but invincible: A study of resilient children.* New York: McGraw-Hill.

Wilhelm, R. (1967). *The I Ching; or book of changes* (Cary R. Baynes, Trans., 3rd ed.). Princeton, NJ: Princeton University Press.

Wise, P.S., Smead, V.S., & Huebner, E.S. (1987). Crisis intervention: Involvement and training needs of school psychology personnel. *Journal of School Psychology, 25,* 185–187.

Wollman, D. (1993). Critical incident stress debriefing and crisis groups: A review of the literature. *Group, 17,* 70–83.

Wong, M., Rubin, R., Ramirez, N., Lieberman, R., Dotson, S., Colwell, B., & Bernstein, R. (1998). *A quick reference guide for school crisis management.* (Available from the Los Angeles Unified School District, Mental Health Services, 6520 Newcastle Ave., Reseda, CA 91335–6230)

Wright, K.M., Ursano, R.J., Bartone, P.T., & Ingraham, L.H. (1990). The shared experience of catastrophe: An expanded classification of the disaster community. *American Journal of Orthopsychiatry, 60,* 35–42.

Young, M.A. (1998). *The community crisis response team training manual* (2nd ed.). Washington, DC: National Organization for Victim Assistance.

Young, M.A. (2000, January/February). Addressing trauma and violence in our schools. *Psychology Teacher Network, 10,* 5–7, 11.

Zilberg, N.J., Weiss, D.S., & Horowitz, M.J. (1982). Impact of event scale: A cross-validation study and some empirical evidence supporting a conceptual model of stress response syndromes. *Journal of Consulting and Clinical Psychology, 50,* 407–414.

Index